P9-CMF-981

Second Sowing

The Life of Mary Aloysia Hardey

Second Sowing

THE LIFE OF MARY ALOYSIA HARDEY

by

Margaret Williams

Illustrations by Anne Pracny

Sheed & Ward · *1942*
NEW YORK

Nihil obstat

ARTHUR J. SCANLAN, S.T.D.

Censor Librorum.

Imprimatur

✠ FRANCIS J. SPELLMAN, D.D.

Archbishop, New York.

New York, July 25, 1942.

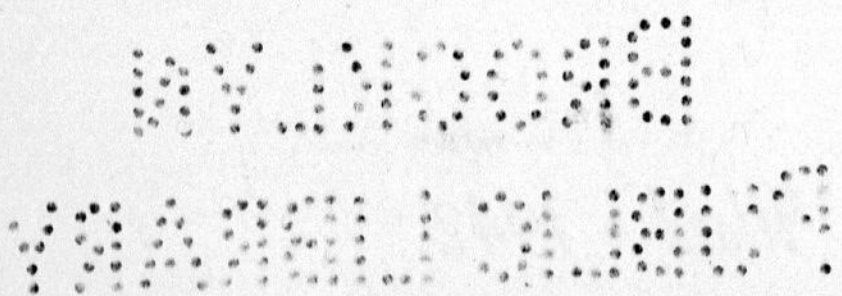

MANUFACTURED IN THE UNITED STATES OF AMERICA
BY BURR PRINTING HOUSE, INC., NEW YORK

Aloysia Hardey

CONTENTS

DEDICATION

TO

Reverend Mother Helen Lucas

From every sowing there comes a harvest, and from the harvest fresh grain is sown for a new increase. From life through death to life is the Christian cycle. Mother Hardey's work began before her day and has been carried on into our own by other workers. To one such inheritor of her traditions, who inspired and made possible the writing of Mother Hardey's story, "Second Sowing" is most gratefully dedicated.

Manhattanville College of the Sacred Heart
Feast of the Sacred Heart, 1942.

Second Sowing

The Life of Mary Aloysia Hardey

I

ONE AND MANY

It is late afternoon, in the year 1826; the day is any day you please, the place is a broad-lawned garden skirting the edge of the Mississippi River which, a little aloft behind its levee, moves coolly by, less friendly than the pillared house that looks towards it across the flowers. The house is the newly opened Sacred Heart Convent of Saint Michael's, Louisiana, and the children settling down on the grass for a moment's rest after singing and dancing French *ronds* at some length are its first pupils. They sit in a tight ring; their broad skirts are spread out, perforce, in whirls of purple bombazine piped with velvet. Their hair is drawn back in curl-subduing nets, but their eyes, quite unsubdued, are all turned to the person in the center of the ring. She is a young Religious of the Sacred Heart and wears, surprisingly, a white veil; for though she is dignified and fulfills her duties as *surveillante* with mature ease, she is a Novice not quite seventeen. She has a low but compelling voice, and the children listen, motionless. While she speaks the sun begins to retreat, as time must, leaving only a picture to live in shadowed memories.

One of those children had a most retentive memory. Sixty years later she wrote of what she saw and heard that evening, that those of another age might also see and hear. She wrote in the slow-moving, courteous style of the nineteenth century in the years of its leisured maturity, but the glow and the love of youth are in her words, which give a fit starting point for the life of Mother Mary Ann Aloysia Hardey: [1]

> We loved Mother Hardey very much; we saw in her everything that a Religious should be, humble, simple, devoted. How often, when we were gathered around her on the green lawn of the Convent garden, she talked to us of duty, and still more of the love of the Heart of Jesus. She never grew tired of talking so, and we never grew tired of listening to her. It was not a sermon that she gave us, nor mere words by rote; she spoke from a heart so full that it could not be held in. Sometimes she told us fascinating stories about the foundation of the Sacred Heart in France, about the way in which it had spread so rapidly, and about the good that it was called upon to do in the New World. I still seem to hear our loved Mistress speaking. Her ways were so simple that the littlest child found it easy to come close to her, yet her dignity of bearing was such that the oldest of us respected her. The rare qualities of her nature formed a setting for the supernatural gifts and graces which shone out in her like rich gems.

Who was Mary Ann Hardey to be talking to the children in such a fashion? She was scarcely more than a child herself, and had been in religion but a scant two years. She was a Novice, just learning to live the life of her Society, and she had never been abroad. Yet we hear her telling enthusiastic and circumstantial stories of the foundation of the Society in France, as though she had been through it all herself. Further, there were then only three houses of the Sacred Heart in America, all in the Mississippi Valley and in a state of pioneer

[1] See notes on page 477 for the sources of quotations and historic references.

hardship, yet she gravely talks of the great good that the Society is to do in this raw new land, quite sure that it will spread there as fast as it has done in France. She is the last person to suspect that she herself is to be an instrument of that wide and rapid spread, yet she is very confident that it will take place. This inexperienced girl talks like a witness and a prophet to the children of Saint Michael's, and the paradox is that she has the right to do so.

The clue to the paradox lies in the simple fact that Mary Ann at the age of fifteen had given herself over, body and soul, mind and will, into the power of something greater than herself. She had given her life, sight unseen, to a Society, knowing that in so doing she was giving herself to God not in her own way but in the way of the Society, a large, sure, strong way, found by a Saint and made broad by many other saintly women, a way of the spirit crystallized into practical rules and customs and confirmed by the Church as God's in the very year of which we are writing. She had given herself to it with a youthful whole-heartedness which was to last increasingly into old age, and in return the Society of the Sacred Heart gave her, to be used as her own, its spirit, its manner and its traditions.

Tradition, says a modern educator, is "the most powerful controlling factor in any human environment." [2] That which controls human environment is transmitted by living human beings; a vigorous moral body is built up by the influence of one personality upon another, by the action of loyal and loving minds upon docile minds, carried on across the years in such wise that time is but the measure of growth. The Society of the Sacred Heart had been founded only in 1800, and so, although it was itself the outgrowth of age-old forces within the Church, its distinctive modes of life were not yet of very long standing. Yet traditions it had, traditions which made up in energy for what they lacked in duration. They had been brought painfully across the ocean in 1818, and had at once accomplished the remarkable feat of making life in a small wooden house on the Missouri River substantially the same as life on the Rue des Postes in Paris, the accidental differences serving but to mark the essential unity. Blessed Philippine Duchesne had carried them straight from Saint Madeleine Sophie, but they had reached Mary Ann through still another intermediary, Mother Eugénie Audé. Each step in the transmission had brought about not a lessening but an increase in the force of the current which gathered strength with each new life swept into its stream. The Novice could well speak to the children of the happenings which she had not seen in France, for they were more than the repeated memories of other people; they were a flame kindled and carried from mind to mind, and the children caught the glow.

With such a hold on the past it was safe to speak of the future. Mary Ann was eager for the spread of her traditions; her own part in the realization of the dream was irrelevant to herself. It is we, looking back upon the whole story, who see her as an outstanding and unselfconscious actor. We feel in her, as her auditors at Saint Michael's felt and acknowledged, the ascendancy of a strong personality, gifted exceedingly. Yet her gifts were not of the singular but of the social order, the gifts of an organizer rather than of an innovator, of a guardian rather than of an explorer, gifts which required—and received—the cooperation of others for their full exercise. She merged both personality and gifts in the Society, which used them. From this comes another paradox: Mother Hardey is most completely herself when most identified with the movements of a larger body.

Her share in the task for which she was used lay not among the difficult beginnings, but in the perhaps more crucial period of expansion. While she was still at St. Michael's, Blessed Philippine Duchesne, in the small Convent at Florissant, was being shaped on the anvil where white-hot desire is forged into sanctity by suffering. The power of her tremendously strong spiritual life enveloped Mary Ann Hardey's light-hearted beginnings, for there was to be a relation between their lives. To quote from an early French biography: "If we compare the Society to a tree fruitful for the glory of God, Mother Duchesne was the hidden root from which the tree draws its life and Mother Hardey the vigorous trunk whose many branches covered the land of America with its beneficent shade." Lately the infallible voice of the Church has set the bells of Saint Peter's ringing with joy by proclaiming aloud that Rose Philippine Duchesne is Blessed, heroic in sanctity, because she let God do His work in her to the fulness of His own desire. Our rejoicing has been great, not only because of the glory that has come to her, but also because we know that we hold in our hands the good things that she bought for us by such a life; they are ours to use. We may wonder, perhaps, just how they have reached us through the intervening years. Mother Hardey's life, interwoven not only with that of Mother Duchesne but with many others less conspicuous but formed after the same pattern, is part of the answer.

If the circumstances of her mission were less picturesque than those faced by Mother Duchesne, they were none the less exacting. It may take as much courage to face a battery of business men over a matter of property as to pursue an Indian tribe into its retreat, armed only with the Gospel. To buy a house in a crowded city may be less romantic than to build one on a frontier, but the vision that inspires both actions is the same. They who sow in tears are rightly called heroes after death; they who tend and cut the grain and make a second sowing may have paid as heavy a price of labour and be no less deserving of honour. The fact that a certain measure of honour may come to them during life sometimes makes the task of such harvesters the harder, when they are moved as much by supernatural views and by love of the cross as were their predecessors. Mother Duchesne's life was moulded by the French Revolution, and by hardships in a rough new land. Mother Hardey's life kept pace with the advance of civilization through the span of the inventive nineteenth century; if her first apostolic journey was made in a mule cart, she soon took to a train. Mother Duchesne was a messenger of Good Tidings from the Old World to the New. Mother Hardey was American through and through; her life was bound up with the growth of her country, and contributed to the growth of the Church within it. But at the end the wheel came full circle, for she went to pass her last years in the France from which her Society had come, and to die at its Mother House. Her novice enthusiasms had their rounded realization.

She did her appointed work with singular rectitude, correctness and ease. She was direct and literal in thought, quietly powerful in action. The unusually perfect balance of her faculties has tended to obscure her personality for those of a later generation who cannot hear her voice or watch the play of her expression. To some she has come to be colourless, even unsympathetic, by force of sheer righteousness. The fact is that Mother Hardey has become merged in the work that she accomplished, as she herself would have wished to be. Yet, as we study that work and gauge the forces at play, it grows clearer what manner of woman this was who could so identify herself with them, a woman worthy of study and of admiration, and sure to win love when known. Those who knew her loved not her abilities but herself. This identification of the person with her work is stressed in a letter written at the time of her death by the Reverend Robert Fulton, Provincial of the Jesuits:

> I have often said that Mother Hardey will hold the first place of American women in our Church History. Besides her material

and visible achievements, what is most striking about her is the extraordinary affection she inspired in the members of her Community. This is entirely beyond parallel. In those achievements how much labour involved! How prolific the results! In that universal, I had almost said passionate, affection, what a proof of rare qualities in her to attract it. Mother Hardey's life will be the history of your Community.

This paradox of the relation of an individual to a body is one which is troubling the world today, for better or for worse; but the political problem has a Mystery as its divine counterpart. The two-edged fear roused by the words "Dictator" and "the masses," turns into inspired hope when we say instead "Leader" and "union," and from that into adoring faith when we say "Head" and "Body," Christ and the Body of Christ. Within this Body which is the Church no member is independent of another, for "the eye cannot say to the hand 'I need not thy help,' " and the more each member is its virile self the more fruitful is the interdependence. The very division of gifts calls for union, that the members may supplement each other, "for the perfecting of the saints, for the work of the ministry, for the edifying of the Body of Christ." In the life of Mother Hardey this truth is seen at work with peculiar clarity. It was a life of giving and of taking; she gave what she had and took what was given to her, only to spend it for the Church, the Society and her country. One alone could do little enough, but one in a Society could strive with multiple strength towards "the measure of the age of the fulness of Christ"—in America. It was a work for one and many.

In the Body of Christ is the Heart of Christ. For Its glory the Society of the Sacred Heart had been founded, and for Its love Blessed Philippine had braved a wide sea and a wide, strange land. Devotion to It expanded in the measure of Its penetration by souls, playing a more integral part in the inner and outer life of the Church as year by year "all things grow up in Him who is the Head." The child at St. Michael's, listening to stories in the outdoor evening-time, could not fail to be drawn to It, for "Mother Hardey spoke to us of the love of the Heart of Jesus. She never grew tired of talking so, and we never grew tired of listening. . . . She spoke from a heart so full that it could not be held in." The Novice's later days were to be amazingly busy, taken up with problems of government; she would measure her life against the history of a vigorous young nation growing up. She became a builder and a doer. But beyond the length of her travels, the breadth of her foundations, the depth of the whirl of more or less mundane affairs both picturesque and drab that claimed her time, lay a fourth dimension of prayer in which the heart of herself lived at home. Without holiness she might have done the work that she did, but it would not have borne the fruit that it has. When her contemporaries compared the story of her activities to the *Book of Foundations* of Saint Teresa, they were not thinking of her travels. She prayed as deeply as she travelled widely, and grew holy under the double pressure. Spiritual lives are the lives that count in Church History, and Mother Hardey's spirituality was, once more, that of a Society. Like it, she was "wholly consecrated to the glory of the Sacred Heart of Jesus."

The sun is setting at Saint Michael's and the children are lost in the night. Each day must close before the next begins, but with the lengthening out of time retrospect becomes a new reality. "I still seem to hear our loved Mistress speaking" wrote our recording child after many years. Late comers too can hear her, for the traditions of which she spoke are still in transmission, and Mother Hardey's own life is by now a part of them.

II

FROM THE ARK AND THE DOVE

THE LITTLE VILLAGE of Piscataway appears, to the eyes of the traveller driving through it on a summer afternoon, to have fallen asleep many years ago. It lies cupped among the gentle hills of Prince George's County in southern Maryland, folded into oblivion by woods and farmland. A dignified Georgian house or two stand aloof from the smaller dwellings along the road, many of which have been abandoned as though the stream of life were ebbing there. Yet the village lies just across the Potomac from the more remembered Mount Vernon, and the signs placed here and there along the road by the Maryland Historical Society impress even the hurried tourist with the fact that this seemingly negligible little town is endowed with the dignity of a great past. Perhaps it is not so much the ebb tide as a quiet eddy that holds Piscataway in its dreamy, leaf-shadowed charm. General Washington crossed and recrossed the spot in Revolutionary days, but where the creek of clear brown water twists along the highway and broadens into the river, earlier events took place which were significant for the planting and spread of the Church in the United States. The soft air that rests over the forests and hills and multi-coloured fields of Tidewater Maryland is redolent of stirring Catholic traditions, and here in Piscataway, most fittingly, Mary Ann Hardey was born on the eighth of December, 1809.

The story of her family and the history of her native State begin together and run parallel. Although she left the environment of Maryland while still a child, its spirit was in her blood, and the racial gifts that she brought to the service of her Society were a birthright. We might almost say that they came over the sea in the *Ark* and the *Dove*. When the sails of those two vessels rose in the stiff, bright November wind, and poised for flight in the harbour of Cowes on the Isle of Wight so many years ago, there was a Nicholas Hardy (as the name was then spelled) among the pilgrims crowded on the narrow decks. He, like the many other high-souled adventurers around him, was willing, for his faith and freedom's sake, to let the shores of England slip forever over his horizon.

The place in England which Master Hardy thought of as home that day is not known to us, nor anything of the life that he had lived till the day when he took to the sea. His name does not occur among those of "near twenty gentlemen," [1] nor on extant lists of other passengers on that voyage. These lists are recognizably incomplete, as the number of colonists was estimated by Lord Calvert at about three hundred and twenty, and the names of the "Redemptioners," or indentured servants, who accompanied the expedition were not recorded. These latter were often men of rank and name who had lost their fortunes, sometimes through penal fines, and who pledged their services to more opulent settlers for a limited time in order to pay their passage. Still more often they were "any lusty able young man, that is willing to labour and take pains." [2] Whoever he may have been, Nicholas Hardy was among the number of hard-pressed Catholics across whose well-nigh hopeless future had flashed the promise held out to such as he in "A Declaration of Lord Baltimore's Plantation in Mary-land, wherein is set forth how Englishmen may become angels; the King's Dominions be extended and the adventurers attain land and gear; together with other advantages of that sweet land." This enticing prospect had been printed and circulated in pamphlet form in the February of 1633. It is no wonder that many men like Master Hardy were stirred to action on reading that:

> The chief intention of my Lord is, and also the same ought to be of all others who venture fortunes with him, to plant Christianity there. An intendment so full of Christian honour, making men Angels who undertake it, as never more noble enterprise entered in English hearts. The regions are *Alba ad messem*, ready to receive the law of Christ. The Indians themselves sending farre and nigh for teachers, to instruct and Baptize them. . . . What doubt then can bee made but many thousands of Soules may be brought to Christ by this most glorious Enterprise; and it may indeed be called most glorious, seeing it is the saving of Soules, which was the work of Christ the King of Glory. But, for all that men are not so noble-minded as to hold their level purely at this end, so great and glorious, but commonly Pleasure wealth and honour are the Adamants that draw them; God's dearly-good Providence hath wrapped also all these together in this one action, that neither higher nor lower inducements might be wanting.[3]

The Latin version of the same advertisement added that "surely such a design is worthy of Christians, worthy of angels, worthy of Englishmen." It reads "dignum angelis, dignum anglis," recalling the play on words made long before by Pope Saint Gregory the Great when the sight of the Anglian slave-youths in the market in Rome who were "non Angli sed angeli," kindled his desire to send missionaries to England. The flame of his zeal was still spreading in 1633.

The day of sailing was November 22nd. At the last moment Father Andrew White, who was to be the scribe as well as the Apostle of the venture, was hurried quietly on board with his companions Father Altham and Brother Gervase, for it would not have been well to publicize the presence of Jesuits among the colonists. The moment was grave. George Calvert, first Lord Baltimore, who had paid for his faith with his political honours, who had spent himself only a few years before in attempting to found a colony in Nova Scotia in the interests of religious toleration, and whose singularly upright, clear and generous mind had formed the plans for the Maryland venture, had but recently died. In view of the difficulties in England during those days of intrigue and penal oppression, his son Cecil, second Lord Baltimore, had suddenly decided that it would be better for him not to sail in person to *Terra Mariae*, and the adventurers rallied under the direction of Leonard, his younger brother. So at Cowes a messenger boarded the boat with a letter from Cecil, containing careful instructions for the journey and for the future. The first of the series of fifteen injunctions reads:

> His Lo^pp^ requires his said Governor and Commissioners th^t^ in their voyage to Mary Land they be very carefull to preserve unity and peace amongst all the passengers on Shipp-board, and that they suffer no scandall nor offence to be given to any of the Protestants, whereby any just complaint may heereafter be made, by them, in Virginia or in England, and that for that end, they cause all Acts of Romane Catholique Religion to be done as privately as may be, and that they instruct all the Romane Catholiques to be silent upon all occasions of discourse concerning matters of Religion; and that the said Governor and Commissioners treate the Protestants wth as much mildness and favour as Justice will permit. And this is to be observed at Land as well as at Sea.[4]

It was a practical beginning—in which expediency had to pave the way for zeal—of that spirit of religious toleration and freedom of conscience which has since been recognized as

Maryland's contribution to the government of the United States.

It is likely that Nicholas Hardy sailed in the *Ark*, "our strong ship of four hundred tons; a better could not be built of wood and iron." [5] Only a small group, presumably of seasoned sailors, could venture on the *Dove*, a little pinnace of scarcely forty tons. What Nicholas lived through in the next few weeks has been recorded in the words of his companion, Father White. Their hearts rose together in good spirits when "on S[t] Cecilias day, the 22 of November 1633, with a gentle northern gale we set saile from the Cowes about 10 in the morninge." Together they shared the excitement of a race out of harbour with a French ship, having "a greate recreation to see that ship and ours runne for the fame with all the cloath they could make, an howers space with faire winde and weather, and pleasant sound of trumpetts." The *Ark* won, of course. Together they suffered heart-ache when "the winde grew still lowder and lowder, makeing a boysterous sea, and about midnight we espied our pinnace with her two lights, as she had forewarned us, in the shroodes, from w[ch] time till six weeks, we never see her more, thinkeing shee had assuredly beene foundred and lost in those huge seas." Together they gave thanks when the pinnace finally appeared off the Scilly Isles, "God provideing a convenient guard for that small vessel." They passed through times of fear together, as when "the like cloude gathered in a fearefull manner, terrible to the beholders, so that ere it began to blow it seemed all the sprightes and witches of Maryland were now set in battaile array against us. This evening the master saw the sunne fish to swimme against the sunnes course, a thing evidently shewing fearfull storms to come." But the perils were passed at length, so that by the time land was sighted they had "soe prosperous a navigation, as our mariners never saw so sweet a passage."

The land too was grateful to the eye when they came into

Chesapeake Bay on March 3, 1634, for "This baye is the most delightful water I ever saw, between two sweet landes. In this place on our B: Ladies day in Lent we first offered (*i.e.* offered Mass), erected a crosse, and with devotion tooke solemne possession of the Country." The place where they landed was Saint Clement's Island, and the event of that momentous day is described in the Latin account which Father White wrote for the General of the Jesuits in Rome:

> On the day of the Annunciation of the most Holy Virgin in the year 1634 we celebrated Mass for the first time on this island. This had never been done before in that part of the world. After we had completed the sacrifice we took upon our shoulders a great cross which we had hewn out of a tree, and advancing in order to the appointed place, with the assistance of the Governor and his associates and other Catholics, we erected a trophy to Christ the Saviour, humbly reciting, on our bended knees, the litanies of the Sacred Cross with great devotion.[6]

It was well that it was Lady Day, for had not King Charles I laid it down in his Charter to Lord Baltimore that "wee of our further grace, certain knowledge and meere motion, have thought fit to erect the same Countrey and Ilands into a Colony, as out of the fullnesse of Our Royall Power and Prerogative, Wee doe, for Us, Our Heires and Successors, erect and incorporate them into a Province, and doe call it Mary Land, and So from henceforth will have it called"? Men saying the name might pay reverence thereby to Queen Henrietta Maria, knowing her large share in the procuring of their most munificent Charter, but as the years passed the larger claims of the Queen of Heaven were acknowledged by the owners and lovers of Maryland. Today a massive white cross stands on the island where Nicholas Hardy first heard Mass in a new world, erected by later Pilgrims and dedicated on the tercentenary of that very Lady Day.

But Saint Clement's Island was too small for a permanent settlement. We do not know whether Nicholas was among those who accompanied the Governor as he sailed up the Potomac in the *Dove*, seeking to make friends among the Indians and to find a permanent home. In the words of Father White:

> They went to Pascatoway, the seat of the Emperour, where 500 bowmen came to meet them at the water side. Here the Emperour, lesse feareing then the rest came privately aboard, where he found kind usage, and perceiveing we came with good meaneing towards them, gave leave to us to sett downe where we pleased. The King being aboard, his men by the water side feared some treason, till by interpretours we assured them otherwise. The Indians began to loose feare and come to our coart of guarde, and sometimes aboard our shipp, wondering where that tree should grow, out of which so great a cannow should be hewn, supposing it all of one piece, as their cannows use to be. They trembled to heare our ordinance thinking them fearefuller then any thunder they had ever heard.[5]

After this friendly beginning the pinnace crept back from Piscataway, and at length the wanderers chose for themselves an idyllic spot near where the Chesapeake and the Potomac meet. "This baye is the most delightfull water I ever saw, between two sweete landes . . . The Potomac, which we have made St. Gregories, is the sweetest & greatest river I have ever seene so that the Thames is but a little finger to it." The place pleased them, as well it might, for "it abounds not alone with profit but with pleasure, *Laus Deo*," with which verdict Father White concludes his *Briefe Relation*. A little stream flowed down into a tidal arm of the Potomac, and this they named Saint Mary's River. The town which grew up on the high bluff overlooking it was called Saint Mary's City, continuing the tradition of Lady Day, a town built upon land bought, not wrested, from the Indians, for to avoid all occasions of dislike and Colour of wrong, we bought the space of thirtie miles of ground of them, for axes, hoes, cloth and hatchets. . . . Is this not miraculous that a nation a few daies before in generall armes against us and our enterprise should like lambs yeeld themselves, glad of our company, giveing us houses, land, and livings for a trifle? Digitus Dei est hic, and some great good is meant toward this people.[5]

Round about this space of thirty miles, stretching in all directions, lay the grants of land parcelled out among the settlers. The grants were generous, for it was stipulated in the "Conditions propounded by the Lord Baltimore to such as shall goe or adventure into Maryland," that "What person soever, as aforesaid, shall transporte himselfe, or any less number of servants than five, he shall have assigned to him, his heires and assignes for ever, for himselfe, 100 acres of good land within said Province; and for and in respect of every such servant, 100 acres more." As the Redemptioners gradually regained their independence they too claimed land, and before long many were the homesteads that scattered the country-side, "built in as decent and uniforme a manner as their abilities and the place will afford." The settlers were as decent and uniform as their houses, for each was required to bring from the old country "two Munmoth caps or hats, three falling Bands, three shirts, one Wastecoat, one suit of Canvas, one suit of Frize, one suite of Cloth, one course cloth, or frize coate, three pairs of stockings, six pairs of shooes, Inkle for garters, one dozen of points." The figure of Nicholas Hardy thus emerges before the mind's eye sturdily and plentifully clad in garments more suggestive of the Puritan than of the Cavalier, but it is not hard to picture the face under the Munmoth hat as of the gay and gallant type of man who built our southern colonies into clusters of warm-hearted and high-living homes. What the women who followed the men in such numbers should wear was not stipulated; they could evidently be trusted to bring a suitable wardrobe with them, and to increase it as the years passed. The Last Will of Mistress Jane Fenwick mentions red cotton coats, spangled petticoats, and taffeta suits, with plenty of scarves, gloves and head-clothes both plain and fancy.[7]

It is evident that soon these "decent houses" had become not only comfortable but elegant. The location of Nicholas Hardy's home is veiled from us by a mist not of tide but of time, but wherever it was, he rooted his family traditions deep in the pleasant soil. Nicholas could not then have foreseen that the huge tract of property granted to Cuthbert Fenwick,[8] one-time indentured servant who rose to be a leading legislator of the Colony, would later pass into the hands of the Hardey family. Still less could he have foreseen that the house named Rosecroft built on that land, crowning a bluff high over the Saint Mary's River, commanding a view incomparably fair of woody points receding into widening distances beyond the water, would be, for two brief years, a Convent of the Sacred Heart.

The family of Nicholas became part of the place that had received it so warmly; its traditions grew like the boxwood planted at Rosecroft from slips brought from England, slowly, thrivingly, deeply at home. The name of Hardy (or Hardey) does not appear among the extant records of the Colony until 1687, and even then the references are not specific enough to enable us to trace its history in detail. It is family tradition that has handed down to the present day the fact of the presence of Nicholas and his sons among the Calvert settlers, and when, at a later date, individuals emerge from the time-mist, their actions are such as we might expect from a family that had formed an integral part of the growth of Maryland. The State Archives[9] reconstruct for us the scenes in which the first Hardeys took part. Great moments stand out from the circumstantial account of the barter of guns and of food-stuffs, of the levying of fines in the form of so many pounds of tobacco. They reveal the fact that in Saint Mary's City the purest type of democratic government was practiced from the time of the first meeting of the Legislative Assembly in 1635, at which every freeman voted, a meeting which caused Lord Baltimore himself to withdraw the right of initiating legislation which could have made him an autocrat in his Palatine Province. At a subsequent Assembly an oath was taken by the Governour giving official enforcement to Lord Baltimore's policy of religious toleration:

> I will not by myself or any other, directly or indirectly trouble, molest or discountenance any person professing to believe in Jesus Christ for or in respect to religion. I will make no difference of person in conferring offices, favours or rewards for or in respect of religion, but merely as they shall be found faithful and well-deserving, and endued with moral virtues and abilities; my aim shall be public unity and if any person or officer shall molest any person professing to believe in Jesus Christ on account of his religion, I will protect the person and punish the offender.[10]

It was not long before this principle was applied to Jews as well as to Christians, as in the case of Dr. Lumbroze in 1658. Through all the ups and downs, the strange reversals, betrayals and recoveries of Maryland history, that principle was to persist until in 1789 it passed, largely through the instrumentality of Bishop John Carroll, Charles Carroll of Carrollton and Daniel Carroll, into the Constitution of our country as its First Amendment: "Congress shall make no laws respecting an establishment of religion or prohibiting the free exercise thereof."

While the political leaders of the colony were thus establishing civil and religious peace, Father White and his companions began their work for the spread of God's kingdom. Today a monument bearing their names stands in a wood near a bend of the Saint Mary's River not far from Rosecroft. The sadly neglected state of the road leading to it shows that few visit the semicircular altar, containing bricks from the chapel of old Saint Mary's City, upon which Mass was said at the time of its tercentenary in thanksgiving by those who had inherited the gifts of those apostles. From the beginning the history of the Maryland Jesuit Mission ran parallel with the history of the State, but on the plane of the spirit, so that never did the families of Maryland, even in the difficult days of persecution, want for soul-Bread. The pioneer priests wrote in their *Annual Letters* to the Mother House in Rome accounts of their hardships and of their consolations, with the latter predominating, as is the way with those who feel the touch of God's hand in trial. "As for the Catholics," they wrote in 1638, "the attendance on the Sacraments here is so large that it is not greater among the Europeans, in proportion to the number." As for the Indians, they were won by the affection, understanding and patient labour of the missionaries with a speed and a completeness hardly equalled in the annals of the American Apostolate. The most notable conversion brings the narrative again to Piscataway, and one would like to think that Nicholas Hardy was among the "many more" who accompanied Governor Calvert to that spot where woods and water fold together in loveliness and which a future Frederick Hardey was one day to call home.

We stated last year what hope we had conceived of converting the Tayac, or the Emperor, as they call him, of Pascatoa. From that time, such is the kindness of God, the event has not disappointed the expectation; for he has joined our faith, some others also being brought over with him; and on the 5th of July, 1640, when he was sufficiently instructed in the mysteries of the faith, in a solemn manner he received the sacramental waters in a little chapel, which for that purpose and for divine worship, he had erected out of bark, after the manner of the Indians. At the same time the queen, with an infant at her breast, and another of the principal men, whom he specially admitted to his counsels, together with his little son, were regenerated in the baptismal font. To the Emperor, who was called Chilomacon before, was given the name of Charles; to his wife that of Mary. The others receiving the Christian faith, had Christian names allotted to them. The Governor was present at the ceremony, together with his secretary and many others; nor was anything wanted in display which our means could afford. In the afternoon the Tayac and his queen were united in matrimony in the Christian manner; then a great holy cross was erected, in carrying which to its destined place the king, Governor, secretary, and others, lent their shoulders and hands; two of Ours in the meantime chanting before them the Litany in honour of the Blessed Virgin.[6]

These early years were a Golden Age of colonial prosperity, but too many successive years of hope fulfilled is not the way of history, and the first serious trouble which threatened the colony affected Nicholas Hardy in a directly personal way. The restless, malignant Captain William Claibourne, entrenched on the Island of Kent which he claimed for himself though it lay within the boundaries of the charter of Maryland, repeatedly stirred up religious prejudice against Papists in order to serve his own ends. He seized upon every opportunity to harass the Calvert Government until his final armed revolt in conjunction with the marauding Puritan Captain Ingle in 1643 ruined many a homestead. Among those who rallied to his side was a certain man named Hardy. The reaction of Nicholas Hardy, who was not of the same family and who had heartily borne arms in defence of the Catholic settlers, was unmistakably positive. The name had been disgraced. He inserted the letter "e" before the "y" in his own signature, requesting that his heirs should do likewise, so that no relative of his should ever be confused with an apostatizing rebel. Mother Hardey had reason for her pride in the spelling of her name.

But Nicholas' grandchildren were not so well off; it could not have been any easy thing for them to hold to the Faith with the same full and hearty loyalty. Beyond the borders of Maryland the Church was making strenuous headway throughout the still scantily mapped reaches of North America. In 1682, the very year in which Governor Dongan of New York built his tiny chapel on Bowling Green in the teeth of both English and Dutch prejudice, the Indian girl Tekakwitha let her life of high and silent holiness burn out like a lamp in a cruder birch-bark chapel in the forests of Canada. Still other chapels built by the vanguard of the French missionaries were springing up in the desert places of Texas not far from the trails where the first martyr blood to be shed in the New World, that of Father Juan Padilla, had fallen. But in Maryland, where its establishment had been most pacific, the Church fell upon evil days. In 1688 John Coode, the chameleon trouble-maker, organized an "Association in Armes for the Defence of the Protestant Religion," to frustrate a fantastic plot laid at the door of the sturdy Catholics of the Colony. Terrorism, not unlike that fomented by Titus Oates in London a few years previously, resulted in the overthrow of the Calvert Government, the official establishment of the Church of England, and the removal of the Capital from Saint Mary's City to Annapolis. The apostasy of Benedict Calvert, fourth Lord Baltimore, made the skies dark indeed.

The persecuted Catholics could not know that hope and a resurrection of their first principles of liberty had come to their shores with the arrival of young Charles Carroll, just before Coode's rebellion. His grandson, a greater Charles Carroll, wrote of the event in after years:

My grandfather, being a Roman Catholic by religion, resolved on withdrawing from the oppression of that period by emigrating to this country. He selected Maryland chiefly because toleration was by royal charter extended to it, and afterwards confirmed by provincial statute. Upon leaving the Mother Country he changed, with a felicity of thought almost prophetic, the motto of his family *In Fide et in Bello fortes*, to *Ubicumque cum Libertate* in allusion to the cause which induced him to leave the shores of his native land.[10]

Carroll imparted this high-hearted idealism to his grandsons who were to do such great things for America and for the Church, but in the meantime, where were such families as the Hardeys to hear Mass? The Penal Laws rested heavily upon Maryland throughout the eighteenth century, and the prohibition against building churches could only be evaded by constructing chapels under the same roof as private houses. To places such as "Priest Neale's Mass-House," built on Deer Creek in 1747, Catholic families came from great distances to Mass and the Sacraments. Names such as Spalding, Neale, Brent, Fenwick and Hardey, which are woven like bright threads through our Church History, testify to long fidelity and to a high price paid for it. The Jesuits had continued along the path of unremitting zeal blazed by Father White, and true to their traditions had founded a School at Bohemia, Delaware, in 1738, an "American Tusculum," where the classics were well taught and where the pupils who chose to follow the classical course paid three pounds a year more than the others in recognition of the fact.

In 1755 the first ship-load of exiled Acadians touched at American ports, and soon from the Atlantic to the Mississippi centers of Catholic life felt a quickening impulse at the touch of these confessors of the Faith. Those who made their way to Baltimore lived in a large unfinished brick house placed at their disposal by a kindly Irishman, Mr. Edward Fotteral. In their spiritual destitution they called upon Charles Carroll, who sent them his own chaplain, and Mass was said for the first time in the Primatial See of the United States upon a home-made altar. Everywhere the story was the same; the needs of the Church were crying out for greater attention. In far-off London Bishop Challoner was quick to hear, and he informed Rome that the Church in the Colonies would soon be ready for its independence.

At this point of the story individual members of the Hardey family step once more into the light.[11] In the shadowy background is a William Hardey, the grandson, possibly the son, of the pioneering Nicholas. Then in direct descent comes George, then another William. At some time the family moved from Saint Mary's to Prince George's County and even farther, for Anthony Hardey, the son of William Hardey and Elizabeth Lanham, was widely known in Virginia as well as in Maryland. Others settled further north in Howard County. Anthony lived, for a time at least, at Alexandria, where tradition brings his active young figure out of the colourless region of supposition into the clear sunshine rippling upon the Potomac and its wooded banks in the days when George Washington was a boy. If shadows of grave events and of responsibilities to come ever fell across their minds, the two young men did not let it darken the walks and sports that they shared together in the opulent country-side. When the name of Washington later became the best known and loved in the new nation that he had helped to shape, Anthony Hardey could not refrain from letting his family know that he had, once at least, been superior to the great General and first President; he had outdone his comrade in athletics in the days of his youth. His boasting was expressed in the courtly phrasing of those days of quick deeds and of slow, careful utterance—he had vanquished George Washington in sports, "but not for worlds," he explained, "would I have harmed my comrade, for I considered him a type of all that is gentle and manly in youth." Washington's early acquaintance with such characters as Anthony Hardey may have been a factor in his generous appreciation in later days of the patriotism of his Catholic fellow-countrymen.

Then revolution broke out and war swept in red lines through the blue, green and gold pattern of the sunny Atlantic colonies. Anthony was back in Maryland by this time, for we find his signature affixed to the following declaration drawn up by the citizens of Prince George County: "I do swear that I do not hold myself bound to yield any allegiance or obedience to the King of Great Britain, and that I will be true and faithful to the State of Maryland." [12] He then proved his loyalty by fighting as First Lieutenant in the Middle Battalion of Prince George's County, while a fair young Hardey, presumably his sister, is remembered to have danced with Lafayette one night, and her ball-dress was folded away somewhere in the traditional attic where it lay for a hundred years or so, taken out now and then as though its silken flow still held the candle-gleam of romance.

When the nation emerged from its trial by arms men of the same faith as the Hardeys could breathe deeply in the new air. The bravery of the Catholic regiments had won recognition; Washington as Commander-in-Chief had answered the fanaticism of such men as John Jay by abolishing the vicious parodies of "Pope-Day." Most significant of all, the Reverend John Carroll, who had been a Jesuit until the suppression of the Society and who throughout the war had been quietly doing his duty as Pastor at Rock Creek, Maryland, was in 1784 named Prefect Apostolic of the Church in the New Republic. "I trust," he wrote in his letter of acceptance "that the foundation of religion will be so firmly laid in the United States that a most flourishing part of the Church will in time be developed here, to the consolation of the Holy See." During this hopeful time Anthony Hardey acquired an ample estate of some three hundred acres just north of Piscataway, known by the curious name of "Refuse" because a crotchety former owner had "refused to take up that piece which he was then running out for, for which reason he said he would call his piece the Refuse." Here he settled with his bride Teresa Coombes, and brought up his three sons and two daughters as blue-blood Marylanders. When his wife died he married Mary Green Hatton, and home-life went on.

The next twenty years, during which Anthony Hardey's sons were growing to manhood, were momentous ones which saw the beginning of the fulfilment of John Carroll's trust. They saw the foundation of Georgetown College, the opening of parishes in New York, Boston and Charleston. They saw the printing of the first Catholic Bible, and the first impress of the faith on public opinion through journalism. They saw enormous initial difficulties faced and overcome by the young Vicar Apostolic, who was consecrated Bishop of Baltimore on the Feast of the Assumption, 1790. And as though to show that his nation-wide work was to rest on the foundations of prayer, the same year saw the arrival of the Carmelites in Maryland. Although the Ursulines had been established in Louisiana Territory since 1727, Carmel was the first Convent to be opened on the actual soil of the United States. American girls had been going over the sea to the Carmel at Hoogstraeten since 1754, and now a small group of them returned, shepherded by Father Charles Neale, to be what Bishop Carroll called his "safeguard for the preservation of the Diocese." Already the spiritual life of the land was being energized by that Devotion which stands singularly for love, a love to be fostered first in the hiding-places of prayer and then to find its way abroad in active giving; the Devotion to the Sacred Heart was weaving itself from side to side of the continent. On the far western coast Father Junipero Serra, the Franciscan Apostle of the Indians, had painted an image of the Divine Heart on the wall of his dearest Mission Church at

Carmel-by-the-Sea; as years passed it faded into the yellow *adobe,* but the words written around it can still be read, "O Sagrado Corazon." To the east a stone church dedicated to the Sacred Heart lifted its spire over the valley of Conewago, while in Georgetown the Religious Community started by Mother Teresa Lalor chose the Rule of the Visitation, the Order to which the spread of the Devotion had been so specially entrusted. It would not be long before a Religious Society bearing the name of the Sacred Heart would reach America.

Thus the energies of the spiritual life had been released for full play in the eager young nation, and as though in confirmation of the fact the corner-stone of its first Cathedral was laid in Baltimore in 1806. In the same year Anthony Hardey's third son, Frederick William, came from Piscataway to Baltimore to claim his bride, Sarah Spalding.

III

AS CHILDREN WILL

A PERSONABLE young gentleman of the Hardey family had no reason for misgivings as he mounted the brief flight of white stone steps leading to the home of the Baltimore Spaldings; he could pull the bell-rope with assurance. In blood, in fortune and in faith the two young people were made for each other, thought Mrs. Spalding complacently, and she left Frederick sitting stiffly on a horse-hair sofa designed to assure formality to any courtship while she went upstairs to call Sarah. There was a moment of silence while the young man stared at the family portraits so like those in his own parlour; then the whisper of a silk skirt was heard slipping down along the banisters.

Although the first Spaldings to come to America may not have crossed with the Calverts in the *Ark* they arrived very soon after, and like Nicholas Hardey's, their homestead graced the fields of Saint Mary's County before 1650.[1] On Sundays when they met for Mass with the other citizens in a church of pioneer proportions they might have been forgiven for remembering—and mentioning—how the great Spalding Abbey in Crowland, Lincolnshire, towered up in the middle of the town that clung around it. The Abbey had been one of the thirteen spared by Henry VIII at the time of the spoliation, so no break had occurred in the traditions that the old Church gave as a christening gift to each generation of Spaldings. The name of the Abbey, or that of its predecessor in the same spot, emerges for one brief instant from the blank spaces of a still more distant history, that of Anglo-Saxon times. In the foundation charter granted in the eighth century by King Ethelbald to Crowland Abbey, the lands of the latter are said to extend "usque addificium Spaldeling," built on the lonely stretches of moor once sanctified by the prayers and presence of Saint Guthlac where "the green plain stood in God's protecting."

The inheritors of such a name were justly proud of it. They were related, in some way difficult now to trace, to the Virginia family of the same name, and they could also claim kinship with the Fenwicks. The Maryland branch did more than keep their ancestral faith intact; they spread it abroad. Kentucky, the first State west of the Alleghanies to be admitted to the Union, was also the first to receive and foster Catholic Missions.[2] Its beautiful valleys were cultivated very largely by Catholic migrants from Maryland, among whom was a Benedict Spalding who settled at Rolling Fork in 1790. Such men were actively loyal to their faith, and demanded so effectively that priests be sent to them that by 1806 the Church was thriving in that hardy, pioneer State. When, a few years later, religious life had taken root there under log-cabin conditions, a Mother Catherine Spalding was the first Superior of the Sisters of Charity of Nazareth. Still later the name was graced by two Prelates, Archbishop Martin J. Spalding of Baltimore, and Bishop John Lancaster Spalding of Louisville.

Frederick and Sarah were married in November, 1806.[3] The ceremony in all probability took place in Saint Peter's,[4] for long the pro-Cathedral, a plain little brick structure which could claim the honour of being the first Catholic church erected in the Primatial See of the United States, but which was then shrinking modestly into its place in history, while more resplendent churches were rising. The corner-stone of the Cathedral which was to overshadow them all had only just been blessed, but Saint Peter's, dignified in its fine old simplicity, was fit for a beautiful wedding. Mrs. Spalding, lavish by nature, spared nothing to make it so, for both families were patriarchally numerous, graced with the social distinction of their colonial race. Baltimore brides even in 1806 wore dresses of heavy white satin,[5] and Sarah Hardey, still in her 'teens, did honour to her low-necked gown with its long puffed sleeves and regal train while she played with a fan and spangled reticule. The veil of rich lace fell straight down from the high-piled hair. Frederick, had he strayed into the twentieth century, would be a more unfamiliar sight in a cutaway coat, high stock and knee breeches which had not yet outgrown the pre-Revolutionary mode. One would like to picture as clearly the celebrant as he stands there in the angular sanctuary. Can it be Bishop Carroll himself?

The beauties of Prince George County unrolled like a carpet along the way of the newly married couple, as mile after mile of winding dirt road brought them nearer to their new home. Hills lifted their tree-softened crests just high enough to enclose that home in its own little paradise. Piscataway Creek curved aimlessly in and out through the newly cultivated fields, till with sudden resolution it broadened its brown and dimpling surface and swept west to meet the blue Potomac. Their juncture was wide enough then to make the village into a port of some importance. In 1806 boats could still make their way up the creek whose small but obstinate voice was heard on quiet nights talking to the stones, while the larger river moved on in silence. Just across its shining surface rose the bluffs of Mount Vernon, and both banks were tense with the memories of Revolutionary days. A few miles to the north a new city was shaping itself into the Capital of the United States, and the future of Piscataway was as alive with promise as its past was rich with history.

The town was so small that each dwelling in it assumed a singular importance. The Georgian type of house, built of brick with white facings and tall white columns, was here replacing the older style of Maryland home with its creamy clapboard walls and gambrel roof, though huge brick chimneys still flanked the ends of every house telling of the warmth of many fireplaces within. The new Hardey estate quickly grew into the landscape. Rows of outhouses sprang up around it, sheltering a colony of devoted slaves. The line where garden merged into woodland became more sharply defined, enclosing a place of busy bounty. Other members of the Hardey family or of the Spalding would arrive by the carriage load to spend a week or two at a time, giving and receiving with Maryland open-handedness. Considering that the National Census of 1776 [6] shows that eight separate homesteads of the Hardey clan were established in Prince George County even then, and that twenty-six more marriages were celebrated in the next few years, we can picture what a family dinner—if complete—would have meant by 1806. The days passed very pleasantly without ever being too easy, for a sacred mode of living was engrafted upon the strenuousness of semi-primitive conditions. These circumstances had moulded Sarah into a mature and queenly housewife by the time the footsteps of her first little daughter, Ann, began to patter on the floor, and in the winter of 1809 her second child was born.

Mary Ann Hardey was proud that her birthday was the

Feast of the Immaculate Conception, for there was a national as well as a personal significance to the fact. On December 8, 1672, Father Marquette had received his orders to seek for the Great River,[7] and when, in the spring of the following year his canoe had drifted into the long current of the Father of Waters, "we began," he said, "all together a new devotion to the Blessed Virgin Immaculate which we practiced daily, addressing to her special prayers to place under her protection both our persons and the success of our voyage," and he named the mighty stream "River of the Immaculate Conception." In 1760 Our Lady as Conquistadora lifted her white banners over a large part of our continent when she was declared Patroness under the title of her Immaculate Conception of all lands owing allegiance to the crown of Spain. Later, in 1846, the fourth Provincial Council of Baltimore would name her Patroness of the Catholic Church in the United States under the same title. It was fitting that Mother Hardey, whose work was to begin on the Mississippi River and follow the course of the development of Catholic education throughout the country, should also owe her first allegiance to the Immaculate Conception.

The baby had time to grow exceedingly pretty before her grandmother Spalding came down from Baltimore to see her a year later. The golden hair had clustered into curls and the blue-grey eyes were wide and alert. Grandmother grew entirely too fond of her, and began to plan how she could take this entrancing child back to Baltimore where her own house now seemed very empty. An opportune epidemic of whooping cough furnished her with an occasion. Little Mary must be shielded from it at all costs, so "good Grandmother Spalding" as she was always called, drove off in triumph taking with her this favorite grand-child and Aunt Betty Edelin, the coloured Mammy. The Spalding carriage jolted along in the wake of the brilliantly painted public coaches which cut so fine a figure on the roads and behaved so badly in bogs and mountain passes. Such a long and difficult journey, thought Grandmother, should not be repeated too often for a very little girl. Once they were safely in Baltimore she would find reasons why her visit should be indefinitely prolonged. She was successful, for Mary remained the darling of her Grandmother's home till the age of five, a time almost long enough to spoil the charming and vivacious child completely.

Dressed in a long wadded coat of merino with a childish poke-bonnet to redeem it, Mary rattled about the streets of the third largest city of the country in a carriage-and-pair. At home she flitted in and out of the drawing room, dropping curtseys to all the distinguished people who came to call upon Mr. John Spalding, looking in her sashed muslin frock which reached to her ankles like a picture framed in the white wood of the doorway. She had occasion to stare at more than one Bishop, for those were the days when Baltimore, having just become a Metropolitan See, was throbbing with the administrative life of the American Church, and all high ecclesiastics found their way to the Spalding home. The new Cathedral of the Assumption was finished by this time, and when Mary heard Mass under its ample dome she could catch a glimpse of Archbishop Carroll, carrying the weight of his years and responsibilities up the altar steps to raise them aloft in Sacrifice.

Grandmother Spalding thought nothing too good for the pretty child; the child was inclined to think nothing good at all unless it squared with her own wishes; Aunt Betty had a hard time trying to please both. One day Grandmother generously bought a new pair of red slippers for Mary, who took a dislike to them. Betty produced the slippers with flattering words, first coaxing, then scolding, then threatening. The child sat in obstinate silence with her feet under her long skirts, and a deadlock ensued. Then suddenly one small foot was extended. Betty, with a crow of approval, slipped on the red shoe, but before it could be secured a vigorous kick sent it flying across the room. History is silent as to the outcome of the incident, and as to the possible repentance and reformation of the culprit. As a matter of fact, stories like this are only known to us through Mother Hardey herself who in later years would tell them, twinkle in eye, to her religious daughters whom she rightly suspected of seeing in her the model of every possible perfection. Edifying sequels—if any—were of set purpose omitted.

But an end came finally to this charming life in old Baltimore. The War of 1812 brought matters to a crisis. President Madison declared hostilities with the British in June. For the first two years the Hardeys were unconcerned—beyond due patriotism—for the fighting took place only on the high seas or along the Canadian borders, but in August, 1814, Redcoats were suddenly seen in the valley of the Potomac and their manoeuvres were visible from Piscataway. During the raid on Washington, with its alarms and excursions and its news that the White House was in flames, Sarah Hardey could be glad enough that Mary was at a safe distance in Baltimore. But matters were different when the British suddenly veered to the North. The fleet came up the Patapsco River to Baltimore itself, and General Ross, swearing that he would "eat dinner in Baltimore or in hell," led the army overland in the same direction. Then it was Grandmother Spalding's turn to be troubled, and to keep little Mary in a back room where the sound of the cannon would come muffled to her ears. All day and all night of September 12th the sound of the grim defence of Fort McHenry echoed through the city, till with the "dawn's early light" Francis Scott Key saw from his prison ship in the harbour that "our flag was still there."* The Brit-

* A granddaughter of Francis Scott Key would later be Mother Hardey's sister in Religion, Mother Mary Key Blunt, who died at Kenwood in 1939.

ish withdrew and Baltimore was safe, but by this time Sarah Hardey had made up her mind that Mary would, in every way, be better off at home.

Five years is not too young to undergo a crisis, and Mary remembered till late in life the pain of her adjustment to these new circumstances when she found herself, bewildered, in a family that she did not know. She had been the spoiled and solitary pet of her Grandmother's home, and now, as the first excitement caused by her return died down, she found herself but one little girl among four, neither the eldest nor the youngest nor the most loved. Ann was the responsible "big sister," Matilda was the baby, she and the third sister (whose name we do not know) were nobodies. She wandered disconsolately about the unfamiliar rooms, looking furtively now and then at her mother. Sarah did not force the child's love but waited till loneliness broke down the barrier; then the warm, natural, semi-outdoor life of home did the rest. Mary's gaiety came back.

More than any other force, she felt the strong sweet ascendency of her mother. Sarah was an incomparable mother, accomplishing her household tasks with a capable ease which left her heart free to spend its best on her husband and children, giving of her time and energies to whatever was worth doing, yet keeping deep spiritual reserves in her own soul. This was necessary for others as well as for herself, for she had, through force of circumstances, to be the link between God and her children. At intervals Mass was said at Piscataway by a priest from Bryantown, but there was little possibility of other religious practices, so Sarah supplied. Prayers were said in common with all the solemnity possible, and a holy picture was placed in each room of the house. Truth was the daily bread that the mother broke for her children, and the presence of God clung lovingly about her. "My mother was a saint," was Mary's all-embracing tribute in later years.

Such a mother soon made up for lost time in Mary's training, but all was not plain sailing for a child inclined to domineer. One day she behaved unbecomingly, in fact stubbornly, with her playmates, and her mother, knowing how beneficial is public humiliation for such as she, used the time-tried method of putting her in a corner with her face to the wall. Too proud to cry, Mary vented her rage by giving in to an old habit; she began to chew her fingernails furiously. No one paid any attention. Finally one of her uncles walked into the room and took in the situation. "Look out for that child," he said seriously to Sarah, "what she is doing now shows that she has strong passions." Mary stopped biting her nails while her relentlessly clear reasoning power asserted itself. If to bite her nails was a sign of something bad she would never do so again; and she never did. There was to be no half-in-half for Mary Hardey in matters of conduct. She was one to see a good thing, to want it, to get it.

In the meantime a momentous change was pending. One of Frederick's brothers, Charles Anthony Hardey, had migrated a short time before into Louisiana. For a while this elder brother had apparently vanished into the unfamiliar tangle of French and Spanish place-names that fringed the southwestern boundaries of the United States, but then letters began to come, enthusiastic letters that ended with tempting offers. Since the Louisiana Purchase in 1803 a stream of boats and wagons had been carrying adventurous Americans into the bayou land. The words of President Jefferson as he signed the Act of Purchase seem to have been taken as a program of action by many a citizen: "We have lived long, but this is the noblest work of our whole lives." The enormous stretch of indeterminate land which he had thus annexed under the name of Louisiana Territory, had in a few short years broken up into its component parts, and when in 1812 the lower end of the territory lying west of the Mississippi had been admitted as a state into the Union, bringing with it the kaleidoscopic remnants of the French and Spanish dominions that had already alternated there, a fresh wave of migration was set up. It was part of a tremendous surge, due largely to economic causes, which sent the population of the United States rolling westward after the close of the War with England in 1815. The State of Maryland was one of the foremost in sending family after family of its best citizens to seek new homes, and now came the letters from Anthony Hardey to tempt his relatives to join the wave. Characteristically, it was Sarah who saw the full opportunities of the offer, and it was she who urged Frederick to accept. It meant turning immigrant, leaving a settled land for an unsettled one, but where would any of our pioneers have been but for the women who followed or even led them to the west? These national movements were to affect Mary Hardey throughout her life, and so it was that at the age of seven she herself became a pioneer.

It was not restlessness or weariness of home that made Sarah eager to go; she meant to take her home with her. Grandmother and Grandfather Spalding understood the urge and did not oppose it, knowing that their daughter would carry with her all that the most conservative heart could wish. So they generously added to her patrimony by presenting the family with numbers of slaves and quantities of furniture and household goods. When the time for departure had actually come the number of slaves had reached one hundred, or so says legend, while for Sarah four little girls were already problem enough.

The start was made in late spring when floods had subsided and boggy roads were dry, so as to reach the deep south in the relative cool of autumn. It was just a year too soon for the migrants to take advantage of the first National Road then under construction from Cumberland on the Potomac to Wheeling on the Ohio.[8] Its macadamized surface was not quite ready for travel, so the Alleghenies had to be crossed in covered wagons along such roads as had already been beaten out by the Great Migration. Day after day the procession creaked and rumbled on, and if the rate of travel was tiresome there was compensation in the enchanting vistas of hills folding back in ridge after ridge about the shining headwaters of rivers that rushed in the green-tinted impetus of their youth through high and curving beds close to the sky. It was worth spending many days in the beauty of the Cumberland water-gap, where trees could be companionable with clouds, not to mention the nights when the four little girls curled up by the campfires while the men took turns in watching over their sleep. Mary was intensely active and observant, and this camping life had charms for such as she.

At last the Ohio River lay before them, no longer greenly rushing, but languidly indifferent to mud and traffic. Every variety of craft was plying up and down near Pittsburgh in the warm gold of the late spring sun. There were steamboats, still a sight to be stared at. They had recently acquired a second deck and twin smokestacks rising to a phenomenal height. Moving lazily among them were the great one hundred ton freight-barges drifting downstream or being poled up against the current. Intermediate in efficiency were the flat-boats worked by ungainly spindle oars at the sides, their squared ends bumping awkwardly against the river ripples. These best suited the practical needs of the Hardeys, and soon the whole colony of family, slaves, animals and baggage had been transferred to a series of flat-boats which set off in procession down the river.

Mary found life considerably more tedious now than when it had been possible to get out and walk by the crawling wagons from time to time, ostensibly to lighten by her few pounds the burden of the toiling beasts. They were all very cramped on the flat-boats, but a gently reproachful look from her mother was enough to silence her restlessness. She would look at Sarah with the peculiarly penetrating and steady gaze that was becoming characteristic and then try to imitate her. It was much for a lively child of seven to check her need for movement and to sit still under the awning at the back of the boat, helping to mind the baby who was of an age to crawl dangerously. The oars flashed and dipped, flashed and dipped; the crooning of the negroes in the boat behind kept time with them, the monotonous shore-line began to blur as the grey eyes blinked. Sarah smiled over her sleeping children, and prayed, as her way was whenever there was space for prayer.

The river wound along the boundary of the new State of Ohio, with the solemn wall of the forest rising to either side, broken now and then by some brave man's attempt to found a home there and even by flashy estates in pseudo-Italian style. They passed Cincinnati rising in its cup of hills, already "a beautiful little city in the midst of a highly cultivated country" with a market "equal in goodness to that of Philadelphia, but much cheaper." [9] Then south dropped the river, till its current grew swift and turgid in the excitement of its junction with the Mississippi. Charles Dickens, a few years later, lavished lugubrious rhetoric upon this forlorn place lying "at the junction of two rivers on ground so low and muddy that at certain seasons of the year it is inundated to the housetops, a breeding place of Ague, fever and death." [10] Then the flatboats moved along the River once of the Immaculate Conception, following in the wake of steamboats to avoid the snags and sandbars that played tricks with the twisting stream.

The hardwood forests with their familiar catalpas and maples vanished and Louisiana rolled away to their right, flat but with a mysterious undulation. The trees that stood knee deep at the edge of the stream were strange with Spanish moss. Funereally black in the damp shadows of the forest, pale green-grey where the slanting sunlight reached them, silvery in the changeable hours of dawn and dark, the streamers of moss bewitched the land. They quivered with undefined movement in a breeze too slight to lift a leaf, yet they made no sound as leaves do. Mrs. Hardey, whose thoughts seemed like words in the silence, wondered how far behind that magic curtain lay their home-to-be.

Their debarkation would be an elaborate affair, and it was necessary to go all the way to New Orleans where they hoped that Charles Anthony Hardey would meet them. From Natchez on, expectation grew high. Mary, more interested in people and their doings than in incomprehensible scenery, found that the days, from being long and dull and heat-ridden, had become almost too short. The vague swampy boundaries of the river were cut clean now by levees, and over their tops the little girl could see the white columns of plantation houses set in queenly opulence among the fields of rising cotton or cane. There were roads with carriages moving on them, piers with gay boats tied to them, there were full-throated Negro voices drifting in the mellow noons. As they neared the city the forests grew thin and the traffic on the water grew thick. The Hardey flat-boats seemed to be in everybody's way, and Mary found herself gazing at close quarters into the faces of seamen of many nations. Rangy Americans, bronze of face and mighty of muscle, guided their cargoes of furs from Saint Louis or of flour and pork from Ohio, and cast sharp glances at the French, Spanish, German, Canadian and mulatto boatmen, all good Louisianians, who were also intent on their cargoes, while from the direction of the delta strange foreign sailing-ships manned by Europeans nosed their way as near as possible to the wharves. Two continents had become aware in the last few years that New Orleans was the gateway to wealth. And not far away, on the left bank, lay the plains of Chalmette where in the January of the year before Andrew Jackson, in an old Spanish cloak and boots, had fought the last battle of the war with the British, uniting Creoles, Yankees, "free blacks" and settlers from the German Coast in a common American defence of the exotically beautiful city.

Through the forests of masts Mary could now see that rose-tinted city lying behind the levees in a hollow lower than the river-bed. The raw new ware-houses and offices of the American quarter fringed the already historic Creole town. Sarah searched the strange scene with eyes that were hungry for one thing. She lifted Mary to the top of the low cabin and pointed to where a sharp spire rose above the blur of houses. It was the Cathedral of Saint Louis. Mr. Charles Hardey was prowling up and down Decatur Street in expectation, and suddenly Mary saw a tall figure, looking so much like her own father, appear over the bales of cotton on the nearest quay. There were shouts and smiles of welcome, and presently the child felt herself lifted in her uncle's arms. Then she was soundly kissed, swung through the air, and set down on southern soil.

It is doubtful whether the Arabian Nights were among the bedtime stories to which Mary was accustomed, but even had she known them they could have presented nothing more strange to her imagination than did New Orleans. Even though much of what we now find picturesque in the *Vieux Carré* was then modern enough, it was romantic to the Marylanders. The narrow streets were dainty with the iron lacework of balconies hung from the blue and rose and green tinted houses whose walls opened unexpectedly into patios where fountains splashed in the Spanish manner. The air was alive with voices speaking many tongues, yet drowsy with the call of church bells. The Hardeys gazed curiously at the *Cabildo*, replenished their supplies from the great open French Market near the levee, and refreshed their hearts in the restful splendour of the Cathedral. Not many of the Americans who were pouring into Louisiana through the City of the Mardi Gras were of the same faith as the Creoles, both Spanish and French, who were its real makers and owners. The Hardeys could be more in sympathy than most of the migrants with this southern pageantry, wherever the sign of the cross rose over it.

It is hardly likely that Sarah failed to take her two eldest little girls to the Ursuline Convent, for it might well be that they would some day be sent there to school. The oldest Convent in the United States lay in a high-walled garden and when the door opened to them Mary had her first sight of a Nun.[11] The Ursulines had come to New Orleans in response to an appeal from Governour Bienville in 1727, and the fearsome story of their crossing, menaced by storm, famine and pirates, still lives in the letters of Sister Madeleine Hachard. She tells further how they stayed in Bienville's house until their own was completed in 1734, and then the Convent annals take up the story and relate how they entered their new home late one fine afternoon:

> We all left the chapel in processional order, the citizens opening the march, followed by the children of our orphanage and day school, and over forty of the most respectable ladies of the city, all bearing lighted tapers and singing pious hymns. Next came twenty young girls dressed in white, who were followed by twelve others dressed as angels.
>
> The young lady who represented Saint Ursula wore a costly robe and mantle and a crown glittering with diamonds and pearls, from which hung a rich veil in graceful folds, and in her hand she bore a heart pierced with an arrow. . . . Last of all came the Nuns and Clergy, the former bearing lighted tapers and the latter a rich canopy under which the Blessed Sacrament was borne in triumph. The soldiers marched on each side. . . . Thus we entered our new abode amidst the chiming of bells, the noise of fifes and drums, and the singing of hymns.

This house can still be seen today in the *Vieux Carré*, its plastered walls painted a soft grey, its steep roof tiled, its generous windows closed with heavy cypress blinds. Even then it wore the air of dignity, remote and simple, that it wears now after two hundred years, in the long peace of its old age. As the visitors stood in the cool entrance they looked at the stair-rail of exquisitely hammered iron, bespeaking the crafts of culture. The Ursuline who received them did not need to tell, even had she wished to do so, of the part that the Nuns had played in the life of the City since they had taken it by storm at their beautiful procession, of how they cared for the sick and sheltered orphans, and far more of how they moulded the gay young girls of New Orleans into women indeed who could carry the radiation of grace into the lives of men. Mary may have understood little, but the Nun smiled at her and took her to the chapel, turning the roving little eyes to the Tabernacle.

But their journey could not end in this peaceful place, and before long the caravan was under way again. This time it progressed in lumbering ox-carts wherever the ground was firm enough, or on rafts where the slumberous waters of the bayous spread their nets through the swamplands. The black water sometimes disappeared under a carpet, beautiful but treacherous, of blue hyacinths. Semitropical undergrowth choked the brakish edges of the ponds, while towering overhead the cypresses made perpetual twilight. There was danger in the water from alligators and moccasin snakes; there was a solemn stillness under the twisting, dying branches which deadened the evening call of crane and bullfrog, but now and then the jungle-like vegetation opened out suddenly showing dry plains that smiled in the light of a normal day.

The party at last pushed its way into the Opelousas district, named for the once-powerful Indian tribe that had roamed there, now converted into the winning Parish of Saint Landry where orchards flourished and where the fields reached out in stretches broad enough to be called prairies. The little town of Opelousas was in reality only a nucleus for the seventy or eighty far-flung plantations where cotton or sugar or cattle were raised. Some were owned by Creoles, the Louisiana aristocracy, some by the new-come Americans, and most by the Acadians.

For all this land, following the Bayou Têche along the way from New Orleans to Opelousas, would one day be called the Evangeline Land, thanks to the pen of Longfellow. The Acadian heroine of romance had not yet been given her literary fame in 1816, but Acadians there were in plenty.[12] It had been two generations since the first of these homeless exiles from Nova Scotia had wandered into Lousiana seeking shelter under the French flag only to find that it had given way before the Spanish one. In 1755 over six thousand French Catholic families had been driven from Acadia at the point of the bayonet while the flames of their burning homes made the night red behind them. Ten years later some forty-eight of these families who had managed to cling together appeared in New Orleans after having tried their fortune in Santo Domingo. Kindly officials directed them to the empty, fertile lands of the Opelousas and Attacapas regions where they gratefully settled. They were a people apart in 1816, shy with strangers yet abundantly hospitable, clinging with simple loyalty to their faith, their language and their customs.

So it was that Mary Hardey, peeping over the wagon edge as the carts jolted at last into Opelousas, saw men trudging home from the fields in long blue cotton smocks. She saw girls with bright fichus over their shoulders, wearing full flaring skirts of a contrasting color. She heard the quick flow of French as the *Cajuns* turned to stare after the passing wagons before trudging home barefoot to the neat farms clustering a few together here and there. She would have been entranced could she have followed them all the way and seen these *habitants* at home, playing the games of Old France in the evening *veillées*, frightened by the apparitions that they alone could see when the *feu follet* danced over the marshes or the *sabbat* rode the night air, praying with the heartiness of their ancestors at all hours of the day. What she could see even now was the fruit of their industry as she passed the larger homes of those who had prospered, come out of the woods, and taken their place in the more influential life of Louisiana.

Charles Anthony Hardey was a proud man when he guided his brother's family into his home at last. It was warm with firelight, and from the open window he showed them where their new house should stand. But a few months after their arrival this kindly guide and elder brother died, leaving Frederick the heir to his estates. By that time the new-comers had a home of their own, a home of creamy white, broad-pillared for coolness and for beauty, while plantation life crystallized rapidly around it. Here Sarah Hardey came into her own, as a southern woman with a little world to rule, and her first care was to establish relations with the Curé of the Church.

So she called one day at Saint Landry's.[13] This mission chapel had been erected as early as 1770 by the Spanish Capuchins, and its baptismal register reflected, in its language and unconscious betrayals of feeling on the part of the Pastors, the alternations of French and Spanish influence over the harassed Louisiana Church. Father Rossi, who had a scattered and polyglot flock to care for, greeted them warmly, his French courtesy predominating over his broken English. He was glad to have American Catholics in his flock; there were not many of them in this part of the world. By sharing a common faith with the older inhabitants they would help to form some sort of unity in his Parish.

Yes, he had a school of sorts, he told Mrs. Hardey, taught by some enterprising young women of the town and supervised by himself. Ann and Mary were duly enrolled. The elder would soon be ten years old, and was admitted to the First Communion class. Mary, who would be eight that winter, insisted upon coming too. As she was too young for the solemn act which would take place in the spring she was relegated to a back seat. She took her place there meekly enough but listened with all her might, and the keen little mind was at work. One day the Pastor asked a question, a key-question, about the Blessed Eucharist. The children seemed unusually dull, and in the awkward silence Mary could contain herself no longer. She pushed her way to the front and spoke out with an incisive clarity which startled the priest, while her eyes shone with intelligent excitement. Father Rossi gently drew her aside from the others, and the two had a long talk. Later on, when the day of First Communion dawned, Ann and Mary in long white dresses and veils went side by side to the altar rail, and two shiningly happy little girls were driven home from Church to a patriarchal breakfast.

A space of four years of home life followed, in the course of which the family circle was rapidly enlarged. Eventually there were five girls and three boys in this enviable home. We know that one of the sons, Charles Anthony, was born in 1819, and another, George Raphael, the following year. The names of the other boy was probably Siebert, but those of two of the girls have escaped all records. Ann and Mary became the vicegerents of this little kingdom, and the latter soon developed a marked talent for housekeeping. The household was enormous, for the slave-quarters stretched in whitewashed rows behind the main building and every evening a great bell hung in a turret outdoors called everyone, black and white, to evening prayers which Massah Frederick said aloud. The plantation was a world in itself; sunlight and rain passed over it, and the eight children responded and grew like the jasmine that twisted over the pillared porch.

Mrs. Hardey knew how to develop a sense of responsibility among them. Mary was given a sacred trust; every day it was to be her duty to carry a bag of provisions to an old negress, no longer able to work, who sat in her cabin and waited till Mary's small shadow cut the sunlight at the door. She was taught the privilege of serving, but at the same time she had a little slave about her own age whose duty it was to serve her. Mary was very fond of her black playmate and generously heaped upon her more than it was her right to give out of the pantry to which she had a key. In spite of the village school the children learned most at home. Mrs. Hardey had hung pictures on religious subjects—of an undetermined school of art—on the wall of every room. The children sat under each in turn, and were told Bible stories in explanation. Missionary priests frequently stopped at the plantation, and Mrs. Hardey brought each of her children in turn to kneel before the visitor and kiss the hands that had the right to touch the Body and Blood of Christ. It is no wonder that high admiration was woven into Mary's love for her mother, of whom a life-long friend wrote years later at the time of the latter's death:

> The qualities of Mrs. Hardey were of a high order, and her example was a rich inheritance to her family and friends. It was said in her obituary notice that "in intellect and worth she towered above others of her sex." This was not an exaggeration. In the judgment of many who knew her well she was not equalled even by her gifted daughter.

Two letters which Sarah wrote to her younger sister Ellen soon after the death of "good Grandmother Spalding," reveal her gently refined conservatism, and still more her vivid faith:

> Your kind letter of the 6th of June came safely to hand, with the melancholy news of my dear Mother's death, news that I expected to hear, for from the account brother Michael gave me

in his last letter I could hardly flatter myself that she would live through the summer. I am sorry to hear of my father's state of health. I hope he has not lost his speech. You must tell me in your next letter. Ellen, if it should be the holy will of God to take both our parents, bear it with fortitude and thanksgiving to Almighty God for His infinite goodness in sparing them to you till the age of maturity, and for letting you have the pleasure of waiting on them in their last moments. . . . Let my Ellen be ever so prudent she needs a guide and counsellor. You cannot be too prudent in regard to your visiting and your visits. You are lonely, no doubt, but you know you are always in good company. When your earthly friends are obliged to leave you, call on the Holy Names of Jesus, Mary, Joseph—company that will ever remain with you, provided you wish to remain with them.

Later, when their father too had died, Mrs. Hardey urged Ellen to join her in Louisiana:

I hope you will consider the welfare of your soul and body and accept the invitation of a brother and sister who think you could do better by coming here than by remaining where you are. My dear, do not think I would send you this invitation without providing you with an escort upon whom you can rely as you could on a father or brother.

Your nieces all go to school this year; it will soon be over, then I shall have the pleasure of their company all day. I assure you, Ann and Mary are great company for me, and also a great assistance. One is a good nurse, the other a good housekeeper. They had a real trial this fall when I was sick. Ellen, you must take care of the books that our father procured for the instruction of his children. You must write to me often and tell my brothers also to write.

In the meantime events were shaping in the nearby village of Grand Coteau which lay but a few miles south of Opelousas. Some people by the name of Smith, who had immigrated somewhat earlier than the Hardey's from Maryland, were living there. The families had become closely connected, for two sisters of Mr. Hardey had married two brothers of Mr. Charles Smith, a wealthy planter and cattle-raiser. The latter had, in 1792, married Miss Mary Sentee from Pennsylvania, an Anabaptist who had recently come into the Catholic Church. The ceremony took place in Saint Landry's Church, then the only one in the vicinity. As the years passed the couple realized the need for another in Grand Coteau itself, and soon the Church of Saint Charles Borromeo was under construction. But in the spring of 1819 Mr. Smith suddenly died, leaving his widow to continue the work. She decided to consecrate a large portion of her fortune to Catholic education. When Bishop Dubourg came for a canonical visitation in 1820 she asked him if she could not found a school for girls in Grand Coteau. Quick as a flash came the answer: she should do so at once, and entrust the new school to the Religious of the Sacred Heart, an Order but recently come to his diocese from France and which was now established at Florissant, near Saint Louis. With surprising speed the plan was carried out. The records of the subsequent Convent of the Sacred Heart states the matter in old-world phrases:

> The time having come when God had determined to form unto Himself a people made up of faithful servants and adorers of the Heart of His Son Jesus in a virgin land hitherto unknown to civilized nations, he called thither a Christian from Maryland, inspired him with beneficent sentiments, and made use of him for the foundation of a church, a house of the Sacred Heart and a Jesuit College in this privileged land.

So it came about that in the spring of 1822 the wife of this beneficent Christian from Maryland paid a visit to the Hardey family. She came at a timely moment, for Mrs. Hardey was just settling an important matter. Ann had gone away from home the year before to the School of the Sisters of Charity at Emmitsburg, where many of her older cousins of the Smith family had preceded her. Should Mary go too? Mrs. Smith was ready with a solution. What could be better for Mary than the new school at Grand Coteau? It had opened the October before with five pupils, including Mrs. Smith's own niece, Mary Sentee, and by now there were ten or twelve. Mother Audé, the Superior, was a most distinguished person and an able teacher. Mrs. Hardey listened with happy relief.

That night the affair underwent a final discussion. Mary, then twelve years old, conquered the lingering doubts of her parents by her own intense desire. There was only one real obstacle. Planters could be land-rich and money-poor, and cash for Mary's tuition would not be readily forthcoming. Silence fell on the group. Suddenly Mary herself had an inspiration, one of those swift, practical perceptions of ways and means which later became so characteristic of her. The Nuns, she remarked, must find it difficult to get all their washing done now that the school was so large. They had no slaves as yet. Why should not Mrs. Hardey have their laundry done by her own slaves, and thus help to pay expenses? It would not be much trouble to drive a wagon over and back from Opelousas at intervals. Mr. Hardey, half in amusement and half in pride, smiled his consent to the arrangement and the matter was settled.

By way of parenthesis it may be added that a compromise was eventually reached. The old account books of the Convent record every few months: "pour le quartier de Mademoiselle Hardey, $35." The regular tuition was $45 a quarter and the deduction was balanced by the labour of Mrs. Hardey's slaves. Had Mary lived today she would presumably have squared the account by working herself, not in the laundry but in the library as a student-assistant under the N.Y.A. Shortly before she left school, the regular tuition was reduced to $35, "pour la plus grande gloire de Dieu."

It was now the end of May and there was no vacation during the summer in those days. Mr. Hardey knew that the school was run strictly on the lines of a French *pensionnat* which granted a brief two weeks holiday between terms in September, and a rare *sortie* at other times, so Mary had best go at once. There was as much sewing and packing and sense of farewell as if she were indeed going to Emmitsburg. When she finally drove off on the brief journey the whole family and all the slaves assembled to wave her off, while her devoted Mammy, Aunt Sophie, wept noisily.

The carriage rolled rapidly along a well-beaten road. On all sides stretched a prairie-like sweep of land, flat to the eye yet graced by an almost undefinable roll as it lifted toward the slight elevation upon which lay Grand Coteau. Clumps of gigantic live-oaks assumed almost the proportion of hills, so sharply and greenly did they stand out against the sky. In the distance roamed half-savage herds of cattle, while the road was fringed with fields of cane. Then the carriage turned off abruptly into an ill-defined new road that led into a more thickly wooded quarter. A turn revealed a wooden house, obviously new. It was only some fifty feet long, but the deep gallery stretching along the front gave it an air of space and stability. A few brave attempts at gardening had not yet resulted in much, and all around it the untamed woods shook out their moss flags and sang their primeval songs to the winds. With a beating heart Mary approached. The bolt dropped and she looked up to where a Religious of the Sacred Heart stood in the welcoming doorway.

IV

OLD WORLDS FOR NEW

In the first strangeness of life in a new house, Mary's eyes looked about for someone upon whom they could rest with confidence. They soon began to follow every move of the energetic, attractive Superior. With French precision Mother Audé called the newcomer by her double name, pronouncing it Marianne. The children followed suit, and Mary Ann she remained throughout her school life. There was one little obstacle at first to mutual confidence; Mother Audé's broken English was sometimes difficult to understand. It distressed the child to hear her new Mother expressing herself in an unworthy fashion and she determined to meet the situation more than half-way. For some weeks she said nothing about the matter but applied herself with all her might to the study of French, practicing on her Creole and Acadian companions. At last she felt the strange words beginning to come with some ease to her tongue. "Mother," she cried in triumph, "you need not speak to me any more in English; I know French!" It was not an empty boast, for what Mary Ann put her mind to she mastered with amazing facility.

Such energy was indicative of the way in which her responsive soul was discovering the meaning of what lay behind her new life. The other children, new as they were, were moving along a path made easy by custom, but only Mother Audé seemed to know where the path led, and whence the customs had come. The house and the country about it were completely new to her, but she went forward unafraid, strong in her knowledge of what lay behind. Mary Ann watched her, and became aware of old worlds behind the new. She noticed that Mother Audé would do nothing without referring to a Mother Duchesne who lived at Florissant to the north of Grand Coteau, somewhere in the empty middle spaces of the continent. Still more noticeable was the impetuous joy that moved her whenever a letter came from a Mother Barat, "our Mother," who lived in Paris over the unthinkable sea. Then she would tell the children stories at happy hours on Sundays about other houses where those two mothers lived and worked, until Grand Coteau was seen as the fringe and not the center of a greater whole. With the coming of the month of June it was clearer where the Center lay. When the children went, veiled and with what pomp their fewness would allow, to the chapel where candles were being lit for their devotions to the Sacred Heart, one of them at least began to understand what name and what reality linked them in a common cause with the children in other distant houses where candles were also being lit because it was June. Mary Ann could not have pieced the whole matter together then as she could later. In order to trace it back to its beginning she would have had to know far more history than she did, but little by little she gathered the outline of a story alive with pictures and with memorable names which ran somewhat as follows:

The school at Grand Coteau was observing its June devotions with exciting gravity in 1822 because of another June day in 1675 when, at Paray-le-Monial, God himself had first asked that a Feast of the Sacred Heart be kept. That day had seen the crystallization into a simple and easily apprehensible form, of a mystery believed by the Church from the beginning; it saw currents and powers of loving as old as the Incarnation fused into a single glowing point. Both the mystery and the love were wrought that day into a symbol which was likewise a reality, and were given a name not new but from then on more utterable. Sister Margaret Mary Alocoque, a Visitandine praying before the Blessed Sacrament, saw the Lord Jesus face to face; she saw His Heart, thorn-bound and aflame, and was told to look upon It. She was told to tell of It to others, to bid them look with faith upon what she had seen in vision. She did so, and the Devotion to the Sacred Heart spread by its own appeal through a troubled world.

It has been said [1] that the God of philosophy, God as knowable by reason alone, was discovered as far as might be by the daring and hungry intellects of the pagan philosophers of old, but that the people who were not philosophers, whose hearts were hungrier than their minds, failed to find that God as thus known had a heart, and so made gods to their own craving. It was the Incarnation that bridged the gap; when God became human, the Heart of Our Lord was the answer to all seeking. The Ages of Faith rested content with the implicit possession of the mystery, loving its symbol and its name. It was after the rending of Christendom, when even those who clung to the indivisible Body of Christ needed a new help in the chaos of strife, that a clearer revelation and more tangible forms were needed to concentrate the old love into a point where luminous strength could be found most easily. In the eighteenth century Philosophism tried to return to the God of Philosophy, but because it knew better was forced to reject of soul as badly as the peasants needed bread. From France even that much of God. The unphilosophic needed satisfaction outward through the world Devotion to the Sacred Heart made its way.

Its way was "marked by signs which do not allow us to mistake the finger of God therein."[2] It acted as a solvent upon the rigours of Jansenism. It inspired the foundation of Confraternities which expressed the spirit of the Devotion in prayers and spread them broadcast to the needy of heart. It gathered power when the full weight of the sanction of Rome came behind it in 1765 with the permission to celebrate its proper Mass and Office, and when the Assembly of the Clergy of France, in response to the desire of Marie Leczinska, resolved to spread the Devotion through their Dioceses. Individuals, townships, men in public life, turned to it in times of plague, danger, persecution and war. This was its Palm Sunday. Its Passion came with the Revolution, when hatred of religion sharpened an attack on every outward symbol of the Devotion, and high-souled women like Victoire de Saint Luc died on the scaffold for having given such symbols to those who treasured them.

The Revolution drove what priests it could not imprison into hiding or over the frontier. One of them, Léonor de Tournély,[3] fresh from his ordination, found himself in 1791 exiled in Belgium. Times grew worse; the heavy pressure of events drove men to despair or to high heroism. It drove Father de Tournély into a Capuchin Monastery in Antwerp to make a retreat, in which he prayed over the proposal that had been made to him by his companion in exile, Prince Charles de Broglie, of founding a new Religious Order. He prayed before a Crucifix, and found the answer while contemplating the opened side of the Crucified. His Order would be known as the Fathers of the Sacred Heart, while waiting for an opportunity to join the Society of Jesus as soon as it should rise again after its temporary suppression.

De Tournély was a young man when the understanding of

his call came to him. He was not to have time to grow much older, but so complete was his response to his understanding that he reached the swift maturity of holiness. While the little Community that called him Father was being driven by poverty and hard events to tramp the roads from city to city, his aloof watch-word remained "Calme du ciel." Compelled by the simplicity of his God-hungry heart to move onward and up along the straight line of contemplative prayer, the needs of others pulled him downward and out. It came to him in his wanderings from one revolutionary land to another that things would go evilly indeed if the children growing up in the midst of turmoil were not saved for the Church. With surprising completeness his mind formed the plan for a Religious Order of women to meet the need, and he gave it a name: the Society of the Sacred Heart. He knew that the movement of its life would be according to the rhythm of his own soul: inward and up in prayer, downward and out in zeal, like the double movement in the breathing of a living thing. He knew that its motto would be "Cor Unum et Anima Una in Corde Jesu," and that the education of those who had most to give to the Church would be its main apostolate.

He called upon the Princess Louise de Bourbon Condé to be its foundation stone. She tried generously to answer and followed him down the Danube to Vienna, but the pieces of the pattern did not fit together in her soul and she withdrew. Father de Tournély said quietly: "This beginning is not what God wants. But He wills the work. I may be mistaken about the means and the time, but the Society will be." When he died in 1797, at the age of thirty, he still repeated, even while the light of heaven was breaking upon him, "It will be; it will be."

Father Joseph Varin,[4] one-time soldier and now militant priest, heard the words. They fell upon good ground. Father Varin had been torn from following his own self-glorious ambitions at the very time when his mother, unknown to him, was giving her life on the scaffold for religion's sake. He gave his own life to the Fathers of the Sacred Heart, comforted for the costly sacrifice of his career by the promise: "My friend, you will always be a soldier." Now he was ready to take Father de Tournély's place at the head of the small but virile band of Apostles, and his chief preoccupation was the fulfilment of his spiritual Father's last wish: "the Society of the Sacred Heart will be."

Three years of wandering and of mistaken attempts to find a Foundress brought Father Varin to Paris in June, 1800. Life in an attic was by this time nothing new to him, and in such austere surroundings he one day interviewed a young priest from the country who wished to give his services to the Fathers of the Faith, as the Association was then called, the name of Sacred Heart being under political suspicion. This was Father Louis Barat, who told his new guide that only one responsibility rested upon him; he had a younger sister whom he was training, for what end he did not know. A strong light broke upon Father Varin's mind; he knew that his search was over when he heard the name of Madeleine Louise Sophie Barat.[5]

She was then twenty years old, and when Louis told the brief story of her life, Father Varin's conviction deepened. It was not hard to see that those twenty years had been God-guided. Little Madeleine Sophie, frail, vivacious, lovable, was the youngest child in the home of Jacques Barat, a wine-cooper. She had grown up among the cobbled streets and the circling vineyards of Joigny in Burgundy, loving to play on the sunlit hill-slopes but compelled instead to study in her attic room for hour after hour, until the pages began at length to glow with that other sunlight of the mind and she grew to love her books. Her stern older brother, who was also her God-father and tutor, had known that this would happen when he set the impetuous, warm-hearted and extraordinarily gifted child to her hard task. It was strange that a country girl, moving about her housework slight of form and serious of face, with eyes that turned easily to the outdoors, should have the lines of Homer and of Virgil singing easily through her memory in their own Greek and Latin, and should slip sometimes out of sight in order to laugh aloud to her heart's content over "that crazy Don Quixote," read in his own Spanish. In later years she admitted once to her nuns, while her eyes searched the Adriatic one clear day as if to reach as far as Greece: "In my childhood I was fire and flame for that country of genius, of art, of strong combats, where spirit and valour ended by triumphing over force and numbers."

So at Joigny, in the small two-story grey house, Madeleine Sophie silently garnered her grain for the future. The simple dignity given to her every move by a home life strong as the earth and warm as a fire-side, blended naturally with the mental power given by her unusual education. She had the aloof beauty of bearing which belongs to those in whom the gifts of the Holy Ghost are distinctly present. "As far back as I can remember," wrote her nephew in after years, "her gracious, modest beauty, her gentleness, her calm and musical voice, exerted a real fascination over me. The picture of her has remained deeply engraved in my heart, like a statue of virginity, or the incarnation of that Wisdom whose name she bore." Her power lay in the energy of her love; she was undivided and tenacious in her loving. She might have clung long to the bright, good, natural things which first claimed her affection if she had not been somewhat rudely trained by her brother to let go as soon as a higher object was seen. She was waiting for the time when it would drive her from home into a cloister, if one could be found in a land that was rapidly becoming cloisterless.

While she was waiting the Revolution broke over Paris in the full tide of its terror, and the rumble of the tumbrils reached Joigny. There were dark hours in the Barat home, when Louis lay in prison and when Madame Barat would have failed under her grief but for the sympathy and energetic tact of her youngest daughter. New confidence came when two small pictures, one of the Sacred Heart of Jesus and one of the Holy Heart of Mary, found their way into the family and were placed on the cottage wall. The pictures were like seeds, instinct with the deep, devotional life of the movement that had produced them, and they took silent root in Madeleine Sophie. She was ready by the time her brother, released from prison and newly made a priest, came home and called upon her for renunciation.

She was only sixteen when she drove off with him to Paris in the stagecoach, dressed in a most uncitified fashion and silent under the pressure of the thought that had so often moved like a shadow over her rare hours of play among the vineyards; "is there then no real joy on earth?" She was facing a life of stern study, and of prayer that would become secretly sweet—four hard years of discipline, with the Fathers of the Church instead of her beloved classics for reading matter, with her brother's imperative hand to chisel her spiritual life, and with a lonely city room for a home. She had become a sensitive and deep-souled young woman, with carefully hidden powers of prayer and a hunger to be a Carmelite, when Father Varin at last met her in the autumn of 1800.

"I found," he tells us, "a frail young person, very modest and timid. 'What a foundation-stone!' I said to myself." Thus Father Varin's more gentle and confidence-inspiring direction replaced that of Louis, who had done well his work of laying the foundations. Gradually he told her of what Father de Tournély had learned from God, and let the vocation to the still unfounded Society of the Sacred Heart shine before her open eyes. An energetic word was needed to draw to it the whole-hearted gift of herself. "This is the kind of life to which you are called," he said. "Very well," answered Sophie, "I shall think it over." "There is nothing to think over," came the quick reply; "when the will of God is known there is nothing left but to obey."

From then on events moved swiftly. November came, and the morning of the Feast of the Presentation saw a back room in a dwelling on the Rue de Touraine lit and adorned with all the small splendours of a make-shift chapel. The candles gleamed on the faces of a Madonna and Child over the altar, painted with the soft richness of the Italian manner. At Mass Madeleine Sophie and her three companions made their act of consecration, and the Society of the Sacred Heart began to be. "I knew nothing, I saw nothing," she said later, "I took what was given me."

The energies of long desire then came into play, as they were doing all over France where the Church was rising stronger than ever from the flames of the Revolution. The new Society needed a School, and one was found—very poor, crowded and happy—at Amiens where the Community took root in the following October * and where vision crystallized into a way of life. Then a leader was needed. Those who seemed likely to be leaders were tried and found wanting till the youngest and most timid of them all heard herself named Superior. Once more the omnipotent words, "God wills

* An interesting "might-have-been" is here suggested. Father Varin was connected at this time with a certain Father Paccanari who was fostering in Italy a Religious Order of Women known as the *Diletti*, who for several years were affiliated with the new Society of the Sacred Heart. In the same year that saw the foundation of the latter, 1800, Bishop Carroll of Baltimore wrote to Father Paccanari urging him to send his Religious to America to let them take root and grow there where the need was so great. The offer was not accepted; if it had been the history of the Society of the Sacred Heart would have been very different indeed from what it is. Bishop Carroll did succeed, however, in obtaining some of the Fathers of the Sacred Heart, as we shall see later.[6]

it," were invoked to make Madeleine Sophie accept the responsibility that she was to carry for sixty-three more years and which she began at once to exercise with the charm of her young maturity, with the gently irresistible power of her grace-saturated nature.

Numbers were needed now, and from the four corners of France women who had been prepared, unknown to themselves, for just this vocation turned towards Mother Barat as towards a magnet. After two trying years of over-crowding and illness, Father Varin sent them, among the words of encouragement which were their constant strength, the hope of a new house as well. The work must begin to expand. "And there is one soul there," he added, "worth going to the ends of the earth for." So, in November, 1804, Mother Barat set out across France on the first of her endless journeyings, to find in a battered and rich-memoried old monastery the woman who was to bring America in its turn into the orbit of the Sacred Heart.

The life of Rose Philippine Duchesne [7] had been, for its first thirty-five years, bound up with the walls of Sainte Marie d'en Haut, a Visitation Convent which rose with grim grace on the side of a hill overlooking Grenoble. She had made her First Communion there as a child at school, already eager, austere, strong-willed. Then she entered as a Novice, overcoming the opposition of her likewise strong-willed family by the simple method of going behind the grille and refusing to leave, until at last the Revolution drove her out. She kept her eyes fixed upon the home of her heart through ten years of exile from it, years of adventurous service of the Church in the war-marred country-side, till she managed to buy back the now half-ruined building. The bitterest of all her experiences was to find that the one-time Community, recalled by her, could not take up the threads of the old life again in the face of the desolate hardship in which her own strong soul gloried. They went away, leaving her in a bleak valley of shadows. But the night broke into incomparable day when word came to her of the new Society with the name of names which, though it could not yet be borne openly, spoke of the spirit within.

The long stage-coach journey reached its end on December 13th, 1804, when Mother Barat reached Grenoble. As she said later:

> I found myself at the entrance to a little corridor, very low, very damp. I saw Mother Duchesne coming; she threw herself on the ground to kiss my feet, saying to me the words with which the Prophet-King exalted the holy mission of the Apostles and their successors: "At last I see upon the mountain the feet of those who bring peace." I let her do it, through sheer stupefaction. I was overcome at the sight of so much faith and humility, and I did not know what to say or do.

What she did was to make the old monastery into which the snow drifted, warm with delight, where she trained strong Religious and won the hearts of children. She could remain only a few months that time on the mountain to which she ever after referred as her Tabor, and to which she looked back in the busy after-years with the nostalgia of a contemplative, but her stay had been long enough to show that the motto "One heart and one soul" would be a reality wherever the Society should spread. It was long enough also to bring a gentle restraint to bear upon the rugged and impulsive character of Philippine, but not long enough to teach her fully the difficult lesson of prudence. It was just as well perhaps, for it was morning on the mountain and in the clear light Philippine saw the horizon lying to the West.

Stories that she had heard in childhood from an old missionary from Louisiana awoke with the vigour of a vocation. She wrote to Mother Barat, who was by that time at Amiens trying to reconcile herself to the fact that she had just been elected Superior General for life, and proposed that the young Society, with two houses, few Religious, and no resources, should expand at once beyond the seas. The answer that she received revealed the fact that her astonishing, not to say rash, proposal was no surprise to her wise young Mother. It was the first manifestation of a Divine plan which had long been maturing in the secret places of prayer. "Your letter," wrote Mother Barat, "has touched me to the quick; I felt that my desires had been granted. Yes, that is what I have been asking for you ever since the Lord gave you to me. I have often come back upon it most ardently, in the conviction that He wants that devotedness from you, and that complete sacrifice." Then referring to great Saints of previous times she wrote:

> Are we so far removed from the ages of sanctity? And may we not hope to see some among us treading in their footsteps? Shall I own it, dear child: when I think of the graces our Lord has given you since your childhood, I cannot help hoping that as He has gifted you with an affectionate and grateful heart you will love God as some of these great souls have done. The circumstances in which you are placed are somewhat similar to those which helped to make them Saints: a new Order, assisted by men full of the spirit of God, and above all the Heart of Jesus speaking so forcibly to your heart.

What her vision did not show her was that she herself would be raised before Mother Duchesne to the honours of the altar.

The expected months of waiting lengthened into twelve years. Mother Barat moved about France like an incessant shadow, founding houses and then still more. She went in public coaches and in the uncovered carts of tradesmen, in all weathers. At the halts in villages she called the rough, shy country children about her for as long as might be, and left grieving because she could not stay with them. Yet while rumbling along the dusty roads, she had to do violence to herself to resist the temptation of slipping away to lose herself in the wood, to be Superior and Foundress no more, so strongly did solitude attract her. The first of such journeys brought her to Poitiers where, marvelously, a group of young girls with vocations and no convent in which to follow them were waiting for her. She made a Noviceship for them in the stillness of a deserted monastery and there she fashioned her fellow-workers, pillars-to-be of the Society, like Mother Maillucheau who had taken the name Thérèse because she could not help praying. Mother Barat's words were their meat; they nourished their souls with them while they swept the great bare house, or taught the first children in the small Boarding School and the large Free School. Like children themselves they sang songs of joy in her honour by the light of the moon when she came back from her journeys.

A house at Niort came next, founded in stark want and kept alive by the faith of Mother Suzanne Geoffrey. From Amiens new houses were opened at Gand and at Cuignières. Mother Barat went from one to another, and often to Grenoble. The children learned to look impatiently for her coming. "We would walk with her in the woods; then stop and have a picnic on the grass, while listening eagerly to the gentle voice which charmed us, entertained us, taught us, all at once." Within the cloister, still stronger bonds were formed; and Mother Barat knew that it was time for the Constitutions to be formulated more clearly, to make this union lasting. She and Father Varin spent long days conferring together on the matter at the Chateau de Chevroz, days which Mother Barat tried to lengthen by prayer till she forgot the hour of supper and a little boy had to be sent to fetch her from the dark church by lantern light.

The work accomplished there gave her strength to face the first serious storm that threatened the Society; Amiens was passing through a crisis of misunderstanding. Outside influences had estranged the hearts of some there, and caused the house of Gand to withdraw from its union with the rest. It was only in December, 1815, that Mother Barat's clear vision, made powerful by patience, brought healing. She called a group of Councillors chosen from each house to meet with her in Paris. Unity, energy and light took hold of all minds when on December 16th they renewed their vows together, and from then on the Society gloried openly in the name of Sacred Heart.

This same meeting had called Mother Duchesne from Sainte Marie to Paris, where a new house was shortly opened on the Rue des Postes. There she found herself named Secretary General, but did not let Mother Barat forget her promises. "I ask for nothing," she would say sorrowfully, "only say Go, and I will go at once, without anything but the grace of obedience." As Mother Barat said later:

Things were in this state when, on the 14th of January, 1817, Monseigneur Dubourg, Bishop of Louisiana, arrived from America and had the kindness to come and see me. Mother Duchesne knew it; she happened to be Portress when he arrived, and had nothing better to do than to beg me not to let such a chance go by. Without seeming to share her certainty, I answered that I would mention the matter if Monseigneur himself introduced the subject, but that I would need eighteen months to form my plans. The next day the Bishop came to say Mass. I talked with him during his breakfast. He told me that, as he wished to establish religious Communities in his vast diocese, he very much wished to have Religious of the Sacred Heart there, and urged me to consent. "Ah, there we are," I said to myself; "Mother Duchesne's affair is going well." I answered that if the plan could be carried out I had a person ready to give him, and I told him of the vocation of Mother Duchesne. Monseigneur Dubourg wished to see his future subject, who knelt at his feet. You can guess her joy, with what transports she showed it, and how she thanked her good Master.

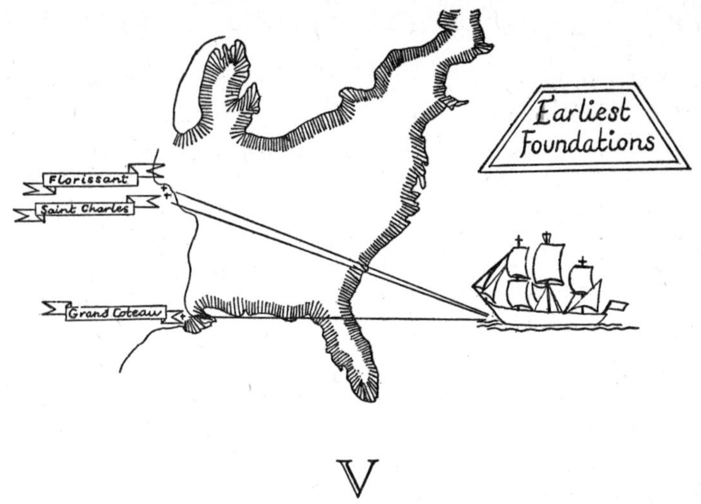

V

NEW WORLDS FOR OLD

At this point in the story the scene tended to become reversed in Mary Ann Hardey's imagination. Child of the New World as she was, she could not picture the ship *Rebecca* with its full sails slipping further and further from the shores of home till it grew tiny in the grey of the west. To her mind it came towards home from a land far to the east, growing larger and brighter as it drew nearer to America. She could see the five Nuns saying goodbye with their eyes to Bordeaux on March 21, 1818, Holy Saturday; she could recognize only Mother Audé, but she knew the names of the others: Mother Duchesne, stronger, older, holier than the rest, Mother Octavie Berthold, Sister Catherine Lamarre and Sister Marguerite Manteau. She saw the boat tossing in the great storms that threatened its passage or drifting helplessly back and forth over the Tropic of Capricorn in a long calm; she heard the Nuns singing the *Ave Maris Stella* on the deck till the wind blew fair again, and she saw it skirting the shores of Cuba, flower-bright in perpetual summer. It was drawing closer and closer. Mary Ann had been only nine years old at the time, newly come to Louisiana, but it was exciting to her now to think that the subsequent events had taken place not so very far from her plantation home while she knew nothing about it.

It had been on May 25th (a day to be glorified in the future as the Feast of Saint Madeleine Sophie) that the *Rebecca* crossed the line where the bronze waters of the Mississippi thrust their way into the blue gulf. For five more days the Nuns had watched the delta lands slip slowly past them as the ship edged her way towards New Orleans. The tangled growth along the water opened here and there to show miles of waving marsh grass fringing an empty sky. May 29th was providentially the Feast of the Sacred Heart that year, and they renewed their vows at an early Mass on ship-board. All day Mother Duchesne kept repeating that renovation in a formula all her own: "I consecrate myself to Poverty, but how rich I am in Thee. I pledge myself to Chastity, Thou art my soul's delight. I vow myself to Obedience; to serve Thee is to reign. I dedicate myself to the education of youth; thou art the Shepherd of their souls." What happened that evening is told in the words of Mother Audé herself:

> All day we crept slowly up the river. The country along the banks became more smiling and open. Wide fields of cotton and corn under cultivation bespoke the industry of the inhabitants. While we were gazing at these new sights came a message that a carriage awaited M. Martial on the river-bank to take him and us to the city, for we were still some twenty miles downstream. As an actual fact there were two carriages and it was about seven o'clock. By eight our satchels were packed and we were being let down into a small boat by means of the famous arm-chair which we had eyed so often with fear and envy during the crossing. . . .
>
> It was with the deepest emotion that we set foot on this soil,

which is for us, in the eyes of faith and the designs of God, the Promised Land. Mother Duchesne's heart could not contain its sentiments of gratitude. In spite of the marshy ground she knelt and kissed the very soil. Her eyes were wet with tears, tears of joy, the kind Father Varin desired for us.

"No one is looking," she whispered to us. "You kiss it too." If only you could have seen her face! It was radiant with a joy that only the Heart of Jesus could inspire in a soul filled with His grace and bent on glorifying His Sacred Heart.

It was a glorious night. The stars that studded the deep blue heavens were mirrored in the silvery waters of the stream. Fireflies sparkled in the low bushes. . . . At a plantation we bought some fresh bread which we had not tasted for seventy days.[1]

Thus they drove under the starlight at two in the morning into the Crescent City, at a moment when its pulsating life was all but still. Morning brought them Mass and Communion in the Ursuline Convent, and the warmest of welcomes, one never to be worn out through the years to come, from the Religious. Mother Saint Michel Gensoul, the Superior, looked upon the new-comers as the fulfilment of a prophecy. She herself had received her call to the Louisiana Mission from Pope Pius VII and once, when in deep discouragement, she had been comforted by a message from an unknown person of great holiness that "some day the wild shores of the Mississippi will be peopled with religious houses."

Six weeks went by while awaiting a letter from Bishop Dubourg. In the meantime the new-comers taught catechism to groups of little negro children, gave presents to the few stolid, poverty-stricken Indians who were hanging about, and made the acquaintance of the quick-silvery, charming daughters of the Creole families. Gradually there dawned upon Mother Duchesne a suspicion which soon grew into an almost despairing certainty that she would never be able to learn

English. Then she fell ill of the scurvy, and when she recovered wrote to Mother Barat of her distress of body and of heart, and of her unshaken peace:

> I fear that I have often repeated and even contradicted myself in my letters to you, for I told you things as they happened, and repeated different opinions; moreover the heart feels sacrifices the value of which is hidden behind the veil of faith and of hope and cannot be seen. But love, even in distress, cries out: "My God, with joy I have offered you all things." I felt this very much when the doctor told me that I had the scurvy. Octavie begged me not to be alarmed. I was not troubled, but very serious at the thought that God wanted nothing more of me, that Eugénie could guide the little barque which would be better off than before, that, happier than Moses, I had entered the promised land. I had brought there those who were to fight the battles of the Sacred Heart, and I had left more than he had, since he came out of captivity and I from another promised land. I assure you that death held nothing but attractions for me, for I have every reason to fear that I may spoil the work we have undertaken. God has shown me nothing but His charms.

On July 12th they began their tortuous journey upstream on the steamer *Franklin*, deprived for six weeks of Mass and obliged to wear secular dress. The beauty of the river banks as cypress and palmetto yielded to hard-wood forests, languorous bayous to sturdy bluffs, could not distract entirely from the discomfort of the long days and longer nights in the pen-like, overcrowded, mosquito-ridden quarters of the noisy boat. It was a relief when they stopped at a port where Indians crowded to the shore to look at them; when, at Saint Geneviève, a Father Pratte came aboard to tell them that in his village the houses had neat gardens and carried crosses on their roofs under which French settlers lived as the first Christians might have done; and when, at Kaskaskia they were able to go ashore and see for themselves how the old missionary priest lived. He had a plate, a spoon and a bed in his cabin, and his life was one of superhuman toil. He was only one of the far too few priests who had in their hands the building up of the Body of Christ among these peoples of every tribe and tongue who, by the hundreds and the thousands, were pushing a nation westward.

On the evening of August 21st, with the summer heat at its height, the *Franklin* reached Saint Louis. Captain Reed, rough of hand and gentlemanly of heart, led them ashore past the limestone bluffs, through the muddy streets, to the episcopal palace which was "poorer than the poorest farm in France." Here Bishop Dubourg welcomed them from his heart and from his poverty. Mother Duchesne thought of where she had seen him last, this courtly, rich-voiced Prelate. Then he had blessed her in their Convent on the Rue des Postes in Paris, and given her *au revoir* for America. Now his head almost touched the ceiling of his hut as he blessed her again, his fellow-worker in a field of which he best knew the difficulties. "You say that you have come to seek the cross," he had written to them at New Orleans. "You are in the right place to find it and have not far to seek. If I were not sure of finding these blessed dispositions in you I would tremble and not rejoice at your coming." As it was, he rejoiced.

The little Community received hospitality at the home of Monsieur Bernard Pratte, the brother of the Curé of Saint Geneviève. Five eager little girls, whom the Nuns secretly pronounced spoiled but irresistible, crowded about them. Emilie and Thérèse were filled with pride at learning that they, together with their cousin Pélagie Chouteau, whose name was that of one of the founders of Saint Louis, were to be the first children of the Sacred Heart in America. This Creole family was one of those that kept an old-world grace together with the family jewels and silverware in their wooden houses, and while listening to Monsieur Pratte's enthusiastic plans for the future Mother Duchesne began, half-reluctantly, to see the truth of something that Bishop Dubourg had already insisted upon. They had come with their hearts set upon teaching the Indians but the practical Prelate was aware that far more good could be accomplished for the present if such teachers would first train those who would inevitably be leaders for better or for worse in the new civilization that was forming. Work among the under-privileged would never be lacking to them, but those with greater advantages were equally ignorant of the faith that was their true power, and often equally in need of culture. An Academy, as much as possible like those in France, must be the immediate care of this, his first Community of Nuns.

The cross had come with the fleur-de-lys to Saint Louis. It was still a city of three mud streets and a crumbling Spanish fort, where French mingled with the authentic Irish brogue and with many variations of English, but it was aware of its own future as it plied its fur-trade and availed itself of the confluence of great rivers. It had been founded by Pierre Laclède and Auguste Chouteau in 1763 as a trading post, and already it was the rival of New Orleans not only in business but even in the grace of its social life. It would be a good place in which to begin, agreed Mother Duchesne as Monsieur Pratte talked on.

But the Bishop, in financial straits and with ideas of his own, decreed otherwise. So on September 14th when a mellow autumnal haze lay like a bloom over the rolling land, a carriage drove them out of town in a north-westerly direction. Father Richard, their future Pastor, was the driver; the Bishop trotted beside them on horse-back. A raft ferried the party over the Missouri River, sullen in colour but strong in its relentless looping movement on to the Father of Waters. Steep but pleasant bluffs welcomed them to the other side on the upper slopes of which stood the village of Saint Charles, with its log church and very near it the Duquette house, now theirs by lease. It was a single-story house built of upright oak posts, and its steep roof ran out over a gallery front and back. Apple, pear and plum trees bent close about it, but the garden proper was an overgrown tangle.

The door opened before them into a large central room. "This," said Mother Duchesne, "is for our Master." What matter if there were only six other rooms badly in need of repair, one of which was to be occupied by Madame Duquette, the kindly owner of the house? The central room was the Master's. Boxes were dragged from the carts and opened; chapel furnishings packed in Paris many months before were set in place. With the dawn of September 8th, our Lady's birthday, the candles were lighted, the Bishop vested, and in the hush of the first Mass the Master came.

At once children from the village began to straggle in, barefooted, independent children of all ages and all degrees of ignorance. There were more of them than the house was meant to hold, which was not saying much, and thus in an undisciplined babble of French and English the first free school west of the Mississippi began its sessions. On October 3rd Pélagie Chouteau and Emilie and Thérèse Pratte arrived to be the *pensionnat.* The two schools progressed simultaneously, occupying perforce much the same space and equally bereft of books and desks. The boarders did not object in the least to rolling up their beds every morning and hiding them away during the day; if the Nuns could be cheerful about lack of room so could they. Mother Audé and Mother Berthold plunged recklessly into teaching in English, for the children fell in love with them. Delight spread among the villagers. Little pictures of the Sacred Heart painted by Mother Duchesne were appearing in their homes; their children were learning to read, to count, to sew, to be good. In Saint Louis Monsieur and Madame Pratte smiled with satisfaction over their daughters' letters, for they were not only happy letters but written in an elegant script.

It would seem, as a specially kind attention of Providence, that several of the Nuns were gifted with beautiful voices, and even those less favoured were constantly singing. The sound of their singing floats out to us from the pages of their journals and letters, and soon we hear the voices of the children joining in, to the evident pleasure of them all. At first they sang hymns to the Sacred Heart composed in French by Father Barat, then a whole Benediction, then a High Mass and Solemn Vespers on Sundays. They sang at the ceremony of First Communion when eleven little girls of the Free School walked two by two to the Church, led by Mother Berthold who had the sweetest voice of all. They sang at the Midnight Mass on Christmas Eve when the day-scholars were somehow housed for the night, lest they should miss the grace of the *Veillée* and of the great Coming. The constant joy of these "psalms, hymns and spiritual canticles" flows through the accounts of the first hard years of each new Convent of the Sacred Heart as it came to be founded, for first of all the Religious, obeying Saint Paul, "sang in their hearts in grace to God"; then they sang aloud in chapel and school-room till the children could not help but sing.

In sharing this joy the children could not realize in what suffering it had its roots. As they ate heartily of their plain but well-served meals they did not know that the Nuns were often hungry. November brought almost a famine. For fifteen days bread and even flour were hard to get for those who had no ready money. An early winter froze the springs and even the borders of the river, so that muddy water had to be fetched from afar, bucket by bucket, at an exorbitant price. No one could be found to work the garden or care for the cow, and all this labour had to be added to already endless hours of teaching and housework. The winter days were grim for them with poverty, anxiety and loneliness, for it took months for a letter to bring them comfort from the Mother House. Yet still they sang, and when Holy Week came they expended their best efforts in an attempt at pomp. They draped the sanctuary on Holy Thursday with white cotton cloth, wishing it were silk, but a gust of wind through the draughty room blew the drapes into a candle flame. When the resulting fire had finally been put out the Sacred Host was found intact under the charred corporal, and by Easter Sunday the chapel had been restored enough for the Lord to rise again in it.

Summer came, and on August 31st the prizes and ribbons of merit were solemnly distributed, though sadness weighed on the School and on the village. The Bishop had decided upon a transfer of the Convent to the village of Saint Ferdinand in Florissant Valley some miles away across the river. On the First Friday all the children came to Mass at which they sang again their First Communion hymns. Father Richard spoke to them for the last time and then left abruptly, too disconsolate to eat his breakfast.

The children were still more afflicted. They and their mothers trailed after the Nuns as far as they could go, clinging in tears to their hands and skirts in the course of the cumbersome departure. Two small boats carried their baggage down to the river, where it was piled on the sand while a still smaller cart made seventeen trips back and forth in the blazing sun to carry it to Florissant. Then, added Mother Duchesne:

> I was supposed to close the march that evening with the cows and the chickens, in company with Sister Marguerite. But the cows were so rebellious at finding themselves tied and at having to walk in the heat that we had to put off our departure till the next day in the cool of the early morning. Then we could make them go with the help of some cabbages which we had placed in the cart. I divided my attention between the care of the relics

and that of the chickens. We crossed the Missouri and I ranged up our charges, she the chickens and I the cows, and fed them with motherly tenderness.

The site of their new home had been well named, the Flowering Valley; [2] Mother Duchesne's eyes softened with pleasure as she saw it in the evening light stretching gently down from the bluff of La Charbonnière, tinted with the harvest and filled with peace. Cold Water Creek meandered in a silver line through the heart of it. On the banks of the stream clustered the houses of a village, a French settlement with a church in the center of the neat gridiron of streets, each of which bore the name of a saint to bless the houses of its sturdy *habitants*. Stalwart in its cedar logs the house of the first *commandant* stood out in bold relief. Once the home of French and Spanish officials, then of a group of Trappist monks, it now belonged to Mr. John Mullanphy of Saint Louis, already well known to Mother Duchesne.[3] This energetic Irish Catholic was not only a fortune-builder but a benefactor of all manner of good works of whom a later generation could say, "his greatest claim on our remembrance is the life he led." He believed that Florissant was destined to become a thriving centre of commercial life which might in time outstrip Saint Louis. This was not to be. Florissant is still today a tiny and peaceful place even smaller than of old. Yet "over Florissant and its environs is spread an other-world atmosphere distilled of the sanctities and heroisms of several generations of genuine Catholic life," [2] and one of the richest chapters in its history opened with the arrival of Mother Duchesne that September night escorted by cows in her uncouth cart.

The Pastor of Saint Ferdinand's Church was a Trappist, Father Dunand, who had been supervising the erection of their new Convent. It was unfinished as yet, so their carts rumbled instead to the "Bishop's Farm," a euphonious name for a rough log cabin lying among the Common Lands that fringed the town. This dwelling gave them an opportunity to live for three months a life that surpassed anything that even Mother Duchesne could have craved in the way of poverty and primeval inconvenience. The plank door of the cabin opened into its one room which was eighteen feet square. A voracious fireplace in one wall swallowed logs eight feet long, so that the inmates had to take their choice between roasting and freezing. In a loft overhead, reached by a ladder, the Nuns lived and slept, leaving the room below to be the class-room, parlour, dormitory and refectory of the boarding-school, made up of children who had come with them from Saint Charles, and which actually began to increase in numbers under these forbidding conditions. Their chaplain, Father de la Croix, had vacated this abode for a corn-crib, "open to the winds like a bird-cage," into which he had to crawl on hands and knees till a box-like cabin was put up for him with a box-like chapel adjoining, into which fell vegetables stored in the rough loft overhead. The Nuns gathered fruit and berries until the weather grew too cold; they milked the cows, cold weather or not, while the Bishop stood by teasing them and secretly admiring this virile high-heartedness. Most of all he admired Mother Duchesne, while admitting that she had not as yet acquired "quite the suavity of Saint Francis." His esteem for them and their way of life had grown steadily, especially since he had found that it was useless for him to try to get them to change in the least the Rules which they had brought from the Center and which were the source of their strength.

In the midst of all this came a steadying grace. Father Felix de Andreis, Superior of the Lazarist Mission at The Barrens and also Vicar-General of Saint Louis, came out to the Farm in October. At once Mother Duchesne recognized in him a kindred soul. The children sang a hymn to the Holy Name of Mary, "and," wrote Mother Duchesne, "the beauty of the song kindled in him more strongly than ever the fire of the love of God and of the Blessed Mother. We saw him grow pale, then flush, then tremble, till he seemed lost, reminding us vividly of Saint John of the Cross lost in ecstasy at Saint Teresa's song on Divine Love." He was a brilliant and cultured man, besides being a saintly one whose cause has since been introduced in Rome. He came again to the Farm in December, and for eight days preached a retreat that lifted them high in spirit on the arms of the cross. They sat spellbound before his dark, emaciated figure, while he filled the cold chapel with the strong fire of his spirit.

The day after the closing of the retreat an anniversary all their own was commemorated, half wistfully and half triumphantly. It had been on December 14th at eleven o'clock that Mother Barat had first entered the cloister of Sainte Marie d'en Haut fifteen years ago and claimed Mother Duchesne for the Society of the Sacred Heart, and now at the same hour five homesick missioners went to the chapel to sing a Magnificat and a Hymn to Saint Francis Regis who was the chosen patron of their labours. All day their memories kept floating back, and Mother Duchesne repeated the familiar story, lingeringly. Her heart had need of easing, for as she wrote to the one whom she loved best:

> I realize that my soul is alone, but I have too little feeling to be afflicted by this. I do not know in what state I am, and though unfaithful I do not tremble; though impatient I taste but the sweetness of Jesus. I rarely yield to others yet I am sure of God's love for me. . . .
>
> "God alone" and "Ita Pater" have a new meaning in these surroundings where I feel that Divine Providence will not abandon me. I seem to be clothed by It, to touch It with my heart and my hands. . . . Consolations are mine no more; my heart seeks a support and can find none but "God alone."

It was a hard blow to learn soon after this of the death of Father de Andreis, for he had understood her in her loneliness.

By now their new house was nearing completion, and on December 23rd the moving began. The younger children drove through the snowy fields tucked safely into the wagons with mattresses. The other girls enjoyed themselves hugely, walking with Sister Lamarre, who wrote:

> You cannot imagine a funnier sight than we were. It was bitter cold, and Mother Eugénie in the abundance of her charity had wrapped our bodies in blankets and our hands in shawls, leaving only our feet a little liberty. Enveloped in all this covering we set out on our walk. Never had we laughed so much in all our lives. We looked like a band of Indians, and by way of amusement we called ourselves a family—father, mother, children. And I? Oh, I was grandma.

Mother Duchesne, as usual, kept the hardest task for herself. She and Mother Audé came last, on Christmas Eve. They waded through brambles in pursuit of a stubborn cow, dropped their earthly wealth into a snow-drift, and froze their fingers in finding it; then the warm doorway of a new home opened. Only a few hours remained before midnight and they were spent in clearing the chapel of lumber, hanging sheets over the unfinished places and spreading clean cloths on the altar like swaddling clothes in a manger. Lanterns gleamed on the snow, and like new shepherds the Irish workmen came silently in for Mass. By way of being angels the little choir of nine children lifted their high voices in song after song. They had not yet done singing by evening of the next day, Christmas Day, for there were Solemn Vespers and Benediction. The Bishop had come to bless the new house, and as the lamps were lit the children gathered around him in the parlour. What though their one rickety table had collapsed under his Lordship's breakfast that morning? They had at least a chair for him to sit on. They stood in a prim half-circle before him, dressed in their uniforms of purple velvet trimmed with black ribbons, and "sang couplets to express their gratitude."

Then work began and the months gathered momentum. New pupils came, bearing names familiar in the history of Saint Louis: Labbadie, Cabanne, Gratiot, and the familiar Pratte and Chouteau. A Free School was opened in an adjacent building erected by the axes and hammers of the townsmen. Their new three-storied brick house seemed incredibly roomy, though it was soon more than full. Feast days brought gleams of consolation as when on July 22nd the children acted a little play called "The Crossing of the Rebecca," and a huge packing case from Amiens brought a piano—what new ardour now for the perpetual singing! But only overwork had made success possible, and in the late summer one by one the Nuns paid the price by serious illness. But the next winter was worth it all, for on February 19, 1821, the corner-stone of the first Church west of the Mississippi to be dedicated to the Sacred Heart was blessed. It was a brick church, built so that the sanctuary touched the south wall of the Convent chapel, and an opening was made between the two holy places. This church still holds today in its simple grandeur the peace of Florissant's heroic memories. Around its walls are illuminated placards telling of its associations with Blessed Philippine Duchesne, the confessional she used, the places where she knelt. She still seems to be praying there as she did by day and by night for many years, through a valley of shadows and rare transfigurations on Tabor.

One of the moments in which she cried "Lord, it is good for us to be here," was September 22, 1820. On that day Mary Layton, a young girl from The Barrens who had been brought to Florissant a short time before by Bishop Rosati, took the habit of a Coadjutrix Sister, and became the first American Religious of the Sacred Heart with joy and singing. "We wished," said Mother Duchesne, "to make as impressive as possible this first religious clothing to take place in Upper Louisiana since the beginning of the world."

That was only the beginning. In March Emilie St. Cyr, aged sixteen, took the habit of a choir religious and Mary Ann Summers, aged fifteen, that of a Sister. Eulalie and Matilda Hamilton soon followed and before many months there was a fully established and ever-growing Novitiate. If some of the Novices were so young that it was necessary to lengthen their habits once or twice before they had finished growing, they were yet stalwart enough to accept penances and privations of the good old monastic stamp and to sleep on the floor wrapped up in a buffalo skin. If they sometimes went off into fits of uncontrollable laughter, as when they saw Mother Duchesne gravely saying Office quite unconscious that she had forgotten to remove her paper sunbonnet, they were yet mature enough to inspire the children with awe for their religious dignity. They were a virile, lovable band to whom Mother Barat wrote:

> What a grace God has given you in calling you to be the first Americans to consecrate yourselves to Him in the Society of the Sacred Heart. This blessing must stimulate your gratitude and fidelity, that you may be fervent models of regularity to those who will join you, drawn by your example and the sight of your happiness.

The growth of an American Novitiate was the condition which Mother Barat had laid down for further expansion. It was now fulfilled and in June, 1821, came Bishop Dubourg's request that they accept Mrs. Smith's offer of a foundation in Grand Coteau.

At this point in the story the picture again reversed in Mary

Ann Hardey's imagination; she saw Mother Audé and Sister Layton coming nearer and nearer down the river from Florissant, after Mother Duchesne had courageously made this first division in the ranks of the Religious. Mother Audé would gladly have stopped here in her story-telling, but this was just the part that the children wanted most to hear. So she complied, and we can catch her very words, for this is how she wrote to the Mother General of the journey down the Mississippi on the Steamer *Rapid*:

> Our journey as far as Plaquemine was monotonous enough, but here the monotony ceased. The crew had put your poor daughters off the boat at ten o'clock at night on an extremely muddy bank where we had to wade for a quarter of an hour, happy to reach the inn with shoes on our feet. We were lodged in a little room draped with the webs of spiders who dropped down in a friendly way on our faces. We were alone; we could content our hearts with talking of you, of our good Mothers and Sisters; we could pray; we were as happy as could be far from our dear family.
>
> After a day more of travel we disembarked, and there were still four miles to the inn at Attakapas. It was impossible to go on foot on those wretched roads, and there were no carriages, not even a wagon. We had to get on horseback. I had some difficulty in climbing up and staying on my charger, whose mane helped me more than once not to go off head-first. We spent the night at the inn . . . and on the 25th we reached the home of Mrs. Smith, who received us with every possible kindness.

Mother Audé went on to tell of the first perilous nights when they slept on the floor of their own new house which was still littered with building materials and open to the winds and to inquisitive animals. She did not relate how ill they had both been, and how she had dragged herself about on hands and knees to supervise the workmen. She made the children gasp with the tale of how she had put her hand into a hole in the wall one day only to hear a sharp hiss which made her jump back while out glided a five-foot snake, bulging with the chickens that it had recently swallowed whole. Mrs. Smith, the solicitous benefactress whom the children all knew so well, had promised that her slaves would bring them food daily until they were well settled. Mother Audé did not add that Mrs. Smith was not infrequently afflicted with absent-mindedness and her slaves with laziness, so that the kind offer was forgotten for days at a time, nor did she tell how Mrs. Smith had expected that her position as temporal foundress would give her the right to live in the Convent among the Nuns, without becoming one. This would have been entirely contrary to Rule, and Mother Audé's combined tact and firmness had been sorely tried before Mrs. Smith had accepted the compromise of living at the Convent as a guest, but outside the Community cloister.

So all had ended well, and for the children these stories had resulted in a happy reality. They could go off to bed after hearing them, content that each day should pass and give place to the next. They did not know that while they were asleep Mother Audé would go down to the kitchen and wrestle with her problems, including the next day's dinner. For a long time she was the cook. Then at a late hour, when the planning and potato-peeling and cleaning were done, she would sit down on a bench in the corner and, holding the cover of a large cooking pot on her knees by way of a desk, would write to Mother Barat. "Pray for me, dear Mother," she wrote, "that Our Lord may increase my courage and receive the sacrifices that I offer Him in place of the prayers that I often cannot say, and of which I have such great need." The comfort that she longed for, tender but uncompromising, came over the sea in a letter that crossed hers: "Have confidence, my Child," wrote Mother Barat. "The Heart of Jesus will make up for all that you lack, and your foundation will prosper. Only be generous and faithful. Let yourself be nailed to the cross. If it now seems too big for you, you will soon grow to its measure and it will lift you above all earthly things."

VI

MADEMOISELLE MARIANNE

Mrs. Hardey was somewhat startled when, on her first visit to the daughter of whom she was so proud, this young lady of twelve behaved in an unexpectedly babyish way by bursting into tears: "They give us worms to eat," she insisted, "I saw them in the bottom of my soup-plate." Mrs. Hardey's eyes sought Mother Audé's, but the matter had laboriously to be translated into French before light dawned. Then Mother Audé's laughter made Mary Ann stop crying. It would seem that French soup made with spaghetti had never appeared upon the Hardey table, and Mary Ann's imagination had run away with her when, in the unfamiliar and dimly lighted refectory, her dazed eyes had seen certain wriggling substances at the bottom of her plate. Now she had the grace to laugh at herself. Some fifty years later it was noticed that Mother Hardey—the imperturbable, the self-possessed Mother Hardey whose impressions were so difficult to guess—could only bring herself by a marked effort to face spaghetti soup. Furthermore, she was always sympathetic with impressionable children.

Although inclined to be reserved and to judge coolly of a situation before letting herself be swept away, Mary Ann was too keenly interested in things to hold aloof for very long. Her school-mates, whose numbers were continually increasing at odd moments—thus adding to the difficulty of adjusting the curriculum—ranged in age from six years to fifteen. The eldest was Mrs. Smith's niece, Mary Sentee, still openly joyous in the grace of her recent Baptism. The other names were, for the most part French: Louise Montbrain, who could recite poetry "à merveille," Félonie Poiret, an old friend from Opelousas, and Zelia Bousseau, who was the first child of the Sacred Heart in America to be awarded a "First Medallion," that highest of school honours. She later married Alexander Mouton. The children's accomplishments and previous cultivation varied as much as their ages. Some were charmingly aristocratic little ladies, others had a way of "swearing like men," a habit which they speedily dropped. All were lovable, loyal and responsive. Among them Mary Ann took her place as a member of "la troisième classe." It would be hazardous to try to equate this class with any modern system of grading; it simply meant that she was within three years of being a "finished product," in the light of prevailing standards.

Novelty helped to make interesting what might otherwise have been hard at first, for the *règlement* of a French boarding-school was carried out with surprising precision. Grand Coteau was not the Hôtel Biron, that recently acquired and gorgeous mansion on the Rue de Varennes which was attracting attention in the highest circles in France. There were no long corridors or sweeping staircase in this simply constructed house, yet the children walked in decorous if abbreviated files whenever they went from room to room. Even the most necessary furniture was often lacking, but that was no reason for a crude or ungraceful manner of holding oneself, or for a too-hurried curtsey. A bell, rung with self-righteous exactitude by one of the older pupils, broke the day into a round of duties, while a wooden signal assured ordered movements with its dry little clap. The children were proud to be behaving like their sisters across the sea.

Small duties loomed large by reason of the high motives given for their accomplishment under the pressure of a steady, moulding control. The sense of responsibility began at the early—the very early—rising when the white dormitory curtains were pushed back by sleepy hands reaching for the holy-water. It followed the scarcely less sleepy little feet to the chapel where eyes gradually forced themselves wide open in answer to the challenge of attention at Holy Mass. It presided in the refectory where turn by turn the children with the best French accent were given the honour of reading aloud to their companions who were expected to handle *couverts* and *gobelets* without the slightest sound. It was present at class hours, as might have been expected; but it was equally prevailing, though less obtrusive, when the rigid silence broke into more or less lady-like shouts in the fragrant, wind-blown outdoors when the children danced *ronds* under the pine trees. It shared with them the rare but gloriously long days of full *congé* when the bell was hidden in a corner and the woods called. Then a picnic took them far afield, back into the untamed tangle of swamp and forest that stretched into the unknown behind the house, along the reaches of the Bayou Bourbeaux where the cypress knees twisted up fantastically, and where wild grape vines looped from tree to tree in swings strong enough to hold the more adventurous children aloft and set them rocking back and forth in the warm shadow-flecked light. It was waiting for them at the twilight return—that blessed sense of duty—to tuck the tired picnickers in at night under the long mosquito nets that looked so ghostly in the moonlight when the last lamp had been put out.

Mary Ann found her greatest excitement in the life of the

class-room, which was a revelation to her.[1] Here the few precious text-books, carefully covered, were passed from hand to hand for study or for reading aloud in turn. Few the books may have been, but each was a *classique* in its own field, and the young minds that pored over them and copied them and learned long passages of them by heart lost nothing by being restricted to a limited range of the best. The difficulty of getting the best was formidable. Mother Duchesne had written in one of her first letters home after her arrival in New Orleans: "Do not forget, dear Reverend Mother, to send us the Rule of the School, the Plan of Studies, an astronomy, an atlas, a geography, the poem *La Religion* by Louis Racine, and *Esther*, and a Breviary." It was an interesting experiment, though hardly looked upon in that light, to see what young America could gain from a long and steady exposure to the luminous beauties of Racine and Corneille. What had been good and salutary for the pupils of Madame de Maintenon in the elegancies of Saint Cyr could not but be the same for the daughters of Louisiana planters, though the condition of education in that newly forged State could hardly bear comparison with that of pre-Revolutionary France. It was, in fact, in a sad state of neglect, for little or nothing had yet been done to further public instruction. The Ursulines who were doing such remarkable work in New Orleans could not reach every one, and not many planters could afford to have private tutors for their daughters or to send them abroad. It remained for the "Institute for the Education of Young Ladies," as the tiny school at Grand Coteau was officially named, to prove that a rounded and classical tradition of education could be transferred from mind to mind, almost regardless of circumstances and with the minimum of equipment.

Mother Audé was confident that it could be done. The children rose as she came into the class-room, then, because she was Superior as well as teacher, they made a deep curtsey. She said the *Veni Sancte Spiritus* aloud, but not before her quick eye had made sure that the dress and hair of each child was neatly arranged. It was a pity that they were not yet in uniform; the material ordered was still on its way from New Orleans. It was enough for the present that the high-waisted and very long muslin dresses of pale but gay colours were in good taste. The children sat down. If Mary Ann's feet crossed each other from force of habit they soon uncrossed again. She was intensely interested in the lesson that followed.

Mother Audé had mastered the slim copy of the Plan of Studies, drawn up in 1820 with the *Règlement* which had reached her but a few months before. She knew well enough that it could not be applied in all its details to the oddly assorted little group of Americans before her, but she had seen it grow in the making, and she trusted to its elasticity and to the living spirit that underlay its letter. Her lesson this morning was a clear and vivid exposition of some phase of *Chronologie,* as history was modestly called. She saw in history the "great School of Morality" that Bossuet had there found, and in her method of teaching it she carried out to the last iota what was laid down in the Plan of Studies both for the *Résumé* methods and for the Exercise that would follow the class later in the day:

> The method of *résumé* is considered most advantageous, not only for the actual mastery of history, but for the several features included in the method itself: it teaches the children to express their ideas clearly, it gives purity, fluency and facility to their style, and it infallibly removes from them that awkward embarrassment which people never fail to experience who have not acquired the habit of writing.

Under such a thorough and illuminating method Mary Ann soon overtook her companions, though she had started eight months late. She developed an irreproachable and very

French handwriting. She mastered the "complex problems, divisions and geometric calculations" prescribed for the *second cours* of arithmetic, and the items of science painstakingly gathered from an atlas and a globe. The teaching of catechism was delightfully interwoven with that of the Gospels and of Church History, while Literature generously included the "study of epistolary style, letter-writing, and *Fables de M. Loriquet.*" The latter were frequently acted out, both at recreation and on more solemn occasions when costumes added their touch of histrionic illusion.

As Mary Ann thumbed and memorized M. Loriquet's little book of Fables she was unaware of all that the name meant. Father Loriquet had been headmaster of the famous Jesuit School of Saint Acheul at Amiens when the first Sacred Heart School had been opened there. He had given precious help to Mother Barat, not only by providing her with text-books of his own writing but by bringing the strong and practical Jesuit tradition of education, with its militant counter-Reformation touch, to bear upon her early efforts. Other influences too had been doing their silent work in those formative days. Streams of thought and practice, driven underground by the Revolution, were rising to the surface again, refiltered; not only the priests who guided but the nuns who taught in the bare little class-rooms of Amiens were inheritors of a past, and had not lost their inheritance during the strenuous and stripping times through which they had passed. Mother Barat herself had learned in her youth all that her brilliant brother had learned in the College of Joigny with its old-time *régime* of classical, mathematical, historic and linguistic studies. Mother de Charbonnel had experimental knowledge of life in an Ursuline Convent. The Ursulines had been educating French girls for over one hundred years when the Religious of the Sacred Heart drew from them ideals of vigorous study, an exquisite standard of the relations between Mistresses and pupils, and many a precious custom. Mother de Marbeuf had grown up in a Benedictine Abbey where the flavour of the Mediaeval had lingered longest and where the Liturgy taught its lessons with the fullest splendour. Others again of the Nuns had come from Saint Cyr, and adapted some of the ideas of Madame de Maintenon to the Sacred Heart method changing them freely, as when the blue, green, pink and red ribbons worn over the shoulder were made into badges of merit rather than indications of grade. Thus very early the education of the Sacred Heart came to have a character drawn from multiple sources but fused into a distinctive spirit of its own.

This spirit was glad to show itself to the world, and had done so with charmingly frank modesty in September, 1805. In that month an exhibition was held for the parents, displaying both the scholastic exercises and the elaborate handiwork of the pupils of Amiens at which visitors were entertained by a "Dialogue of Madame de Maintenon, a Proverb of Saint Cyr, a Lyrical Scene, and some interludes of symphonies and choruses." A note appended to the program of these events adds:

> We have had many enquiries as to the method followed in this school, whereby even abstract studies are made interesting to the children. . . . It may be enough to state that we try to unite the useful with the agreeable. We aim at instructing while amusing our children; that is to say we have adapted the method so much admired by Racine at Saint Cyr, the method of the immortal Fénelon whose lessons, so delightful in their simplicity, will always surpass all modern theories.[2]

So, when May Ann Hardey's golden head, with the long curls smothered in a hair-net, bent over the Fables of Father de Loriquet her mind was drinking from a stream of wholesome learning, flowing from very far back. Mother Audé smiled with silent satisfaction at the child's absorption. What would become of the mental powers so visibly awaking in the bare school-room deep in the Louisiana woods? Strong powers they were, thorough in assimilation, luminous in interpretation, rapid in execution. The imagination was clear, if not poetic or highly coloured, and if there was an interplay of emotion with intellectual activity it was always under the control of a deliberate will. Yes, Mary Ann was a good student who would one day, without further formal instructions than that given at Grand Coteau, be a great educator.

But education is, after all, more a matter of teachers than of books, and here too Mary Ann was blessed. Mother Audé of course made the first impression, for she was not only Superior but directly in charge of the children as Mistress General. Eugénie Audé, beautiful and multi-gifted, was then barely thirty years old, but her quick, youthful manner was tempered by an aristocratic grace which she had kept from the days when she had been sought after in the court circles of France and Italy. Mary Ann, like everyone else who came under her ascendency, felt the attraction, but she could hardly have known the story of the strong and sudden grace necessary to change the brilliant young belle into the ardent Religious. That grace had come at a strange moment. Eugénie had returned late one night from a ball, and given herself the satisfaction of a last, lingering look at her own reflection in the candle-bright mirror. But it was not her own eyes that returned the gaze. The face of the Man of Sorrows looked out at her from the mirror and the Divine eyes met hers. She responded by entering the Novitiate of the Society of the Sacred Heart. Shortly after her vows she went to Quimper, and while there completed her generosity by offering for the American missions. Her offer was accepted and consummated with unexpected swiftness. She was sent for by Mother Barat and reached Paris after five days and nights in a stage-coach just in time to make her Profession, in what recollection was possible under the circumstances, on the very morning of the departure of the Missionaries. She had brought her beauty, her tact, her energy, over the sea to use them for any duty that came to hand, till Bishop Dubourg had asked her whether she had learned to milk cows at the court of Napoleon.

Mother Anna Xavier Murphy had reached Grand Coteau from Europe only a few months before Mary Ann's arrival, and it was she who had perhaps the deepest influence on the child. She was an Irish woman, young, enthusiastic, humorous and forthright. She had been educated by the Ursulines at Cork, but had entered the Sacred Heart Noviceship in 1820, taking the name of Xavier as an index of her missionary longings. Mother Barat discerned not only her unusual fervour but also her sterling qualities, and shortened the time of her training to let her sail for Louisiana with Mother Lucille Mathevon, the future Apostle of the Indians, at the end of 1822. The three months' crossing brought them to New Orleans in February; there she wrote a letter to Mother Barat that reveals much of herself. After giving an account of their departure she goes on to say:

> The sight of the limitless expanse of sea roused in me a sensation that I can never describe, but it was very delightful. When a stiff wind caught us we were uncomfortable enough for three days. I was sick at times but never the least bit afraid. Mother Lucille was simply frightened to death, and sometimes I could not help laughing at her exclamations of terror. She invoked every saint in the calendar and at times jumped from her berth to pray with arms extended in the form of a cross, begging mercy from heaven, but I was too sleepy to act the part of Aaron. Even in the worst storms I could sleep. . . . One day the waves rolled so high as to inundate our cabins and other apartments, giving them a very timely housecleaning, for it was the Christmas season.
>
> I revelled in the beauty, the magnificent scenic grandeur, which nature continually displayed at every hour. I could only contemplate it in silent wonder and bow in adoration before the

Creator of such marvels. I had no need of a meditation book. Sunrise and sunset were gorgeous, and then there was moonrise or the starry heavens lighting the ocean with a glint of silver. I was so enchanted I could scarcely think of other things. . . .

Mother Lucille is delighted with her destination at Florissant with Mother Duchesne. It is all the same to me; the place makes little difference so long as it is in America.

In the meantime, Mother Lucille was writing her own account of Mother Murphy to the Mother General:

I really ought to speak about Mother Xavier, dear Reverend Mother. How fortunate I was to have her as a companion! She won the hearts of all the Americans on board. If we were respected and even loved by them I must attribute it all to her. . . . When we were in very grave danger on the ocean and I was terrified I used to pray, "Lord, save me for the sake of Xavier whom I am taking to America. I am not worth casting into the sea, but Xavier will make you known and loved." She has just the type of mind that appeals to Americans.

The last remark found its proof in Mary Ann Hardey's instant attraction to Mother Murphy, though she admired all the Nuns, and was especially interested in Sister Mary Layton as the first American Sacred Heart nun. Hers was a hearty lovable nature that laughed at hard work. There were three or four others, all novices, of whom only Mother Carmelite Landry was to persevere. The habit which they wore was still in its process of evolution from the Burgundian dress worn in her youth by Madeleine Sophie Barat. It was becoming conventual in a gradual and inconspicuous way. The fluting of the white frill bordering the cap was larger than it is now; the hair over the forehead was as yet unconcealed by a black band; the sleeves were gathered in at the wrist. But the austere blackness of the garb, with its silver cross and consecrating veil, set the Nuns in a race apart for Mary Ann. She had that sensitive awareness of the supernatural often seen in children who have a religious vocation and do not yet know it. One day she heard Mother Murphy make a remark beginning, "When I was a little girl." Mary Ann, still very much of a little girl herself, stared at her. "What," she cried abruptly, "were you ever a little girl?" Mother Murphy saw that her bewilderment was real and did not rebuke what might have been considered an impertinent remark. She explained, half-smilingly, how ordinary people, human beings like everyone else, are sometimes called by God to a life made special and heavenly because given to Him. The child listened in silence but a deep response woke within her, vague at first as an idea but powerful as an impulse. As she walked away she drew an immediate and practical conclusion. "From that moment I date my conversion," she recounted later. " 'Since the Nuns were once like me,' I said to myself, 'why cannot I be like them?' And for that end I began to correct my faults."

The faults seem to have been of two kinds, the first being due to harmless naughtiness. Later on Mother Hardey could always be trusted to say the worst possible of herself, though with a saving half-wink, so the following episode which she used to relate gives a fair idea of the extent of this naughtiness:

At Bishop Dubourg's visit to Grand Coteau, Mother Audé prepared the children for the reception of their venerable guest, trying to inspire them with the respect and the politeness with which they should greet him. A welcoming ceremony had been prepared, and when everything was ready Mother Audé withdrew to seek His Lordship. The children had made up their minds to do exactly as their devoted Mistress wished, but alas! fear got the better of their good will and as soon as they heard the voice of the Bishop they fled like frightened birds and hid under the staircase. You can imagine the disappointment of Mother Audé; and to think that I was the leader of the escapade!

Such irresponsibility soon disappeared after the aforementioned "conversion," but the other kind of fault was more subtle and it took greater insight on Mary Ann's part to correct it. Her success in studies was phenomenal, and after her "conversion" her success at being a model pupil was quite as marked. Add to this a natural and really powerful gift for leadership and it is easy to see what might have become of her. Mother Audé had long talks with her in the little hole under the stairs that served as the Office of the Mistress General, and a certain amount of systematic snubbing before the other children was used to check vainglory.

But Mary Ann was too deep to respond to any but a deep appeal, and this came with the definitive call to the supernatural life, something inexplicable to those who have never felt it, irresistible save by a bitter turning away to those who have. Once more it was Mother Murphy who served as the instrument, not knowingly but by simply being where she should have been at the time, in God's hands and at her post of duty. The children were moving noisily about in that restless and dangerous moment between two occupations known as "the five minutes," when anything may happen to discipline. Mother Murphy was in *surveillance*, and Mary Ann's eyes were, as usual, fixed upon her. She stood quietly and alertly at her post, and controlled the situation without a word, while there rested upon her person that benediction from within, that undefinable element of manner which betrays the Presence of God. Once more understanding woke within the child like a chord of music at the touch of the Presence of God. An interior voice said to her: "What others have done you can do." She knew without a doubt that she would be a Religious of the Sacred Heart, and nothing from then on would be too hard to do, would be too high a price to pay. The conquest had already begun, for it is in itself a hard and humbling thing to know that God is calling and that one is unworthy to be called.

Then, swiftly, came the end of the year. Examinations were over; the Prizes had been given, and the children were highly pleased with their own success in reciting a little Dialogue in the presence of Father Rossi and Mrs. Smith. The next day, August 7th, would be their last day before going home. That morning the bell was just ringing for breakfast and Mother Audé was leading her now restless little flock to the refectory when a great event occurred. As she wrote later to Mother Barat:

> I was in the midst of my little ones, now numbering seventeen, when a man came in to say that three Religious were coming towards the door. Surprised, I asked him if he had not brought me a letter, if he were not making a mistake. "No, I tell you, they are here," he insisted. "They have come from Saint Louis." I could not hold back the joy of my heart. "O children," I cried, "it is *ma Mère,*" and my tears began to flow. The children crowded around me, repeating, "*ma Mère, ma Mère.*" They clung to me and began to cry too. I broke away from them and ran to the door to see if she were there. I saw Mother Duchesne, I was in her arms.

They were a bedraggled little group, the travellers about whom the whole household of Grand Coteau gathered with such joy. There was Mother Duchesne, erect and valiant as ever, Mother Josephine St. Cyr, who had just made her first vows, and Sister Frances Mullanphy, a Novice. Waiting in the background to greet her loved Mother Audé was Thérèse Pratte, now fifteen years old. It had been Mother Duchesne's first experience of travel on the fearsome bayous, and she was still shaken by the excitement of being pursued by a canoe full of savage Indians, friendly in reality but looking horribly like cannibals, of riding in the black of night in ox carts through bogs where there were no roads, of poling on slow rafts where no land could be found. But now all was forgotten. "What a memorable, what a happy day!" wrote Mother Murphy in her Journal. "With what delight we beheld this cherished Mère, and with what maternal affection she embraced us!"

But this delightful day was also the last day of school, a proverbially hectic day in all schools. Mother Audé was determined that Mother Duchesne should have a favorable impression of the children, excitement or no excitement. They were called together, and while Mother Murphy drilled them in their deepest and slowest curtsey Mother Audé hastily wrote an address of welcome. But who would read it? It must be someone of poise and manner, someone who could read it well with the minimum of practice, and who could be trusted not to get nervous. Mary Ann Hardey, though only in the school three months and not in the highest class, would certainly be the most representative.

Evening came, and the little school gathered in solemn expectancy. Desks were hidden away, chairs arranged in a faultless oval facing the seat of honour. A rustle, a murmur, Mother Duchesne was in her place. Mary Ann rose and stepped before her. She curtseyed and read the French address impeccably. At appropriate intervals her grey eyes rose to meet the steady, penetrating gaze that rested upon her. If the hands of the clock could have folded together at that hour and the significance of the past and future been revealed in the unity of the present, what would it have meant for Mother Duchesne to know what this child would be, to know what a large part of the harvest that she herself could not see while still in the toil of the planting, would be reaped by those young hands, reaped and scattered as fresh grain in fields lying the length of an ocean from Halifax to Cuba?

The address ended and in silence Mary Ann sat down. She

still looked at Mother Duchesne. The impression that she received has been recorded by another child of those times:

> In appearance, Mother Duchesne was not prepossessing. She was rather florid looking, though fair. This was probably due to her exertions in the garden and in the laundry, for no work was too hard for her to do. She had pale blue eyes and high cheek bones, but her face was strong and tender in spite of her lack of beauty. She had a great love for little children, gathering them around her whenever possible, though she spoke very little and very broken English. The girls all loved to be with her.

Now Mother Duchesne smiled, called Mary Ann to her, and asked her name. One by one the other children came. Then spontaneously they sat down on the floor around her while Mother Audé slipped away. Mother Duchesne was alone with her little Americans as she had so often seen herself long ago while praying in far-away Grenoble that this might come to pass.

The next day the holidays began in earnest. It was the long vacation, lasting for the whole of two weeks, and Mary Ann found herself home again in Opelousas. While she was enjoying her family and running loose on the plantation the Nuns were making the most of their opportunity. Mother Murphy wrote in her Journal:

> Vacation for fifteen days, very *à propos* as the absence of the children procured us the delightful gratification of being all together with our *Chère Mère* who had the mortification of being without Mass the Sunday after her arrival. "But the just man lives by faith," which is indeed the only nourishment congenial to this climate.

This Journal, which recorded the events of the house from day to day, was kept by Mother Murphy in a mélange of French and English of uncertain idiom. Through it we see life as it was lived in that Community full of pioneer strength and joy. One week of their precious two they spent in retreat, and as no priest could be procured Mother Duchesne herself gave the meditations. The other week saw them preparing for the children once more, who returned on August 22nd, and "appeared quite satisfied at being restored to us. That evening Mother Duchesne read the School Rule for them, and made the several appointments. The next day classes commenced."

A week later there was a scene of which the children knew nothing:

> August 22: *Jour de naissance de notre chère Mère Duchesne.* No Mass, but she passed the whole day at the foot of the sanctuary. It was at the recreation after supper that she told us she had that day accomplished her fifty-third year. On account of not knowing it we were deprived of expressing the sentiments which such an event necessarily excited in the hearts of her daughters. May her valuable life be long preserved; may she live to see her children and her children's children peacefully established in Louisiana.

On September 2nd there is a briefer, more poignant entry in the Journal:

> *Notre chère Mère* Duchesne left us. Judge of our feelings on the occasion. But it is unworthy a daughter of the Sacred Heart to express them. *Dieu seul, Dieu seul.*

So Mother Duchesne vanished again behind that mysterious tapestry that hid the bayous. A long silence followed before a letter came to tell them of a journey grim and more peril-fraught than any experience yet encountered in the new world, of suffering born with stark, impersonal heroism. She and little Thérèse Pratte had set off in the blinding September heat. The first of their adventures had its comic side, when the horse, "a poor animal which reminded me of the Apocalypse resolutely refused to go on, and both he and his companion ended by falling into a quagmire. My pupil and I tried to draw them out but in vain. Finally a negro played the part of a horse, for after we had unloaded the cart he managed to draw it." But matters became more serious when they reached New Orleans and found the city in the grip of the yellow fever. Soon they were in the midst of unrelieved nightmare:

I entered the steamboat (the *Hecla*) with a sort of horror; contagion was raging. I felt my own fever mounting. The Captain, his mate, and a third person succumbed. A young man coming from Lyons was so ill that he was put off at a village; they say that he died there, but he had a priest. I suffered in every way, seeing men die like beasts with neither human nor Divine help, deprived even of that tender compassion which brings relief to all ills; songs of merry-making were heard on all sides.

I thought that it would be prudent to stop at Natchez, one hundred miles from New Orleans. It is the last city this side of Saint Louis. Once there we learned that we could not be received through fear of contagion. We got off on the opposite shore and stood on the beach waiting for a passer-by to find a shelter for us. We were refused in several houses; finally a man received us. He offered us the bed in which his wife had died a short time before, on which the sheets had not been changed. I was at the crisis of my fever, but I sat up as straight as I could to hide it, and kept hidden for four days, doctoring myself. God blessed what I was able to do, and soon I found that I was better.

At this point the curé of Natchez, hearing of their plight, found shelter for them with a kindly family. They tried to procure the comfort of the Sacraments for Mother Duchesne, but the priest who attempted to come to her carrying the Blessed Eucharist could not cross the river because he was too poor to pay the ferry money. Finally they embarked again on a different boat:

Never had I so felt the need of Mass and the Sacraments, having seen death so near. There were still ten or twelve days of river-travel ahead. That made sixty days of the most rigorous fast that I have ever had to make, even in the days of the Revolution. In the midst of these dire privations I saw how ceaselessly the arms of Divine Providence were stretched out over us. We passed the steamboat on which we had first travelled. It could not go; its boilers had burst. The steam had killed two men and burned others; thirteen had died of the yellow fever. . . .

I made my retreat on the boat; everyone on board spoke English, and so, finding myself alone with God, I took advantage. There was a man among us dying of the fever. I saw him several times during his illness. I hope that God had mercy on him, for he had no religion and had never been baptized.

Mother Duchesne baptized him, and knew that the suffering had been worth while. When the sobering news of this journey reached Grand Coteau months had passed. All felt that Mother Duchesne had been in the wine-press; it had wrung from her broken body and her famished soul prayer so pure and strong as to be worthy to wrestle even with God and draw down floods of mercy upon this grace-parched land. What was the temper of a soul for whom endurance was not enough, who must take her suffering in both hands and lift it high? Weak from fever, tormented by noise, by insects, by the proximity of rough human bodies on the crawling steam-boat, with no Sacraments or sanctuary, Mother Duchesne chose to make her retreat. "Finding myself alone with God, I took advantage."

The brief two and a half years of Mary Ann's school-days passed all too swiftly. They had found her a child and left her a young woman, albeit only fourteen years old. Through Mother Murphy's inimitable language we can see many of the events which had a moulding power upon the children, and upon this child especially, this observant, responsive child. The account opens, characteristically, with singing:

1822, June 6, Feast of the Sacred Heart: *Mère Eugénie et moi* united with all our dear Society by renewing the solemn engagements we had made at the foot of the altar; *ensuite, Salut* (Benediction) which terminated by a *cantique* which so engaged priest and children that they continued singing until the bell of supper.

The deprivation of Mass, which affected children as well as Nuns, began early:

June 17: Our chaplain, M. Jeanjean took his *congé*, leaving us like the once-solitary daughters of Jerusalem, without priest or Sacrament. The good curate of Opelousas, M. Rossi, takes pity on us and says Mass sometimes.

July 22: Sweet Feast of *notre chère Mère Barat.* During this day of remembrance how often did my spirit bound to the Hôtel Biron and there mingling with the idolized group I embraced and offered for this cherished Mother the most ardent wishes of my heart.

July 26: My birthday. No Mass but every privation here has a *je ne sais quoi pour moi* in this cherished land of my adoption.

November 1: Had High Mass, the first sung by our children, who also appeared in their uniforms for the first time.

Whenever visitors came, Mother Murphy recorded that they left "all embalmed with our little establishment." Each new event, introducing a custom or weaving a memory, "embalmed" the children also, in the French sense of the word:

December 8: Feast of the Immaculate Conception. After the *Salut* in the evening a little altar was most tastefully arranged at the foot of the sanctuary. *Nos enfants* entered two by two holding in one hand an olive branch which served as a link between them and in the other hand a lighted taper. The act of consecration was audibly read by one of them, *ensuite* a *cantique.*

December 25: *Fête de Noël.* Had high mass and sermon at midnight which lasted till three o'clock. You may suppose we had no objection to our beds. All visited them except Mère Eugénie who remained before the Blessed Sacrament which was exposed all night and during the day till *Salut* in the evening. There were twenty-six persons communicated in our little chapel among whom were several black men and women.

January 1, 1823, *Le Jour de l'An.* Gave the Prizes. *Nos enfants* were ornamented with the trophies of their industry by M. Celini and M. Rossi. *Notre digne* Foundress (Mrs. Smith) also joined in decorating the interesting little group of whom she seemed to exclaim by her approbationary look of satisfaction "*Voilà mes bijoux et ma plus belle parure.*" The most amusing part of the ceremony was the description of their feelings at the moment when the crowns were placed upon their heads. "Indeed, when the crown was placed upon my head I thought that I was going up into heaven." I often think how charmed *chère Mère* Barat would be with the native simplicity of the children here.

Mary Ann had already made her first Communion, so she was an onlooker in the ceremony which took place every year on Easter Sunday. The children were given practices in the course of their training which might seem to us to require unusually high spirituality, for "they appeared to have the fervour of angels. After receiving absolution they entered the class and on their knees demanded pardon. Not satisfied with this they requested to kiss the feet of those of their companions to whom they had given some pain. This had a great effect upon the other children." After the ceremony Mother Murphy, deeply moved, concluded her account with the words: "For my part it was one of the happiest moments I have ever experienced, to witness which I would cross five oceans." More beautiful ceremonies came with Corpus Christi:

May 9: *Fête Dieu.* All arranged in the evening in the greatest order, *six de nos enfants* dressed as angels. All was deranged by the rain. However we went to the *reposoir* which was fixed in the woods rear of the house. At our return a sermon was given in English; many assisted, *malgré* the rain.

Rain could be terrible as well as annoying in Grand Coteau:

September 14: What a night, and what a melancholy view presented itself the ensuing morning—fences broken down, trees torn up, in fine all is horror and devastation, all hopes of a *récolte* blasted from the dreadful storm.

The Convent account books also throw light on Mary Ann's school days. They reveal the fact that the first considerable sum received in payment of a tuition was instantly sent north to Mother Duchesne who was always in greater need than they, and similar entries occur at regular intervals. We can see the house being furnished and made cheerful by the purchase of desks, clocks, quantities of white and even red paint. Occasional payments for a wooden partition show the attempt to multiply rooms in a small house by making them smaller still. Domestic animals gradually transform the fringes of the woods into a farm, while the purchase of a book here, a bolt of blue cotton there, altar furnishings and medicines, shows poverty being transformed into simple comfort by good husbandry. By the time Mary Ann left school Grand Coteau had acquired the stable charm of a home, while a number of negro slaves also found that it was home. Old Martin, Phyllis with her three wee children, Frank and the wife whom Mother Murphy redeemed for him from another owner, these were not only made as happy as possible in their snug little cabins, but were gradually won to the light of faith and to the love of the Sacred Heart that was the reason for Grand Coteau's existence.

One cold morning of Mary Ann's last year at school, while the children were dressing in the dormitory, Mother Murphy beckoned to them to come to the window. A startlingly beautiful sunrise was pouring its splendour through the spires of the trees to the east, and Mother Murphy, reverently excited, was likewise pouring out a little flood of talk in the praises of God the Creator, when suddenly a grey cloud blurred the glory and it vanished. There was a silence. Mary Ann was, as always, contemplating Mother Murphy rather than the sky. How much could her maturing mind have guessed of the thoughts that were passing in the soul of her loved Mistress, and which were afterwards confided to the Journal?

> The rising of the sun this morning was imposingly great. I called the children to look at it, and to consider what must be the greatness and splendour of that Being who created so beautiful, so magnificent an object. While I was indulging in the reflections which such a sight naturally inspires, it suddenly disappeared. The contrast which succeeded suggested to me the comparison of a soul that, in the commencement of her conversion or when determined to give herself solely to God, at that moment usually basks in the sunshine of the consolatory delights which the sensible attraction of grace suffuses. But after some time this consolatory feeling is withdrawn, when the poor soul, like the horizon this morning, suddenly appears dark, silent, good for nothing. In this season of privation, when like the plaintive daughters of Jerusalem, she only lives in recollections, what is it that nourishes and supports her? The spirit of faith. "The poor man lives by faith."

Whether she guessed such thoughts or not, Mary Ann had by now become a markedly thoughtful young person herself, and the time was coming when she too must live somewhat more by faith alone. Clouds were not far ahead, though their eclipsing of the sun would not be for long. The last spring and summer passed quickly. She was wearing by now the coveted First Medallion, bespeaking her leadership in the school. On September 18, 1824, came "Solemn distribution of Prizes. All present appeared pleased with our children, who repeated their geography and three pieces admirably well." As Mary Ann drove away next morning in the family carriage and looked over her shoulder at the house among the bright gardens and the moss-hung pines, she knew that she would soon be back.

VII

MISS MARY AND SISTER ALOYSIA

THERE WAS NO CLOUD over the joy of the Hardey family at having her home again, no longer Mary Ann but "Miss Mary." Like a queen she stepped into the first place in the affections of everyone from her father down to the littlest pickaninny running about the slave quarters. She was at fourteen a fairly tall girl with an easy, dignified carriage. Her golden hair fell, when she let it, below her waist. Her complexion was clear, even brilliant, and emphasized the wide-set grey eyes, the straight mouth, the pronounced chin. Now, as a young lady, she was given everything in the way of dress and ornament which could set off her charm, and became her father's comrade, her mother's home-maker, and "good angel and playmate," as her brother Charles said, to the younger children.

Carriages rolled back and forth between the plantation houses of Opelousas, stopping before one open door after another in a constant round of friendliness. The figure of Mary Hardey was seen with ever increasing frequency, moving about the shady lawns of an afternoon or entering the subdued but gleaming ballrooms of an evening. It was a gay and charming life and Mary too could be gay and charming, though at times a veil of reserve would fall suddenly between her and her young companions. These would, at the same age, be boys and girls today but were then young ladies and young gentlemen with hearts of their own, but also with strong-minded parents who had the honour of a family to maintain. But sometimes it was more than reserve that made Miss Mary, for all her attractiveness, slightly difficult to deal with. A sudden reaction against pleasure, signs of an almost violent struggle, would appear when least expected.

Mrs. Hardey soon guessed the truth and had too deep a sense of spiritual values not to accept it. Mary had a vocation, and it was costing her very much at the moment to follow it. In a fit of unwonted timidity she begged her mother to break the news to her father; she then waited the outcome with some fear. He, instead of becoming angry, took a pooh-pooh attitude which was rather galling to her pride. The news leaked out and was passed whisperingly about among her friends, who agreed upon a common plan of action. They would whirl her into their carefree life; they would give her no time to think; they would see her married before she knew it. Mary was too quick not to know what was afoot. She met their insinuations with energetic resistance; when broached openly upon the subject she defended her purpose with fiery ardour, "in a spirit of contradiction" as she said deprecatingly later on. But alone in her own room she had other and harder battles to fight, with no contradiction but what came from her own nature. It seemed to her that she could not, would not, live in obedience and in constant renunciation all her life. She was under no illusions about religious life; hers was no romantic school-girl attraction. So the inner battle went on for months while Mary alternated between hours of all-forgetting enjoyment at home or in society, and hours of lonely prayer, of clinging to the ideal of sacrifice that lay at the root of her vocation.

A year passed thus. The summer was a gay one, and September came bringing its serious thoughts of "what is to be done this year?" One of her friends, a perspicacious and determined girl, realized that a crisis was at hand and resolved to turn it her own way. She planned a brilliant party for the evening of September 28th and invited all the people most calculated to break down Mary's resistance, including one young man to whom no girl in her senses could be indifferent. Mary would leave the ball if not engaged at least captivated.

The friend appeared at Mary's home early in the day, punctiliously asking the permission of Mr. and Mrs. Hardey for their daughter to attend the dance. All day she laid siege to Mary, and as evening drew near went home, sure of her success. After supper Mary went to her room to dress. Alone in the blue September twilight she realized that the moment for a choice between God and herself had come. Over there to the south, behind the darkening curtain of the wood, lay Grand Coteau where the Blessed Sacrament waited in the small chapel. There was a cloistered part of the house into which she had never penetrated; that too was waiting. Nearer at hand was another house, pillared and gracious, alive with lights and with the small twitter of tuning violins. "One more night to have a good time in; it's not wrong," she kept repeating between her prayers for help.

Then Mary put her ball dress out of sight, lit the candles on her desk, and sat down to write two notes. She called the slave who was waiting to drive her to the party and told him to take one of the notes instead. It was a politely regretful refusal. Then she went upstairs and with a beating heart slipped the second note under the door of her father's room which was directly over hers. It told him that she was leaving the next day for Grand Coteau.

She spent most of the night packing, but whenever she stopped moving about she could hear her father's feet overhead pacing back and forth. The next morning she waited in terror till she thought that the family breakfast was over before creeping downstairs to the dining-room. Her father was sitting there, and merely remarked over the top of his newspaper that he would be glad to drive her to Grand Coteau himself that day. The sooner she went, the sooner she would come back. Mary stiffened and went off to find her mother. The latter knew better what was happening, and when the carriage drove off she said a final farewell, a silent one, for the little brothers and sisters who shouted "come back soon" from the verandah, and the affectionate slaves who stopped their work to wave at her as she passed, were not to know that this was more than a passing visit to Grand Coteau.

When the door of her old school finally opened Mary flew into Mother Audé's arms. "I've come to stay," she cried in a burst of joy. Mr. Hardey stiffly explained that he had yielded to this caprice only to cure it. "You will be back in a week," he said to his daughter as he bade her goodbye; "in the meantime is there anything that you want?" Mary thought, then a distressed look crossed her face. "Yes, I forgot my mirror. Will you send it over to me?" Mr. Hardey drove away with his feelings lightened by a gale of laughter.

Mary did not find herself alone in the Noviceship. On the Feast of the Mother General, Sophie Maygown and Philippine Jourdain had taken the habit. They had been given the names of Sophie and Philippine in honour of Mother Barat and Mother Duchesne, they proudly explained. Being in the cloister at Grand Coteau was a different matter from being in the school, and Mary spent a good deal of time elaborately avoiding her former companions. She was in another world now, and had been trying to acclimatize herself to it for only a few days when the old familiar world once more asserted its claims sharply.

Mary was told that Aunt Sophie, her old coloured Mammy, was in the parlour and wanted to see her. She flew downstairs, and like the child that she really was clung to the old woman whose comfortable frame suggested home, petting, firesides, and—yes—the cookie jar. But Aunt Sophie seemed distraught. She rocked back and forth, drying her tears with a bandana. "O Miss Mary, Miss Mary," she sobbed, "come home!" Mary fought back her own tears and shook her head, but when Aunt Sophie gasped out that her father was ill, was dying, was calling for his daughter, her heart stood still. For a long time the Mammy pleaded; Mary could only shake her head, dumb with grief. Finally Aunt Sophie, crying more noisily than ever, climbed into her gig, and Mary saw her turbaned head bobbing down the road that led towards home. Then it disappeared, and the house was very still, as still as death. Mary felt her feet moving out the door, down the walk under the solemn bearded trees. They broke into a run as she reached the road. On she ran, stumbling, sobbing now, unthinking, only knowing that her father wanted her.

She had gone a full mile when sheer weariness forced her to stop. In the silence of the country-side her mind cleared; she remembered that she had forgotten to pray. She prayed now, her head bowed under the empty sky, and the will of God turned her back strongly along the way that she had come. She walked the length of that endless mile, into the Convent, straight to Mother Audé's room, where she told her all that had happened. "I am glad for your sake that you have come back," was the grave and gentle comment on her act. But Mother Audé was really much moved by the occurrence, and at once sent one of the Convent slaves over to Opelousas to enquire after Mr. Hardey. The man came back with the news that Massah was enjoying his usual good health. It was indeed well that Aunt Sophie's ruse to get her adored little Mistress home again had not succeeded.

Whether it was because she feared that indetermination might shake her again or whether she acquired a scruple concerning her use of the famous mirror, Mary's next act was a rash one. She cut off her beautiful long hair, none too artistically, and appeared before the Community in a bobbed condition one hundred years ahead of the fashion. This time the rebuke she received was by no means gentle. So the weeks passed in the usual ups and downs of postulants. At one time it was feared that her health was suffering, and she was made to take long horse-back rides around the property. She very much objected to this as a concession, but obeyed and the rides proved effective. When her soul suffered she managed to find some energetic cure within herself. One day the old repugnance at the thought of perpetual obedience, of giving up her own will to that of another, rose again to torment her. Calmly she turned the tables on herself. "The surest way of being able to do my own will," she said, "is always to will that which my superiors will for me." So she threw herself headfirst into obedience, and whenever she was asked if she knew how to do something she would answer, "No, but I can learn." She showed such skill and patience in untangling a skein of knotted silk one day that Mother Murphy declared aloud that she should be immediately rewarded with the habit, and Mother Audé agreed.

The length of time for postulantship was not fixed then as it is now, and Mother Audé was sure of Mary. There was a serious point, however, to be settled before the Prise d'Habit. It was customary then in the Society of the Sacred Heart for a Novice to take a Saint's name at her clothing. The name that Mary Hardey chose was not only inspiring and difficult to live up to, but a link binding her to one of the most potent traditions of the young Society. It was the name Aloysia, taken remotely in honour of Saint Aloysius, but directly through love and admiration for Mother Aloysia Jouve, niece of Mother Duchesne, who had died at Grenoble in 1821, the account of whose death had contained these significant words: "At the age of twenty, full of strength, of energy, of facility, of zeal, Aloysia believed that she was destined for the appealing missions of Louisiana, but in the designs of God she was to become their zealous protector in heaven. . . . Pray for us, dear Aloysia, for you are with God." [1]

Mother Barat had found Adèle Euphrosine Jouve at Grenoble under the care of her aunt when she first went there in 1804, a brilliant, beautiful, ardent child, and had watched the transformation of her nature as God won her to Himself at her First Communion and still more at her entrance in religion. A flame-like imitator of Saint Aloysius in his penance and his fidelity, she took his name. She confessed to enjoying the sound of soldiers on parade, for it reminded her, she said, that she was a soldier of Jesus Christ. She dreamed of heroic sanctity, of the missions, of martyrdom. Gifted with high powers of prayer and a remarkable capacity for hard work she became a challenge to all who knew her, the joy of her aunt, and the greatest comfort of her Superior General who exclaimed almost passionately: "It is thus I had dreamed they all would be." Then at the age of twenty-two God fulfilled all her hopes by crossing all her desires. An incurable illness reduced her to suffering and immolation while she continued, on crutches, to carry out the duties of the responsible offices which had been laid on her young shoulders. When not quite twenty-five she died in an act of transcendent love. A cry of sorrow and yet of triumph went up from the whole Society; how could it not but gain from the death of one so holy? At Grenoble wonders of grace and cures of body began to be worked in such numbers that Aloysia might have become the first canonized Religious of the Sacred Heart had she not, obedient even in death, ceased to work them at the express wish of Mother Barat who feared this intervention of the marvelous so early in the life of what she liked to call her "little Society." In Florissant, where her inconsolable aunt was praying to her, Aloysia's intervention was felt in the sudden and really extraordinary growth of the Noviceship, the hope of the Society in America, while at Grand Coteau Mary Hardey took her name with the veil of religion and prayed to share in her spirit. Who can say what measure of the work accomplished later by Mother Hardey was done by her and what by the heavenly patroness who had poured the fulness of her life thus early into the common treasury of the Society? In the Louisiana for which she had longed she became the patron of a novice destined in her turn to spread the work of the Society, "full of strength, of energy, of facility, of zeal."

So Miss Mary became Sister Aloysia on October 22, 1825, while Sister Frances Mullanphy made her first vows at the same ceremony. Perhaps the wee chapel at Grand Coteau had never been so crowded before, filled as it was with Hardeys and Smiths and their numerous friends and connections. She was not the first member of the family to be clothed in the religious habit. One of her cousins, Jeanne-Loretta Smith, had already joined the Sisters of Charity at Emmitsburg, and, as Sister Marie Regina, would one day be Superior of all their American houses. But that ceremony had taken place too far away to be a family affair, and now several other young Smiths, among them a few more future Sisters of Charity, watched the transformation of Mary with round eyes. Among the school children was her youngest cousin, Eliza Smith, a naughty, charming little orphan seven years old, whom Mr.

Hardey took into his own home to console himself for the loss of a daughter.* [2]

At the ceremony Mr. Hardey became not only convinced of the reality of his daughter's vocation but proud of it, and he rose to the occasion when Mother Audé told him that his sacrifice was to be even more complete than had been expected. A new foundation was about to be made at Saint Michael's, near New Orleans, and Aloysia had been chosen—a signal honour—as one of the foundresses. Mr. Hardey bowed his acceptance, and offered to provide an ox-cart to take the Religious to the boat. That night Mother Audé, writing of the proposed foundation, called Mother Barat's attention for the first time to her promising new daughter:

> I am taking with me a Novice, Mary Ann, who comes of an excellent family and whom we have had for two and a half years in the boarding-school. She was always one of the first in her class and won the medallion. She would do honour to us even among the French Novices. Pray, dear Mother, that she may persevere, for I think that some day she will be of great service to us. She is not quite sixteen!

The remote cause of this sudden change of scene in the life of Sister Aloysia was the hungry zeal of Mother Duchesne, who was a missionary through and through. She who felt herself so awkwardly remote in outlook and language from the people of her new land, managed to bridge all gaps when there was question of spreading the faith. She somehow knew the names and the needs of every fellow worker in the Mississippi Valley and beyond it in both directions. She gave away

* In the far future this child, as Mother Marie Clotilde, a Visitandine Nun, was to make the foundation of the Monastery of Villa de Sales in Brooklyn while Mary was establishing the Religious of the Sacred Heart in New York. She lived a life of remarkable holiness and her body was later found to be intact upon its exhumation in 1890.

everything that she could lay her hands on, even to her own clothing, when a hard-pressed priest appeared at the door, and her heart would follow him wistfully out into the wilds.

She was aware of the immense good that had already been done. She knew the story of the Kentucky Church, of Father Stephen Badin, the first priest ordained in the United States, who had laboured there; of Bishop Flaget of Bardstown and his endless rounds of fruitful visitation in the wilderness and semi-wilderness, Bishop Flaget who could hardly be mentioned without the epithet "saintly."[3] She knew that the Dominicans and Trappists laboured fruitfully in Kentucky, and she was still more keenly interested in the fact that the first Religious Orders of women in the Middle West had begun their existence there. In 1812 the Belgian missionary, Father Charles Nerinckx, had placed the veil upon the heads of the first three Sisters of Loretto. The new Religious had scarcely begun life in their log-cabin Convent when Father John David performed a similar ceremony in another log-cabin Convent for the first three Sisters of Charity of Nazareth, among whom was Catherine Spalding,[4] the distant relative of Mother Hardey whose life was to resemble hers in its constant round of foundations. Kentucky had a right to be proud of its rôle in American missionary life.

Mother Duchesne was aware too of the shadows on the picture, the schisms and scandals in New Orleans which she tried to repair by ever more rigorous fasting and penance, and the blight of ignorance that lay everywhere. This last was what she felt she could really remedy, by ever so little. She had been shocked to learn that ignorance had placed pictures of Bacchus and Venus in the Church at Portage des Sioux, and she had promptly sent more seemly ones to replace them. As Bishop Dubourg wrote in the notes of a pastoral visitation of Opelousas: "Ignorance causes much harm in a Parish. This evil cannot be remedied except by means of missions which may eventually be established in the places most distant from the Church. . . . The Pastor must multiply his familiar instructions on the most important parts of Christian Doctrine, particularly to the children." [5] This surely was in her sphere!

Her favorite reading was the *Annales* of the Society of the Propagation of the Faith. These modest pamphlets reached her regularly from the time of their first publication in 1822, for it was to her own Bishop Dubourg that the Society was at least partially indebted for its existence.* By means of them she was able to follow missionary movements throughout the world. She was ready to believe anything. "They say that China is converted," she wrote to France. "Can this be true?" In any case, as she engagingly reminded Mother Barat, she was already half-way across America and only a few weeks more of ocean-journey separated her from China. Of course, if China were already converted, there was still Peru! It is no wonder that with such visions in her mind's eye Mother Duchesne was only too willing to listen to a new plan, slightly more modest than the conversion of China or Peru but requiring not only zeal, which was never lacking, but money and subjects, both of which were always lacking. It was a plan that would unwittingly launch Aloysia Hardey on her long career of expansion, which if not precisely of missionary character was at least *de propaganda fide*.

The scheme originated with Father de la Croix, the same who had so obligingly lodged himself in a corn-crib in order to give the Nuns his house, and who had served the Convent in Florissant faithfully when not off on those hair-breadth ad-

* On his begging trip to Europe, Bishop Dubourg had started a movement among his supporters in Lyons for raising money for the Louisiana Missions. In 1820 Pauline Jaricot, inspired by a letter from her brother in the Seminary, had experimented with a simple and systematic method of securing funds. In 1822 Bishop Dubourg sent Father Inglesi to Lyons to pursue the matter and at a meeting on May 3rd an Association was formed adopting Pauline Jaricot's method and spirit. At once the *Annales* began to be published.

ventures among the Osage Indians which endeared him to Mother Duchesne even more. In 1823 he was recalled from Saint Ferdinand's by Bishop Dubourg and given charge of the Church of Saint Michel de Cantrelle lying on the further bank of the Mississippi where it curves and swings to the east not far above New Orleans.[6] Facing it across the river was the parent-parish of Saint Jacques de Cabahannocé. All about Saint Michel lay the plantations of the Acadians, thriving, opulent centers of Catholic homelife, where the girls were unhappily growing up without education. Father de la Croix was determined upon having a Convent of the Sacred Heart close to his church. He answered Mother Barat's prudent objections to the new foundation by taking up a collection among his parishioners and even among the priests of other Parishes with such energy that he amassed a fortune of seven thousand dollars in a few weeks. She was won over by so much zeal, but Mother Duchesne, willing to give her life and her all for any movement that would spread God's Kingdom, was never willing to accept a position of authority unless compelled to do so. She begged to escape being made Superior, writing in her habitual strain: "Mother Eugénie is well known in that part of the diocese; she will give a good reputation to the house which she will be able to maintain by her zeal, her prudence and her talent for managing the children. . . . Here even more than in France the old and the ugly count for nothing." For once she had her way.

Thus it came about that an unwonted stir went through Grand Coteau at one o'clock in the morning of October 25, 1825. The day before had been remarkably busy with a visit from the Governour of Louisiana, Henry Johnson, who was keenly interested in educational work. There had been singing, addresses, and exhausting civilities of all kinds, so that now the Convent was sleeping soundly, all except those leaving for Saint Michael's. Departure at this unusual hour was a ruse on the part of Mother Audé to escape the farewells of the Community and children. Only Mother Xavier Murphy, who was to replace her as Superior of Grand Coteau, was on foot, brave and bright, whispering "Dieu seul" under her breath in a steadying manner. The party numbered seven: Mother Audé, Mother Xavier Hamilton, who had made her first vows but a short time ago at Florissant and who was to be Assistant of the new House, the coadjutrix Sisters Labruyère and Mullanphy, and the Novices, Philippine, Sophie and Aloysia. The three latter, all in their 'teens, were trying to remember that they were Religious seriously answering the call of obedience, and not children off on a midnight escapade. Clouds were scudding over the westward-drifting stars, and it looked like rain as the travellers made their way to the house of the Curé to receive his blessing. Mr. Hardey was waiting there to say goodbye to his daughter and to pack the party into the waiting ox-carts. The negro drivers recognized Miss Mary and grinned in the lantern light, then the carts rumbled off into the dark through the ghosts of palms and cypresses along the edges of the inky bayous.

The threatened rain came and drenched them through and through, so that the next day's sun had to dry them, still en route. As they neared Plaquemine they changed their vehicles for the inn-keeper's wagon. The surly driver decided that their combined weight was bad for the wheels, so he left them by the side of the road while he went to fetch another cart. It took him till midnight, their second sleepless night. It was cold, and the three Novices, who were undeniably enjoying themselves, had a good excuse for jumping up and down to their heart's content. The next day found them stranded in an inn, where a tedious wait for the boat exhausted their supply of provisions. When they finally boarded the river-steamer they saw half their baggage tumbled into the water and roughly fished out. It was in keeping with the character of the whole journey that the boat finally landed them at Saint Michael's at three o'clock in the morning.

Father de la Croix, a sanguine Fleming, did not mind the hour in the least. He was vibrant with satisfaction, and lodged them in his own house while he, as formerly, went elsewhere. The next day was the Feast of All Saints, and the Pastor triumphantly paraded his new flock to the Parish Church for Mass. Word of their arrival had spread through the village and its environs. As Sister Aloysia passed up the aisle she could feel the curious gazes of a packed congregation. She felt—not saw—them, for, as Mother Audé, whose business it was to see everything, recorded with satisfaction, the Novices kept their eyes lowered and saw no one. They were led to a bench placed conspicuously inside the altar rail, and here, true to their traditions, the Nuns opened their new apostolate with a burst of song, for Father de la Croix, who knew their talents, calmly asked them to sing the Mass. Unabashed, they did so. Benediction followed, and the ravished congregation joined in the more familiar *Tantum* and *Laudate*. "The people showed really extraordinary emotion," wrote Mother Audé, "and many of them wept."

For three weeks they lived perched in the rectory before their new home was ready. It lay in the heart of the tiny and very proud town of Saint Michael's, only a few yards from the Church where for a long time the Nuns were obliged to go for Mass. The town had a right to be proud. The members of its Corporation bore names of purest Acadian ring: Arcenaux, Dugas, Dumaine, Bourgeois, Hébert, Poiret, names which soon appeared on the School-register of the Convent as well. Loyalty to the faith and to their own Parish Church in particular was taken for granted, devotedly and at times belligerently. Aloysia had at first no further contact with the town than that made through downcast eyes at Mass. When she let those eyes stray beyond the boundary of the Convent garden it was upon the river that they rested, or upon the fringes of wood that held the far, flat fields in a cup of silence. The river went its own moody way very near to her door. Already levees had begun to control its erratic course, and at times the swollen waters crept threateningly near to their tops. Busily the boats plied up and down, but the river kept its own mighty counsel and swept on. It gleamed silver when the skies lent it their own glory; left to itself its colour was sullen with the weight of long journeyings.

Their new house was of colonial style, red brick walls, green shutters, white pillars guarding the broad galleries. A touch of elegance given by the mahogany trimmings within made Mother Audé prophesy that it would be the Hôtel Biron of America, and she was not wrong, though for the moment it was as bare as it was elegant. The three Novices, who were soon joined by some new recruits, were delighted with their opportunity of practicing a few mild heroics. They sat on their heels for want of chairs and lived mainly on rice and milk for a month. There were not enough plates to go round until a peddler appeared one day, displaying fine tin-ware. A set of plates was purchased—on credit. The Nuns were enjoying the luxury of a tin plate apiece the next morning at breakfast when the peddler abruptly appeared in the refectory. He claimed his wares, having found a more immediately lucrative opportunity for selling them. The plates were washed and returned to him on the spot, with much laughter and no rancour. This sort of poverty would not last long and they made the most of it, "warming ourselves at the Saviour's Crib, and at times in the kitchen." Their state appealed so strongly to Mother Barat that she wrote with her habitual longing: "What a sacrifice not to be able to come to see you! To console myself I sometimes plan to do so; I do not want to die before seeing the banks of the Mississippi."

Before Mother Barat had quite given up this hope, prosperity came. Aloysia, moving about at her housework or sewing quietly in a corner of the Noviceship, heard the voices of children playing on the galleries. She heard too the noise of hammering where the new chapel was under construction, but by March this sound had ceased, giving place to that kind of silence which is like a hush of surprise in every place where a lamp burns before a Presence. On Easter Sunday the first Mass was said, and as Mother Audé wrote:

> The whole world with its riches, pleasures and satisfactions could not pay for one moment the sweetness that I felt when the Blessed Sacrament was placed in the tabernacle. Upon coming out from Mass, where we sang all the prettiest songs that we knew, my Sisters and I wept with joy; even the children, new as they are, were moved, and scarcely knowing why, they did not want to leave the chapel. Their eyes were fixed upon the tabernacle and I had to give the signal several times before they heard it.

After this the voices of the children became omnipresent; the school was increasing beyond all expectation. It is a remarkable fact that throughout most of the way opened up by Divine Providence to Mother Hardey things tended to happen on a large scale; big houses full of children would call for still bigger undertakings. She who had seen the hiddenness and abjection of Mother Duchesne's habitual way knew well where the roots of her own success lay, but the outward difference remained. The Novice at Saint Michael's, unaware of the future, heard the voices of the children with some misgivings. While still a postulant she had one day confided to her Superior that she could never be a classmistress, for she felt unable to teach, which was only another way—although she did not know it—of saying that she did not want to teach. Mother Audé had received this ultimatum without comment, and Sister Aloysia considered the matter closed. Now, however, she was sent for. One of the class-mistresses was ill; would Sister Aloysia kindly substitute for her? Glad to be obliging, the Novice graciously accepted and began to teach. The other mistress recovered and was given new work while the Novice went on teaching. "I went on for seventeen years," related Mother Hardey later, "and such is the grace of obedience that teaching not only became easy for me but even attractive."

Thus she began early to lead that double life which is made one by single-heartedness, the life of prayer and work, of contemplation and activity, the intake and outgiving of the Divine which Father de Tournély had seen in the beginning as the life-breath of the Society. In Aloysia's case there was to be no preliminary period of training in perfect quiet. Life was too strenuous in those days for Novices to be secluded from apostolic work, for there were often no other workers to be had. So, in the cloistered part of the house, Mother Audé raised her White Veils in Spartan fashion, anxious to make of them Religious who would be *de la race* in the eyes of their Superior General; while in the school-rooms the children unwittingly did their part in the process of forming their Mistresses. She was almost instantly successful, and her pupils found that they could take no liberties with her inexperience. She seemed strangely gifted with maturity from the beginning. Young maturity is a vastly different thing from precocity. It was not so much her gifts as the harmony reigning among her gifts that made Aloysia accomplish things with such apparent ease. It was not so much the resources of her own nature as the fact that she yielded those resources into the hands of others that made her powerful. It was not only because she worked prodigiously but because she could let go of work when praying that she became while still so young God's fit instrument. During her years at Saint Michael's no other moulding forces than those at play within her own small world were brought to bear upon her, but they were enough to change her from an inexperienced girl into a trained Superior ready for hazardous responsibilities, for they found her responsive.

Mother Audé saw to it that Aloysia was not dazzled by herself. Private humblings alternated with public reprimands, and the children would stand with downcast eyes while their *surveillante* was blamed for their misdeeds. Tragedies of novice life become comedies in retrospect, and Mother Hardey liked to tell later on how she had complimented herself one day upon the fact that she never broke things, whereas the next morning she sent a bundle crashing through a window in a hasty attempt to put things in order on hearing Mother Audé's step drawing near. In any case the mere exigencies of life left little time for complacency. The best of the work of training was done in the more leisurely hours when the assembled Novices listened to letters like the following from Mother Barat:

> Do not forget that you are the cornerstone of the American Noviceship, and consequently the foundation of the Society of the Sacred Heart in your vast country which has such need of spiritual help. This places upon you the obligation of generous fidelity, of refusing nothing in God's service. Only give Him your whole heart and soul, and all will be easy.

So if Sister Aloysia found all easy, she must have given her heart and soul, while unaware that Mother Audé was delighting Mother Barat with letters about her:

> Our little Novices are being formed. One of them in particular, Mary Ann Hardey, who has taken the name of Aloysia, is made for succeeding with children; her appearance, her gifts for study, her docility in taking advice, her excellent judgment, her attachment to the Society, all this makes us look forward to receiving great consolation on her account. . . .
>
> Aloysia is like an experienced Mistress with the children; she has a marked aptitude for study, and makes progress. Her exterior is

most attractive; she has a frank and open character, a solid judgment and a strong vocation.

When similar eulogies reached Mother Duchesne she remarked discouragingly, "Sister Aloysia will not live long; she is too perfect." In spite of this prophecy, however, she became covetous, and wrote a little later humbly asking if Aloysia could be spared for the new foundation at Saint Louis. "If you take Aloysia you might as well take the whole house," answered Mother Audé rather tartly.

VIII

RESPONSIBLE

In October, 1827, Mother Duchesne wrote a letter to Mother Barat which spoke in the name of all the houses of America, voicing their common joy in a strength-bringing race:

With you we thank the Heart of Jesus for the grace of our Approbation, and we want you to know of the pure happiness it brings us. It gives us courage to suffer in upholding by our labours, as far as we can, the work which God Himself has done, and one in which He mercifully allows us to share. Each succeeding foundation gives us new joy since it spreads the glory of the Heart of Jesus and draws to Him souls seeking to embrace religious life.

By this Approbation the Holy See confirmed the Constitutions and Rules of the Society. His Holiness Pope Leo XII had signed the Decree on December 22nd of the year before, and "we are now," wrote Mother Barat, "among the Orders approved by the Church, holding a place in her Hierarchy." The Fourth General Council of the Society had lately been held, and its Decrees did much to strengthen the bonds of unity now made sacred by the approved of the Vicar of Christ. Points concerning cloister and the vow of poverty were clarified and made stricter; a vow of stability was to be added henceforth to those made at Profession; the religious habit was regulated to its present form. By March, 1827, Saint Michael's proudly felt that it was more than ever *de la race.*

It was a fit moment for Sister Aloysia to take her place definitively in the ranks of the newly strengthened Society, and she thought that she saw the heavens opening when she learned that her Noviceship was to be shortened by seven months, and that she was to make her first vows on the Feast of the Five Wounds. Sister Sophie and Sister Philippine, who had come with her from Grand Coteau, changed their white veils for the black at the same ceremony, which was performed by Father Richard. With a new quietness the Aspirant went back to her work when the day had closed.

There was a shadow over the house for the next few weeks. Mother Xavier Matilda Hamilton was dying at the age of twenty-four. Mother Duchesne's mournful remark about the early death of the virtuous was only too often justified by the facts, and the crosses in the graveyards of those first houses tell their own tale of fatal illness among the very young. Mother Hamilton was distantly related to the Hardeys, and her family had come from Maryland at about the same time. Her home had been the refuge and mainstay of many a needy priest in Missouri. Temperamental and ardent, Matilda had gone through violent spiritual struggles which had ended by winning for her the name of "Angel of Peace," and by making her ready for heaven in May, 1827.

Mother Hamilton had been Mistress General of the School, and Aloysia was still grieving for this loss when the burden of responsibility was laid for the first time upon her own shoulders, a burden to grow increasingly heavy and never to be lifted. Before she had reached her eighteenth birthday she found herself named Mistress General. Later on, she tried to joke away the implication that she had been chosen for responsibility on account of her virtue. "If I made my vows at seventeen," she said, "it was because in the House of Saint Michael's only the Superior was more than a Novice just then, and priests complained at seeing the School in the hands of three white veils. Then, as my two companions were very small and thin, and thus could not properly represent authority, I was chosen on account of my height." But whatever the reason for her appointment, this absurdly young Mistress General took the copy of the Constitutions that Mother Audé gave her and went to the chapel to meditate upon her new Rule. She had no time to lose in fears, for her duties were all around her.

There they were, more than fifty of them already, ranging through all the ages of childhood, eager, obedient, high-spirited, very winning in their sashed and piped dresses that nearly swept the ground. Behind the children were their parents, driving formally up to the Convent on Thursdays in their handsome carriages manned by liveried negro coachmen. More rare, yet still more formidable were the dignitaries who came from time to time to Saint Michael's and whom she must now meet. Thus it was that Bishop Rosati found her, still shy and tentative, and became her fast friend. He had succeeded Bishop Dubourg in Saint Louis when the latter, oppressed by circumstances with which he could not cope, had left his vast diocese in other hands and retired to Europe. The new Bishop was more than pleased with Mother Hardey and with her work, and wrote of what he had seen to Mother Duchesne:

> May God be blessed! It is easy to see that He has merciful designs for this country since He not only gives us the blessing of a brilliant and Christian education, but the unhoped-for grace of several

religious vocations. . . . The good that is being done here is very great, and we look forward to even greater things.

The still greater things were already in process. Prophetically, the Mistress General's first care was the planning of a new wing to hold her growing school, and by the following year it branched out from the old Convent like a hand extending into the future.

When the cold of November fell in 1829 a south-bound boat brought Mother Duchesne to Saint Michael's for the first time, while Mother Murphy arrived from another direction. This happy meeting had a serious purpose behind it. From France Mother Barat had been watching the growth of the Society in America. The handful of missionaries were now a band of sixty-four of whom only fourteen, including the original five, had come from France. The other fifty were all Americans. The work was by now being carried on in six houses, for in 1827 Mother Duchesne had, thanks to the generosity of Mr. Mullanphy, opened a school and orphanage in Saint Louis, and the following year the old wooden house in Saint Charles, now more than ever in ruins, had been valiantly reopened. In addition an attempt was being made to incorporate into the Society a small Community of Sisters of Loretto who were discouraged by the isolation of their position at Bayou La Fourche. This latter venture was not to prove a success—although some precious vocations were to come from among the few children there—and the house was later closed. Its Superior, Mother Hélène du Tour, now came with Mother Murphy to Saint Michael's. This rapid expansion had made Mother Barat anxious for more concerted action among the Superiors, and she had asked Mother Duchesne to preside at a Provincial Council.

Mother Hardey was appointed secretary, and went to Mother Duchesne for instructions. It was seven years since the little girl at Grand Coteau had read an address to the visiting Reverend Mother, and now the two had a long look at each other. Mother Duchesne saw that this dignified and singularly attractive young Mistress General was of metal worth testing, but it was difficult to find an approach through such exterior perfection. She chose this very dignity as the vulnerable point, and more than once during the course of the Council found fault with the bearing of her secretary which she laid to "American pride." Mother Hardey at once disarmed the charge by the humility with which she admitted its truth, and Mother Duchesne smiled her satisfaction.

For her part Mother Hardey managed, for all her discretion, to study deeply the face that inspired such veneration. The features of Mother Duchesne, always rugged and austere, were more deeply lined than they had been seven years ago, lined not only with the strokes of pain but with the tender lines left by sympathy and by an often thwarted desire to reach out to other people. There was a loneliness in her bearing that spoke of depths impenetrable to others, but in her shadowed eyes one saw the smouldering, often the flame, of a love that went out to God and man in one leap.

The Council was brief and things were not altogether pleasant. Mother Duchesne, always diffident on account of what she considered the failures of her own mode of government, was fearful of going beyond her authority. Mother Audé, whose work had always met with obvious success, had long been in the habit of appealing straight to the Mother General in matters of government, without referring to Mother Duchesne. As the latter did not possess the clearly defined powers of a Provincial this was hardly an actual breach of loyalty, but it certainly did not make for mutual understanding, especially since Mother Barat had continually urged that Mother Duchesne should be consulted and obeyed. There was a sense of strain at the Council which ended by accomplishing little in the way of actual legislation on the many small points on which uniformity of action was desirable.

Mother Hardey was nothing if not discreet, and her position as secretary made her a silent witness of all that happened. This was her first experience of the intricacies of feeling that arise when people of very different temperaments are working together for the same ends, and if it caused her pain it must also have deepened her understanding of character. She would learn in time how to accept maladjustments as inevitable, how to allow for the tension that is often the price of balance between personalities, how to see the limitations of others with no loss of love or admiration, while admitting one's own limitations.

The Council closed, and Mother Duchesne sent glowing and perhaps a bit wistful reports to Mother Barat of the flourishing state of Louisiana houses. It meant much to her to have seen and known them, and when the day's work was over and the winter darkness blinded the windows to the outside world the Community could gather about her. Then, with the problems of the Council forgotten, she felt at home with her own. The very first of these recreations on the night of her arrival was a gay one. Old Sister Boudreau had entered but a short time before, an already elderly widow. There was a radiant, childlike simplicity about her which brought the spirit of Saint Francis of Assissi to the gathering, for she sang and then danced her delight in her revered Mother's presence.

Mother Duchesne had endless things to tell about Florissant, things of which the grimmer side could only be gathered by hearing between the words. She could hardly have told them that the Florissant Journal bore the entry: "the worldliness of the pupils who have left us, their forgetfulness, the indocility of those still with us, calumnies, all these things keep us under the pressure of the cross—to which we must add poverty and illness"; but she could relate that their spirits were so high in spite of all this that yearly, on the anniversary of their sailing for America, the young Nuns demanded a holiday for sheer joy, and *grand régal*—such as it was—in the refectory. Her greatest consolation had been the coming of Father Van Quickenbourne with his sturdy band of Jesuit Novices. They had settled on the Bishop's Farm, of vivid memory. She dwelt upon the spiritual richness that their arrival had brought; she did not say how the Community had pinched and scraped and gone a little bit hungry and cold that these Sons of Saint Ignatius might be satisfied and warm. She told of the devotedness of Father Van Quickenbourne himself, coming to say Mass even when he was mud to the ears with crossing the swollen stream in wintry weather; she added nothing of his extreme severity to herself, rebuking, punishing, chiselling her ardour because he knew that she was worth forging into a Saint at the price of a few tears. It had been he who had brought her, hidden under his cloak, the two first pupils of the little Indian school that was her delight. She made everyone laugh by relating how the children of said school had a way of disappearing out of the window into the tree-tops whenever the Abbé Dussaussoy appeared suddenly in their midst. The Novice in charge had come in tears to Mother Duchesne, who had exclaimed: "Does he think that because he is our Mother General's nephew he can upset our school like this?" But, she hastened to add in telling of the incident, she had given herself a good penance for having spoken in such a fashion of a priest, and another penance to the Novice for having listened to her! The Novice, by the way, was Anna Josephine Shannon who would one day be Superior of Saint Michael's in its palmiest days. None of them knew how this same Novice had come across Mother Duchesne one day sitting beside the cabbage patch in utter weariness, saying her rosary while the tears of hard and hidden grief rolled down her cheeks, and had withdrawn aching in heart because she had caught a glimpse of the price that Saints pay for the sanctity they do not know they possess.

Mother Hardey could guess much of that price, watching the play of expression on Mother Duchesne's face as she talked with bright abandon to her daughters of Saint Michael's. She did not dwell on the state of bleak ruin in which they had found their little house in Saint Charles when they went back to it, but she did relate how after the Bishop's Mass the next morning she had heaped his coffee cup with nice white salt instead of sugar, forgetting that the only sugar obtainable in their poverty was brown. She said nothing of the troubles connected with starting a school in the isolated house in Saint Louis which had been given them, but she told triumphantly how she had dispelled its reputation as a haunted house by going herself to meet the noisy ghosts at midnight and finding them to be cats who had come down the chimney to hold their revels in the parlour. She mentioned with a sigh the extreme unsuitability of the basement room that served as a chapel in the same house, but caused a burst of laughter by describing the crickets that disturbed her at her prayers—those long night-vigil prayers—as "huge spiders that sing like birds." Then, with her inevitable humility, she described the virtues and attractive qualities of all the young Nuns that worked with her, adding only, "as for me, the children in the neighborhood call me the poor old witch." Mother Hardey, who had the gift of seeing through and beyond what people said, gazed in wonder on the face of the old witch, beautiful with a beauty beyond her power to fathom.

Mother Duchesne departed a few days later, and it was well that Mother Hardey did not know that she had seen her for the last time. She went first, in company with Mother Murphy, to Bayou La Fourche where they had done what they could to regulate the situation in that experimental house, and then went on to Grand Coteau. The bayous were always a somewhat terrifying mystery to Mother Duchesne, and this time the languid waters so delayed travel that Christmas Day found them far from home with no Mass nor glad *Noëls* to break the wintry silence of the cypresses. By the twenty-sixth they had reached Portage, and the older children drove out to meet them, singing the Christmas songs at last. The roses and camelias bloom forever at Grand Coteau, and Mother Duchesne stayed till February in this earthly haunt of the peace of heaven. The greatest joy of her stay was the company of Mother Murphy. She wrote of her, "Mother Murphy is the one of our Mothers with whom I can talk most intimately. We could not but help wishing that we could be together at Saint Louis, but who could take her place at Grand Coteau?"

Four quietly busy years passed for Mother Hardey, during which she unobtrusively slipped into her twenties. She saw her first work visibly blessed, as though in gentle encouragement from God. The school was overflowing, and so was the Noviceship. The sense of well-being was felt throughout the Parish. Father de la Croix, who had returned for a few brief years to Belgium on account of his health, had utilized his stay in the Mother Country by amassing a considerable sum for the building of a new church, a wonderful brick church of more or less Roman architecture boasting ten columns. When the edifice was nearing completion in December, 1832, a gift arrived from Belgium, a great bell bearing the legend "Catholici Belgae fratribus Americae." The bell was baptized Eugénie-Louise, for Mother Audé and Monsieur Louis Lebourgeois, benefactor of the Church, and its voice began to call in melody at morning, noon and night through the still air. On the ninth of the following March it rang long and gloriously for the dedication of the new Church by Bishop Neckère of New Orleans.

The joy of that day lingered on the air throughout the

following month of May, and Mother Hardey's days were as bright as the sunshine. On the thirtieth she was too busy with preparations for the ceremony of the crowning of Our Lady to notice the sudden disappearance of Mother Xavier Van Damme from her post of duty. Then Mother Audé came to look for the Mistress General. One glance at her face told Mother Hardey that the shadow of the cross had fallen dark and sudden. All that spring the Asiatic cholera had been making its way down the valley from the shores of Canada where it had been brought by immigrants. The alarm had not been general until, on the warm soil of Louisiana, the disease had taken its most virulent form. Saint Michael's lay directly in its path, and even now Mother Van Damme, well but a few hours ago, was at the point of death.

Acting with incredible speed Mother Audé isolated the four or five other Nuns who felt the first clutches of the disease, and sent word through the Community that all were to move at once to the most distant wing of the building. Such was the religious discipline in vigour in the house that not a question was asked, and many actually remained in ignorance for some time of what was happening. Upon Mother Hardey fell the first duty of dispersing the children. With swift efficiency she set in motion a chain of communication through the village and plantations. A stream of carriages, carts and boats appeared from nowhere, and by night-fall all the children, except the orphans, were far from the stricken house.

But the planters were thinking of the Nuns, and they too acted swiftly. The next morning a special steamer appeared before the Convent with word that an empty house at Donaldsville where the disease had not yet reached had been hired for them. The neighbors had hastily furnished it with all the necessaries, and the Community was urged to come. Mother Audé, standing at a safe distance from the Captain of the boat, made her simple answer. Mother Van Damme had died in the night and three others were at the point of death now; their Mother could not leave them. As for the rest of the Nuns, some were stricken and all wished to be of service where they were, for they could not abandon their orphans. The steamer withdrew, and a new admiration for the Religious spread through the country-side.

Mother Hardey took her place beside her Superior. For two weeks neither of them slept or ate more than was barely necessary to keep themselves alive. Four Nuns and two orphans died within the first few days, and their funerals took place in the dead of night. Mother Hardey possessed a gift untested before now; she was an instinctively skillful nurse and proved it by a remarkable feat. Among the orphans a third seemed beyond recall. The Doctor found the Mistress General, regardless of danger, lavishing personal care upon her. After a brief examination he turned to Mother Hardey. "This child will die," he said, "nothing can be done and you are needed elsewhere. You had better go." She obeyed, but a little while later she came back for a last look. The child was still alive. A great determination took hold of Mother Hardey. For twenty-four uninterrupted hours she stayed by the orphan's bed, battling against death by her prayers, her will-power, and all the remedies which common sense suggested to her inexperience. When the Doctor found her there again he pronounced that she had won.

Gradually the plague withdrew, and word of all that had happened reached Mother Barat. Mother Audé wrote:

In those terrible days God gave me the consolation of seeing the Sisters who were taken from us die like saints, and the others, calm, resigned, and even happy, expressing but one desire—to be true to their last breath to the consecration they had made of their whole lives to the Divine Heart of Jesus. As for Mother Aloysia, we were constantly helped by her devotedness and her charity. She has been everything for us during these days, and we thank heaven for having spared her to us, for every day she is more valuable throughout the whole house.

When the danger was over Mother Audé herself fell ill, not from the cholera but from the reaction to exhaustion, and Mother Hardey, young enough to take no rest from her own weariness, nursed her back to health. All seemed well when God's hand fell again with unexpected suddenness. Four more Religious died within a few days of each other, one of apoplexy, and three of a form of yellow fever that crawled through the valley in the wake of the cholera. "Has God closed the last link of this cruel chain?" cried Mother Audé. "He alone knows."

The chain did close by July, and they were grateful to hear that Grand Coteau, where a procession in honour of Our Lady had been held with tranquil and powerful faith in her protection, had escaped altogether, and that in Missouri none of those attacked had died. It was time to resume normal life at Saint Michael's, and time too for Mother Hardey to be recompensed for her terrible months of trial. Mother Audé felt that the soul-testing experience through which she had just passed might well count for her Probation, those six months of prayer and contemplative life which precede the final vows of a Religious of the Sacred Heart. So it was by a short and terrible journey along the highway of the cross rather than by a leisured lingering in the paths of peace that Mother Hardey reached her *Dies Domini*. She made her final consecration on July 19, 1833, and received her cross and ring from the hands of Bishop Neckère. Her two companions in the ceremony were Mothers Louisa Lévèque and Helene Green. Philippine and Sophie could not share the joy of Profession with her that day. They were both ill of lingering consumption, and were professed later on their deathbeds. Of Sister Sophie it was written: "She died after long suffering borne not only with patience but with joy, a joy which broke forth always and in a way that showed that it came from the depths of her heart." This same joy was Mother Hardey's that nineteenth of July, and she carried it with her not into heaven but to harder work.

On September 17, 1833, a letter brought one more sorrow. Mother Octavie Berthold was the only one of Mother Duchesne's first companions who had remained by her side throughout the fourteen years since their arrival. As a young convert from Calvinism, she had been in the Noviceship with Mother Aloysia Jouve before following her call to America. Drawn ever closer to God by a deepening interior awareness of His presence, she had prayed that He would take from her the natural attractiveness that she feared might interfere with the mission of giving Him and only Him to souls. He took her at her word, and a slow disfiguring disease brought her years of suffering, during which she could say in spite of the temptations which tried her serenity:

> I feel drawn to a closer union with Him. During the last six months especially He has attracted me very much towards a life of intimacy with Him. Sometimes the sense of His greatness and infinite sanctity overwhelms me, for it shows me the loathsomeness of my own soul; at other times when I am near the tabernacle or with the children or in the refectory or in the room where I sleep, I feel an almost sensible consciousness of the presence of God which lasts four or five days, and this state always precedes new bodily sufferings.

She complained towards the end, "I have nothing more to suffer; Our Lord treats me like a tepid soul to whom He does not even send temptations." "Our Lord will see to that," replied Mother Duchesne. He saw to it by allowing a temptation to despair to rack her last hour, over which Mother Duchesne's prayers triumphed. This last sharp purgatorial flame cut loose her soul and she died crying: "Now there is only Jesus."

By this time Mother Audé's endurance was at an end, and Mother Barat called her to France for the General Council of 1833, as Assistant General for America. It was hard enough for Mother Hardey to see her go, but in addition she found herself named Assistant to Mother Julie Bazire who became the Superior of Saint Michael's. She did not know that Mother Audé had written: "Aloysia could perfectly well be superior, but she is but twenty-three years old and has only had her cross a few months. I see no other obstacle than that, for she has prudence, virtue and talents." Such an exception was too great a one to be made even in Mother Hardey's case, so it was as Assistant and Treasurer in addition to her Offices of Mistress General and teacher that she faced life without the guide and mother who had been by her side from the beginning. Mother Audé left in the spring of 1834; the months passed and contrary to all hopes she did not return. Mother Barat had found her health too shattered to send her back to Louisiana, so it was as Superior at Marseilles that she continued to follow "mon Aloysia" from afar.

In her isolation Mother Hardey felt a new bond with her Mother General, and began that correspondence that was to mean so much to her through the years. Her first letter gives a rather formal account of the house with its many new pupils, its happy Community, its fervent Noviceship. The next begins tentatively to ask advice, protesting, half afraid to let herself go, that "when I look into my heart, it seems to me that its strongest desire and its most ardent one is to please you, and to please you in everything." Finally she feels at home:

> I have given you the news of our house, I have spoken to you of everyone, and for once I have forgotten myself altogether! How I wish that I could give you equally good news on that score! But no, I have to admit that I am very often unfaithful; but it seems to me that I am becoming a little less so. I want to do my best not to be altogether useless to the Society that I love more than myself.

At last came the longed for answer, a letter to herself from Mother Barat:

> Try, my daughter, to help as much as you can to maintain regularity, silence, religious exercises, and the virtues of our holy calling in your house. . . . If regularity and fervour reign, be sure that Jesus will bless it and will send you subjects. But if virtue grows weak, if each one prefers her own interests before those of Jesus, all will drag and wither, and what a misfortune that would be in a country where Angels are needed to draw and gain hearts to Jesus Christ.

While thus making herself responsible for all, she was filling her Treasury ledgers with neat entries. The first volume records that after the travelling expenses of the foundation journey had been met, there had been little to begin on. Money trickled out at first: 25¢ for "a handkerchief for the little negro," $1.20 for a hat, then recklessly, $50 for two cows. A surprisingly large amount—$3.40—went for a single bottle of cough syrup, and the staggering sum of $150 to the music master. Then, like the most natural thing in the world, $106 was sent to Mother Duchesne. Later registers show the running of a large and well-regulated school: five hundred pens purchased at a time, quantities of plush, velour, muslin and ribbon, First Communion candles, wax flowers, "livres classiques," and special sums charged for "summer baths"; winter baths were evidently of slight account. The acquisition of a "scientific dialogue" is followed by that of a mirror with a careful explanatory note: "for the pupils."

In March, 1836, Mother Murphy paid a visit to Saint Michael's and Mother Hardey marvelled at her. She suffered constantly from fever but nothing could dim the bright sparkle of hard-won joy that was hers by nature and by grace, and she said simply: "My soul is stronger than my body, I think, for my mind is always at peace. It seems to me that the more imperfect I am the more God loves me." She was the life of the Community during her stay at Saint Michael's, organizing holidays for them, writing gay poetry in their honour. She left after too brief a stay, and the next word that reached Mother Hardey concerning her was the account of her serene death. Mother Murphy's own peace had risen supreme over the waves of sorrow that swept Grand Coteau on the night of September 6th when all hope of saving their loved Mother was lost. She died at midnight, and the next evening was laid to rest in Coteau's quiet cemetery where roses bloom today over her grave.

In a very short time word came from Paris that Mother Bazire would go to take Mother Murphy's place and that Mother Hardey was to be the Superior of Saint Michael's. It was the end of 1836, and the tempo of Louisiana life was increasing rapidly. More elaborate steamers swept by Saint Michael's at more frequent intervals; cargo boats passed more heavily laden. The frontier, a vaguely verticle line, had moved on like a shadow to the west, and the developments of the east were following fast upon it. A horizontal line, rougher along the edges, was appearing between the north and south, threatening to split them apart. Political life was growing apace with the growth of the great national parties, and culture was spreading in uneasy, erratic spirals from the few centers of thought, from Yale, Harvard, Princeton, Georgetown, and the University of Saint Louis. The missionary age of Catholicity was passing, and settled diocesan life took its place along the Mississippi. A new age was beginning, in the midst of which Saint Michael's was blossoming with the ease of a southern flower when the care of it was placed in Mother Hardey's hands.

She seemed made to carry responsibility. If all the tributes paid to her later in life by the men with whom she was in constant contact—the educators, business men, lawyers, prelates, and fond fathers of school-girls—were collected, the general impression made would be that of sheer admiration at her capacity for government. Clear-headed, swift-willed, tactful and firm, she could bring both people and things into an organized harmony in which vision was made a reality by efficiency. "She is a woman who could govern the United States," said Bishop Hughes of New York. If the tributes were collected from another quarter, the impression made is not different but deeper. The women she educated, the souls whom she counselled and sustained, the unfortunate whom she helped, these all speak of the breadth and the virile tenderness of her heart. She was their perfect and unfailing friend. "She was born to rule," said Bishop Spalding, "but to rule by the power of love and gentleness." But this is not all; there were also the Religious who were her spiritual daughters, and for whom she was the mother beyond price. It was the Religious who better than all others could feel the force of what lay behind both head and heart, a soul nourished by the things of heaven, its strength guarded by silence. "Let us think of God and not of ourselves," was her own unconscious explanation of herself. It was because she did not divide these energies but spent them all—head, heart and soul—upon whatever she had to do, that she was so well qualified for the charge that began when she was given Saint Michael's to govern.

Frightened at first, she turned to Mother Barat:

> O Mother General! How could you put this burden on your poor little Aloysia and make her so unhappy when for the twelve years that she has belonged to you she has found nothing but joy and happiness in the prompt and entire fulfilment of your will? But, Reverend Mother, I shall not shrink; I promise it as a true American. If to succeed I have only to follow your counsels I can answer in advance for my success. . . . I do not know how things will go, but whether for better or for worse, you shall know everything.

Mother Barat had herself a genius for governing, and she had taken the measure of Mother Hardey. She wrote:

Your two letters of last March and April were sent to me here in Rome, dear Mother and beloved daughter; you can guess what pleasure they gave me. I love the simplicity and confidence with which you deal with me. I hope that the Heart of Jesus will bless you, and that your own heart is calm and at ease. Thanks to you, dear daughter, I now know all about your house, and it will be easy for me now to keep in touch by a few lines from time to time on each essential point.

Your gift of fifteen hundred francs has just arrived; it will be used for the foundation of the Roman Noviceship that we have just established in a new house, the Villa Lante. These poor children, numbering fourteen, have been perishing for want of air. This Noviceship has no income, and so it is your gift and those which other Superiors send me, which will support it. . . .

How glad I am that you are still able to keep the Office of Treasurer, in spite of your other responsibilities. Very few know how to manage the Treasury, but you must have help for the details. How much one can save by order and precision! For us Religious, our economizing must be based on Holy Poverty, so there must be nothing useless, even for the sacristy. But enough for this time about that, dear daughter. What I cannot too earnestly recommend to you is to build your perfection, your own and that of others, upon interior spirit. You do well to save time for prayer.

I shall try to get the things that you wish, but alas, I am far from Paris. Others will do it for me, for I shall not return to France until next spring. I wish that I could then turn my steps to Louisiana! I feel quite strong enough for that, but it is impossible to even think of it. Later on it will be easier for you to come to France, and what a consolation that will be for me!

In the meantime, my daughter, grow holier every day, to glorify the Heart of Jesus and to make many other souls glorify It. That must be our one passion. This Divine Saviour is so offended, so forgotten! And by whom? This thought makes me tremble. What need there is for His Spouses to strive to make up to Him. I know, my daughter, that your heart understands this need. It is a consolation for me to find one more who wills to love our good Master without measure.

In spite of the trust placed in her, Mother Hardey was undeniably young and she could not help looking it. Soon after her nomination a gentleman came to place his child in the school. Mother Hardey met him in the parlour and made the necessary arrangements. "And now," said the father rather tactlessly, "I want to speak either with the Superior or with someone old enough to be responsible for my daughter." "Certainly, that would be wise," agreed the Superior, and slipped away to send an older Religious of commanding presence to complete the interview. On another occasion, when a business agent insisted on seeing the Superior, Mother Hardey was obliged to insist with equal firmness that she was the person in question. When the business was done, the man inquired with blunt admiration how so young a person had come to be in charge. "I am as surprised as you are," she replied quite unruffled; "I think that the mistake will soon be discovered."

Her first serious responsibility was prickly with difficulties. Significantly, it had to do with property and building. Already, in the preceding year when Mother Bazire was still Superior, the townspeople had exhibited the defects of their good qualities by "showing a little too much zeal," as Mother Murphy had put it, for the honour of the particular House of God for which they were responsible. A dispute had arisen with the Trustees of the Parish Church concerning the little strip of property between it and the Convent, and there had actually been a riotous scene in which fifty angry men had pulled down the enclosure wall built by the Religious. The matter had been smoothed over for the moment, but the uneasy situation remained and threatened further annoyance.

Moreover the housing problem was also becoming acute. The original Convent had not been planned for the two hundred children who were now packed into it, and to keep adding wings on disputed property would only be a dangerous compromise. Mother Hardey soon determined to build afresh, at a safe distance. Suddenly an offer for an advantageous piece of ground presented itself, one which must be refused or accepted immediately without time for recourse to the Mother House. It was a hard decision, but Mother Hardey made it and then wrote at once to explain matters and get the necessary sanction. Mother Barat had already given her liberty of action in cases where distance would interfere with execution, and soon reassured her fears. The property which she had bought at auction was a beautiful stretch of many acres reaching back from the river at about a mile's distance from the old Convent.

Mother Hardey's enthusiasm ran high and she sent to New Orleans for an architect to plan the building, who, by the way, was so impressed by what he found out through his dealings with her that he came into the Church soon after. With one of her sure prophetic strokes of judgment she ordered a house three times longer and a story higher than any that the Society had built so far in America, on a scale of simple but imposing amplitude. She could read the future enough to see three hundred children moving about those spacious rooms. So the foundations were laid, and the walls had begun to rise when Mother Hardey was interviewed by Bishop Blanc of New Orleans, who had succeeded Bishop Neckère. He was a familiar friend of the Sacred Heart already, but he had taken alarm at the scale of the plans for the new building. She must retrench them, he said; they would prove harmful to the Ursulines in New Orleans. Mother Hardey knew better, and moreover the work had progressed too far to be abandoned without great loss. She requested time, and before long her action was supported by the Mother General, who wrote: "Undoubtedly, if the Bishop gives orders we must obey; but then I should protest, and perhaps in that case I should move your work elsewhere."

The Bishop finally admitted the justice of her cause, but in the meantime a painful complication arose. It had not yet occurred to Mother Hardey that anyone who seemed worthy of her trust could betray it. She took a third person into her counsel, an influential man who had always proved himself a valuable friend in business matters. She showed him a confidential and very freely written letter from Mother Barat. It was underhandedly copied and shown to the Bishop who promptly called again at Saint Michael's, seriously angry and blaming Mother Barat. This was more than Mother Hardey could bear, and for once she betrayed her youth by a flood of tears in His Lordship's presence. He left somewhat mollified, but the disagreeable consequences of the affair dragged on for long. Instead of being lessened, Mother Barat's confidence in the prudence and loyalty of Mother Hardey only increased, and she wrote to comfort her:

> The affair that you tell me of has caused me pain. As you say, we must take greater precautions next time that such a thing shall not happen again. Divine Providence has allowed these contradictions in order to try you, and also, my Daughter, in order to increase my attachment to you and to your house. You belong to the Sacred Heart, and you are one of my first American daughters; that is enough. Besides, I naturally love your nation on account of its excellent qualities. We shall always understand each other; I see that. So do not be distressed at whatever you may hear said; such idle talk makes not the slightest impression upon me. I shall appeal directly to you when I need enlightenment, and shall feel perfectly at peace.

In another letter she added still more explicitly: "I give you this counsel all the more freely and trustfully because your manner of government pleases me and seems to me to come from God. He will always bless your obedience."

Little was the Community, and still less the School, troubled by these events. To them, Mother Hardey seemed to live only to make them happy. One of them wrote: "She is loved by her Community as well as by people outside, and what brings out her precious qualities is the fact that she knows nothing about them herself. Our Lord seems to take pleasure in pouring out His blessings on everything she does." The year 1838 in particular seems to stand out from the records in a series of vignettes.

The first is a picture of the month of May; an unusual current of fervour is flowing through the school for the Sodality of the Children of Mary has just been established. "It is surprising," says a letter, "how much good the sodality is producing, and how eager the children are to merit membership in it." It was already a tradition in schools of the Sacred Heart that the most difficult children should let themselves be converted by Our Lady for at least the duration of her lovely month; for there will be a procession, and a crowning of the Queen of the May at its close, at which virtue will be more than its own reward. This particular May the children talked excitedly in the parlour on Thursdays about the little shrines erected in each class-room, until the families who lived near-by took to sending exquisite basketfuls of flowers every morning; they too became Our Lady's slaves.

May deepened into June, into the richness of the month that meant most:

> All this was a preparation for the ceremony of First Communion on the third of June when we had the happiness of presenting eighty children at the altar. Monseigneur Blanc came a few days before the ceremony, and as the chaplain had too much to do, what with the instructions and exercises of the retreat, the Bishop helped to hear the children's confessions. On the day itself

he pontificated and gave the children a beautiful sermon at the seven o'clock Mass. . . .

The Bishop returned before the Feast of the Sacred Heart and gave us several instructions during the Triduum of preparation. On the Feast there was a triple ceremony of religious clothing, first vows, and profession. . . . The Bishop officiated in the Church and all the priests of the section of the State were present. High Mass was sung to the accompaniment of the new organ, and our chaplain outdid himself in his sermon on the Sacred Heart.

Mother Hardey had, at the express wish of Mother Barat, given up her classes in the school, but she was among the children as often as she could be. On June 21st:

The children had *grand congé*, and as it was the Feast of Saint Aloysius they feasted Reverend Mother with verses and songs, gave a very interesting little play, and presented her with some altar linen and a very handsome altar cloth—all made by themselves. Reverend Mother had not the heart to refuse them a second *congé* the next day, and this was a *congé sans cloche*. Never had the children had so good a time as on this day. As for the Community, we too had a marvelously good time in our own way. Reverend Mother gave us all different employments for the day—helping in the kitchen, pantry, and everywhere. Those who had no charge of this kind were with the children, for there was need of greater vigilance because of the greater freedom. The day opened for them with breakfast in the open courtyard behind the building, for the weather was magnificent, and it ended with a long drive through the countryside in wagons or carriages.

Song again flashes like a bright refrain through the tale of 1838. The annual vacation began that year on December 10th, and on the evening of the 8th there was a procession in honour of the Immaculate Conception. The next day:

Bishop Blanc presided, with eight priests. The programme included some short plays, with musical selections on piano, harp and guitar. Next morning there was a Mass of thanksgiving for the graces of the year. . . . Then, within the space of two hours, our large house was emptied for the vacation.

The recreations that year were spent sewing for the new Lazarist foundation at La Fourche, for poor missioners knew well where to turn for help and Mother Hardey had learned from Mother Duchesne how to give it. Bishop Bruté of Vincennes also knew where to go. "Ascetic, *litterateur*, educator and tireless worker in the ministry, Bishop Bruté is an outstanding figure of interest and of charm in the story of the early development of Catholicism in the United States." [1] His face, his clothing, spoke of hard and holy living when he came the next month to recover his broken health in the peace of Saint Michael's. The children sat about him in circles, dressed in their winter uniforms of crimson bombazine with black velvet trimmings and wide sashes. Since the occasion was at least semi-formal, they also donned their short black velvet capes which made them look so much older than did the embroidered muslins of summertime. They listened entranced to the Bishop's gallant tales, then organized a drive among themselves and their families for his relief.

Mother Hardey was directly in charge of the novices, among whom was her own sister, Matilda. A little cousin, Cecilia, entered later. She was in the infirmary most of the time, and the children sang under her windows on the Feast of her patroness, just before she went to Grand Coteau to die at the age of twenty. One of the most interesting of the Novices was Margaret Galwey, a future Mother Vicar. She was not in her first youth when she entered and had long been accustomed to expressing and following her own ideas. Mother Hardey made the overcoming of her will easier by an accompanying appeal to her sense of humour. One day Sister Galwey remarked rather petulantly that she hoped her living quarters would not be changed; she objected to sleeping in a new bed.

The next day they were changed. The day after that they were changed. In the course of the week she had slept on every floor in the house including the attic. "Mother Hardey taught me," she said later, "to find rest in every corner of the Sacred Heart."

There were still others whose faces brightened when Mother Hardey approached. She was loved in every one of the neat brick cottages that fringed the coutyard where the slaves lived, and she too loved each black face that turned at her approach with a flashing smile. At intervals ebony babies were brought to the parlour that she might find high-sounding names for them, and when one of the slaves died the Nuns would follow the dark body to the cemetery, candles in hand, to speed the bright soul to heaven. But none of them loved Mother Hardey as did Liza. Bishop Dubourg had given Liza to Mother Duchesne at Florissant, a little orphan from nowhere. She was sent to Saint Michael's at the time of its foundation, where, capable and effervescent, she attached herself adoringly to her mistresses. She followed them everywhere, and even penetrated to the cloister by means of the keyhole. What she saw made her anxious to join the Community; but Mother Hardey, her spiritual adviser, assured her that she was far too precious to the Nuns in her present capacity to be spared. Liza did not want to be black, and declared that she was an Indian. One day Mother Hardey found her crying inordinately in her cabin, a bundle of wet bandanas beside her. She had been told that if she could cry a hogshead of tears she would turn white. Her directress pursuaded her that the result would not be worth the effort, "and, anyway," she added, "you will be white in heaven."

Liza thought that Mother Hardey was too easy with the children, and told her so roundly, but she thought everyone else too hard on Mother Hardey. She took all her advice to heart, and when it was suggested that she get married she did so not once but twice. Each experiment ended unhappily, and when her second husband absconded with all her worldly goods Liza gave a sigh of relief and returned to her devoted service of the Nuns. We shall meet her again, with her little oddities and great love, when we return later to Saint Michael's.

In 1839 Mother Hardey paid a visit to Grand Coteau, arriving on the evening of Good Friday while the whole household was gathered in the chapel for the singing of the *Stabat Mater*. The school was three times as large as it had been when Mother Hardey was among its pupils, and the children were established in the new building which Mother Murphy had planned and built for them. The Community still lived in the original house, for the bricks intended for further construction had been given to the Jesuits when they had opened a College nearby, to the great consolation of the Nuns. The gardens had been elaborately laid out so that flowers were more abundant and constant than ever, weaving perpetually their charm of fragrance and colour, crêpe myrtle, jasmine, roses, camelias.

One day Mother Hardey met Mrs. Pierce Connelly, a beautiful and fervent young convert, who invited the reverend visitor from Saint Michael's to visit the little cottage, Gracemere, on the edge of the Convent property, where she lived with her husband and four entrancing children. Mr. Connelly taught in the nearby Jesuit College, and Mrs. Connelly, when not giving lessons in piano and guitar to the Convent pupils, divided her time between her pretty home and hours of prayer in the Convent chapel. She had only been a Catholic a few years but was walking with giant stride in the pathway of the saints, and she confided to Mother Hardey that the Nuns had given her the privilege of making an eight-day retreat with them each summer. Youngest of the children was John Henry, not quite two years old, and as Mother Hardey left he stood in the doorway laughing after her with his large dark eyes while the baby hand waved. The picture of him was still in her mind's eye as she went back to Saint Michael's. The next January came word that John Henry had fallen into a vat of boiling sugar while playing in the garden, and had died in his mother's arms. Mother Hardey did not then know that his death had been the unexpected acceptance of that heroic mother's act of oblation in which she had offered the whole of her happy life to God to be done with as He willed, but as the years passed and Mrs. Connelly became Mother Cornelia Connelly and founded, in suffering and ever fuller oblation, the Society of the Holy Child, Mother Hardey understood.[2]

A meeting of a General Council of the Society of the Sacred Heart was held in Rome in 1839. The multiplication of houses, which had doubled in number since the approbation of the Constitution twelve years before, seemed to call for some adaptations and even changes in the latter. The Council opened in June, and proved to be the cause of a crisis in the history of the Society, one of those difficult periods of experiment and misunderstanding which either wreck an organization or try as by fire the stuff of which it is made. The remodelling of the Constitutions was a thorny enough matter in itself, but there was the further and equally thorny question of whether the residence of the Superior General should be fixed thereafter at Rome or at Paris. Many of the Religious who were the foundation-stones of the Society, who had taken part in its government from the beginning, either had died or were prevented from taking part by age or circumstances. Among the younger members were a few, and those the most influential, who were inclined to be somewhat radical in their views and over-hasty in their mode of procedure. The wise and patient Foundress alone saw all sides of the measures proposed, and foresaw the disastrous consequences of some of them. In their attempt to bring the Constitutions into closer conformity with those of the Society of Jesus the reformers altered a very large number of Articles, and when word of these changes was indiscreetly spread abroad a more or less open protest arose from many quarters both within and without the Society. Mother Barat saw that only time could test the wisdom of the new measures, and asked for "a loyal trial of three years," at the end of which, she promised, another Council would make the final decision.

On the 12th of July Mother Barat, whose heart was heavy with premonition, called the Councillors together at the Villa Lante in Rome. At the end of a beautiful alley of acacia trees on the slope of the hill that rose above the house was placed a picture of Our Lady of Sorrows. It had been painted two years before as a thank-offering for the grace of preservation from the cholera, and before it Mother Barat now made her act of trust that the Queen of Martyrs would keep the Society and guide it through its darker days. The picture was wreathed with garlands. The voice of the Mother General rose in the stillness. "Be, O divine and afflicted Mother," she prayed, "the guide and the sovereign Protectress of this little Society."

The new Decrees were sent to each of the forty-one Houses. Saint Michael's received its copy well before the end of the year, and the letter in which Mother Hardey voiced her instant and full readiness to make the loyal trial asked by the Superior General sped straight back to Rome:

During vacation Monseigneur de Forbin Janson came to give us our eight-day retreat; we took advantage of this time of prayer to read the Decrees and as soon as the children returned they were all put into practice with extraordinary ease. There is no one who is not delighted with the various changes. As for myself, it had always seemed to me that nothing could be more perfect than our Constitutions, that it would be impossible to improve them, but now I see that the changes which have been made are exactly what were needed. May we not be more proud than ever to belong to this dear Society? Yes! and we wish to prove how happy we are to be its members. Everyone took generous resolutions after the retreat.

This letter gave such pleasure to Mother Barat—who had not, to her sorrow, met with the same alacrity to obey in every quarter—that she had a copy of it inserted in the Society's Annual Letter for 1839, adding the following tribute to Saint Michael's: "This house continues to be among the most flourishing of our establishments with two hundred and twenty pupils and many orphans. The Noviceship also is increasing. The good spirit in it is ever the same, and all its members are one with us in the Heart of our good Master." * To Mother Hardey herself she wrote:

> What a consolation you have given me by your submission in receiving and putting into practice the new Decrees! I was afraid for a moment that you would find some difficulty in doing so; your prompt obedience will please Our Lord. So pay no attention to X's letter telling you to delay. I much prefer your readiness to obey.

It is true that most of these Decrees were later found defective and were not to be lasting, but as long as authority had asked for their observance they were the best that could be, as far as Mother Hardey was concerned.

Among the members of the Council was Reverend Mother Elizabeth Galitzin, the Secretary General, who had been the moving spirit of the would-be reforms. It was she who was now chosen to visit the Houses of America of which she had

* Previous to this, the Annual Letters had been written out by hand and sent by each house directly to every other house. 1839 was the first year in which the various accounts were collected at the Mother-House where they were multigraphed and sent thence to every house of the Society. Thus the Letter of 1839 was a most important one. It opens with an account of the Consecration to Our Lady of Sorrows.

been appointed Provincial, as Mother Audé was unable to continue in that position. A breath of excitement passed over the five Convents as Mother Galitzin took to the high seas in the autumn of 1840.[3]

The name was already famous in missionary annals of America. Prince Demetrius Augustine Galitzin, a cousin of Mother Galitzin, had come to America in 1792, a restless young member of the Russian aristocracy making the "grand tour." Under a sudden stroke of grace he offered himself to Bishop Carroll for missionary work in this needy land, was ordained a few years later, and set to work in Pennsylvania, first at Conewago, then at Loretto in the wilds of the Allegheny Mountains. For forty-five years he toiled with prodigious activity and fervour, building log churches, exorcising the evil spirits from haunted houses, carrying on controversies by means of pugilism and literature. Unable to mount a horse, he rode through the woods in a sleigh at all seasons, over sun-baked summer trails as over drifts of mountain snow. With gusty eloquence he preached in a medley of languages to uncouth congregations, and his earnestness did what his words alone might not have done, for the tears of zeal ran down his cheeks as he pleaded and waved his arms. Roughly dressed and unpredictable in conduct, he yet won his way, and when he died in May, 1806, a powerful but broken old man, he had won and kept a whole people for Christ. "He has done an infinite amount of good and great things in God's Kingdom" said Father Lemke, the companion who knew him best.[4] His County of Little Cambria was called in the following years "the Catholic County."

And now another Galitzin, who promised to be quite as interesting in her own right, had landed in New York early in September and was on her way to Saint Louis. Her story was well known, even in America. She was a Russian Princess from Saint Petersburg, a daughter of Prince Alexis Andrievitch, one of whose ancestors had suffered martyrdom without dying as a result of his conversion to Catholicism through the cruelties inflicted on him in the Ice Palace of the Empress Ann, where he had been forced to submit to a mock marriage for the entertainment of the court. Elizabeth resembled him in fortitude of character. She was brought up in the schismatic faith of her fatherland, and the bitter laws against the Catholic Church were still in force when her mother secretly embraced it. The young girl, then fifteen, was so horrified by this conversion that she wrote out in her own blood and renewed daily a vow that she would always hate the Church, and the Jesuit members of it in particular. But God was stronger than her implacable will, and during the course of a single night, while she lay in sleepless prayer, He bent her to the truth. Trained in sternness, brought up in loneliness, the austerity of her youth and still more the autocratic trend of her own nature continued to mark her even when she had come through long struggles into the Society of the Sacred Heart, and had felt the gentle and magnetic influence of Mother Barat. Her energy and her abilities placed her early in positions of authority, and thus it was that she arrived in Saint Louis in mid-September to find the aged and humble Mother Duchesne kneeling before her, surrendering the trust of the American missions into her hands. Mother Galitzin did at once what Mother Barat could not bring herself to do; she accepted Mother Duchesne's resignation as Superior. She then made a rapid but thorough visit of the Missouri houses, explaining the new Decrees, visiting the classes, and suggesting that certain dilapidated furnishings should be repainted red.

Mother Hardey was prepared for generous dependence, for Mother Barat had written to her:

> Strive to enter fully into Mother Galitzin's views for the greater glory of the Sacred Heart of Jesus and the good of souls. Yet, my Daughter, it will not be contrary to the perfection of

obedience to make known to her the customs of your country and the inconvenience which might arise from the adoption of certain measures or regulations proposed by her. She will profit by your counsel and experience.

December had come by the time Mother Galitzin had embarked upon her journey south. It was very cold, so cold that the traveller wrote to her mother in Saint Petersburg that she believed there was no really warm country on earth, and she longed for the mildness of the Russian climate, adding: "I have to resign myself to finding sweet and lasting warmth only in the world to come." Had she stayed long enough to be overtaken by a Louisiana summer she might have changed her mind, but as it was the Community of Saint Michael's slid over a layer of crackling ice as they gathered in the garden to await the carriage. The down-stream boats did not then stop at a signal from the Convent as they did later when a larger building commanded the river, and Mother Galitzin had to go nearer to New Orleans to disembark. A feeling of awe had reduced the Nuns to unwonted solemnity, a feeling which Mother Hardey confessed to sharing: "I admit that I could not help feeling very uneasy at the thought of receiving a Princess with my rustic manners, but after all she had been sent by our First Mother, and that consoled me." The carriage arrived. A slight simple-mannered woman in secular dress alighted and looked hurriedly around. Mother Hardey went forward, but before she could utter her carefully prepared words of welcome she was interrupted. "My dear," said the Princess in rapid English, "send someone down to the boat quickly. There is a man on board who has very fine cabbages and you can make a good bargain; you should not miss such an opportunity." Everyone laughed and a messenger was sent post-haste after the cabbages. The Princess Galitzin was forgotten and Mother Galitzin took her place with easy, affectionate charm in the midst of her new family.

She stayed but a few weeks this time at Saint Michael's before going on to Grand Coteau. Mother Hardey hastened to write to Mother Barat:

> It would have been difficult, even impossible, to find anyone who could represent you better; her bearing and manner make a most favorable impression in this country. She has already won the confidence of everyone here, and every heart is devoted to her. As for me, I feel so at my ease with her that there is nothing even to my most secret thoughts that I would not be willing to confide to her. Yet I am not a person who is easily communicative with those whom I do not know very well.

Mother Galitzin returned to spend another month with the Community at Saint Michael's, and Mother Hardey carefully regulated with the Mother Provincial all the details of the house. She begged for observations on her own conduct, and Mother Galitzin, hard put to it to find matter for correction, reproached her on the same point that Mother Duchesne had hit upon: a certain aloofness of manner that amounted at times to coldness. Mother Hardey took everything to heart, for there was in her character a lucid simplicity of outlook, a singleness of purpose, which caused her to take the most obvious and literal line of conduct whenever possible. If her natural perspicacity showed her something of the questions and complications involved in the new Decrees which Mother Galitzin had come to enforce, she kept a wise silence on the matter. If she felt the difference of nationality and the exigencies of a somewhat autocratic temperament, she did not allow them to put a barrier between herself and one who had a right to guide her own inexperience. She followed the Community retreat during Mother Galitzin's stay, and sought earnestly to learn all that she could from one who had come from the center of the Society. She took every remark made concerning her government or her personal conduct as something to be acted upon at once, while all during the retreat the deeper levels of her soul were, as she confided to Mother Barat, occupied with a persistent call, a challenge from God, to plunge more completely into that spiritual life through which she could make reparation for the unresponsive members of Christ's Mystical Body.

This grace of insight was prophetic of what was to come next. The Mother Visitatrix had more on her mind than the welfare of individual houses, for she was concerned with the whole range of the work of the Sacred Heart in America, and knew that it must now reach out more widely than before. In the early spring she told the Community that a foundation in New York City had been decided upon. She herself would leave for there in March with a small band of Religious from Saint Louis, and another band would leave from the South soon after. Mother Hardey's mission had begun.

IX

YOUNG NEW YORK

Mother Barat's interest in New York went back to 1827. In that year a band of four missionaries had sailed from France to reinforce the Communities in Louisiana, and instead of going by way of New Orleans they had landed in New York and taken the wearisome coach and canal-boat route overland. They had crossed the ocean in company with two dignitaries-to-be, the future Archibishops Eccleston of Baltimore and Purcell of Cincinnati. The boat approached land early on the morning of the Feast of Saint Ignatius, and Father Purcell, sharing the eagerness of the Nuns to hear Mass on that day, took them ashore himself in a rowboat. Many years later the Archbishop used to regale the Community at Clifton with a version of the event which suggests that he was making a "tall story" out of it. One of the Nuns, he related, had such devotion to the will of God that her favorite prayer was "Ita, Pater." While in the rowboat she fell overboard, and when pulled from the water of New York harbour was still spluttering "Ita, Pater." In any case, the four travellers were at Mass in the Cathedral shortly afterwards, and Bishop Dubois made their acquaintance during their stay at the home of the Lewis Willcocks. As a result he wrote to Mother Barat in October:

There is no doubt that a Society such as yours would do an immense good in my episcopal city, that it is even necessary to it; but considerable funds would be required to meet the most pressing needs! The Catholic population is so poor, being made up almost entirely of Irish immigrants, contributions from the Protestants are so uncertain, property in this city so dear that I dare not go ahead . . . But without apostolic workers, without means to prepare the most necessary establishments, I have the grief of seeing an abundant harvest rotting on the ground, for want of workers and temporary resources. Have the goodness, while I am writing, to prepare subjects for me. If I succeed in my plans I could, upon my return from Rome, bring back with me a colony of your angels of virtue and of zeal.

Mother Barat, to her grief, could not grant the Bishop's request at once. It always distressed her to be obliged to refuse a foundation for lack of subjects or of means. It humbled her with a feeling that perhaps the fault lay with her; would not a stronger tide of zeal and love in the Society have made all things possible? But Bishop Dubois was still hopeful, and when Mother Audé passed through New York on her way to France in 1834 he gave her the following letter for the Superior General:

I do not think that our difficulties are insurmountable; a few efforts, a few sacrifices, would bring about brilliant results. Through education, your Religious would bring back piety and fervour into the highest ranks of Society, as the Sisters of Charity have done among the poor, and piety once sown in these hearts would open up the sources of charity. Conversions would take place among the more influential people; their example would draw others; the Catholic religion would take once more the place that belongs to it. God alone knows what a revolution might take place among people weary of multitudes of sects, which are always contradicting each other, people who need only to see truth freed from the pettiness of the uneducated to accept it.

Mother Barat once more said the word that so often proved her wisdom, "We must wait," but after the death of Bishop Dubois his successor, young Bishop Hughes, determined to see the matter through. He, a self-taught man of the people, recognized in the views of his predecessor, a Frenchman with memories of the old-world order of things, an aristocratic outlook that was not his own. But he also recognized the truth that cultural leadership is apt to be found among the more leisured, and that from those to whom much is given much may be expected. A turbulent controversy with the Public School Society was giving him great trouble at the moment, but he knew that as much might be done for the Catholic life of New York in the quieter atmosphere of a "Select Academy" for young ladies as in the more crowded schools of the City. What would happen if no one had the long-sighted patience to undertake the education of the "poor little rich girl"? He must persuade Mother Barat that now was the time for a foundation in New York.

He did so in person in 1840, in the sedate little parlour of the Convent on the Rue Monsieur. Mother Barat once described the American character as "reason personified," but the Bishop had been Irish before being American, and there was a touch of Celtic passion in his words. His usual manner of gaining a point was a compound of winning charm and flat resolution, and he refused to leave until she granted his request.

Mother Galitzin passed through New York on her way to Louisiana a few months later. The Bishop conducted her on fruitless carriage drives around the city in search of a house. None was found, but there was a mutual exchange of promises:

she would brings Nuns to New York the following year, and in the interim he would find them a house. Mother Barat was not quite prepared for such speed, and wrote:

> For goodness sake, do not go so fast in the matter . . . God continues to strike us by taking away excellent subjects; how can we dare add to our foundations? It is true that I want this new post extremely; it has become necessary in the interests of Louisiana. We shall make great efforts, but a year's delay would have been a help to us. Think it over before God.

A compromise was reached, and it was determined that Nuns from Louisiana would begin the foundation and others from France would come later. So on May 6, 1841, Mother Galitzin accompanied by Mothers Shannon and Thieffry arrived in New York. They drove to the episcopal residence on Mulberry Street only to find that the Bishop was still house-hunting for them. They were taken temporarily to the Convent of the Sisters of Charity near Saint Peter's Church, where they were made to forget their disappointment.

In the meantime, Mother Hardey had set her face to the east. It was her way to look straight ahead of her as soon as she knew the road. The Community of Saint Michael's was already familiar with the level look, steady, simple and unself-conscious, which they saw that April morning. God's will was plain, the steamboat was ready, the spring was on the river. The Community pretended not to notice the unwonted secular dress. She pretended not to notice the tears in many eyes. Young Mother Ellen Hogan followed her into the carriage which with relentless speed reached the bend in the road. No Religious of the Sacred Heart has a lasting home less wide than the Society, and as the Community went back into the house one of them caught the feeling of the moment when she wrote: "Our dear Mother Hardey has been called to New York; some among us have lost in her our first class-mistress, others their first companion in the Noviceship, or else their first Superior. It is easier to feel than to express how hard this separation is."

The next day the Community were on the lawn again for another more distant farewell. The Mississippi boats were by now sumptuous three-deckers over which huge twin smoke-stacks towered twice as high again. Mother Hardey's boat went by with a great show of smoke and a loud salute to the Convent, while two bonneted figures on the deck waved and waved until Saint Michael's grew small beside the lengthening silver ribbon of water that unwound sinuously behind them. It was the first of endless journeys for Mother Hardey which, although accomplished with relatively greater ease as the years passed, were never to lose either their penitential or their apostolic character. The cloister could not be carried out openly into the world in the days when the tales of Maria Monk found not only readers but believers, so a secular dress had to be adopted, without betraying either love of the world or too much contempt for it. Mother Hardey was always correct and unobtrusive, in the habit or out of it. It was perhaps fortunate that by the time her long series of journeys had begun, the clinging, high-waisted dresses and the hats top-heavy with flowers of the early century were becoming old-fashioned. It was easier to adapt oneself to the ever-widening flounces of the 'forties and 'fifties, to the voluminous shawls and deep-set bonnets. The natural grace of such a costume lost nothing on Mother Hardey's erect figure.

The panorama which had first unrolled before little Mary Hardey's childish stare on the flat-boat journey of old now reversed itself and passed with swifter motion before her interested eyes. The river-banks had changed as much as the boats on them, and so had the City of Cincinnati. Here Bishop Purcell gave them a kind welcome, and used his influence to assure them the same in Philadelphia. He wrote to Mr. Mark

Anthony Frenaye, a future benefactor of the Society in that city:

> Madame* Aloysia Hardey and Madame Hogan who are on their way to New York to commence a boarding-school have no acquaintances in Philadelphia. I therefore most earnestly recommend them to your care. I am sure the good Sisters or Madame Lejus or some other Catholic lady will be delighted to lodge them for twenty-four hours, if they can stay for so long in your fair city.

But Mother Hardey's journey was so speedy that she could not have stayed long in any fair city. Methods of transportation were at a crisis in 1841, when the full acumen of American genius was focused on means of locomotion. Machinery was pulsing on rivers and canals, and even proving its superiority over horse-power on the eastern sea-board. Mother Hardey could have gone all the way to New York by water: steam-boat to Portsmouth, canal-boat to Cleveland, steam-boat to Buffalo, canal-boat along the Erie to Albany, and a final magnificent sweep down the Hudson, and all—so said the advertisements—for $14.75; time: one month. This latter item was a consideration, for though the packets on the canals bore such names as *Flying Cloud* and *Lightning*, they bumped along the bank at the plodding rate of the horses that drew them. The time-honoured stage-coaches reduced the time to a week, with nights at an inn instead of in a cabin with forty-two bunks. Handsome six-horse coaches dashed along the new National Highway, passing the slow-moving Conestoga wagons which carried the greater part of the nation's freight under their spreading canvas tops.

* The use of the word "Madame" as a term of address for the Choir Religious of the Sacred Heart throughout the nineteenth century was due to the fact that the Society originated shortly after the French Revolution when it was not possible to employ specifically religious names. It has since been dropped in favour of "Mother."

But in the East excitement over the newly built wisps of railroad was spelling the doom of the stage-coach, and considering Mother Hardey's adventuresome spirit it is not unlikely that she actually chose to go from Philadelphia to New York by train. Although the newspapers lamented the fact that "scarcely a day passes that we do not hear of a locomotive running off the railroad," Mother Galitzin had braved train travel while in America, and wrote to her mother in Saint Petersburg that its jolting had completely cured her of a chronic fever. The speed was tempting, thirty miles an hour, but schedules were uncertain. By the time the sputtering engines with their smoke-stacks, looking like over-grown bells turned upside down, had jerked their box-like cars out of the station, they were as completely lost to knowledge as a ship at sea till sighted at some vague time from the next station, at which point the men all ran out to take hold of the train and assist the wooden brakes in slowing it down. If Mother Hardey succumbed to the novelty of this experience, she and Mother Hogan left Philadelphia at 7 A.M. on the Perth and Amboy line and went to New York for $3 apiece, with "all luggage at the risk of its owner," and a steamboat ride thrown in at both ends. The last boat brought them triumphantly to Pier Number 2 in the North River, in the early afternoon of May 17th.

A century ago the tops of the tallest buildings in the sky-line of New York did not rise much above the level of the trees that interwove the warm brick and brown tones with a shimmer of green. Had Mother Hardey been the most imaginative person in the world—which she certainly was not—she could hardly have glimpsed even a suggestion of what that sky-line would be some day: of how the city that could not grow beyond its river-banks would spring instead into the air, carrying stone and steel upward till it tossed them like motionless foam into the high and windy sky, weaving patterns of shadow and sun by day and of fountains of electric stars by night; how the power of its life, so stern under those cloud-line fantasies, would pierce into the earth beneath and set the rocks humming with the movement of its restlessness; how through the crawling canyons of its streets tides indescriptible of wealth and of poverty would ebb and flow together. But even had she been able for one revealing moment to have seen the strange reality of a century ahead, the faith that she held so simply was more towering and more sky-scraping than builded steel, more driving than trains running under rivers and rocks. She had come to open another Tabernacle, and she knew what Life would radiate out from it to the subduing of steel and stone, of hearts and souls. The words of Mother Barat were ringing in her ears: "You have much to do there for the glory of the Sacred Heart and the good of souls."

The boat drew into Pier Number 2, and Mother Hardey's eyes searched among the irregular streets for traces of New Amsterdam, of the English colonial town, of the briefly proud capital of a new United States. What she saw was a progressive city. "Missionaries" to New York had by now no illusions about working among primitive conditions. One must be modern, very modern, to overtake the stride of even conservative New Yorkers, no matter how staid the silk hats and the poke bonnets worn on the restless heads. Here and there in those brimming streets, their presence betrayed by a flash of gold on a spire, were the churches, very few, that held the Ultra-Reality, the Person for whose sake she had come and for whom she could advance into the future with the best.

The travellers walked to Bowling Green, bright in its May freshness, and found where the Broadway omnibuses started.[1] The horses set off with a will; there was racing among bus drivers in the days before red and green lights. They went past Wall Street, once indeed the outer wall of the town but now collecting bank buildings along its narrow edges, past Maiden Lane whose name, recalling twilights and hedges of old, sat ill upon its commercial prosperity; past Canal Street where the stream that drained the Collect Pond and the vanishing beauties of Lispenard Meadows had but recently been closed over with paving stones. From there it was but a brief drive further to the Cathedral, where Bishop Hughes welcomed them with an apologetic look on his face.

This young Prelate, handsome, energetic and buoyant, who was to be Mother Hardey's unfailing friend for the next twenty-five years, had brought rich experience to the government of his new See.[2] As a child he had borne contempt and proud poverty under the petty injustices of the Penal Laws that still weighed heavily on County Tyrone, Ireland, where he was born. He had worked on his father's farm, stopping suddenly now and then to kneel behind a hay-stack and beg Our Lady to let him be a priest. Learning Latin by rushlight was too slow a way to his goal, so he crossed the seas in search of a swifter one. At Mount Saint Mary's Seminary at Emmitsburg he had to tend the garden while waiting for a vacancy, but the eyes of the Rector, Father (later Bishop) Dubois, were on him, and he was ordained priest in 1826. He was then thrown headlong into parochial work in Philadelphia when the Trustee system was at its scandalous worst. The management of Parish affairs by a board of lay Trustees was one of the greatest difficulties that the Church encountered while learning to deal with a lusty young Republic jealous of its liberties, and Father Hughes had a hard struggle with turbulent and schismatic elements in his congregation at Saint Mary's Church. Controversies with prejudiced Protestant Divines roused his ever-ready fighting blood and called out his powers of brilliant and witheringly honest speech. This daring Irish priest, who was heartily loved and wholesomely feared, became an ardent American patriot while his first loyalties were given to the Church. It was natural that he should feel himself to be the man to show the world that Americanism and Catholicism were compatible.

Such fearless ability caused him to be named Coadjutor to the aging Bishop Dubois in January, 1837, and such was the excitement in New York at his consecration, the first ever to be held in the young city, that platforms had to be built around the outside of Saint Patrick's Cathedral, level with the windows, to accommodate the crowd. Among the witnesses of the scene was the future Cardinal McCloskey, who spoke of it long afterwards:

> I remember how all eyes were fixed, how all eyes were strained, to get a glimpse of their newly consecrated Bishop; and as they saw that dignified and manly countenance, as they beheld those features beaming with the light of intellect, bearing already upon them the impress of that force of character which peculiarly marked him throughout his life, that firmness of resolution, that unalterable and unbending will, . . . all hearts were drawn and warmed towards him.

The Bishop now apologized profusely to Mother Hardey for his failure to find her a house, and drove her back along the way that she had come to join Mother Galitzin at the Convent of the Sisters of Charity on Barclay Street. It was a fitting place for the Religious of the Sacred Heart to begin their work in New York, for Saint Peter's Church next door to the Convent was not only the mother of Churches in New York City and State, but the proud pioneer of Catholic education in the same area. Saint Peter's Free School had been opened by the Board of Trustees as early as 1800, and the enrollment soon numbered hundreds of children. At first the teaching had been carried on by laymen, but in 1831 the Sisters of Charity had come from Emmitsburg to work, most appropriately, in the shadow of the Church were their Foundress, Mother Seton, had received the gift of faith. A little brick house on the east side of the Church was the home which they so kindly shared with the new-comers. The latter soon numbered seven, for Mother Boilvin and Sister Gallien came from Saint Louis to join the colony. Increased numbers made no difference to their hostesses, for as the Journal of the foundation says in its courtly way:

> Our Mothers and Sisters found in these excellent Religious tender and devoted Sisters who willingly shared with them their table and their home. . . . They do not cease to give us proofs of the most touching affection. Far from being troubled at seeing us settled in this city they are the first to procure pupils and postulants for us. All this proves them to be true Spouses of the God of Charity.[3]

Weeks went by while hunting for a house, till the middle of June brought the day when the Religious would most have wished to be in a Convent of their own. The Sisters of Charity, guessing this, decorated one of the side altars in the Church of Saint Peter, and there on the Feast of the Sacred Heart the Mass of Renovation was celebrated for the exiled Community. In telling of the event the Journal could not help adding: "At Benediction almost the whole burden of the singing was carried by our Mother Provincial, greatly to her own astonishment, for she had always thought that she had no voice; however, our melodies greatly touched the priest."

As Mother Hardey went day after day for Mass in the Church of Saint Peter's, its history and the other Catholic traditions of the City had time to grow upon her.[4] Those traditions went back to August, 1634, when New York-to-be had been blessed with the presence and prayers of a martyr. The kindly Dutch settlers of Fort Orange had smuggled Father Isaac Jogue onto one of their vessels, after having helped him to escape from the Iroquois, and had brought him safe to clean, pretty, little New Amsterdam. Its steep-roofed houses stood in rows about the fort, each with its trim garden; the view was laced in every direction with shining blue water, and in the evening the violet smoke of peace curled from the chimneys. The Dutchmen dressed the tattered priest in respectable burgher's clothing, and let him roam at will through the farmlands of lower Manhattan. There he met and brought grace to a few Catholics in the variegated population before boarding a ship for France. He would return one day to death among the Iroquois.

When New Amsterdam had become New York under the English, James II appointed a Catholic, Thomas Dongan, as its Governor in 1682. He came from England accompanied by the Jesuit, Father Thomas Harvey, and the first Mass was said in a room of the Governor's residence on the spot where the Customs House would later rise. Then a small chapel was built just south of Bowling Green, and Mass was said there daily while the ships circled about the jutting land on which it stood. Other Jesuits from Maryland came to found a Latin School for the boys of the Colony who ran to class at the ringing of the old Dutch bell of the Fort. Education and the faith went hand in hand. Under the influence of Dongan the first Legislative Assembly of New York echoed the acts of its sister-colony, Maryland, by declaring that "no person or persons which profess faith in God by Jesus Christ shall at any time be anyways molested, punished, disquieted, or called in question for any difference of opinion on matters of religious concernment."

Persecution swept away this promising beginning, but the faith came back, as its way is, and established St. Peter's Church. The building that Mother Hardey found, low and simple in its Greek architecture, was new, having been erected only four years previously to replace the crumbling older structure which had been the first on the island to lift a cross on its sharp tower.[5] Mother Theodora Guerin,[6] who passed through New York at this same time, has described the impression she received of Saint Peter's,

> of its elegance, of its being as light as if it had been made of crystal, of the dazzling whiteness of its walls, of the pews which were of solid mahogany, of its galleries with four rows of seats placed in tiers which gave it the appearance of a theatre. The Church was filled with men. There were at least as many men as women, and all comported themselves perfectly well. We did not see one woman who did not have on a bonnet.

We may be pardoned for adding, by way of an irrelevant digression, another quotation from the same letter:

> Here the shepherdesses wear bonnets, and even the milkmaids while milking their cows. The milk is carried around in quite a stylish conveyance drawn by two horses at such a rate that one might think it were the President's carriage rolling along. The men who distribute the milk from door to door are dressed up as if for a wedding. It is impossible to have an idea of the extravagance of the Americans without having witnessed it.

This shining new edifice inherited the history as well as the congregation of the older one. The first Saint Peter's had been gorgeous with civic and religious pomp on that November day in 1786 when the French and Spanish legations and high officials of the new American Government had brought the brilliance of their uniformed presence to the solemn High Mass of its dedication. Its walls soon after had seen the tragic outburst of schismatic factions when the Reverend John Carroll, then Prefect Apostolic, had been tumultuously evicted from the Church as he was mounting the altar steps to say Mass. But erratic priests and high-handed Trustees alike had been subdued at last when on March 25, 1805, Elizabeth Seton had made her first Communion there in "a triumph of joy and gladness that the Deliverer was come, my defence and shield and strength." From then on Parish life grew in energy. Things happened which proved that the fervour of the Ages of Faith could still live, and Mother Hardey must have drawn comfort from the almost incredible story of the conversion of the Barber family. Virgil Barber, a Protestant minister, had called at Barclay Street seeking the truth, moved by a pamphlet on the life of Saint Francis Xavier belonging to his Irish servant girl. He not only found the truth but handed it on to others so efficaciously that a few years later he became a Jesuit and his wife a Visitation Nun. One by one his five children heard and followed the call to religious life, while his father and several members of another branch of the family gave themselves and all they had to the service of God.

New York, together with Boston, Bardstown and Philadelphia, had become a separate See in 1808 when Baltimore was erected into an Archbishopric. The first Bishop chosen, Reverend Luke Concanen, was in Italy at the time, and there he died before he could reach his See. But a providential leader was found in Father Anthony Kohlman, S.J., the Administrator.[7] He was an Alsatian who in his youth had been one of the holy, happy and energetic members of Father de Tournély's little band of Fathers of the Sacred Heart in Austria, and he brought the zeal kindled in him by his Father in God to the service of a motley flock of fifteen hundred Catholics in New York, where an Apostle must be able, as he was, to speak German, French and English, not to mention the Brogue, if he would be all things to all men. Father Kohlman not only organized the amorphous Diocese but founded the New York Literary Institution, and he was the moving force behind the Novena to Prince von Hohenlohe which resulted in the cure of Mrs. Mattingley of Philadelphia, a miracle which startled the country into an awareness of the supernatural. The second

Bishop, Reverend John Connolly, had to face the economic revolution that came with the opening of the Erie Canal in 1825 which flooded New York with a new labouring—and Catholic—population, while his successor, Bishop Dubois, met with endless other troubles of his own, as when his new seminary at Nyack burned down as soon as built. He had fine supporters among the Clergy, but he needed Religious Orders, Schools, Colleges, and this, declared Bishop Hughes to Mother Hardey, was the need that she must help to supply.

As she went in and out of Saint Peter's she became familiar with the faces of the influential men upon whom the Catholicity of New York largely depended. There was the tall, distinguished Pastor, Father John Power, who was already friend and confessor to her Community. There was Father Felix Varela, the Cuban patriot, who had brought his brilliance and his devoted service to the land of his exile. There was the striking and aristocratic figure of Charles Constantine Pise, the only priest ever to be chaplain of the United States Senate. He was the author of the first indigenous Catholic novel, a tale called *Father Rowland* which, in the manner of the day, made its plot into a handsome but stiff frame for its lessons in apologetics. He was then engaged in stimulating the intellectual life of New York City by journalism and energetic scholarship. Most Catholic periodicals of that era had a brief and stormy life, finding it too difficult to steer their way through Hibernian politics, but the *Expositor* held its own on a high mental and literary level, preparing the way for the spread of Catholic literature.[8]

Mother Hardey's southern feelings must have aroused her to unusual interest when she first met Pierre Toussaint on his way to Mass.[9] He was a negro, a one-time slave and now fashionable hair-dresser, who spent all his spare time and more than his spare money on corporal and spiritual works of mercy. Everyone in town who knew anything of him knew that Toussaint was a demonstration of what the Faith can make of a man. After the death of their beloved little niece, Euphémie, he and his wife had consoled themselves for having no children by educating a number of neglected little negro boys. He had risked his own life time and again while caring for the victims of yellow fever. Fashionable ladies sought his hair-dressing parlour during his hours of work, but at other hours he was in any place where suffering needed him, noticing opportunities for friendly words and neglecting to notice insults. Such gifts of mind and character went with his distinguished bearing that a noted Boston convert wrote of him:

> His life was so perfect, and he explained the teaching of the Church with a simplicity so intelligent and so courageous, that everyone honoured him as a Catholic. He would explain our devotion to the Mother of God with the utmost clearness; or show the union of the natural and supernatural gifts in the priest; or quote our great spiritual writers in a way to account best for the faith that was in him. When I was young I used to hear Protestants speak with reverence of two Catholics—the great Fénelon and the humble Pierre Toussaint.

His black head was often seen bowed before the altar, for the whole Congregation of Saint Peter's was particularly devout to the Blessed Sacrament, and at one time the Church enjoyed the rare privilege of daily Exposition. The heart of prayer throbbed intensely in the heart of the intense young city.

The search for a house went diligently on, extending even to the wilds of Brooklyn and of Staten Island, but it would not do to begin in the country and at last a house quite close to the Cathedral itself, at 412 Houston Street on the corner of Mulberry, was found. It was in a shocking state, having for some years been a boarding-house for single gentlemen who kept their rooms as they pleased without interference from

Mrs. Seton, the landlady. But this lapse in dignity was only an episode in the life of the fine old three-story house. It had been a boarding-school for young ladies kept by Madame Chégary, a French *Emigrée,* and its reputation for elegance had reached even to Louisiana. An old picture gives us a glimpse into the back garden where young ladies are disporting themselves. The elder ones stand in romantic and statuesque attitudes, designed to show the grace of their tight-waisted gowns. The smaller children in pantalettes are playing less self-consciously on the grass with little white dogs. Although the lawn was unkempt when Mother Hardey first saw it, her practiced eye could people it with other young ladies, no less genteel and perhaps more earnest.

But the wily Mrs. Seton wanted no young ladies on her lawn. She had promised to let the Nuns have the house as soon as the last lease expired, but whenever a room fell vacant she promptly rented it again so that no end to the process was in sight. Mother Hardey made a vigorous decision. "In this way," she said, "we may be kept waiting indefinitely. We must assert our rights by resorting to prompt and decisive measures." So she herself, with two postulants who had bravely joined the Community, took possession of the next room that fell vacant. They held their precarious position, taking room after room as the tenants left, working their hardest in the meantime. Mother Hardey was in her element, sweeping and scrubbing the unseemly place, facing small annoyances with gaiety and grave decision with assurance.

In the meantime word had spread that a school was in preparation, and the parlour was besieged. Mother Hardey's manner made an instantly favourable impression upon all who met her, and lasting friendships were formed. "During those weary days," writes one such friend, "I frequently visited Mother Hardey and I was always impressed by her air of peace, recollection and cheerful acceptance of the sacrifices which daily presented themselves. I made myself her commissioner and I thus had ample opportunity for observing her sustained calmness and self-forgetfulness."

"Little Old New York" is the modern sentimental name for what Mother Hardey saw as she looked south from the windows on Houston Street, but to her it was neither little nor old. It was creeping up the East River, and though on the Brooklyn side the green fringes of forest held their own, Cherry Street on the Manhattan side, once the center of colonial social life and the home of the first President of the United States, was beginning to reflect the bustle of business. A great fire through this section a few years ago had made the city conscious of its lack of a public water supply; pumps still stood along the flag-paved streets. Recent epidemics of fever had sent many people country-ward, and Greenwich Village, with its haphazard streets and cosy houses, was the first of many such to grow up along the Hudson as far as Spuyten Duyvil Creek. A handsome City Hall had been erected in 1812, three sides of marble and the back of sandstone, for, said the Corporation, the City would never grow further north than Chambers Street. This back wall had sheepishly to be painted white, for Mother Hardey was looking at it from the North side. All about her was the tingling impatience of a town in the act of becoming a city. When she looked out at night she saw a garish sight, for the new brilliance of gas-light was spreading from street to street, though some blocks in between checkered the effect with their old oil lamps swinging dimly from poles before every seventh house. In cellars on Wall Street the first daily newspapers tried to keep up with progress, and Mother Hardey must do the same.

She and her helpers went daily to Mass to Saint Patrick's Cathedral just around the corner. The shady streets were pleasant, and the Minetta Brook nearby tempted fishermen. Where the leafy light and shadow fell tremulously then, sharp checkerboards of yellow and grey fall now, etched unmercifully on the sidewalks between tenements where poverty pushes its vendor's carts. Within the Cathedral, begun in 1809, Mother Hardey found pseudo-magnificence.

Tall clustered columns on each side divided the body of the church into three naves surmounted by Gothic arches. The painters had designed on the flat rear walls terminating the edifice behind the altar a continuation of these arches and columns that form a distant perspective and produce a vivid illuson on strangers not warned in advance, giving them the impression that the altar stands midway in the church.

On her way back from Mass she passed, with a glance of regret, the building which had housed the promising beginnings of the New York Literary Institution. The little Jesuit College had flourished for a few years, and gained even greater reputation after its move to the country, on Fifth Avenue near Fiftieth Street. Here it had earnest students and brilliant teachers, including Father James Walsh with his astronomical instruments, but the existence of the College threatened that of Georgetown and it had been closed. Mother Hardey knew what had already happened to more than one Religious Order in New York. The Ursulines from Ireland had gone back. Trappist Nuns had also come and gone, as had the Trappist Monks. The Sisters of Charity had persevered, but they were indigenous to the ungrateful soil. What would the Religious of the Sacred Heart do? Treasured in Mother Hardey's memory were Mother Barat's words: "In spite of the crosses which you will meet, do not lose confidence in Our Lord. Pray and keep close to His Divine Heart." So she prayed obediently as she went into Houston Street and washed the stairs and laid the carpets all but single-handed in the summer heat.

At last the place was ready, the rest of the Community arrived from Barclay Street, and the Bishop came in the afternoon to add to the pleasing confusion. Mother Galitzin wrote to the Mother House:

> We are in a charming site and the house is the same. The school part, the chapel, the parlours, are very nice. Simplicity reigns in the Community in its full vigour, thank God. Even the parlours are simple in their elegance. They have pretty carpets; we could not do without them, as they have them in all the houses here. The Sisters of Charity even have them in their kitchen . . . Our chapel will be a real gem. I have made the designs for the altar and the Tabernacle. Everyone is delighted. I cannot say otherwise for it is in very good taste.

As soon as the Blessed Sacrament was reserved in the new chapel, cloister closed round the Nuns, and their days began to move on with hope and content. Mother Galitzin, whose talents were multiple, painted three pictures, one of them representing Our Lady of Sorrows who was chosen as Patroness of the house. Bishop Hughes blessed the place from top to toe, then spread word that a school was waiting for pupils. A steady stream of visitors began. They were captivated by the novel sight of the children's dormitory with its rows of curtained alcoves, "elegantly draped." Then the children began to come. The first to be enrolled was Rosine Parmentier,[10] whose vivacious little Picard face spent long hours bent over her samplers. Her father, André Parmentier, had laid out stretches of scientifically cultivated gardens in Brooklyn, where his widow now lived, spending her time and her fortune on works of charity and hospitality. Rosine was to live on into another century, keeping the house on Bridge Street open as a focus of Catholic social life, known to young and old as "a type of all the elegance and grace of the *ancien régime*."

Real work could only begin with the arrival of more helpers, and at last on September 17th:

From early morning we awaited the arrival of our Mothers and Sisters from France . . . At last at seven o'clock we heard carriages stop at our door and the bell rang. Mother Shannon hurried down and received the colony for which we had been longing: Mothers Bathilde Sallion, Elizabeth Tucker, Marie Talbot, and Sisters Anne Battandier and Marie Louf. Our Mother Provincial, understanding from the noise that went on below that it was really our Religious who had arrived, came downstairs promptly. The joy was great on all sides. While everyone was thus occupied good Sister Gallien thought that it would be a fine thing to set the bells ringing as a sign of rejoicing; but as in this good city of New York the bells are rung for fire, all the neighbors gathered at the door, knocking loudly and saying that the house was on fire. It was with difficulty that we persuaded them otherwise.

Standing among the new-comers was a young Sister of Providence who had crossed the sea under Mother Sallion's care. Sister François Xavier looked frail, but the sparkle of her spirit was in her eyes.[11] The group of her Religious, led by Mother Guerin, who had gone to found a Convent in Indiana the year before, had literally to build their convent from logs still growing in the woods. She told Mother Hardey how the Nuns had found the Blessed Sacrament housed on a shelf in the one-room hut where the priest lived, for sanctuary lamp the light that struggled through the brushwood that screened the unglazed window. She did not know that she herself would be one of the master-builders of the Saint Mary's of the Woods which would grow and stand when the woods themselves had fallen.[12] She was the first of many pioneer Religious whom Mother Hardey was to speed on their way, placing the seal of her hospitality on their work for the Church in America. Sister François wrote home:

At last I am in New York . . . In this City I found good friends, Messieurs Beyerley and Parmentier who have aided our

Sisters at Saint Mary's so much. They offered me their house. True, I feel better at the Sacred Heart than anywhere else, but I should consider myself very much honoured to stay with such fervent Catholics. But I refused. I live here exactly as in a Community in France. I go from my room to the chapel, from the chapel to the refectory, from the refectory to the recreation room where I find very amiable, cheerful and perfect Religious, though very much exposed; for here they must live as people in Brittany would live who have an anual income of 40,000 francs. The House is superb.

In October Mother Galitzin went away to continue her visitation, leaving Mother Sallion temporarily in charge. Mother Hardey, as Mistress General, took the school in hand. Every morning a greater number of carriages rolled up to the door, each leaving a smartly dressed little day student or two on the step; the education problem, it seemed, would be more complex here than in the south. She noticed without seeming to that the boarders, already at work when said carriages passed invitingly under the windows, lifted their heads as each day-student fluttered by to her desk. Mother Hardey did nothing stringent at first; she must learn to know her world. She relaxed the *règlement* just enough to make the little urbanites begin by liking it.

On the Eighth of December a feeling of being at home took possession of them all. The altar shone with the pomp of candelabra from France, and visitors elbowed their way in to see Bishop Hughes give the white veil to two postulants, and First Communion and Confirmation to some children. The joy of the morning found an outlet in afternoon processions, and when the Bishp tore himself away towards dusk he remarked that it was the happiest day he had known since leaving Rome. Here was nothing to arouse the ever-ready offensive and defensive of his nature; here was only charming promise of good things to come for his Diocese.

But all was not easy, and the Journal entry for Christmas remarks:

> We did not have the consolation of Midnight Mass, as his Lordship thinks that it would have a bad effect on this very Protestant city. That was a real sacrifice which we have offered to the Heart of Jesus, happy if it will obtain the grace that we ask of Him so insistently, that He may bring truly Christian sentiments into the hearts of our children. These young people have great enthusiasm for their studies, but they are very cold towards God, and it is only little by little that we can bring them to the practice of solid virtue.

Mother Hardey had a genius for inculcating precisely that; solid virtue. During Lent such a wave of fervour moved through these cold-hearted little devotees of study that the Mistress General was obliged to check their ardour for sacrifices. When the month of May brought its double sunshine of the skies and of the spirit, the city of New York was searched in vain for a suitable statue of Our Lady. None could be found, so a tiny and somewhat battered one only ten inches high was placed on the May altar. Devotions were none the less solemn for that, and the Bishop, who frequently knelt among the children, was impressed. He told his clergy about the practice, and before many years it had begun to spread through the parishes, helped by the same flighty little day-students, transformed into Children of Mary. A good labourer was at work in Young New York.

X

TO WEST AND TO EAST

It might well have seemed a duty to the small and overworked Community of Houston Street not to look beyond their immediate needs, but it is not the way of zeal to be over-prudent. It seems that from the beginning there was a seed of growth, of energetic expansion in the New York house, for the names of Bishops eager for a Convent of the Sacred Heart flit in and out of the Journal from the first year. But before expansion could begin Mother Hardey was drawn to West and to East. The journey to the West was made in spirit only; that to the East, to the old world, took place in actuality. Both brought her vision, strength and grace.

The Church has said of late, in infallible tones, that one actor in the scene of 1841 is to be called Blessed. Mother Hardey could have foretold as much, knowing Philippine Duchesne. For in those same summer and fall months another foundation was being made, different indeed in prospect and in circumstances from that on Houston Street and reaching out in the opposite direction. Mother Duchesne was on her way to the Indians. Are we going beyond our rights in guessing what mental pictures went through Mother Hardey's mind as she knelt in the Houston Street chapel, in the absorbed attitude that caused a quieting of the spirit in those who merely looked at her, and prayed for her fellow-worker in the Middle West?

At Sugar Creek, in the Indian Territory was a Reservation for the tribe of the Potawatomies. On June 29, 1841, a steamboat set out from Saint Louis heading west against the muddy current of the Missouri River. There were four Sacred Heart nuns on board whose thoughts were flying ahead of them to Sugar Creek. Mother Mathevon, Mother O'Connor, Sister Amyot, all vigorous women in the prime of life, might well be recognized by their fellow-passengers as missioners facing scenes of hardship with fit courage and equipment, but who was this other woman, obviously in her seventies, who completed the group? Anyone could see that she had lately been ill, and that her strength had long ago been spent in great labours. Mother Duchesne herself was the only person on board who thought that she was young. She walked up and down the deck with a quick, eager step. How could she think otherwise when for nearly forty years she had longed for just this? It was Indian children whom she had pictured during her night watches on Holy Thursday in Grenoble so long ago; dark-skinned children unknowing of God had called to her until it seemed to her impatience that she must cross the sea without a ship if none could be found to carry her. She had come at last, as far as the ship could bring her, but through all the hard work and misunderstanding of the ensuing years her eyes had still turned hungrily to the West. Now she was really on her way. No wonder that the motley crowd of passengers on the steamer looked with curiosity and respect on that frame, rugged yet so frail that the wind might have blown it away, on the strong, weathered face, on the eyes whose peering look betrayed the failure of their sight even while seeming to read the horizon.

Cart travel succeeded the days on the river boat. Mother Duchesne seemed unconscious of the jolting. Prairie lands unending were around them now, and high grass moving all one way in the wind. Two dots in the distance became two Indians at last, wheeling about them with gesticulations and whoopings of welcome. Mother Duchesne's old eyes glowed. These two were but fore-riders of the tribe which soon appeared in hundreds as the settlement was neared. There was a cross on the top of one of the wooden houses, the first that they had seen since leaving Saint Louis, though crowded villages had clustered on the river-banks along the way. The Nuns were led to a wooden bench outside the Church. The mounted men, feathered and painted, wheeled about in faultless circles. There was an endless ceremony of hand-shaking which was hardly over before the dark came. In the excitement of such a day the fact that no house had yet been built for them seemed of slight importance. That night Mother Duchesne slept in an Indian cabin.

It was mid-summer and very hot, and their cabin had one room. The Religious called its four corners by such high-sounding names as refectory, dormitory, Superior's room, parlour, but it remained one room. At any hour the Indians came in unannounced by a knock, sat down for as long as they liked, watched the Nuns in silence, and left impressed but undemonstrative. They showed their respect by occasionally hanging a fresh scalp over the door. Cooking was done on a fire outside, and once while Sister Amyot turned to find a frying pan a prairie dog ran off with a month's supply of meat. Mother Duchesne tried to help but her limbs could not move fast enough to keep out of other people's way, so she went off into a corner with a pile of rough mending.

A school was opened after only a few days, for circumstances were of small account in a place like this and it was no use waiting for proper housing and scholastic equipment. Each morning the Jesuits in charge of the Mission ran around catching the little girls and bringing them to school before they learned to like being first washed and then taught. Again Mother Duchesne tried to help, but the young Redskins, so said the Jesuits, had best be taught their prayers in their own language which the other Nuns were fast acquiring. Mother Duchesne could not remember the long-syllabled words. Again she went off, this time to the church which was nearby, and prayed.

She saw the Indians crowding in to their own prayers, to Mass, to the Sacraments; she felt the breath of a fervour like that of the first Christians moving among them. She knew that the Sacred Host had more than once left the hands of the priest to seek the lips of an old Indian woman. Her thoughts leapt abroad, farther and farther west. There were more Indians, tribe after tribe of them, as far as the Rocky Mountains. She found a piece of paper and wrote to the Mother General who had always understood her:

> I feel when I hear of the Rocky Mountains, or other missions of that sort, the same longing desires I had in France to come to America, and in America to be sent to the savages. They tell me that people live to be a hundred in the Rocky Mountains. Now that I am quite well again, and being after all only seventy-three, why should I not have ten more years of work before me? Then at other times, it seems to me more perfect to await the events which will decide my fate.

The undying apostle in her had written those lines, but the consummate saint in her had added the last words. While waiting she found that she could do nothing to help in the cabin, for even the new one built for them by the Indians, one room at a time, was over-crowded. She had only to let herself swing free into the wide waters of prayer, that inland sea of silence where she had long learned that God was to be found. During four hours in the morning and as many in the afternoon she remained motionless in the church, sightless too, for the Indians could creep up unnoticed and kiss the hem of her patched skirt. In the evening one or other would come to the cabin with his only obtainable fresh egg and leave it there for "the woman who prays always." The weather grew colder and colder, but that made no difference.

All about her were the circumstances of the mission life to which she had always felt herself called. Now that she could not do the work herself, she was there, a lamp burning itself out before the Presence. And during those same days, fifteen hundred miles to the east in a metropolis, Mother Hardey was kneeling in the same Presence, taking what time she could from the driving routine of a school day to weigh before God the possibilities of new foundations in the neighbouring cities and beyond. Indian life was to be broken up by relentless forces, and scattered; Mother Duchesne let the seed of her apostolate fall into the prairie ground and die there. Simultaneously it sprang to life in far places where a civilization was being moulded which would eventually cover the continent. Mother Hardey could draw upon a grace and a strength more than her own, while Mother Duchesne, who had held the whole of America in her keeping since the first days of the Society of the Sacred Heart, dreamed of the Rocky Mountains and grew weaker and weaker.

Winter came, and it was necessary to dig a path daily through the snow to the church. The hut was lined with canvas which grew taut like a sail when the wind blew. Mother Duchesne fell ill, and even the spring warmth could not restore the strength that she had only thought was hers. Summer came; she had been but a year at Sugar Creek and it was decided that she must go back to Saint Charles. "God alone knows the reason for this recall," was her only comment. She lived on for another ten years as "the woman who prays always," and there was hardly a year of those ten, and of many more after, in which Mother Hardey did not open still another house of the Sacred Heart.

While this was going on in the West, the shrewd eyes of Mother Galitzin had been measuring the worth of her fellow-worker. "Mother Hardey is my right arm," she had written to the Mother General, "and we act together in perfect harmony. I am looking forward with pleasure to presenting her to you. She satisfies everyone and is advancing the reputation of this house." She then proposed that Mother Hardey should accompany her to the Seventh General Council. In answer, Mother Barat wrote to Mother Hardey:

> Our Mother Provincial could not have given me a greater pleasure than to choose you as her companion to the Council, where you will have the opportunity of meeting all the first Mothers of the Society. I have at last the hope of seeing you, if the Good Master will sustain my frail life till then, and what consolation this meeting will give me! Take care of your health, my daughter, so that there may be no obstacle to your departure. As soon as I reach Rome, where I am going in a few weeks, I shall settle the date of the Council and the time for you to leave America.

The summons came in the spring and Mother Hardey's joy was full. She felt like a magnet moving towards the lodestone as the time drew near for seeing the Mother House, Rome, the Society in its length and breadth, and above all in its Foundress. Moreover another joy, an intense and personal one, was waiting for her among the others, that of seeing again her own Mother Audé who was now Superior of the Trinita dei Monti, in Rome. Mother Hardey could see her in anticipation, standing in a deep Italian doorway at the top of an ample sweep of steps. April came, and it was nearly time for the picture to become a reality. One day while her mind was thus in Rome, Mother Hardey entered the chapel at Houston Street and stopped to read a notice hanging at the door. It told laconically of Mother Audé's death at the Trinita on March 6th. Mother Hardey went on alone into the chapel, while her thoughts left Rome to search out heaven. A little later a letter came from Mother Barat telling of the high-hearted death of the one-time missioner whose "dispositions were those of a saint, full of resignation, confidence and the sweetest peace," and adding the detail that a former pupil of Saint Michael's had been in Rome at the time and had come with her negro slave to the funeral mass, that Louisiana might say a last "thank you" to mother Eugénie Audé. The Society draws the ends of the world together, and on May 19, 1842, Mother Galitzin and Mother Hardey set sail towards the East.

The ocean voyage was ten days shorter than when Mother Galitzin had last crossed only two years before; such was the acceleration rate of ocean travel since the first transatlantic steamship with passenger service, *The Great Western*, had thrown New York into a ferment four years earlier. She noticed, with some envy apparently, that Mother Hardey was not in the least disturbed by the vagaries of the waves, and had the whole of the days on deck.

There was much to think about. Mother Hardey was treasuring a letter received the summer before, and she went over its words time and again, sounding them out, making them her own. Mother Barat had written almost a year ago:

> Our foundations seem to prosper, thanks to the Divine Goodness which deigns to make use of such poor and unworthy instruments to promote the glory of the Sacred Heart. Are we not among these instruments, my Daughter? How little virtue we have, when we look into the matter! And yet, our Good Master does not disdain to use us to save souls for Him, and even to form

His Spouses. Oh, what if we were to do the opposite through want of fidelity, of love, of generosity, or through a failure to humble ourselves for fear of yielding up that reserve of pride which perhaps still dominates in us, how guilty we should be! May such a dishonesty be far from you and from me, my Daughter. Let us make haste instead to give everything, to sacrifice everything. The glory of Jesus, procured at our own expense, that is what we must strive for with all our power, is it not, dear Aloysia?

As to the present state of affairs in the Society, I have only one word to say to you. Hold fast to the trunk of the tree, no matter what you may hear! Tell me of your doubts, your uneasiness, for we shall always understand each other. My compass shall ever be the See of Peter, the Vicar of Jesus Christ. Directed by it we can never err, and we should rather die than swerve from its guidance. However, things are calming down by degrees around us. Each one is trying to do all that she can for the good of the Society, so I hope that Jesus will continue to bless us. He will bless you especially, dear Aloysia, if you understand the importance of your obligations. Unite yourself to Jesus and count upon His help rather than your own capabilities, for self-reliance usually spoils everything.

Mother Hardey was obliged to meditate upon this letter in silence. She could not discuss its implications with Mother Galitzin, for by now her natural perspicacity had shown her that the impressionable, strong-minded woman whom she so revered was hardly the person to give her a rounded or sympathetic view of the situation in which the Society found itself at the moment. She knew by now that it was Mother Galitzin herself who had been the moving spirit in framing the Decrees of the Council of 1839, and that when sent to America for the purpose of promulgating them in the houses of the New World she had gone to extremes in abrogating the Rule to suit the ideas she had conceived of it. Mother Hardey, in the spirit of simple, literal obedience which remained forever the same in her, had furthered their observance with all her power, and she had in truth been Mother Galitzin's right hand. But as the three years during which the Decrees were to be on trial passed, she had come to understand that the Superior General herself had not inspired most of them, that they bore rather the stamp of more rigid and impatient minds, and that only Mother Barat's knowledge that tares cannot be rooted up at once without injury to the wheat had led her to place her authority behind them. She knew that a storm had arisen against them in Europe, violent outside of the Society, more moderate within it, and that the question at the heart of the storm concerned the proposed residence of the Superior General at Rome. The coming Council would decide whether the Decrees would be confirmed, modified or repealed. Mother Hardey's part in the Council would be simple; older and more experienced minds would do the thinking, and she would support the decision. Later on in Rome, when Father Rosaven, Jesuit Assistant General, asked her somewhat over-eagerly why she had come to the Council, she said briefly, "to obey." "What side are you on?" he persisted. "That of authority," was the answer.

The ship made for Havre whose steep streets, grey-lined with wooden houses, rose abruptly from the bay in welcome to the travellers. The latter went on shore where France and its ways closed around them. They set out straight for Paris, journeying as fast as might be. Though locomotives were sputtering in America there was, as yet, no choice of conveyance here but the stage-coach. So far Mother Hardey had spent her life on extravagantly wide plantation lands or in very young cities. Now she was driving through a web of old towns and villages so closely woven that the bells of one called out and the bells of another answered. Time had never begun over again here, nor had Revolutions been able to break its continuity. They reached Paris but only to find that Mother Barat was not there, so they hardly gave themselves time to feel at home at the Mother House before setting out to follow her to Rome. Another journey, probably by boat from Marseilles, brought them to the heart of Italy and the miles had not yet become wearisome before they found themselves driving across the Campania and through the streets of the Eternal City. They went to the Villa Lante, but once more failed to find their Mother General. She had been called away some weeks before, and in her place was a summons for the travellers to follow her to Lyons.

Mother Hardey was not sorry to have the grace of a breathing space in Rome, though the stay must be a short one. But the shortest days spent there take on something of the agelessness of the City itself, and she proceeded to fill the days given her with the wealth of a year's living. It was mid-July by now, and the sun poured its heat lavishly over the warm-toned stones of the houses, and traced strong squares of shadow on the streets. The Villa Lante was a wonderful old house, proud in its austere strength, with a royal stairway pouring like a flood from one level to another in a torrent of courtly welcome. Towards evening of her first day, when the heat was ebbing, Mother Hardey was led through the warm gloom of the acacia and orange groves by path after path up the sides of the Janiculum, to be released at last in the tranquility that comes before nightfall on a height overlooking Rome. The sweep of land belonging to the Villa Lante was larger than it is now, and from one corner on the summit of the hill the dome of Saint Peter's could be seen near at hand, just below the level of her eyes. About and beyond it rose and fell the seven-hilled city, while against the opposite skyline the towers of the Trinita dei Monti were traced against the deepening blue. Somewhere in the blur of the low-lying Trastevere nearer at hand lay Santa Rufina, a third Convent of the Sacred Heart. Mother Hardey's eyes passed lingeringly back and forth. There was nothing to reveal to her the fact that some day the Mother House too would be embraced in that view beyond compare, a new Mother House over there on the Via Nomentana.

The flaming distinctness of the sunset hour came and went, and Mother Hardey was led into the little house crowning the Janiculum, the original Villa which had given its name to the estate. There on the wall she recognized the picture of Our Lady of Sorrows, a copy of which hung near the altar in the chapel of Houston Street, Our Lady with the cross behind her and the crown of thorns to gaze upon. She knelt before it, in memory and in forethought. A few moments later, as they were going down the hill in the gradual blur of nightfall, they paused at the end of a long alley. This was the spot where the picture had been placed on the memorable day at the close of the Council of 1839 when Mother Barat, with trust unshakable, had made the Act of Consecration to the Mother of Sorrows which placed the affairs of the Society in her hands. Mother Hardey thought how well it was that the New York foundation had been placed in those same hands.

The next visit was to the Trinita, where her coming was joyfully recorded: "The meeting with our American Mothers was a striking example of the beautiful spirit of union which exists among the members of our loved Society. How close are the ties which bind us when farthest separated, and how easily we become acquainted when we meet!" The high-built Trinita crowned a long flight of steps leading up from the Piazza di Spagna to the brow of the Pincian Hill. It had been built for a Community of Minims, sons of Saint Francis of Paula, in 1495, and the old monastic frescoes still transformed the cloisters into strange scenes of a mediaeval world. Its chapel was a church rich with oratories, its garden swept the hillside with verdure, its towers crowned Rome. It was too soon for Mother Hardey to see at the Trinita the fresco of

Mater Admirabilis, which was to be painted on the side-wall of a corridor two years later by Pauline Perdrau, a postulant. In later years there would hardly be a Convent of the Sacred Heart without its copy of Mater, Our Lady in the Temple, rose-robed, very young and full of grace, but now Mother Hardey passed the blank space on the wall unsuspecting.

Santa Rufina had a visit in its turn. It could boast neither the elevated beauty nor the significant traditions of the other houses; it huddled around its little courtyard in the oldest of the old quarters of Rome, opening its small dark rooms as wide as possible to swarms of small Trasteverini who were in need of everything that it could give. Here Mother Hardey found a Superior as young as herself. Reverend Mother Lehon, strong and wise in spite of her youth, was destined to be Superior General in the far future. Upon leaving, Mother Hardey presented her with a characteristic gift; it was the latest American invention, a steel pen-point. Mother Lehon received it with gratitude and valued it highly, so highly that years later she was still showing it off as an interesting souvenir, while continuing to write with a quill.

In the meantime an old friend of Mother Hardey's was busily arranging for the best visit of all. Bishop Rosati happened to be in Rome at the time, and he saw to it that she was properly escorted not only to Saint Peter's but into the presence of Gregory XVI as well. So once more the great Catholic adventure was repeated. The leather door curtain of Saint Peter's abruptly yielded its weight to the push of one more hand, and the far lamps burning about the Confession drew new eyes down the nave to the heart of Christendom. Sunlight sifting down from incalculable heights; the blaze of gold and marble and mosaics dimmed by distances, the hush about the chapel of the Blessed Sacrament, the silence of the fathomless face of the Pieta, each spoke anew. Then came the romantic pomp of the palace whose monarch rules to the frontiers of heaven and of the earth in all its roundness. The sword-guarded gates were passed, the whisper of ecclesiastical robes on the long stairways kept passing to right and to left; the Bishop's assured step, inaudible on the carpets, went on and on, until Mother Hardey found herself in the presence of the Vicar of Christ. Gregory XVI was an old man then; his reign had not been easy, nor had his policy of conservatism in the face of wave after wave of revolution throughout Europe brought him much comfort. But his face was kind, and a Religious of the Sacred Heart from America was of new interest. The interview grew easy and friendly. At its close Mother Hardey went away enriched with a feeling that now at last she knew what it meant to be a Catholic, with a Papal blessing for Houston Street, and with a small bronze medal from which she never afterwards parted.

On July 16th she left Rome for Lyons with Mother Galitzin. There were three houses there: the Rue Boissac, where the Sodality of the Children of Mary of the World had been started just ten years earlier; Les Anglais, a country house on the high lands surrounding the city; and La Ferrandière, a one-time chateau then also in the country. It was here that they were to stay. As the carriage drew near along the tree-shadowed drives Mother Hardey suddenly felt very young and strange. She dismounted in a daze. A group of Religious stood in the doorway. The friendly hands of those nearest drew her towards the central figure with the whispered words: "Notre Mère Générale." She knelt to kiss the outstretched hand of her First Superior, without daring to look up. She felt the vigorous, affectionate pressure of a very warm embrace, and heard the laughing remark, "How young she is!" Mother Galitzin, always at hand and never non-plussed, made the time-honoured rejoinder: "That, Very Reverend Mother, is a fault which she is correcting day by day." Everyone laughed, and Mother Hardey found herself looking straight into the deep, shrewd, humorous, loving eyes of Madeleine Sophie Barat. Something in her gave way before a flood of confidence as the Mother General led her solicitously into the house. "My American daughter," she was saying with deep satisfaction.

Mother Hardey found herself the last and least in a remarkable assembly. In view of the importance of the matters to be discussed a large number of Councillors had been summoned: all those who had taken part in the last two Councils, all the Provincials and Vice-Provincials, and several other Superiors. Mother Hardey already knew most of them by name and by character. She felt strongly drawn to some of the more venerable of the Mothers whom she knew to be among the foundation-stones of the Society—Mothers de Charbonnel, Desmarquest, Prévost, who had shared the poverty and the vision of the first days at Amiens; Mother Maillucheau, whose gifts of prayer had kept her as on a mountain height throughout her long life. There was Mother de Limminghe, one of the framers of the Decrees of 1839, whose adopted name of Addolorata became her well, and in whose austere bearing and somewhat extreme manner Mother Hardey could recognize a likeness to Mother Galitzin. Mother de Gramont alone of the first Officers was still detained, it would seem, in Paris. The younger Superiors linked with these their forerunners, and all formed in their persons a living history of the growth of the Society, and a register of its spirit. There had been only eight houses when Mother Duchesne had crossed the sea, all in France; now there were forty-six, in many countries, and the "one heart and one soul" must expand proportionately. Revolutions had shaken it, mistakes had taught it, and by now its features had taken the expression of its soul.

The days went by, and for some reason not evident to everyone the proceedings did not begin. Mother Hardey devoted herself to watching her Superior General. It was a fruitful occupation. Mother Barat had held her post now for nearly forty years, but as she had been only twenty-three when the burden had first been laid upon her she was not yet old. The alert step, the rapid yet silent movements, the controlled energy of word and look, were proverbial in the Society, as were the twinkle in her eyes and the spice of her repartee. Yet the power of her personality was veiled in gentleness. Mother Barat talked and laughed with her daughters, and walked serenely with them in the garden; she was simple and approachable, full of eager interest in their affairs. Yet each silently recognized the existence of depths that they could not sound, and were won by a love which they knew to be all for God, yet all for them. It was enough to be in her presence, for virtue went out from her. Mother Hardey remembered Mother Duchesne. She recognized in this brighter, more mobile face, with its ready responsiveness to all things human, the same strength that had made the "Heart of Oak" stand steady in all storms. She had seen Mother Duchesne turn and lean towards her absent Mother as the magnetic needle leans to the North, and now she herself could do the same.

Still the days passed and Mother de Gramont did not arrive. The councillors waited in silence while outside other tongues were talking all too freely, weaving a network of misunderstanding. At last a letter came from Paris, but not from the Hôtel Biron. It came from the Archbishop, Monseigneur Affre. Claiming jurisdiction over the affairs of an Order whose Mother House was in his Diocese, he forbade the Council to convene in Lyons and produced a formidable list of objections to the recent Decrees. The letter was a thunder-bolt. Mother Barat, who had been acting under the advice of the Cardinal Protector in Rome, could not so lightly compromise the position of the Society. She sent a dignified exposition of the state of affairs to the Archbishop, and wrote to Rome for counsel. Then she faced the weary weeks of waiting.

In the meantime the summer was wearing to a close, and the house was full of Superiors who were badly needed elsewhere. Mother Barat calmly took advantage of the situation. She sent all the Councillors in a body to Les Anglais to make a retreat. The house, on the slopes of La Fourvière under the eyes of Our Lady, was wrapped in the lofty silence of high places; Father Barrelle, the most sought-after retreat-master in France, came to guide them.[1] This intense and flaming director of souls, who paid dear in penance for his profound influence, felt that he had a special mission for Religious, and this occasion became famous as "the retreat of interior life." The biography of Père Barrelle records that: "At Les Anglais, the man of God was speaking to strong souls. Never had generous hearts been placed in more virile a hand, drawn by the inexorable logic of grace and of vocation, never had a more pitiless light been brought to bear upon more responsive souls." His opening words to the retreatants struck the keynote of a calming detachment: "The sentiment that must fill you," he said, "is a sentiment of a great peace, for you can and must say that the Lord is with you. He gathered you together for important affairs; it seemed urgent that you should be busy about them, and lo! He says 'not yet, think of Me, and of your own soul. Fear not; your affairs are in my hands'."

The circumstances of the retreat were so remarkable that it is no wonder that Mother Hardey found herself entering into depths of the spiritual life of which she had hardly been aware before. From fragments of letters written later on we can gather that it was at Les Anglais that a craving for prayer came upon her that would but grow in intensity with the years; she became possessed by a sense of the power of silence and of the primacy of abandonment. It would be enough for Mother Barat to write to her later on: "Remember the graces of Les Anglais." She had, however, a few unexpected distractions. It would seem that the office of sacristan was among the few of which she had never had experience, and the matter turned out to be more difficult than it seemed. One day she let the only pair of altar vases which the house possessed crash to the floor. Mother Barat only smiled and advised her to entrust her hands to the care of her angel guardian. But the Superior General's reactions were very different on the day when Mother Hardey miscalculated the number of hosts to be consecrated at Mass. When Communion time came the priest was obliged to distribute all those in the ciborium, and not one was left to be reserved in the tabernacle. The confused sacristan hurried to Mother Barat to tell her that their Lord would not be among them in His Sacrament for many hours. Now Mother Barat's soul was in anguish those days, an anguish deeper than her daughters could know. With the whole of her sorely tried faith she was clinging to our Lord, and to have His bodily presence withdrawn was too much for her just then in the darkness of her trial. Mother Hardey was terrified to see her fall on her knees and burst into tears. "O Lord," she cried aloud, "have our sins forced Thee also to abandon us?" All day she grieved near the empty tabernacle. She felt this abandonment with a saint's acute awareness of God's habitual presence, and her pain was undisguised. It revealed not only the bitterness of the trial through which she was passing, the climax of which had not yet come, but still more the depth of her insight into the hidden ways of God where love or the failure to love, fidelity or sin, are the root causes of all that happens. Mother Hardey, so much less experienced, so habitually unready to make a display of deep feeling, watched from the back of the strangely empty chapel while Mother Barat wept near the altar. She could never afterwards forget what she learned from this sight of the tears of holiness unhidden.

Another soul was under great stress during these days. Mother Galitzin had come to realize somewhat in the translucent atmosphere of that retreat how her own precipitous actions in 1839 had helped to bring on this crisis. With that impetuous generosity that could be her strength as well as her weakness she made a heroic resolve. With Mother Barat's sanction she offered herself to God as a victim for the well-being of the Society, signing the oblation with her own hand. God accepted the offering, though not at once.

The retreat closed, and still no word came from Rome. Mother Barat felt that to hold the Council at Lyons would be to cause an irreparable break with the Archbishop of Paris, and she determined to disband the Councillors. It would not be easy to call them all together again but there seemed nothing else to be done. Mother Galitzin and Mother Hardey returned with Mother Barat to La Ferrandière.

There were a number of Novices there who were awed by Mother Hardey's presence among them. They would walk past her room and steal furtive glances through the door at the American Mother, but she never turned her head to look at them. America to them was a missionary country; their imaginations and their zeal had alike been fed with stories of Mother Duchesne, her heroism and her hardships. New York was the latest American foundation, and here was its foundress sitting quietly at her desk writing letters. One of the Novices at length yielded to temptation. She slipped into the room and approached the desk. "Mother," she said, timidly yet speaking her whole thought, "Mother, please pray that some day I may be your daughter in America." Mother Hardey turned to her with a smile and a searching look, but only bowed her head in answer. The Novice felt both the sympathy of her understanding and the force of the lesson in how to observe silence. She slipped away happily to pursue her request elsewhere, and with good effect; her desire was to come true.

Mother Barat walked with Mother Hardey in the garden, and her step was tireless beside that of the younger woman; or she had long talks with her in the room that she kept so bare of all but the most necessary furniture. She talked over the affairs of the American houses with a vividness of interest and an accuracy of detail which showed how large a part of her thoughts she gave to them. A look of sadness came over her expressive face when Mother Hardey voiced the hope held so urgently by all the American nuns that some day their Superior General would come to them, not only in heart but in person. No; she shook her head. She had been obliged to make that sacrifice long ago. She could not come, but—and she paused as if to pray before adding in her gentle yet irrevocable way—Mother Hardey would be her shadow as Superior of the New York house. Then a flame from Mother Barat's soul came into her voice and her eyes as she urged Mother Hardey to keep union and charity at all costs, through obedience and through a great, unquestioning dependence. The flame sprang out from her and caught; it entered deeply into the tempered steel of Mother Hardey's will till it glowed with a resolve that would never fail. Mother Barat saw and was satisfied. Never, in the twenty years during which she would continue to trust and guide Mother Hardey from a distance would her confidence in the loyalty of this American daughter be shaken, even though appearances might be against it.

The separation came on September 9th, when Mother Barat left for Paris. The next few months were as a Purgatory for her. The web of misinterpretation spun from Bishop to Bishop, from Rome to Paris, grew more tangled through indiscreet rumours and exaggerated reports. Even the French Government took part in the embroilment, and, hardest of all, many of those who should have been Mother Barat's most loyal supporters seemed blinded to the true issues. Mother Galitzin's conduct, in spite of her offering, showed that even generosity of will cannot supply for breadth of vision or for humble docility. She must have tried at this time to bring some sort of pressure to bear upon Mother Hardey, for years afterwards the latter wrote to her Superior General: "As long as I thought that the measures of 1839 were approved by you, I tried to support them; but once I knew your will, nothing could have made me sign an approbation which my conscience disavowed. That cost me much trouble, it is true, for I was with you and could not open my heart to you. But our holy Mother Galitzin thought that she was acting for the best." This fine, tactful, discriminating loyalty was always Mother Hardey's compass on difficult seas.

There was something mysterious in the way in which every sort of trial, difficulty and incomprehension rose up at once in those painful months, until, in April, 1843, the kind offices of Monseigneur Mathieu, Bishop of Beauvais, succeeded in bringing about concord by obtaining from Rome the necessary sanction for returning to the observance of the Decrees of 1826. The storm then died down, the necessary alterations in these same Decrees were made gradually, and certain measures proved to be helpful and wise were kept from those of 1839. It became apparent that the essential unity of the Society had never been broken in spite of everything, and it faced the future with a new unfolding of its God-given powers. As a price for this Mother Barat had suffered inexpressibly but the lamp of her love had gone out in the floods.

Mother Hardey sailed for home on October 17, 1842, on the *Utica*. As the ship moved towards the open sea she looked back at France, and could still feel the quick, strong touch of

Mother Barat's hand giving a blessing. Then she looked to the west. Over the curve of the ocean lay Houston Street. She could not see what lay behind it: other houses, more and more of them, waiting in the varying distances of time and place. She would open them all in the strength of that blessing from Mother Barat, who had said, "Let us found for eternity."

XI

HUNTING GOOD SOIL

For twenty-five years New York was to be the center of Mother Hardey's activities, her home, the stable point in a very mobile life. But once the business of opening new houses had begun, not to mention the still more complicated business of visiting them all as Superior Vicar, a very large part of her time was spent in travelling. For a biography to attempt to follow the chronological order of her days too closely would result in confusion, to say the least. For this reason the narrative will first see her safely established in a House built upon a rock, after which it will follow the growth of her foundations, grouping events according to locality rather than time sequence. This will save us from the breathless experience of being transported thousands of miles between paragraphs, but for a real understanding of Mother Hardey's life it must be kept in mind that she herself was not spared such experiences. For her, a network of constant travel was stretched across her home duties, forming an outwardly double life unified from within into harmony.

But for now it is enough that the *Utica* has reached port. The crossing was a stormy one, and the Religious of the Good Shepherd who were travelling with her—the eldest of whom was only twenty-nine—recorded their experiences:

> The Mother Superior of the Religious of the Sacred Heart and four of her Sisters were on board. . . . The next day the wind was adverse; the sea was terrible; the winds raged. For nine days the Sisters were prostrated by sea-sickness. It was ten days before they could go up on the vessel's deck. The Mother Superior of the Sacred Heart was most kind to the Sisters, although the sea-sickness of the four who were in her charge was severe and continuous. . . . At last, after thirty-one days the Sisters reached New York on November 17th. For five days they remained in that city, the guests of the Religious of the Sacred Heart, who treated them with overflowing kindness.[1]

Mother Hardey saw at once that all had gone well during her absence. Her first thought was for the Good Shepherd Nuns. She helped their Superior, young Mother Marie des Anges, to make arrangements for their further journey into Kentucky, and upon the advice of Bishop Hughes fitted them out with secular dresses for their inland route. With the broadly zealous interest that characterized her, she found out all that she could about their special vocation, about their Mother House at Angers where the recently established central government was giving impetus and power to their work, and about Mother Saint Euphrasia Pelletier,[2] their saintly foundress whom she herself, unknowingly, resembled in many ways. It was Bishop Flaget who was calling the Good Shepherd Order to his diocese, and Mother Saint Euphrasia had sent them off with the words of Saint Ignatius, "Oh why have I not many more faithful servants to immolate to the glory of God!" A memory of Mother Duchesne may have flashed into Mother Hardey's mind. What would she and Mother Marie have said then, could they have known that in a little less than a century Mother Saint Euphrasia would be canonized in the same month that witnessed the Beatification of Mother Duchesne? It was more than a coincidence; it was part of the interdependence of the members of the Mystical Body which was Mother Hardey's reason for being so practically helpful to the members of other Religious Orders whenever the opportunity came her way. The next came very soon, when she welcomed and assisted Mother Mary Xavier Warde who brought the first band of Sisters of Mercy from Ireland to Pittsburgh the following December.[3]

Mother Sallion was called away that same month, leaving Mother Hardey Superior of Houston Street. As she looked about the make-shift place with eyes made more penetrating than ever by all that she had seen in the last six months, she measured it against the back-ground of New York and knew that it was far too small for the work that it was called upon to do. This meant that within the next few years she must find an adequate house, a large, permanent one, aloof, aloft, capable of expansion, perhaps on the rocky heights beyond the city. As she looked swiftly along the ranks of the children in their green merino dresses, sixty of them gathered in formal greeting at her installation as Superior, she could read in the earnest faces of the elder among them a promise that new religious workers would soon be recruited from Houston Street itself. Vocations would be the most visible sign of blessing on her work. Her practiced eye picked out fervent Alicia Dunne, and even her mischievous little sister Margaret, then turned questioningly towards Eliza and Ellen Hogan, Margaret Donnelly, Margaret O'Connor. With the greatest assurance of all she looked at Sarah Jones.[4] Sarah was really too old to be in the school. She was nineteen, but Bishop Hughes had insisted upon her coming for one year. This motherless daughter of the distinguished Judge Jones, great-granddaughter of Alexander Hamilton, had been led most marvellously into the Church. When a child of fourteen a sermon by a Protestant minister had so penetrated her heart that on coming home she went and prayed that Christ would reveal Himself to her. Then, "suddenly I saw with the eyes of my soul Our Lord in His agony in the Garden of Olives. He looked at me with ineffable tenderness and said, 'See how I have loved you! Can you not have confidence in me?' From then on I tried to act and speak and think like Him, and often I changed my conduct in consequence of this thought 'Jesus would not have acted thus'." She turned her whole intelligence along the road down which her heart had gone, and in a few years it led her to the truth, though this meant misunderstanding with her adored father. She appealed to Bishop Hughes for help, and became his favorite spiritual child. When she implored him to baptize her conditionally he was at first unwilling, but she all but compelled him to do so. A daughter of Elizabeth Seton was god-mother. Later she had reason to be grateful for her own strong-mindedness in the matter. One day, when she had been a Nun for many years, her old coloured Mammy came to see her, and in the course of reminiscences related how she had held the baby Sarah at her Baptism, and how the naughty little thing had cried and kicked so hard that not a drop of water had touched her.

Sarah came unannounced to Houston Street, soon after its opening, and asked for an interview with Mother Galitzin. Without preamble she had demanded to enter as a Religious. "We are a teaching Order, you know," said the astonished Superior, trying to draw the conversation back to a proper beginning. "That is what I wish," was the answer, "I am a born teacher." Bishop Hughes, when consulted, agreed that this was going a little too fast, so here was Sarah, making her year of probation under Mother Hardey's special guidance.

With the opening of 1843, Houston Street began to hum

like a bee-hive. The work of Retreats and a Society for helping needy churches were begun. Then came the excitement of several conversions among the non-Catholic children, events which always caused a stir through a city still small enough for all the first families to know each other's business. The approving, the curious, the censorious, came in ever increasing numbers to fill the tiny parlours. Even during the holidays they came, for it was the custom of all the ladies to call on Christmas day, and all the gentlemen on New Year's day. Bishop Hughes himself was the Convent's best publicity. He officiated at most of its ceremonies, and brought every other Bishop who strayed through New York to call. On one occasion he brought nine of them simultaneously, all of whom listened docilely to French dialogues and to music composed specially for such events. Most of them left with ill-concealed determination to have Sacred Heart Convents in their own dioceses some day, to which Mother Hardey could only give the smiling answer, "Yes, some day." Young ecclesiastics were brought to say their first Mass in the Convent chapel, among them the future Archbishop Bayley of Baltimore. One day Father de Smet went through like a skyrocket on one of his never-ending journeys in behalf of the Indians of the Far West, leaving behind him a blazing trail of zeal for the missions which Mother Hardey kept alive among the children by tales of Mother Duchesne and her hunger for the Rocky Mountains. Men whose fingers were on the pulse of the thought of the day came to give lectures. There were advantages, thought Mother Hardey, in living in a metropolis. She had already taken into herself the best of the leisured aloofness of the South, its grace, its fragrance, its chivalry. Now she would respond with equal readiness to the brisker tempo of life in New York, sharing for better or for worse in the give and take of its material and intellectual life.

Looking back into the history of the years from 1841 to

1847 during which Mother Hardey was engaged in hunting for a bit of good New York soil in which to sow her seed, it is striking to see how many other people were doing precisely the same thing at the same time, though the crop of both weeds and flowers that sprang up shows how varied were the seeds planted. The period then opening has been given the self-important title of "Period of Industrial and Educational Development."[5] Mother Hardey was, once again, only one of many. It was not in the way of Providence for her that she should ever be either a lonely pioneer or a defender of a besieged cause. Hers was perhaps a more dangerous because less simple way: to go with the current, yet make it take her where she willed to go.

There could be no doubt about the material advance; its rapidity was phenomenal. The newspapers of the day were full of notices, enthusiastic or skeptical, of new improvements, new inventions. During her absence in Europe a system of running water had been inaugurated from a huge new reservoir at Forty-second Street and Fifth Avenue, and the *Evening Post* for July 5th had recorded that: "Yesterday at sunrise the Croton water was introduced into the distributing reservoir, with appropriate ceremonies before an immense concourse." Mother Hardey did not go to the expense of putting pipes into her rented house, but neither was she among the citizens who, as the newspapers complained, objected to the new system because it was new. She was interested in new things, and as an advocate of the womanly arts, was glad to read, on March 3, 1843, that a patent for a sewing machine had just been issued. She made herself one of the first patronesses of the new device, and some years later became the means of introducing sewing machines into the European Convents, even when she found it necessary to send an American Nun along with the machine, to give lessons in its use. She had reason to rejoice that same year in the appearance of the first mechanical street-cleaners, a vast improvement on the late method of turning loose into the thoroughfares droves of rubbish-consuming hogs. She was probably indifferent to the opening of a daguerreotype establishment, to be followed soon by one that experimented in photography. It would only have been a matter of amusement to learn from the old pupils that a public ice-cream resort named the Alhambra had opened downtown, becoming "the marvel of New York" and that the windows on Broadway were flaunting "Italian verandah curtains," considered a flashy luxury until they had become common enough to be called awnings. The whole town in fact was changing in time to these advances. "Broadway has ceased to be Broadway," lamented a popular Guide Book. "It is almost blocked up with omnibuses, carts, sleighs, barrows. . . . It is said that within a year there will be scarcely a private residence or a boarding house below Wall Street. . . . Ladies will hereafter scarcely extend their promenades farther down than the Park, and what will become of the Battery heaven only knows." "And," added no less a person than Charles Dickens, looking out from his hotel window in that same Broadway, "Heaven save the ladies, how they dress!"

But Mother Hardey was not given to lamenting "the good old days." She was that rare person, an unexcitable progressive. Hers was the attitude of mind reflected in the first telegraph message flashed from Washington to Baltimore in the spring of 1844: "What hath God wrought." If she did not at once avail herself of the first submarine cable put into service this was because it only reached to Staten Island. When it finally reached to Paris she used it freely. Before leaving New York she would be familiar with, even if she had no opportunity to use, elevators, elevated railways and subways.

If she saw signs of materialism in all this, she was aware of other tendencies becoming manifest in those same experimental years, though this required more perspicacity. The chief establishment which then claimed the ambiguous title of "Museum" was that owned by Phineas Barnum. Its wax work displays ran a whole gamut of subjects from the scientific to the sensational, and it boasted two platforms, one for a lecturer on any subject popularly desired, the other for a species of drama known as "The Moral Show." It was to take another decade for Museums of more genuinely aesthetic pretensions to appear, yet a movement towards the Fine Arts had begun. A Philharmonic Society was founded in 1842 and a gallery of Fine Arts two years later, while great singers of Italian opera could be heard in Castle Garden on the Battery, an historic fort transformed into a dazzling theatre with "a beautiful fountain in front of the stage, which plays when the players do not." Literature in New York was far in advance of her sister Arts, and when Charles Dickens visited the City in January, 1842, he was forced to admit, for all his badinage about the general cheapness of entertainment, that "New York has excellent literary institutions and libraries." So it was a good sign when New York went mad over Dickens himself, "that small, bright-eyed, intelligent-looking fellow," as he was called. It arranged a Boz Ball on a gigantic scale, "the tallest compliment ever paid to a little man," in which the characters of Dickens' novels appeared, considerably larger than life. New York could appreciate English writers and was becoming aware of her own contribution to the Commonwealth of Letters through her coterie of "Knickerbocker Authors." Washington Irving was appointed minister to Spain a few months after the Boz Ball; William Cullen Bryant's not yet venerable figure was seen daily going in and out of the Offices of the *Evening Post*, while the less reputable Edgar Allan Poe was haunting the Bronx, his eyes full of fear of his own stories.

Boston, then in its full literary flowering, was inclined to be jealous of New York on this score, but it allowed its rival to share in its best treasures when Emerson lectured there. The sage of Concord threw out a challenge in that spring of 1842. "It is," he said in his lecture upon The Poet, "a proof of the shallowness of the doctrine of beauty as it lies in the minds of our amateurs, that men seem to have lost the perception of the instant dependence of form upon soul."[6] This stressing of the word "soul" threw into focus the deeper elements of the forces then at work. Even a superficial observer, a traveller from abroad, remarked that in America "probably religious extremes are pushed farther than elsewhere."

It was religious hunger, veiled under Transcendentalism, that was driving the Boston intellectuals along the path that searches out truth. The years 1841 to 1847 in which Mother Hardey was feeling her way in New York were precisely those which measured the short life of Brook Farm,[7] where George Ripley and his fellow-idealists were attempting to plant an earthly paradise among the meadows of West Roxbury. Here philosophers raked hay, musicians taught school, and children worked and learned at the same time; here nature was looked in the face and religion sought behind her many veils; here such names as Dana, Dwight, Hawthorne, Bancroft, Fuller, were not only spoken in the library but called across the fields. Apart from Brook Farm but behind it as an inspiration stood Orestes Augustus Brownson,[8] to whom Ripley wrote: "If I had never known you I would never have engaged in this enterprise. I consider it the incarnation of those transcendental truths which we have held in common, and which you have done much to make me love." This man of challenging and astringent intellect, whose powerful thinking inspired the élite among thinkers, Parker, Emerson, Thoreau and Hawthorne, and whose appeal to the multitude aroused the many to think in their turn, whose very fearlessness made him feared and whose love for humanity made him loved, pursued truth unrevealed through partial and changing forms, until in October, 1844, he bent his massive head to pass under the doorway that led to Truth Revealed. Isaac Hecker, the future founder of the Paulist Fathers, the boy who had served as baker at Brook Farm where he had kept a volume of Kant propped open over his kneading board, had just entered that same door. It was the beginning of a succession of notable conversions, keeping time with the movement in England which brought Newman into the Church one year later.

All this may seem to have affected Mother Hardey only remotely, but her work lay in the educational world, a world sensitive to the impact of ideas as they work their way from mind to mind. The year following her arrival in New York had witnessed the climax of Bishop Hughes' dramatic controversy with the Public School Society over the question of teaching religion in non-sectarian schools. The battle resulted in a half-victory for the Bishop, and in a momentous development for the Church. The Public School Society went out of existence, but in its place rose the present system of State-controlled schools in which the Catholic position was still untenable. Parochial Schools supported by the faithful sprang up by the dozen to meet the need, and Mother Hardey, already looking for an opportunity to open a Free School in connection with her Academy, watched the development keenly. Another event equally significant for education took place more quietly. The Theological Seminary and Saint John's College at Rose Hill, Fordham, were in difficulties, while down in Kentucky Saint Mary's Jesuit College had collapsed outright.[9] Bishop Hughes brought success out of both failures by uniting them, and in August, 1846, the little band of Jesuits from the South, led by Father Thébaud and Father Murphy, toiled into Fordham under the weight of their own baggage. The Seminary soon moved elsewhere, and in a very few years Mother Hardey began to feel the force of the intellectual and spiritual power reaching out from Saint John's College as it grew to its full stature in Fordham University.

As though to emphasize the need of thorough education, another current of ideas was making itself felt in those years far more noisily than the current that led toward culture and conversion. Ancient bigotries arose in the 'forties and met the flood-tide of immigration that was sweeping into America from every country of Europe. In that decade two hundred thousand foreigners arrived annually, of whom as many as eighty thousand disembarked at New York in one summer. They crossed the sea in fearfully overcrowded ships where conditions were such that large numbers of them landed already victims of disease and semi-starvation. They were poor to begin with, and so shamefully were they exploited in the city-ports that few ever reached the farmlands that were crying out for them beyond the cities. Labouring, economic and social conditions were altered by this influx, but the status of the Catholic Church was affected even more radically. Over half of the newcomers were her children. In Boston the number of Catholics, which had been two thousand in 1820, rose to forty thousand in 1850. Priests did not multiply in proportion, with the result that:

> The problem of the Church was with the immigrants, and the obsessing work of the clergy was for them. Merely to house them under some kind of a roof where they could hear Mass of Sundays was a task which made other tasks a distraction. And then there were the schools to build, and the hospitals, and the orphanages, all without money. . . . Even the Bishops disappeared in the Deluge; from any national gaze drowned. . . . There were only two Bishops who were widely known in the United States in the days of the Deluge, in its first flood. And one of them was known because he stood outside of it; he was Bishop England of Charlestown, in which city there arrived no immigration: the other was

Bishop Hughes of New York, and he was known because the flood at New York was so prodigious that it made him known.[10]

By an illogical twist of ideas, all that was most bitter in the antagonism of the more ignorant of the American people towards the immigrants became centered upon their Catholicity. Anti-foreign feeling became the rallying point for all the old fanaticisms and hatreds, and so it came about that the Nuns on Houston Street found that they had reason for serious alarm when, in the spring of 1844, the Native American Party broke out into violent demonstrations. Friends began calling upon Mother Hardey to warn her that the situation of the Convent, so close to the Bishop's house and to the Cathedral, placed her in great danger. She listened, took other advice, and waited. She could not forget the outrage of the burning of the Ursuline Convent in Charleston, Massachusetts, only ten years before, and she knew that the poison of an almost incredible bigotry against Nuns had been injected into the veins of the body politic by the publication of the *Awful Disclosures* of Maria Monk. In May came news from Philadelphia to confirm her worst fears, and she wrote immediately to Mother Barat:

I would have sent you the enclosed notes the first days of the month if it had not been for the frightful events which have just taken place in Philadelphia, and which there is reason to fear may be repeated here. I refer to almost general attack upon Catholics and the destruction of churches. The "glorious days" of 1830 saw nothing comparable to the excesses from the sixth to the ninth of May, 1844. All the churches are closed, or rather they serve as barracks for the soldiers, for the city is under martial law. Oh, how Our Lord is insulted, offended, and that during this beautiful month which the Philadelphians celebrate with such solemnity! But it is believed that, in general, great good will result for the cause of religion. The papers, even Protestant ones, which rarely publish facts favourable to Catholicism, relate that upon the only wall still standing of the beautiful church of the Augustinians, the oldest in Philadelphia, the inscription "God sees me" over the high altar has remained intact in spite of every effort to efface it. The fact is all the more remarkable because the flames which completely blackened the wall spared that inscription the golden letters of which stand out more brilliantly than before.

Since the tenth, peace has been re-established, but the fears are now for our own city. Several parents have taken away their children, others have left them here for greater safety. We are all ready, even during the night, to leave the house in case of attack, but things have not reached that point. There is really nothing yet except the greatest excitement. The feeling is that we are only in danger on account of our proximity to the Cathedral and to the Bishop's house. I must admit, Venerated Mother, that I have not had a moment of fear. It seems to me that Our Lord will keep us safe, since we are keeping Him, and during these nights I have not been in the least afraid of death. How is that? I fear that it may be through indifference, for I am hardly prepared to die.

One cause of Mother Hardey's confidence was her knowledge of the character of Bishop Hughes. Not for nothing was he both an Irish immigrant himself and a whole-hearted, enlightened American. An extra issue of the *Freeman's Journal*, the paper which represented the Bishop's interests, appeared with a clear statement of his program: "If it should be part of Native Americanism to attack their houses or churches, then it behooves them, in case all other protection fail, to defend both with their lives. In this they will not be acting against the law but for the law." Mother Hardey, keeping vigil in Houston Street that night, heard the determined tramp of feet passing her door as two thousand of the foremost Catholics of the City gathered fully armed to guard the doors of the Cathedral one block away. The frightened Mayor, who had been told his duty by the Bishop, ordered out squadrons of mounted police on his own account, and the rioters no longer dared so much as to hold a procession. Soon all danger of violence had melted away, while the Bishop fired a last verbal shot which echoed through all the newspapers of the land, aimed not at the noisy church-burning rabble but at the men in high places whose perversion of facts had twisted the minds of the people: "Now therefore, ye deceivers of the public, stand forth and meet Bishop Hughes. But then come forth in no quibbling capacity—come forth as honest men, as true American citizens."

While Mother Hardey was gaining experimental knowledge of her surroundings, events at the Mother House had been working towards a redoublement of strength and of harmony in the work of the Society. Early in 1843 a letter from Mother Barat told her that the long controversy concerning the Constitutions had been settled at Rome. She wrote:

> And now we are all at one. Thank Our Lord for this and redouble your zeal, my daughter, to consolidate in your house that divine charity which reigns in the Sacred Heart in all its purity and to its fullest extent.

In another letter she said:

> Be prepared to arrange things as they were before 1839, but since Mother Galitzin is coming to you with that very end in view, wait for her before making any changes. I beg you to let me know everything that you hear, and if there is any opposition. I do not believe that there will be; I count enough on your good spirit and your attachment to the Society to defend the measures adopted, as well as the actions of your Mother who has suffered so much to prevent the destruction of our work.
>
> I cannot urge you too strongly, my daughter, to keep the fruit of your retreat made in 1842, and to work every day to gain more interior spirit, to become more humble. It is a matter of experience for me, dear Aloysia, that we can only bring to fruit our work for souls if the instrument is united to the source of grace; now, a dissipated soul and a proud heart are precisely the obstacles most

opposed to the reign of the Holy Ghost, and we shall never become interior if these faults reign in us. I do not say that they dominate, since we do not will them, but sometimes we are negligent in tearing them up from the roots. At least, let us work for this with all our will-power; so, let there be unremitting fidelity and constant generosity in walking in the way which leads to religious perfection. It is only souls who are dead to everything who can do good in the country where you live.

So in July, 1843, Mother Galitzin returned to the house that she had opened. Her face was worn by recent illness and still more by the moral storms which had lately passed over her, yet Mother Hardey could read a new and steadying peace in her expression. Mother Galitzin had herself offered to come back to America to undo the work of her former visit by re-establishing the Constitutions of 1826. Hers was a mind that moved in a straight line, a line so straight that it could not always allow for the inevitable curving of events, or for the broadening out of a principle into its practical applications. Her will was equally straight, with the same quality of unrelentingness.

As though she felt the flight of time, the Mother Provincial hastened her business, but before leaving for Missouri she devoted a full day to the children of Houston Street, who played *câche-câche*, picknicked in the somewhat restricted forests of the back yard, then came to sit in tight circles around Mother Galitzin who was an unrivalled story-teller. Within the Community she did her best to make herself the spokesman of Mother Barat with more truth than she had ever done before. To Mother Hardey she confided a dream which had come to her the year before at Lyons. She had seen in it three coffins side by side; in one lay the body of her eldest brother, in the second that of her mother, in the third her own. Two-thirds of the dream, she added, had already come true. Mother Hardey was impressed, but not to the point of doubting that she would see Mother Galitzin again when the latter said goodbye and left for Saint Louis on September 21st.

Three months later she heard that the third coffin had been filled. The letter that brought the news came from Saint Michael's, and Mother Hardey had only to close her eyes to picture vividly all that had happened. It seems that in Saint Louis Mother Galitzin had no longer been able to conceal the fever that was eating away her strength. The Nuns, in their anxiety, had hastened her departure into the milder winter of the south. They did not know that the more terrible yellow fever had broken out at Saint Michael's. She arrived there on November 14th, and in the midst of the holiday in her honour a little girl died suddenly and was buried at night for fear of general alarm. Mother Galitzin refused to let the shadow fall over her. Gathering all her strength she spent it in creating a glow of love and peace that held the house in its charm. She gave extra recreations, she visited the new building that was rising rapidly now according to the plan that Mother Hardey had made for it. She made the children sing to her, and over and over again yielded to their demand for more stories. No one could prevent her from visiting the Nuns who were ill. All that was gentlest and most lovable in her nature shone through those last days before the yellow fever claimed her on December 6th. Strong-willed to the last, she held death at arm's length, putting off even Holy Communion which she wished to receive as Viaticum on the great day of the Immaculate Conception. But by midnight on the Vigil it was too late, and the Feast brought her to her eternal Communion. A hard struggle closed that life of high purpose, and God ratified in suffering her act of self-oblation. Only after death did her expression of agony change to one of peace so winning that even the children refused to go away for their enforced vacation until they had walked beside Mother Galitzin to her resting place under the mossy trees of Saint Michael's.

Mother Hardey's grief was entirely self-forgetful as she tried to console Mother Barat, who was ill at the time, for the loss of the Mother Provincial of America. While she was writing, another letter had already reached Paris. Far away in Saint Charles Mother Duchesne, wrapped in the humble obscurity of her last years during which she took no part in the affairs of Government, had not been able to refrain from telling Mother Barat her thoughts on the subject of the next Mother Provincial. "Both within the Society and without it," she had written, "a Provincial who is herself an American, and of a representative family, will be more favourably received than any other. If I were consulted, Mother Hardey would be my choice." Mother Barat's thoughts were the same, and so it was by the appointment of two Saints that Mother Hardey found herself, in the spring of 1844, named Provincial of the American Houses along the Eastern seaboard, while Mother Cutts assumed charge of those in the Mississippi Valley. She wrote at once: "How your letter of last March has crushed and distressed me! I do not even know how to govern this little family; every day I tremble at the thought of the account that I must render to God, and now you are adding to my obligations. O my Venerated Mother, what will become of me!" Mother Barat did not trouble to answer this query, being of the same opinion as the former Provincial who had said of Mother Hardey, in untranslatable idiom: "c'est une tête comme il y en a peu."

As though this nomination had forced upon her the realization that a more spacious house in or near New York had become a necessity, Mother Hardey agreed to Bishop Hughes' proposal that she should move the Convent into the country as soon as possible. She wrote to Mother Barat:

His Lordship says that it is an absolute necessity for us to move to the country this year, but we cannot raise the money as we have no property. He desires me to say that if you could borrow the money in Belgium we could pay the interest and return the principal later. We cannot do more than vegetate here as long as we have to pay an annual rent of $2,600. Besides, the health of the Religious suffers greatly in the summer, and the school diminishes one-fourth from the first of May until the first of October.

As soon as a favourable reply reached her the work of house-hunting began, Mother Hardey had a very direct and literal way of subordinating human activity to prayer in such cases, and now she began a Novena. By the ninth day property had been found and acquired. The Novena was made to Saint Francis Regis, for her memory went back to Mother Duchesne who had entrusted the American foundations to the Saint of Louvesc from the beginning. In the economy of the Communion of Saints grace is linked to grace in a chain the strength of which lies in its continuity, and Saint Francis Regis, that indefatigable self-spender, hunter of souls, and lover of children, fulfilled his trust. Mother Hardey acknowledged her indebtedness by placing the new foundation under his patronage. The fact that the Convent on Houston Street was not closed but remained open as a City House explains why the patronal title of Our Lady of Sorrows was not then transferred to Ravenswood.

The new house lay beyond the East River. The village of Astoria was most romantically situated on Hell-Gate, and looked out upon a cluster of beautiful islands where farmland and forest still strove peaceably together. Wards and Randall's Islands had not then been subdued by steel and masonry into footstools for the Triborough Bridge, but the City had lately placed its sooty finger upon them in the shape of Potter's Fields and Almhouses. Time was when Hell-Gate deserved the name to which popular use has corrupted the original Dutch *Hellegat*, meaning "beautiful pass." In 1678 it was seen by the Reverend Master Woolley who wrote in his Journal: "In this Hell Gate, which is a narrow passage, runneth a rapid, violent stream, both upon flood and ebb; and in the middle lieth some islands of rocks upon which the current sets so violently that it threatens present shipwreck; and upon the flood is a large whirlpool which sends forth a continuous, hideous roaring." But the very swiftness of the current wore the rocks away to relative calmness, with some help from engineers, and by 1844 the waters, still swift but tractable, mirrored the gigantic cottonwood trees that were the boast of every fine estate along both shores, while a snug little ferry skimmed them at the northern tip of Blackwell's Island.

The newcomers wrote:

> Upon arriving in the country all were delighted with the beauty of our new dwelling. There reigns here a silence which draws us to God, while nothing could be prettier than our situation. The house is surrounded by greenery of all sorts, and through the great trees we catch sight of the river which gives a delightful freshness to the house.

Ravenswood had originally been know as the Delafield Mansion. A local historian wrote of it:

> There existed but few of those costly mansions that now adorn the township, and particularly the northern and western borders of it, the result chiefly of the taste and enterprise of New York merchants. One of the first if not the very first, of these erected in the vicinity of Hell-Gate was that built in 1792 by Mr. John Delafield, a distinguished merchant of New York. . . . This building was fashioned after the English style.[11]

A few years after its erection the house had been visited by Eliza Browne from New England, who included it among the delights of her stay in New York. She was leading a happy dilettante life just then, and the Delafield House, with its tall portico of peerless colonial style, its wide chimneys and air of easy grace, fitted into the picture of her vacation days, of which she wrote home:

> Whenever we have nothing particular in view, in the cool of the evening, we walk down to the Battery, go into the garden, sit half an hour, eat ice cream, see a variety of people, and return home happy and refreshed. Sunday we dined at Mr. Delafield's near Hell Gate, Long Island, the most superb, magnificent place I ever saw, situated directly on the East River, the finest view you can imagine. I was delighted with our visit, so much ease, elegance and hospitality.[12]

The village had once been called Hallet's Cove, but was renamed Astoria at the time of its incorporation in 1839 in honour of the fur magnate. The summer-home of John Jacob Astor, now a fabulously rich and very old man, lay just across the river from the Delafield House. The name made him dream of the first Astoria, his trading-post in the far Northwest that might have given him the monopoly of the world's fur trade in 1812 but for war and the treachery of friends. Washington Irving wrote his book *Astoria* in this peaceful country seat, looking out at Hell Gate of which he said that at half-tide the current roared "like a bull bellowing for more drink" and at full tide "slept as soundly as an alderman after dinner." Irving had just returned from Spain in the year in which Mother Hardey took possession of Ravenswood, and she may have seen him going in and out of his friend's house, the first writer to believe that America was old enough to have her traditions reflected in the mellow glow of his literary art.

By the time the cottonwoods were hinting of autumn's coming, the Delafield Mansion was being changed by hard work into a Convent:

We pass our time in the joy of the Lord, and very usefully. We are hurrying to prepare the rooms for the return of the children. Our time is divided between our spiritual exercises and domestic work, such as cleaning, sweeping, sewing carpets. We are only too happy to spare Reverend Mother some expense, and by this means to expiate our faults against holy poverty. Our furniture has not yet arrived, and the arrangements in our refectory please us greatly. Two large doors serve for tables, and we have three cups for the breakfast of twenty people.

If news that Nuns were in the neighbourhood made its way but slowly among the mansions, it spread like wild-fire through the village. The Irish families who formed the Parish of the Blessed Virgin of Mount Carmel thought of a way of showing their pleasure. While the moon shone bright and the Nuns were at their night prayers, the neighbours crept up to the colonnaded porch and sang serenades. On Sunday their Pastor, eager to accommodate all parties, brought his entire flock to the Convent where he was to say his one Mass. As the chapel was quite unequal to this emergency the altar was moved out onto the gallery where tall pillars framed it reverently during Mass. When all was over it was discovered that some water waiting for use in a corner had been carried away, under the impression that all water from a Convent must be holy water.

The children arrived in installments until finally all the boarders were settled at Ravenswood, leaving the day-students only at Houston Street where a part of the Community remained with them. The space gained allowed Mother Hardey to fulfil her long desire; she opened a Free School in the empty rooms at Houston Street. Better accommodations never meant less work where she was concerned. She was Superior of both establishments simultaneously, which required something very like the gift of bi-location on her part. On great Feast Days the two Communities were reunited for a brief vacation, and there was constant journeying between the two houses. In April of the following year the City House was moved to 114 Bleecker Street.

The Bishop counted upon Ravenswood becoming the leading Academy for Young Ladies in his Diocese, and advertised it vigorously. It was the apple of his eye. He frequently urged upon Mother Hardey the necessity of keeping pace with progress in this most progressive of American cities, and always found her willing to consider his suggestions. On the other hand, he had the utmost respect for her judgment, and still more for the Rules and traditions of the Society that she represented, and he made it a matter of pride to be able to say that he had never urged Mother Hardey to change one of her Rules. Yet he did urge her to adapt her customs, and she complied. From the beginning she had allowed a monthly outing to the pupils, and had given greater liberty in the matter of visits from their families than she had done at Saint Michael's. Such innovations, when proposed in Missouri, had shocked and alarmed Mother Duchesne, and it was well that it had been so. Had Mother Duchesne not been rigid in the maintenance of the least thing that made for unity, had hers not been the ungrateful task of laying the ground plan according to the primary pattern, it would not have been safe for Mother Hardey to raise the walls in whatever style expediency required. But Mother Duchesne had stood firm, and now unity was not lost in expansion. Mother Barat gave her consent to Mother Hardey's modifications, and the Bishop expressed his satisfaction.

Yet Mother Hardey could be exceedingly firm, even drastic. At the price of doubling the work of her teaching staff she had divided the classes of the boarders from those of the day-students at Houston Street when she saw signs that the mingling was not good for the spirit of discipline. At Astoria, when she noticed after the first Christmas vacation (which began incidentally on December 26th) that a cooling of fervour had resulted from those two weeks of rather strenuous urban pleasures, she refused to give further mid-year vacations for a considerable time. She had reason for her fears. A few old pupils, who had been at school for too short a time to be won over to its spirit, had thrown discretion to the winds in their social conduct, which started a chain of criticisms of the Convent. These soon turned into calumnies which found their way to Paris. Mother Barat did not blame Mother Hardey, but she knew that the roots of such troubles lie very deep and she went straight from accidentals to essentials when she wrote:

I was obliged, in my last letter, to tell you of the remarks that I have heard about you. I hope that you will have the good sense to know that I am guided by the deep concern that I feel for you and for your religious family. Your house, on account of its position, should take first rank, and be a model to the others, at least in what regards the pupils, in all that is solid, deep, essential. What are learning and the arts in comparison with the solid virtues which we must teach our pupils? Only so much sand, dust which the wind carried away. Apart from the greatest of all considerations, the unique, the sole interest—that of the salvation of souls—even the most superficial people will always prefer a modest, industrious woman, attentive to her duty, before some dazzling creature who only cares for pleasures and vanity. You must give yourself neither peace nor rest until you have made of all your Mistresses models of good spirit, that is, real Religious.

Mother Hardey took the full blame for whatever had been amiss and when a further and more reassuring letter reached her she wrote in reply:

Your kind letter awaited me at the close of my retreat, during which I had made the sacrifice of your esteem and confidence, as your last two letters had caused me to believe that I had forfeited both. You may then have some idea of my joy and gratitude on learning that you approve of all that I have done for the welfare of the souls confided to my care.

One very significant point had been under discussion in all this. It was the question of introducing higher branches of study than had been habitually included in the curriculum. Here too Mother Hardey was able to show to Mother Barat's complete satisfaction, not only that such studies were a real advantage both to the school and to its students, but that they were an unfolding of the Plan of Studies rather than an addition to it. Unhappily the letters discussing this point are no longer extant. It would be interesting to know more of the exact manner in which Mother Hardey made herself the prophet of the Liberal Arts College which would one day develop out of the school which owed its scholastic standing to her wisdom.

So she continued unperturbed. No matter what might be going on, the children of Astoria were a joy to her. She was in and out among them as much as her time would allow, and perhaps more, by force of circumstances. The house was very small, and Mother Hardey decided that the simplest way of saving space was for the Superior to do without a room of her own. In this she got her way, for a time. She put a little desk in one corner of the children's dormitory, and while they were busy elsewhere she sat quietly at her work. When they reappeared she slipped to some other temporarily empty corner, carrying her papers about with her in an unfashionable handbag. The children were accustomed to meeting her anywhere, and possibly the more perspicacious—or to put it less euphemistically, the more mischevious—had discovered that her bed was a cot kept in a class-room cupboard during the day.

There were orchards on the grounds, and one day in late autumn the children playing there spied a red apple left alone at the top of a tree. They shook the branches, they threw things at it, they prayed aloud. Twilight came with the end of recreation hour and the children went regretfully indoors, but their spirit was up. The apple was a challenge and back they came the next day to the assault. It still defied them. While they were staring hopelessly at it one small child suddenly knelt down and closed her eyes, praying once more, irresistibly, to Saint Francis Regis. With a plump the apple dropped to the ground before her. A shout of triumph greeted its fall and the little girl ran with it to the Mistress in charge of the recreation. "But why," asked the latter, "did Saint Francis not hear your prayers yesterday?" "Oh," said the child, "it is only just now that I really prayed to him in my heart." Mother Hardey laid up the story in her own heart with a prayer of thankfulness. It was not the first time that a great truth had been learned from the fall of an apple. Many of her Religious in the years to come were to hear the incident at a moment when they needed to, and while the lesson sank in they would hear Mother Hardey adding gently, "It is only the prayer of the heart that reaches heaven," as she remembered a red apple tumbling from a blue October sky in Astoria.

Interesting as the children were, Mother Hardey had a more absorbing care in the Novices. There was a relatively large number of them now, for the Novitiate which Mother Galitzin had transferred from Florissant to Conewago in 1841 had recently been brought to New York. Although Mother Hardey was willing to lead a camping life herself she would not permit the Novices to do so, and assured privacy and silence by adding a plain wooden wing to the handsome but too small house. This was their Nazareth, and at its inauguration Mother Hardey, remembering of what it was made, placed it under the protection of Saint Michael. The Archangel accepted his charge. A short time later a candle left burning in an empty room set fire to the curtains. The flames towered up and then sank back and died, leaving not so much as a mark of smoke on the flimsy wooden walls. Here, after two years' delay caused by illness, Sarah Jones took her place among the white veils on January 2, 1846, responding to the full to the training she received, which was faithfully based upon letters such as this from Mother Barat:

> I beg my dear Mother Aloysia to found the Novices upon solid virtues; we cannot anchor them too deeply in the practice of humility, of mortification, of self-forgetfulness, of abnegation. If these virtues are not familiar to them, we are working in vain; we shall gain but little fruit, souls will suffer for it, as will the work of God. Believe me that it is better to be few in number and better religious; imperfect Professed do more harm than good. Is this not your experience? . . . So, work with all your might, my Daughter, in forming your young people to the love of Jesus Christ, to the practice of solid virtues, especially of humility. Remember your retreat as Les Anglais, and try to form that type of perfection in the hearts of others. Everything else is, as an old proverb says, nothing but whipped cream which has no substance and which does not last.

Mother Barat knew that a craving for the interior life, strong and straight, was growing upon Mother Hardey with increasing force. The longing expressed itself in the way in which she sought and put first those aspects of her work which had a directly spiritual bearing. At Astoria, for instance, as at Houston Street, she claimed for herself the privilege of preparing the First Communicants for their day of meeting with the Lord. Once during their preparatory retreat, with the favoured children sitting quietly about her, she asked one of them to read aloud the Gospel of the Passion. The child did so, and when she had finished closed the book and looked up. There was a very long silence. "Reverend Mother," said the reader timidly, "that is all." Mother Hardey came to herself with a visible effort. "Read it again, my child," she said gently, "I could listen to the story of the Passion all my life." The reading began again, this time in a tone of awe. Many years before, when a child herself, Mother Hardey had become aware of the Presence of God through the words and manner of a Religious, and now another child became aware of it through Mother Hardey. When this child in her turn became a Religious she admitted that her insight into the spiritual life had begun when she heard Mother Hardey say, "I could listen to the story of the Passion all my life."

Idyllic as the life at Astoria appeared, its isolation brought difficulties of which the most serious was continual deprivation of Mass, for the Parishes of Brooklyn were on a missionary footing. The devotedness of Bishop McCloskey, the newly appointed coadjutor who came himself whenever possible, could not supply for all their spiritual needs. There were other drawbacks as well, and it soon became evident that this could not be the Convent's permanent home. In many ways the four years passed at Ravenswood had been trying and lonely ones, bringing grief through the death of several young nuns, and a personal sorrow in the loss of Mother Hardey's mother in distant Opelousas.

Then on April 21, 1846, Mother Hardey's problems, "which are troubling me singularly" she confessed, were considerably lightened, for Bishop Hughes broke in upon her like a ray of energetic sunshine. He had that very morning landed after a trip to Europe, and could not wait till he had seen Mother Hardey. He wanted to tell her of his visit with Mother Barat, at which he had had the satisfaction of hearing that the Superior General was very pleased with the school at Astoria. Best of all, he was the bearer of her sanction for transferring that school elsewhere, and he handed Mother Hardey a letter which confirmed his words. Being both a kindly and a somewhat impatient man, he no doubt made her read the letter on the spot, while he looked modestly out the window. It ran:

Your venerated Bishop has kindly offered to take all our commission and to be the bearer of this letter, which must be brief as I leave to my secretary to reply to your business questions, and I count upon Monseigneur to make known to you the result of our conversations respecting your house.

They were consoling to me, for we agreed upon every point. His Lordship has remarkably sound judgment and foresight, as well as a thorough knowledge of business affairs. How happy I should be to have such a guide! This good Prelate will provide with truly fatherly interest for all your spiritual and temporal wants. We have agreed upon the necessity of changing your present abode, and we have decided to borrow the funds requisite for purchasing a desirable location at 4% instead of 7%, which you have to pay in the United States. We shall await the purchase of the property before raising the money . . .

With so much labour and solicitude, dear daughter, it is essential that you keep your soul in peace and in fidelity to God. Be dependent then upon His Holy Spirit, by the practice of generosity in sacrificing your own inclinations and in restraining natural activity. A Superior should be, as far as possible, a living rule to all her subjects. Be faithful, my Daughter, to all these recommendations, and Jesus will bless your efforts and you will thereby procure His glory by your personal holiness as well as by your works.

When Mother Hardey looked up from reading her letter, the Bishop was pointing in a north-westerly direction. Over there, he said, was the ideal place. He was bent on acquiring the Lorillard estate, near the village of Manhattanville, for a Convent of the Sacred Heart.

XII

STRIKING ROOT

ACROSS THE RIVER to the north-east of Astoria, where Manhattan Island began to narrow above Hell Gate, lay Harlem. It is a safe guess that there are few places, if any, on the whole face of the globe that have changed more startlingly in the course of their history than has Harlem. This small area, scarcely one and a half square miles, has been called "the spiritual capital of Black America."[1] A quarter of a million negroes live uneasily within its narrow limits. The poorest of the poor among them swarm in and out of crowded tenements, fighting a seemingly hopeless battle in which their native singing laughter may well be silenced sometimes in bitterness. The educated among them, the doctors, lawyers, artists and thinkers, bring the weapons of intelligence and hope to bear in that battle. Within a few blocks are thrown together all the incongruous elements of life-on-the-defensive; there are glaring, exotic places of pleasure near the grimed places of humble effort at uplift; there are gilded stores and ambulant lunch-stands; there is an Art Center not far from the pathetic stump of the "Tree of Hope." There are far too few churches.

Many dubious prophecies for the future are made by those who thread these streets where African mystery is blended with the starkest American realism, but few thoughts turn backward in time. The experiment is worth making. Here are these same streets in the 'nineties. There is not a black face in sight, for it was only after the turn of the century that a depression in real estate resulted in an influx of negroes. The brownstone homes, the aristocratic apartment houses, are widely spaced, and like to have shade-trees around them. An elevated railroad has recently turned the place into a fashionable suburb, proud of its Opera House, its fine trotting horses. But beyond all this in time is the rural Harlem, the small town of the eighteen thirties, with its trout streams and its farm houses. The shadow of the approaching city has barely fallen over in the form of a paved street or two.

Yet more lies behind, and as the blur of our rapid flight back through the mists of some two and a half centuries clears away, we find ourselves standing on a tidy, well-beaten road in a flood of sunshine. It is the height of the spring in the year 1711, May 19th to be exact.[2] The morning is a momentous one, for a meeting of certain favoured freeholders of the Village of Harlem is to be held in the Town House. The sound of the Dutch tongue is in our ears. Prompt and alert, but not in any particular hurry, the citizens emerge one by one from their comfortable houses on Church Lane, one-story stone or wooden houses whose steep-pitched gable roofs have but lately changed their thatch for shingles, houses that nestle each in its bower of fruit trees. Other citizens come rumbling in by the cart-load from outlying farms. All are making their way to the plot of land near the Church where the Town House stands with the Harlem River behind it, a bright, curving stream pleasant to see and to hear.

The town too was a pleasant sight in colonial days, this Harlem, or *Nieuw Haarlem* of the Netherlands of the Western World. Its life centered in some forty homes, and its time was given to cultivating the rich flat lands that encircled it. At the foot of its one street, between its one church and its one tavern, a single ferry-boat toiled to and fro over the river to Bronck's Land and back. To the north field after field, each ending in a plot of good salt hay at the water's edge, fringed the bank all the way to Spuyten Duyvil Creek where a rival ferry ran, not far from the village of Fordham on the Bronck's Land side. Jan Arcer had there "at his own charge and with good success begun a township, at a convenient place for the relief of strangers." There was a good wagon road to New York, still secretly called New Amsterdam, built somewhat under compulsion by the men of Harlem in payment of their debts to the English. Here and there the charred remains of a stockade showed that Harlem had more than once fought sturdily for its life against Indian attack. When the Netherland spirit of liberty was left to itself, life was peaceful enough; young men might be arrested now and then for transporting a boatload of hay on Sunday, or the good beer sold in Verveelan's Tavern might incite a brawl, but otherwise homes and crops and flowers were what counted. As for the Church, it maintained a high standard of godliness. Some of its members even went beyond the standard, as did Good Wife Marie Cresson who "having had a remarkable experience of a light shining upon her" was told that she should not go to Church any longer, being too holy. She continued to go, being also humble.

The names and faces of the citizens showed that they were not all of pure Dutch descent. In Europe, the religious wars of the sixteenth century had sent many French Huguenots, including Walloons and Picards, to seek refuge in the polyglot Netherlands. Here they had intermarried with the Dutch and united with them in a common resistance to French Prelates and Spanish soldiers. Across the uneven tenor of their lives came word of Hendrick Hudson and of what he had seen sailing in his ship, the *Half Moon*, up a mighty river in the newest part of the New World. In 1625 Johannes de Laet, Professor and Geographer of the University of Leyden, published from the original manuscript Journals a full and thrilling account of the voyages of Hudson, and of the establishment by the West Indian Company of a trading post called New Amsterdam on the southern tip of the Island of Manahatta. This book, *The New World*, was enough for the Huguenots and their Dutch friends.

On October 1, 1836, Henry de Forest and Jean de la Montagne set sail with their patriarchal followings. Once on new soil they refused to be cramped within the palisades of a town, and obtained from Director Van Twiller a grant of the Muscoota, or Flat Lands, lying to the north-east of New Amsterdam. They called their first farm Vredendal, or Vale of Quiet, and it became the nucleus of the town which twenty years later was ready to receive from the Dutch authorities its charter and its name of Nieuw Haarlem. Old Peter Stuyvesant befriended it. Each family that came staked out generous claims for itself, the Dyckmans, the Van Cortlandts, the Brevoorts, and many of French descent.

Thus the faces of the citizens gathered in the Town House on that 19th day of May, 1711, showed history in the making. The occasion was an important one; a statement was drawn up agreeing that the generous stretches of Common Lands lying to the west and north of the cultivated fields should be surveyed, divided, and given out by lot to deserving landowners. One by one the members of the Commission approached the table of the Magistrates, took the quill in their firm fingers, and signed the statement: Jan Nagel, Abraham Gouverneur, Jan Dyckman, Samuel Waldron, Peter Oblienis, and one woman, Maria Myer.

The signatories went home well pleased. Peter Oblienis had but a step to go; his house was among the more important residences on Church Lane, the house of an aristocrat though its floor was sanded and the household cooking was done at a blazing central hearth open on three sides. Peter was a weaver and the owner of enormous if scattered stretches of land. The special reason for his satisfaction this morning was the fact that he had just acquired one hundred acres more. The agreement concerning the Common Lands had stipulated that some should be sold in advance to pay for the cost of surveyors and lawyers. He, Peter, had bought them. As he stopped before the invitingly open half-door of his home his eyes turned to the west of Harlem where Jockum Pieter's Hills, a rocky ridge that formed the backbone of Manhattan Island, stretched north. Opposite his gaze was a low pass through the ridge where four little streams rose to meander in a string of pools through his new property just beyond, a beautiful oval of uneven meadowland reaching down to a cove in the Hudson River.

Peter went into his house and was soon blinking with satisfaction over his pipe. He was pleased with his Hundred Acres, though unaware that they were the site of the future village of Manhattanville. He was equally unaware that in acquiring them he had become the owner of the favoured spot where Hendrick Hudson anchored the Half Moon on his first journey up the Great River of the Mountains, through "as pleasant a land as one need tread upon." Hudson had entered New York Harbour on September 3, 1609, and progressed slowly inward until on the 13th—so runs the log-book kept by his Mate, Robert Juet—"having fair weather, the wind northerly, at seven o'clock in the morning, as the flood came, we weighed and turned four miles into the river; the tide being done, we anchored. Then there came four canoes aboard, but we suffered none of them to come into our ship."[3] The spot where he anchored, historians assure us,[4] was Manhattanville Cove which again, on their way down the River, offered them shelter: "We anchored in a day clear of all danger of them [the Indians] on the other side of the river, where we saw a very good piece of ground, and hard by it there was a cliff . . . It is on that side of the river that is called Manhatta."

But the squared sails of the *Half Moon* did not overshadow Peter's mental picture of his cove as Maria Myer passed his door on the way to her own house just a step beyond. She was a commanding figure, with her silk *samare* or jacket flaring out over her many-layered petticoats, and her beribboned hair coiled over her ears, the widow of Adolf Myer, *schepen* and inspector of chimneys, who had died recently, leaving his will "to his grandsons named for him each a pair of gold buttons, and to his grand-daughters named for his wife each a gold ring."

The next spring the solemn drawing by lot took place and "to Maria Myer and her son Johannes" fell Lot 15 in Division 1. It was an odd lot, a quite irregular one which had no opening on the Hudson, too rocky for farming and rather high for the placid Dutch cattle to take to for grazing. It crowned a rocky ledge in Jockum Pieter's Hill and sloped towards the Hollow Way where the four streams collected in Oblienis' Hundred Acres. It touched his property along one boundary beginning at "a certain chestnut tree, marked and standing on the northwest side of the road." Maria Myer continued to live comfortably on the flats till her death at the age of ninety-two, but Johannes built a farm-house on the very top of Lot 15, where a copper tower would one day rise.

As the eighteenth century gained momentum the character of these country estates changed little. In 1743 Peter

Oblienis died, and in his will left "to his beloved brother Hendrick one British shilling, and his whole estate otherwise to his nephew, Peter Waldron." But the Hundred Acres could not lie forever unbroken by fences. It became divided into small holdings as the years passed, until, in the year 1776, a Jacob Myer owned Lot 15, and a David Waldron the part of the Hundred Acres that touched it. These two peace-loving Dutch farmers were suddenly disturbed when in the autumn of that mighty year the vales and heights of the Hollow Way became the scene of war. The signing of the Declaration of Independence in July may not have meant much to them, but matters were different when, on the twelfth of September, the harassed face of George Washington, Commander-in-Chief of the Rebel Army, was seen for a moment as he galloped straight across the Myer Farm. The family no doubt took refuge in the cellar, for there was no place to which they could flee. Following Washington came more horses, then a stream of wagons full of provisions, then files of discouraged soldiers. They had crossed the Harlem River in full retreat after the Battle of Long Island. The General made his headquarters a short distance beyond Lot 15 in a house belonging to Colonel Morris, now known as the Jumel Mansion at 161st Street. His army camped all along the rocky ridge, and the next day there could not have been much fruit left in the Myer and Waldron orchards, or food in their thrifty storehouses.

Sunday the fifteenth was disastrous. The British landed at Kip's Bay on the East River, and through the cowardice and jealousy of certain Continental troops the City of New York fell into their hands. Confusion, terror and burning filled the island, while on Harlem Heights the Americans "spent the night covered only by the clouds of an uncomfortable sky." Before dawn that sky grew red with the burning of the Fire-brig just off the Cove on the Hudson, while Washington stayed up all night writing dignified but desperate letters to Congress.

There were several small boys on the Myer Farm, and small boys do not run away in such crises. We shall get a good view of the Battle of Harlem Heights[5] if we climb with one of them, let us say Peter, the youngest, to the top of a hypothetical tree at the southern edge of the property. Peter sees Washington ride by at dawn, wearing his big blue cloak. The General took his stand at the Point of Rocks, the last spur of the ridge, today submerged among the houses at 126th Street, near Convent Avenue. Below him lay the Hollow Way (125th Street) and opposite rose Bloomingdale Heights (where Columbia College now stands). Up the Bloomingdale Road and through the woods on a wide front, reaching from the Heights to the Hudson, crept the British. Peter saw the scarlet flash of their coats as they blew their bugles insolently. There were skirmishes, feints, scattered attacks. The Rangers, a volunteer regiment from New England, bore the brunt of it all; and the two noble Colonels, Knowlton and Leitch, paid the price of victory with their lives before the eyes of their grieved Commander-in-Chief. Little by little the British were driven back until Peter saw them disappear from view beyond a buckwheat field on the Van der Water Farm (110th Street.) To pursue them further would have been folly, and Washington blew the signal for retreat. His men "gave a hurra and left the field in good order." As they filed up the Heights again Peter saw the gleam of triumph on their weary faces. One would like to think that some at least of the valiant Rangers were fed and warmly housed that night in the Farm on Lot 15; but perhaps, if they were not offered hospitality, they took it. Washington fell asleep knowing that victory would now come, for, as he wrote to Congress: "The affair was attended with most salutary consequences, as it seems to have greatly inspired the whole of our troops." So the Dutch Farmers found themselves citizens of a new United States, dwelling in the outskirts of its temporary Capital. By 1800 the Dutch Dominion in Harlem was passing; the families were scattered, the lands divided, though Lot 15 remained in the same hands. Beautiful homes owned by wealthy New York families were built along the edges of the oval that enclosed the Hollow Way. Hamilton Grange was only one of many country-seats that drew brilliant companies of visitors from the City when George Washington, Lafayette and later Joseph Bonaparte were entertained in them. It was inevitable that a town should follow the building of homes, and on July 9, 1806, an interesting news item appeared in the *New York Spectator*: "The Village of Manhattanville is now forming in the ninth Ward of this City on the Bloomingdale Road, in front of Harlem Cove on the North River. . . . The proprietors of the soil are now laying out the streets which are to be wide open to the Hudson River, where vessels of three hundred ton may lie in safety." The next year a further notice appeared to the effect that "a house of entertainment" had been opened on the Bloomingdale Road, that there were "conveyances to and from the City daily." A ferry to New Jersey soon followed, then a stage line to town. The stages were economical, for a single driver sufficed; he had a leather strap attached to his leg which passengers inside the coach pulled when they wished to alight.

Among the wealthiest of New York families looking for land near the new village was Jacob Lorillard. Jacob had begun very humbly, for in 1805 he had inserted a cryptic notice into the *Common Advertiser* which read: "During the sickly season Jacob Lorillard advertises that he sells hides and leathers at his tan-yard, corner of Magazine and Cross Streets." He prospered at his tanning trade, for in 1831 the same Journal bore the notice that he had purchased the old State Prison for a Sanatorium, with " a place of reclining over the portico . . . combining all the advantages of a hospital and a home," having eighty-nine rooms equipped with "baths either cold, warm or vapour."

In 1833 Jacob and his wife Margaretta, with their son and five daughters, drove out to Manhattanville where Lot 15 became the chosen site for their new home.[6] To it were added a piece of Peter Oblienis' former Hundred Acres and two more odd lots at the sides. The historic chestnut tree must have stood right in the center of the property till it disappeared forever, as did the old Myers' House. Jacob built his own house on the highest point of the land where the view from river to river was something to dream of. It was a brownstone house of an amplitude and grandeur unseen in the neighbourhood before. Jacob was well pleased and built a second smaller house near the north-east corner of the first for his eldest daughter when she married. He shortly had four more sons-in-law to match the remaining daughters, but the house-building seems not to have gone beyond the first.

All was prosperous when in 1836 the head of this patriarchal establishment died, leaving the whole estate to his wife. She promptly gave it to her six children jointly. After ten years the six of them decided to sell, and notified New York to that effect. One of the first to respond was no less a person than Bishop Hughes, who at once notified Astoria. So, late in April, 1846, another visitor with an eye to property drove out the Bloomingdale Road. As Mother Hardey climbed the sloping road to the house, then turned to look out over Manhattan Island spread at her feet, she knew that she had found the spot prepared from of old for her sowing.

Bishop Hughes, through his secretary Father Bayley, set to work at the negotiations, which proved to be difficult. Early in November he appeared at the Astoria Convent to urge Mother Hardey to make one of her omnipotent Novenas. The whole Community undertook to make the Way of the Cross for nine days. The next afternoon the Bishop reappeared, completely discouraged. The six Lorillards refused to sell without the consent of their mother, who absolutely opposed the present offer. "Be patient," he said as he drove away, "make up your minds to stay here for another year." One of the Nuns remarked to Mother Hardey that of course the Novena would stop now; it would be tempting Providence to go on. "God is more powerful than His creatures," was the reply. "Let us trust Him and continue our prayers." So the Ways of the Cross went on, and the last day of the Novena brought a rather startled Bishop to the door. He had come to tell them that Mrs. Lorillard had died suddenly that morning. He was in fact a bit taken aback by this simple solution of the problem, and used to say afterwards, half in jest and whole in earnest, "Be careful not to oppose Mother Hardey's wishes, for if necessary she will kill you with her Novenas."

Only one difficulty remained. The price of the property, $70,000, was beyond the means of Mother Hardey, who declared that she could pay $50,000 and no more. Nothing daunted, she appealed to the children. Would they undertake to join with the Religious in saying 20,000 *Memorares* during the next few days? They did so, enthusiastically, and on the evening of the third day the Bishop came with a final message; $20,000 had been subtracted from the price and twelve acres of land added to the contract. Thus, on the sixth of the following February, 1847, Mother Hardey, through the intermediary of Bishop Hughes, purchased for $50,000 the sixty-three acres of land lying on one of the highest points of Manhattan Island, where stood a large house visible from afar in all directions. Manhattanville was founded. "It was," said a great lover of the spot nearly one hundred years later, "as though God had waited for a woman with a heart as wide as the world to found a place where everyone could come."

The moving took place in the bleakness of February, over

the East River and up the Kingsbridge Road, till the Community and children were once more encamped in the luxurious destitution of two fine houses with nothing in them. One of the Nuns wrote:

> We shall never forget our installation, for we were very few and everyone had to work hard. We ate in the corridor or in the kitchen, where a few planks laid on trestles served as tables. One Novice prepared the meals and another served them, while in the midst of all our goings and comings Reverend Mother Hardey's smile was our greatest encouragement. Our first Pastor paid us frequent visits, and although we were in the midst of Lent he wanted us to have three full days of *grand congé* to celebrate our arrival in our new domain. Our improvised tables and chairs pleased him greatly, but what delighted him above all was to see how Reverend Mother managed to get for herself all the hardest work. One day His Lordship remarked, "I never see your Mother without an apron on and a broom in her hand, as good tempered in the kitchen as in the parlour. She is one in a thousand."

As Mother Hardey looked from the main entrance towards the south she could see the meadows, fringed with heavy trees, dip unevenly down to the Hollow Way. Behind it the hills rose again, under a blank sky unetched as yet with a pattern of distant sky-scrapers. To her left the land fell sharply away in cliffs, beyond which stretched a panorama of blue peace woven of flat meadows and waterways and homes. To the right a rocky gorge separated her from the neighboring property known as Donnelly's Woods, behind which the village of Manhattanville, suburbanly self-conscious, stirred briskly on the banks of the Hudson.[7] Beyond the river stood up the Palisades, proudly unchangeable; they would hold their own long after the rest of that landscape had been smothered in a tide of humanity.

The people in the Village soon named the new establishment the "House of God," for reasons of their own. Mother

Hardey's first act was to remodel a large brick stable into what was really a Parish School, although there was yet no Parish Church. The drone of one hundred and twenty little voices soon filled the air, and the restless heads would turn at every sound to see if Mother Hardey were coming. Her practiced eye read the story on each face, and wherever she saw the touch of sorrow or of want she found a way of remedying both. Fathers and mothers began coming to the Convent door, always asking directly for Mother Hardey, till family troubles were healed, family means restored, and family spirit rekindled at the Sacraments. As a result, the faces in the school grew rounder and brighter. The two Novices who taught there were proud, when the sessions ended in July, to invite Mother Hardey to the closing exercises. The children sang and recited better than could have been expected, but their young teachers had made one bad mistake. Prizes had been awarded too sparingly and with too rigid a sense of justice. Every one deserved a prize, decided Mother Hardey aloud, and she drew a package of holy cards from her pocket. Something rewardable was discovered in each child, and that night the Parish had one more reason for referring to the Convent on the Hill as the House of God.

In the meantime the children in the boarding-school were rivalling their predecessors of the pioneer convents of Missouri in primitive inconveniences and were equally ignorant of how much heavier a share fell to the Nuns. They wore muslin and calico dresses which, even in the days before factory-smoke, had to be laundered twice a week, so that the Community spent many of their recreations in the basement, with Mother Hardey foremost at the wash-tubs. Water for use in the dormitories had to be carried upstairs bucket by bucket. In this hardy atmosphere studies and the *arts d'agrément* soon flourished, and by the end of its first year the Academy was prepared to show itself to the world. The

Catholic Directory announced that the Bloomingdale stage would stop at the Convent "whenever there are passengers to or from the Institution." In July, 1848, the Prizes were distributed with all the pomp possible. Mother Hardey thought that the occasion would be a good one for making friends with some of her more aloof neighbours, among whom was a Quaker household. Its members were shy of affronting a Convent, and asked a young Catholic girl of their acquaintance to come with them. The prizes were given on the terrace behind the house and were made impressive by a bunting-draped platform and by elaborate singing. The atmosphere captivated the young visitor, and she finally expressed her feelings in a singular prayer: "Lord, if ever I have a daughter, may she be a Religious of the Sacred Heart." The prayer was heard; nearly a century later a very old Religious of the Sacred Heart told the story of how Mother Hardey's friendliness had unexpectedly resulted in her vocation.

Help soon came from Europe, and one July afternoon in 1848 a bewildered set of travellers got off the boat and set out for the wilds of Manhattanville.

At last we were drawing near; five indescribable creatures! Would they let us in? Not one of us knew a word of English. It seemed to us that Manhattanville was miles from the harbour, and that the City of New York was made up of a string of little towns. We passed over rivers, then through crowded streets, then through vague fields. At last, after four hours en route we stopped at the top of a steep hill, not before a Convent but before a chalet. It was half past six. The postulant who opened the door seemed terrified. "Religious of the Sacred Heart," said Mother Moncheur, and we went in almost in spite of the little Sister who ran to tell Mother Hardey that some strange Bohemians were at the door. This venerated Mother came at once, and after blessing and embracing us led us to the chapel to say our *Suscipe* of love in our new mission. In her thoughtfulness she had prepared religious habits for us, and how good it was to put them on again!

Mother Tommasini, through whose Memoirs [8] we can catch many glimpses of early Manhattanville, was a vivacious and very young Italian aspirant who had been driven out of Piedmont by the Revolution of 1848. Mother Hardey, who believed in the sink or swim method, tossed her into the school at once, having first forbidden her to speak a word of English to the children. So she taught them Italian songs which, to the despair of the other Nuns, they were soon humming all over the house. Not much more than a child herself she frequently retired to sing and dance in private as an outlet for the superabundance of her spirits. Her enjoyment was at its height on a certain July 22nd, Feast of the Mother General:

> The whole household had a picnic in the place where the Jewish Orphanage now stands. The children were on one side of the grounds, the Community on the other. The former went to play in the woods while we recited Office. It was the first time that I had said it outdoors, and I enjoyed it enormously, as well as the gaiety and the simplicity of the Americans. In the midst of this country-festival Bishop Hughes arrived, bringing with him Bishop Timon of Buffalo. When their Lordships understood what was going on, they stayed to share our pleasure for almost an hour.

Mother Tommasini was at first considerably in awe of Mother Hardey, whom she found somewhat grave and imposing. Mother Hardey for her part considered that a little more gravity would not come amiss to the mercurial Italian, and missed no opportunity of inculcating it. Through the eyes of the younger Nun we can see Mother Hardey moving about the house, omnipresent, all-seeing, beneficent. She supplied as a matter of course for any class-mistress who happened to be ill, going to the work with particular alacrity if the class was in the Junior School. At one moment she would be at the front door to greet the Bishop, who had a way of inviting himself to supper. No special entertainment was needed, since he insisted on eating with the children, so Mother Hardey would be free to slip away to attend to her duties in the infirmary. She was herself Mistress of Health, and there were three young Nuns to be cared for, all dying at once. Then, as Mistress General, she would lead the children out into the garden where Mass was frequently said for the privileged few in a tiny Lady Chapel.

She would next be seen supervising workmen, for the front of the house was expanding in a chapel to the east and school wings to the west. A Gothic tower was rising over it, while a porte-cochère in front lifted the seal of the Society over its hospitable arches. The smaller house behind was transformed into a Noviceship. Soon it was impossible to tell where the old Lorillard Mansion began or ended. As the convent on Bleecker Street had been temporarily closed, Mother Hardey gave its patronal title to Manhattanville, which became the house of Our Lady of Sorrows.

The chapel was the last to be completed, and on Easter Monday in 1851 Bishop Hughes preached one of his most ringing sermons at the ceremony of the First Vows of Mother Alicia Dunne and the clothing of her sister Margaret, while the high operatic voice of Mother Tommasini poured out a flood of gratitude in song. There was song at all times, as there had been when Mother Berthold kindled the first American children of the Sacred Heart with the hymns of France. The music of the mid-century was far more elaborate and Italianate, drawn out into "sempiternal amens," as Mother Hardey remarked severely, but it rang with the same timbre of spontaneous gladness. At the first Midnight Mass in the new chapel: "the children of the Infant Jesus Sodality were ranged about the New-Born One who was placed in the middle of the chapel surrounded with flowers and lights, and at the moment of the Elevation they sang *Adeste Fideles* to the sound of the harp, while some swung censers and others scattered rose petals from little baskets over the Holy Crib." Eventually, one of the characteristic sights of Manhattanville was the file of carriages that drove up for Benediction on Sunday afternoons to hear Mother Tommasini and her strenuously trained choir sing, in many parts, their *Quam Bonum*. Manhattanville was never to stop singing, though the burden of the music would change in years to come at the word of Pope Pius X.

The first trouble to overshadow the new house was peculiarly painful to Mother Hardey. Bishop Hughes had asked her to take charge of a little group of orphans, as the Sisters of Charity were unable to do so at the moment. She had accepted gladly, and housed the children in a few spare rooms in the Noviceship building. She did not realize what interpretation the world at large would make of her action. The measure had been taken because the Sisters of Charity were passing through a crisis at the moment. Bishop Hughes had represented to them that for the good of the Diocese they should undertake certain works incompatible with the Rule as observed at Emmitsburg. The result had been a separation by which the majority of the Sisters in New York were constituted into a separate establishment on a Diocesan footing. A short time later, the Emmitsburg Sisters became affiliated with the Sisters of Charity of Saint Vincent de Paul, whose center was in France.

Before Mother Hardey realized what was happening a rumour had started that the Bishop was planning to do the same thing with the Religious of the Sacred Heart. Manhattanville was to become the center of a separate Order with Mother Hardey as Superior General. Actually, the two cases were not parallel, and there is no discoverable proof that Bishop Hughes ever considered them so. In the case of the Sisters of Charity he believed, as did those Sisters who complied with his wishes, that separation would be the best thing for their work and their organization. There is no evidence that he thought the same of the Sacred Heart, understanding as he did its international character and the unity that was its strength.

As for Mother Hardey, the least suggestion that she should act independently of the Mother House was a matter of keen suffering. She would sooner have undone her work than call it hers, and wrote straight to Mother Barat of her trouble. The answer soon came:

> Continue, dear Daughter, to open your heart to me, and to let me know everything that concerns you and the family which is so dear to me. It seems to me that you should understand that by now, and so it is wrong for you to dwell upon your fears; they rest on no plausible foundation. I believe that by now I know you through and through, and what I am convinced of above all is your sincere attachment to the Society. As for the rest, you know that people are not perfect, and that we must all make allowances for one another, and you know too, dear and good Mother, that no good can be done save by the cross and with the cross.

Mother Hardey knew well that Mother Barat would not have said, "I understand you," if she had not meant it, but other people were not so understanding. They saw in her a powerfully influential person, looked up to with increasing respect in ecclesiastical and lay circles. The rumours afloat concerning the separation of the American Houses did their work by creating an element of ill-defined suspicion concerning her which continued to cling vaguely to her name. As though to combat this impression, absolutely groundless as far as Mother Hardey herself was concerned, the notices sent out from the Mother House after her death are almost belligerent in their insistence upon her continual, whole-hearted and unhesitating spirit of loyalty and of dependence, a dependence, as they add with engaging frankness, all the more remarkable for being found in an American. One such tribute said:

> It will always be Mother Hardey's crown and glory that she was exhaustless in her efforts to strengthen and maintain the bonds of unity between our houses in Europe and in America. American by birth and American in heart, she had nevertheless acquired in a high degree from those who trained her to the religious life the spirit which characterized the Society in its infancy. Powerful by her sterling virtues and splendid character, her dignified bearing and attractive manners, she made use of these gifts to maintain in all its integrity the spirit she had received and to transmit it to future generations of her religious family.

Alarm concerning Manhattanville took a more practical turn soon after. Mother Barat wrote:

> What is this that I have heard about you? That His Lordship, your Bishop, who has been so devoted to you, and has led you to undertake costly enterprises, has established near you another school, like yours but with a lower tuition, so that your work will be hindered? What are you going to do about it?

Mother Hardey, nearer at hand, had already been assured from her own knowledge of the case that the two schools could flourish simultaneously, but she represented the fears of Mother Barat and some uneasiness of her own to the Bishop, and drew from him a reassuring letter on financial matters in the course of which he said:

> I know that from the day when I invited the Religious of the Sacred Heart to this diocese I have been loyal, and in good faith zealous for their success and, unless awfully mistaken in my judgment, true to their interests. I may say at the same time that in great things, as in small things, the Community has been all that my heart could wish; that they have already done much for the good of religion, and are destined with God's blessing to do still more; that I see no reason for despondency, and that I am now as

sanguine of their success as I have been at any time since their coming to this diocese. . . . So long as I live you must not allow yourself to give way to gloomy apprehensions, whatever discouragements you may experience from other causes, for I consider myself bound to see that your house shall not go down whilst I am able to sustain it, and that in any event we shall stand or fall together. . . . I beg you never to allow your courage to fail. There is no reason for it, and even if there were, the Church cries out every day in a sense which religious persons above all should understand, "Sursum Corda!"

So in the midst of these joys and troubles the time-shadow slipped noiselessly over the mid-mark of the century. In 1850 inventors were toiling over their first plans for a transmarine cable to eliminate time between continents, but before their schemes could take tardy shape the invisible wires between Manhattanville and the Center, spun of effortless prayer, were humming. It was the Jubilee year of the Society, and November was the Golden month. Mother Barat set out from Paris to Rome in the summer-time, and her journey curved from one house to another in such wise that she reached the Villa Lante only a few days before the momentous date. The chill of an early Roman winter fell with the twilight about the rambling and regal old house. Mother Barat came into the Community Room on the eve of November 21st, leaning on the arm of Mother de Limminghe, while rows of faces turned to her in the uncertain lamplight. As the worn but vibrant voice began to speak a tide of warmth and of radiance rose from her presence; it filled the room and reached out beyond it into space, even over the ocean to where Manhattanville was busy at the moment with its own preparations for the Jubilee:

Fifty years ago the Heart of Jesus laid the foundations of our Little Society. What a small instrument He used—a nothing, a mere nothing. He chose it for that reason; He Himself wished to be all; the Heart of Jesus is our Founder. . . . Every Religious Order studies the spirit of its Founder; the measure of its perfection is the conformity of its Members with him.

The next day, Feast of the Presentation, brought its full panoply of celebrations, with High Mass and a series of panegyrics which were excruciating to Mother Barat since the speakers committed the unpardonable blunder of giving to her the name of Foundress, after all that she had just said. This was the one point upon which she believed herself right and everyone else wrong, so when the sermons grew unbearable she slipped out of her stall and went about her business. It was serious business, for she had come to Rome not only to ask the blessing of Pope Pius IX but to secure approval for the final modifications of the Constitutions that had grown out of the discussions of 1839. The most important of these was concerned with the appointment of Provincials, or Superiors Vicar as they came to be called, who together with the Assistants General should form the Council of the Society.

Considerable delays arose, and Mother Barat wrote out a list of her troubles and desires and took it to the Trinita. There on the wall was the painting of Mater Admirabilis, so named by the Pope himself. Miracles and spiritual graces of all sorts were beginning to be worked in that name, and Mother Barat, who always shrank from the extraordinary, was in some doubt about the rosy *Madonina* whom she could not help loving. So she laid her paper on Mater's altar, and the rapid and remarkable solution of all her difficulties was the final sign. The Constitutions were satisfactorily arranged and the devotion to Mater Admirabilis sanctioned at one and the same time. Mother Barat then summoned the Seventh General Council.

Mother Hardey crossed the sea with Mother Cutts from Grand Coteau, an English convert who had come to the Louisiana missions shortly after her first vows to complete the international union reigning there. The two went straight to La Ferrandière where the Council was to be held. This time there was no delay in the proceedings, and Mother Hardey found herself very far from being the least important member of the gathering. The sixty-five houses of the Society were divided into ten Vicariates, eight in Europe and two in America; Mother Hardey and Mother Cutts were confirmed in their respective charges, taking for the first time the new title of Vicar. There was only one point of disagreement. All the Councillors listened with sympathy to Mother Barat's pleas that they would lift the burden of government from her aging shoulders, but the youthful animation in her voice and eyes undid the effect of her words; a unanimously negative vote was returned. The Foundress expressed her feelings in a letter to Mother Duchesne: "Pray for your Mother, whose needs increase with the years and with the extension of her work. I asked in vain to be relieved of this burden that I have carried for fifty years. They were all deaf. I still hope that Jesus will grant me the grace to die free from this terrible responsibility."

This letter was carried to America by the returning Vicars, but not before they had spent a refreshing month at the Rue de Varennes. A Novice who was to sail with them came to Mother Hardey's room to help pack the night before their departure. She was taken aback by the tears flowing unchecked down her Superior's cheeks, a sight rarely seen by anyone, and she ventured a few awkwardly well-meant words: "Reverend Mother, why are you crying? Don't you want to go home? You know how much your daughters love you and are longing to see you." Usually, personal remarks to Mother Hardey met with evasion or snubbing, but this time her answer showed how much she shared in the spirit of the letter from Mother Barat that she was carrying: "Child, you are only beginning your religious life, but if you live long enough you will learn how terrible is the burden of responsibility. If I could be freed from it, how gladly I would obey!"

The return journey was made uncomfortably lively by storms, broken engines and all those ocean disasters which, as Mother Hardey wrote back to the Mother House, "have their funny side for those who do not suffer from seasickness." Her companions were all convinced that they had died several times over in the course of the journey, and the Captain was equally convinced that the ship had been saved only through their holy prayers. Manhattanville was eventually reached, and fairly rocked with joy at Mother Hardey's return. Mother Tucker, who had replaced her during the long absence, had felt the responsibility to such an extent that she had become unduly nervous about noises at night, conscientiously investigating every sound. The night after the home-coming watch-dogs were heard barking outside, but the case was different now. When someone came to report the matter she only said, "Let them bark; Mother Hardey is home again."

The ties with the Mother House were once more strengthened by the arrival, on May 24, 1852, of Reverend Mother Anna du Rousier, who had been sent as Visitor of all the Convents in the New World. America had been in her thoughts for the greater part of her life.[9] As a child she had been sent, after the brutal murder of her father by his political enemies, to the school at Poitiers, and had been one of the group of children who pressed with curiosity and excitement around Mother Duchesne when she stopped there on her way to the *Rebecca*. The parting missioner was afire with zeal, and her words caught hold of the children until they grew clamorous with their promises to join her some day in the field afar. Anna, always shy, kept silence; yet she of all the children was deep and strong enough to one day do what all were then saying. She entered the Noviceship soon after, and at her clothing heard the priest say: "You will be in the hands of God like a leaf which the wind carries away, like a seed cast into far soil to bear its fruit; abandon yourself to the breath of grace." An unusual preparation followed. As Mistress General, then as Superior of the Convent of Turin which had been founded by Royalty for the children of Nobility, she was at first the arbiter and idol of high society in Piedmont, whose daughters she formed into equally elevated Christians. Then without transition she found herself the object of hate, calumny, mockery and violence when the Revolutionaries of 1848 confiscated her house, burned her in effigy, caricatured her on the stage, and drove her from the land with countless other religious exiles. Mother Barat called her to Paris where, after an interval of silent suffering in which even the work of a normally peaceful school seemed to go wrong, she was sent to visit the American houses.

She reached Manhattanville with Sister Antoinette, a sterling missioner from Piedmont, and straightway wrote back to Mother Barat:

> I have found a beautiful house situated in a superb locality. Its prosperity is remarkable. There are over one hundred pupils, twelve novices and eight postulants, so you see that the blessing of the Good Master rests upon this family. I have been edified by the religious spirit of the Community, so much good will is shown by all. The rule of silence is faithfully observed; spiritual exercises are made with the greatest exactness. I have found the spirit of poverty well observed in all the departments, and the furniture used by the Religious is of the simplest and most ordinary kind.

Mother du Rousier then started on her round of visits, but when she reached Saint Louis she learned that Mother Duchesne was very weak, perhaps near her end. It was November 16th, and the weather was November at its worst. Something urged her not to lose a moment, and in spite of persuasions to the contrary she set out at once with Mother Cutts, driving through the blinding wind and rain to Saint Charles. Mother Duchesne was lying now in the cold, cramped room under the stairs that she kept as bare of comforts as the hut at Sugar Creek. When she learned that the strange Reverend Mother at her bedside had come from the Mother House, all her love of the Society passed into the tight grasp of her hand and the eagerness with which she asked for a blessing. Mother du Rousier gave it in the name of Mother Barat, and then in her turn asked a blessing. Afterwards she said, "Oh, I still seem to feel the cross that she traced on my forehead. I trust to that cross to bring me happiness, and I shall try to love it ever more and more."

Mother Cutts must have had very pressing business elsewhere, or perhaps it was impossible for any of them to realize that so strong a life could be flickering out, for she took Mother du Rousier back to Saint Louis the next morning. It was the first day that Mother Duchesne had not read her Office from the battered book that lay closed near her bed. All over its fly-leaves was written a revelation of herself in a sprawling, determined hand. There were litanies to the great apostolic saints with the refrain "Seigneur, suavez votre peuple"; there were hymns in French, English, Latin, all beating with intense feeling, outburst of praise and of contrition; there were lists of intentions, the great causes for which she had spent her outwardly useless life for the past ten years. Then, written very firmly, was "Je ne suis rien, je ne puis rien, je ne sais rien," then, in English with lapses into French spelling, came the words: "I resolve to lead henceforth a penitente and mortified life." "Fiat voluntas tua" she had written large on another page, and splashed it with her tears. Tucked into the book was a scrap of an old letter with the seal of the Society and the post-mark—New York, 10¢—showing through, on which she had written her last desire: "O mon

Dieu, vous pensez à mourir pour moi; et moi, quel amour puis-je avoir sinon le vôtre?"

The night of the seventeenth went by uneasily. Very quietly they tried to light a fire in her room, but she heard them. In the morning she received the Last Sacraments and could say nothing more but "I give you my heart and my soul and my life—O yes, my life, generously." By noon she had gone into Life.

Mother du Rousier herself wrote the news to Mother Hardey:

> Mother Galwey will give you the details concerning the edifying death of Mother Duchesne. Here, the general opinion is that we have lost a saint. The clergy and the Archbishop in particular, speak of her with the greatest admiration. Bishop Kenrick declares that she was the noblest and most virtuous soul that he has ever known. Father de Smet assures us that while living she was already worthy of canonization. Our houses in America owe everything to her. She cut the first furrow with much weariness and privation, and I am sure that I am acting in accordance with the wishes of our Mother General in asking for her the suffrages indicated for a Superior Vicar. . . . God granted me the grace to arrive in time to ask her prayers for my mission. She promised to help me near Our Lord and I count on that, for I believe that she is all-powerful with the Heart of Jesus.

Three continents were linked in that blessing: Europe, where the Society had come into being, North America, where it had begun to flourish, South America, where it was about to take root. Mother Duchesne, never content with one continent at a time, had longed for South as well as North America. Mother du Rousier was at Buffalo on her way east in the spring when word came from Mother Barat that it was for her to carry out that longing. A foundation was about to be made in Chile. But Mother du Rousier had always been frail, and she had suffered much both physically and morally; the undertaking might be beyond her strength. Mother Barat told her to weigh the matter before God, and that if she felt it better so she might entrust the mission to Mother Hardey.

Mother de Rousier went to the chapel and stayed there all night. By morning she had made her choice. She would go to Chile, taking the labour and the dangers for herself, and leave Mother Hardey in the North. The graces to be poured out upon her mission in the future were paid for dear that night. As she wrote to Mother de Limminghe:

> I confess to you alone that I then went through the greatest inner combat of my whole life. The idea of being transported from the shores of Lake Erie almost to the end of South America roused in me such repugnance and revulsion that the entire night following the reception of the letter was passed in a terrible struggle. I really think that I then experienced something of the agony of Jesus in the Garden of Olives. Heart, mind and imagination, all were overwhelmed. The peril of the long journey, isolation, abandonment, the difficulties that I should find, a thousand other fears and apprehensions frightened me so that in spite of my prayers and supplications I felt my soul fail me. However, after repeated acts of accepting all and of giving up all, said from my heart in spite of the storm, the *Ita Pater* calmed the tempest, and a feeling of confidence and of loving peace arose in my soul.

The decision once made, she hurried to New York. In a farewell conference to the Community of Manhattanville she told them that while praying for light on her mission an interior voice had said to her: "I have appointed you that you should go and bring forth fruit, and your fruit should remain." The Community did not realize the implication that they had narrowly missed seeing their own Mother Hardey leave them for Chile. But Mother Hardey herself knew it. For weeks she had kept her will winged for flight, but instead she saw Mother du Rousier, with Mother McNally and Sister

Antoinette, leave for the Chilean mission on the First Friday of August, 1853.

The blood-curdling story of the adventures *en route* only reached her many months later, when Mother McNally sent back an account of that unspeakable journey over the Isthmus of Panama. Perched on the backs of obstinate mules, hungry, frightened, surrounded by genuine bandits, avaricious negroes, callous muleteers, they had faced the peril of storms, broken limbs and threatened assassination before emerging, thanks to their chivalrous Spanish protectors, from the jungle into semi-civilization. The most fearsome moment of the journey had been that at which Mother du Rousier tumbled from her mule and rolled over the edge of a blank precipice. Before she reached death at the bottom her fall had been checked by the branches of a stubby trees where she hung until ropes could be let down for her rescue. While in this situation she had promised Saint Joseph to have a chapel built in his honour if she were saved. On learning this Mother Hardey wrote at once begging Mother du Rousier to do nothing further about the chapel. It would be built at Manhattanville in her name.

By spring of the next year it was standing among the trees on a gentle hill behind the house, a small hexagonal structure lifting a sharp spire. Into it were built Mother Hardey's thoughts about three continents, about Mother Barat, Mother Duchesne, Mother du Rosier. Later, when flames reduced the first Manhattanville to a few charred walls, the little chapel of Saint Joseph stood untouched by flames, unstained by smoke. It became the link between the old and the new, like the oak tree before it that towered and spread with the years. Now time is doing what fire could not do, but when Saint Joseph's meets its own destruction it will have its own resurrection, for places into which faith and love are built have, like people, an incommunicable personality and a life unbroken.

XIII

BRANCHING OUT

IN THE MID-CENTURY, when the frontier was checked perforce in its westward sweep by the Pacific Ocean, when the foreign policy of the United States was making itself felt for the first time through the world, and when compromises at home were all that kept the country from splitting apart on the question of slavery, the educational shuttle was moving ever more rapidly back and forth, weaving an American pattern.[1] No more than in Colonial times is the history of the Church separable from national history in that era of energy and expansion, though the two histories have for the most part been written in separate columns. The development of the Church in those years is statistically startling; the Catholic population of 1844, numbering 811,000, increased to 3,842,000 during the next twenty years, and the educational shuttle had to fly fast. From Manhattanville which looked out over broad horizons, Mother Hardey set herself vigorously to the task, letting not even national boundaries limit her. It is time to follow her through the foundations which she made from 1842 to 1869, beginning with those in her own country.

When Mother Duchesne reached America she had confessed to a feeling of disappointment upon finding that she was not the first to introduce her best-loved devotion into the New World, for in the Ursuline Convent in New Orleans she found a large painting of the Sacred Heart which had been brought from Rome. She did not know that thirty years before her coming a remarkably handsome stone Church had been erected at Conewago[2] in Adams County, western Pennsylvania, and dedicated to the Sacred Heart, the first church to bear the title on the continent of North America. The remote green valley-lands under the shadow of its cross had sheltered the Chaughnawaga Indians, in all probability a Catholic tribe that had been converted in Canada before their migration to the south. Then quietly and without friction the first white settlers had wandered in, mostly Dutch and German, with Catholics among them. Hot on their trail came the soul-hunters, Jesuits from Maryland, till by 1741 the peaceful place boasted a small log Mass-house and a chaplain who dedicated his mission to Saint Francis Regis. This Saint, it seems, never failed to remember the trust that Mother Duchesne had placed in him. Not only was the stone Church subsequently erected there by Father Pellentz dedicated to the Sacred Heart, but exactly one hundred years after Saint Francis had been placed in charge of Conewago the Religious of the Sacred Heart came to the valley.

The foundation was made at the request of Father Philip Borgna, a protégé of Mother Duchesne who had said his first mass at Florissant and there kindled his zeal from hers. He called on Mother Galitzin as soon as she came to New York in 1841, and used as one of his arguments the fact that Conewago had once been the scene of the labours of her illustrious cousin; would she not continue the good work begun in

Pennsylvania by the Apostle of the Mountains, Father Galitzin? She consented, and the foundation represented a union of east and west, for the new community came from the old home of Mother Duchesne and the new home of Mother Hardey. The first group to arrive, led by Mother de Kersaint, was recruited from Saint Louis and Grand Coteau, and a few months later the entire Florissant Noviceship followed them. The second group come from Houston Street. When Mother Hardey returned from France in November, 1842, the well-being of the new house and of all others to be opened in the east was placed in her hands. She set out at once for Conewago.

As she drove up to the comfortable country house in the village of McSherrystown, one mile from the Church of the Sacred Heart, she saw the villagers, Irish and German and very Catholic, hovering about the verandah in the hope of being of some service to the visiting Reverend Mother. They had been hovering in this fashion for the past six months, dropping in at all hours with vegetables or bread fresh from the oven. They had themselves furnished the house throughout, putting into the stable a conveyance of sorts and into the parlour a piano upon which music for solemn ceremonies was executed by the town-sheriff. Their faith was the pride of their Pastor, Father Lekeu, S.J., who had taught them to make a daily meditation.

Within doors Mother Hardey found a very small boarding-school and a very large free-school more than filling the homely rooms. She also found the first McSherrystown postulant already wearing the habit. Not so consoling was the sight of another Novice at the point of death, a presage of the shadow that hung all unsuspected as yet over the breeze-stirred peace of Conewago Valley. When Mother Hardey left she carried away an impression of regretful fear concerning this out-of-the-way house situated a full day's journey from

Philadelphia, as trains went then. With her special gift of foresight she had never shared the over-hasty confidence of Mother Galitzin concerning its suitability either for a school or for a noviceship, but in spite of this she continued to foster it with all her might, in love with the charm and the simplicity of the place. The next spring news of a calamity reached her. Mother Cauche, the Superior, had been walking in the grounds when a workman had carelessly tossed a plank from the roof of the house, which struck her on the head. All summer she was dangerously ill, and Mother Boilvin from Houston Street took her place, bringing to her new work the precious training received as child and novice from Mother Duchesne at Florissant.

At Mother Hardey's visit in April, 1844, she found much to rejoice over. A new chapel, a new day-school and additions to the old house were rising in the spring sunshine, the labour and material being furnished by the townsmen. Every week an overwhelming amount of provisions appeared at the back-door, gratis, while the Nuns had only to mention that a second piano would be useful to have the Pastor furnish it. The thirty smooth-haired and very devout children in the boarding school wore uniforms like those at Houston Street, and for their sake Mother Hardey waited.

These children were dutiful, delightful letter-writers, and fortunately the fond parents of some of them preserved the letters.[3] There was in the school a whole series of little Quiggs, all sisters from a large Philadelphia family, and their quaintly formal phrases ripple with the little joys and trials of school life, at a time when the highest ambition of most school girls was to wear one of the daringly new crinolines. These cared for other things. We can look over the shoulder of Ellen, the eldest, as she sits in the study-hall on December 15, 1844, and writes:

Dearest parents, you know I love you, and would like to spend this New Year's Day with you, but as it is better I should be here, I am quite satisfied, and will show my gratitude by making progress in my studies and in every virtue, and may God protect and bless you for having sent me to the Sacred Heart.

Ellen allowed her little sister Hannah, not yet of an age to study punctuation, to utilize the inside page of this same letter:

I would very much like to write you a nice letter but as it is the first one I ever did will you please to excuse the many faults I wish more than a happy New Year. I cannot express what I wish you but I hope you will spend a very pleasant one I am going to study very hard this year and hope I will become a good little girle I am well my dear Parents I wish you a great deal of happiness.

Hannah had her troubles and confided them to her second letter, which by that time had acquired periods:

We had the examinations of six months, and after that the Premiums were given. Ellen got the prize for good conduct in English class and the Premium for application in French. Mary and Ellen were both promoted to higher classes in English and French, but I had to stay where I was, but I am trying to study very hard and I got the medal the first week after classes began and I have it yet and I think if I try I can get a prize too. . . . Tell all my little brothers and sisters that I do not forget them.

In the meantime Mary Cecilia, who loved to write letters and opened them with the words "allow me the pleasure of once more performing this agreeable duty," was tasting with youthful zest the consolations of religion. She grew anxious about the spiritual well-being of her parents, and wrote:

It would give me great pleasure, Dearest Parents, to have the happiness of seeing you on Easter Morning, approaching Holy

Communion, as I hope I will have the happiness of doing, for it is to me the greatest happiness in the world. We are passing this Lent in the most happy manner. . . . Everything is so agreeable and time passes so sweetly away that this holy season will have ended when we think it is only beginning. It is impossible for me, dear Parents, to describe to you the pleasure and happiness found at the Sacred Heart, where it is the only object of everyone to do their duty for the love of God and the pleasure of their parents, where there are so many different families living together like sisters, trying what they can do to please and make one another happy. When I think of all this, I do not know what name to call a place where there is so much love and happiness, but presently I think of the name—Miss Mary used to call it, "a Little Heaven."

It is no surprise to find the next letter giving news of the reception of both Mary and Ellen among the Children of Mary, and to see that subsequent letters are dated from Ravenswood first and then from Manhattanville, for Mother Hardey called them both to New York when they asked to enter the Noviceship. From then on their letters are long transports of joy. They first assure their mother that they will not need "moreno drapes," for the weather is not cold, and moreover they do not intend "to dishonour the Feast of Saint Stanislas with their secular drapes"; they will change them for the Habit on that day. After their clothing they find "our solitude is like an earthly Paradise, which I would not exchange for all the pleasures of the world," while the practical Mother Hardey writes across an inside page: "Would Mrs. Quigg have the kindness to send, when convenient, India rubber [overshoes] for her two daughters?"

Then, abruptly, the letters came to an end, for Ellen fell ill and Mary wrote: "This is the plain truth; Madame Hardey desires me to tell you that if you like and think proper you may come and take her home, as she is not well." As it happened, both Novices went home to die of the tuberculosis that they had contracted at McSherrystown. This was Mother Hardey's reason for finally steeling herself against the pleas of the children that she leave the house at Conewago open. Four Nuns had died there in the course of a single summer, and several others, including Mother Boilvin herself, were attacked, so in the spring of 1846 she transferred the whole establishment to Philadelphia.

She could not, however, persevere in her resolve to abandon the valley where the Sacred Heart was so much loved, especially when she found that the other Religious Order which she had expected to take over the work in the Parish School could not do so for the time being, and in the autumn of 1848 she herself led a small colony back to Conewago. Four happy, hard-working years followed, in which the Village became so identified with the Convent that it made a municipal event out of the Society's Golden Jubilee in 1850. But in spite of the affectionate generosity of Pastors and people and of the Jesuits from near-by Pigeon Hill, Mother Hardey felt that she could not continue to support a house which was a heavy drain on the rest of the Vicariate, being too remote for an Academy, the primary work of the Society. So when the Sisters of Saint Joseph came to Conewago Valley in 1852 she left the Free School in their hands and withdrew, glad to know that the name and spirit of the Sacred Heart would live on, under the spire of the pioneer Church to bear that name.

The stormy era of Philadelphia Church history had closed when Mother Hardey arrived in March, 1846, to take possession of the house on Logan Square which Bishop Kenrick had provided for her. Catholics in Pennsylvania had enjoyed unusual opportunities for the free and peaceful practice of their religion in Colonial days, but as soon as the Diocese of Philadelphia had been erected in 1808 trouble began. The work of Bishop Egan and of Bishop Conwell after him was all but paralyzed by the scandal of the long and bitter war which the Trustees of Saint Mary's Church and their schismatic pastors waged against the authority of the Church. That matter had scarcely been settled when the City of Brotherly Love broke into flame, the scene of the most infamous of the Native American riots; but that outburst was short-lived, and by now Bishop Kenrick, a pacific, hard-working Prelate, quietly constructive in his aims, could look forward to better days. As Mother Hardey looked out the window the morning after the first night spent alone with Mother Dumont in the bare and rented house, she could see across Logan Square the foundations of the Cathedral-to-be holding up its corner-stone. Down the street in various directions other walls were rising, renovated walls of burned convents and churches, and of new centers of spiritual life. Philadelphia was responding to the trend of the times, and noted converts were following the American aftermath of the Oxford Movement. In 1841 Bishop Kenrick had written on open letter to the Bishops of the Protestant Episcopal Church inviting them "to follow to its legitimate consequences the movements towards the Catholic Church that had begun in England."[4] It was a promising moment for an educational venture, and work began the next day with the arrival of Mother Boilvin and of the school from McSherrystown. Bishop Kenrick himself brought the first books for the library. When he sent a handsome crucifix for the sacristy he received a warm but meagre note of thanks written in pencil, so his next gift was a supply of pens and letter paper.

The house remained on Logan Square for only one year, but its brief annals sound a significant note. The time was approaching for the proclamation of the Dogma of the Immaculate Conception, and for the choice of December Eighth as the Patronal Feast of the United States. Mother Hardey had brought with her from Louisiana, and spread through every house that she founded, a custom which had grown with the life of the Society, that of making the most of that day of unselfish "Praise of Glory." As a child she had carried an olive branch in Grand Coteau's brief but solemn procession, and now on December 8, 1846, Bishop Kenrick summed up what many another American Bishop had reason to say.

> Today, for the first time, this feast has been celebrated with fitting solemnity in our Diocese. You have taken the lead, going ahead of your Pastors, and I cannot tell you the joy I feel in seeing that at the Sacred Heart the Blessed Virgin is receiving the initial homage of a veneration which all the American Bishops are so anxious to see developed among their flocks.

The next spring Mother Hardey was once more back in Philadelphia. One of her repeated problems was that of maintaining balance between rural and urban localities, often by suburban compromises. Her procedure was to begin where she could, then choose where she would, and eventually to have city houses working in conjunction with country houses till all needs were met. Now she went to examine the Cowperthwaite mansion, set in a gently rolling land of plenty, hushed in the lucent peace that moved over the Delaware River. Here the vineyards yielded fruit known through the country-side as the "Glorious Grapes." Mother Hardey lost no time in buying the place, changing its name of Eton Hill to Eden Hall, and entrusting it to Our Lady of Sorrows, while the *Catholic Directory* announced:

> The "Ladies of the Sacred Heart" inform their friends with pleasure that they are again prepared to resume the duties of their institution at Eden Hall, the elegant estate to which they have recently moved from the city of Philadelphia, beautifully situated within view of the Delaware River in a region of country celebrated for its salubrity and picturesque scenery. The grounds are tastefully ornamented with choice shrubbery and shaded by majestic grove and forest trees, with spacious gravel walks, affording delightful promenades for the recreation of the young ladies.

She herself could not stay in any earthly Eden for very long, but accounts of it followed her to New York. They told of how Bishop Kenrick chose to make his first visit on the Fourth of July, stipulating ahead of time that the children should be at study when he arrived, that he might have the pleasure of seeing them roused to their rightful holiday by a sudden ringing of the big bell. They told of the large groups of Parish Sodalities that came by boat and by carriage to picnic in Eden's generous outdoors, on which days "piety and pleasure combined to drive silence from our solitude." They assured her also that Our Lady of Sorrows took her duties as patroness of Eden very much to heart. Not only was the convent saved from the disastrous consequences of debt by her intercession, but owed its beautiful chapel to the singing of the *Stabat Mater*. The hymn was rising with great devotion through the twilight one evening when it reached the ears of Mr. Edwards, a wealthy friend of the house, who was calling on Mother Tucker. He remarked on the sweetness of the song, and was assured that the children had never asked a favour in vain from Our Lady of Sorrows. Mr. Edwards promptly entrusted a troublesome business affair of his to their prayers, and in thanksgiving for its granting gave 15,000 francs towards their much desired chapel. It soon arose, a Gothic gem set in the heart of an Eden that stretched out its walls in all directions around its vine-heavy verandah. It soon lifted its head high in the educational world, being in fact one of the first Academies to receive recognition from the State Legislature. This gave it "privileges which are numerous and very important; they exempt us from taxes and put us on a level with the best non-Catholic institutions of the country." One of its best friends was the saintly Bishop John Nepomucene Neumann, whose cause has been introduced at Rome.[5] Eden Hall never lost the peace, the naturalness, the quiet beauty that had made Mother Hardey name it for the earthly paradise. It became a farm as well as a school, where flowers and fruits were of the sturdiest, and where each animal belonged to the household. Its rural enchantment, its life of thoughtful study, branched tranquilly out from the sanctuary where white Caen stone had been cut into forms of enduring prayer.

But Eden's first years had cost Mother Hardey a great loss. Young Mother Boilvin was the friend and councillor to whom she could turn with the greatest assurance, and now this earnest worker was dying on her feet. Mother Hardey sent her to the bracing air of Canada, but there she ended her life at the age of thirty-six, holding high the lamp that she had lit at Florissant from the spirit of Mother Duchesne. All the houses in the country mourned Mother Boilvin, "one of America's most distinguished religious of the Sacred Heart."

In the meantime the New York City House had reopened and was absorbing a good portion of Mother Hardey's time, for she continued to govern it as Superior from Manhattanville. Only one year elapsed between the closing of the house on Bleecker Street in 1847 and its reopening in another location on the same street. There it remained for three energetic years, paradoxically sought after for its quiet and its good air even by those living in the country. It took only day scholars, children under thirteen who were expected to go to boarding-school for the closing years of their education. It was also a center for the Children of Mary living in the city. Mother Hardey placed Mother Sarah Jones in nominal charge, although she had only just made her first vows. Regularly every month, and more often irregularly, Mother Hardey arrived from Manhattanville, travelling in the butcher's cart to save expense. One day the butcher failed to appear in time, but a farmer's wagon bound for town stood at the door. Mother Hardey begged the favour of a ride. "But you can't go in that open wagon," whispered the horrified portress.

"Why not?" retorted Mother Hardey. "I can lower my veil and pass for the farmer's wife." And she was as good as her word. Mother Tommasini was a frequent companion on these journeys, and being very young sometimes met with misadventures while travelling as a secular:

> One day, on learning that I was to go to town, I had the perverse idea of being dressed for once in that latest fashion. . . . It was the time of crinolines. Choosing the largest, I took a grey silk dress and a lace shawl, putting the whole outfit on over my religious habit. The look that Mother Hardey gave me showed me her displeasure, but it was too late to change anything. Handing me her bag she said: "My Lady may carry this." . . . In the bus I found that I did not know how to sit down in a crinoline. When I explained this to Mother Hardey, her look of contempt showed me that I was in disgrace. Happily there were few people in the bus, but each passenger who got on looked at me in astonishment, seeing me standing before an empty seat. Suddenly a jerk threw me violently back against the seat, and my crinoline rose into the air, revealing my religious habit underneath. . . . Reverend Mother never made an allusion to this affair and I thought that she had not forgiven me, when once at the Mother House, before all the Superiors after the retreat of 1877, she told the story in detail, adding: "You never knew how you amused me."

On another occasion Mother Hardey remarked drily to her oddly dressed companion, "Mother Tommasini, you did well to enter religion."

Mother Jones wrote in after years of those visits to Bleecker Street:

> The days when we saw Mother Hardey were very dear to us; they rekindled our fervour and stirred us to generosity. We loved the evening recreations, especially when her attractive conversation woke in our souls the true spirit of the Society which she loved so deeply. She never grew tired of speaking to us of our venerated Mother Barat, of Mother Audé and the early days in Louisiana,

and we were hungry to hear her. One evening the time-keeper, wishing to prolong these delightful moments, took it on herself to stop the clock. Suddenly, in the midst of the most interesting story, Reverend Mother heard the city clock striking ten. She rose at once, while the culprit owned her fault and was forgiven. "But," added Mother Hardey with a smile, "never do that again or I shall lose confidence in you."

We were very poor in New York; we had no regular beds, and could not afford fuel for fires except in the class rooms, and there we stretched out our mattresses for the night. When Mother Hardey came to visit us she was no better lodged than we were, and bore our privations so gaily that we could see she really enjoyed them.

Our humble house was the place that she chose for her annual retreat. Her air of solitude and of profound recollection made a deep impression upon us, and our hearts echoed the words of the Jesuit father who was her spiritual guide: "I have never known a more humble soul than your Mother."

But Bishop Hughes was not quite satisfied with Bleecker Street; its possibilities were too limited, and Mother Barat wrote: "It will be a thousand times better for you to buy a suitable place in the City; you can not get along without it, considering the kind of work you must do in your country." So in 1851 Mother Hardey transferred the establishment to West 14th Street, where a large Parish School was at once opened in the basement of the new Jesuit Church of Saint Francis Xavier. Before the year was out the Journal recorded that "about one thousand souls are already receiving graces from the Heart of Jesus through this house," and a further expansion was necessary. Mother Hardey courageously bought six lots on West 17th Street and began to build, in spite of the opposition of the property holders in the neighbourhood. For two years the work met with every kind of set-back. The bank in which she had deposited the funds for the building failed, and Mother Barat wrote:

> I am grieved to learn of the state of your finances, . . . but what is to be done, since we are unable to assist you? Your own experience as well as mine testifies that difficulties arise from all quarters as soon as we begin a work which has the salvation of souls for its object. I am not surprised that you and I have to struggle against the dark purposes of our arch-enemy. How consoling it is to know that he is none other than the enemy of Jesus Christ.

Mother Hardey turned to Saint Joseph in her direct, confiding way. The first payment fell due, and the morning's mail brought a totally unexpected gift of the exact amount required. The second payment fell due. This time the morning's mail brought only part of the sum needed. "This is Wednesday, Saint Joseph's day," said Mother Hardey. "We will wait till noon." At eleven o'clock the Superior of another Convent arrived, ready to repay an old debt with a sum far in excess of Mother Hardey's needs.

The Blessed Sacrament was carried into the new chapel on 17th Street on March 9, 1855. The house reflected the generous practicality of Mother Hardey's mind, being, according to those who lived in it, "well-built, well-aired, planned to accommodate large numbers without crowding and to carry on diversified works without confusion." So ornamental was the tall brownstone structure considered, and so impressive its semi-ecclesiastical façade, that a deputation of the formerly disgruntled property-holders on 17th Street called upon Mother Hardey and lifted their high silk hats in elaborate thanks for having added to the dignity of their neighbourhood. She herself thanked God by dedicating the house to Our Lady under the title of the Immaculate Conception; it was the first to be opened since the proclamation of the Dogma the year before. A full life of fifty years spent on the city side-walks lay ahead of it, before it moved, in 1905, to Maplehurst, hiding there in a garden-spot around which the city would one day creep again, as though loath to let it go.

The next foundation carried Mother Hardey westward. Bishop Hughes brought Bishop Timon of Buffalo[6] to Manhattanville one day, and the two Prelates were obliged to track the Community into the Convent woods where a holiday was in progress. It is likely that the talk turned at once to Mother Duchesne, for Bishop Timon's strong-featured and silver-framed face had won its look of holiness during years of missionary service, and the Lazarist Seminary at the Barrens lay very near to Florissant. Tireless, prayerful and gayly courageous, Father Timon had gone into all the places that Mother Duchesne could reach only by her prayers: Indian camps, dens of white man's vice, huts and jostling frontier towns. Faith sprang up wherever he went. Named Vicar-General of his Order, then Prefect-Apostolic of Texas, he had become a master-builder in God's house by the time he was made Bishop of Buffalo in 1847. There, at the meeting of inland seas where first Mass had been said on the deck of a ship in 1697, and rarely after that until the first Pastor came in 1821 to take charge of a host of migrants of unsettled faith, Catholicity sprang into full life at the touch of this "Bishop of Charity." He had been received with a flourish of flambeaux that shone through a drizzling rain on the night of his arrival, had at once joined battle with the inevitable trusteeism and had won, and had then opened hospitals and a Foundling Asylum to which he carried the babies in his own arms. Now education was his problem; would Mother Hardey come to his rescue?

She agreed, and went to explore Buffalo where she received hospitality, as in so many places, from the Sisters of Charity, one of whom wrote of her:

> Mother Hardey appeared to me the most perfect type of religious Superior. At a glance one could see that she was born to rule. Her queenly bearing and noble manners were rendered still more attractive by the beautiful simplicity of her virtues. . . .

Before her departure we had reason to admire, in her generous gifts, what seemed to be the ruling principle of her life: that it is more blessed to give than to receive.

The Foundresses reached Buffalo in the spring of 1849, led by Mother Trincano until the Superior, Mother Brangier, could arrive from France. No other house founded by Mother Hardey went through such acute trials, such faith-testing sorrows as this one. The troubles of the Community were relieved by the unresting, unsparing charity of Bishop Timon whose watch-word, "Do be saints!" drew irresistible power from his own example, and by visits from Mother Hardey, in whose presence "our hearts are at ease."

The school opened in a pleasant house overlooking Lake Erie, but the enrollment was ominously small. The first Mass was said on a plank resting on four chairs; Bishop Timon could give them no better, for he had nothing to give. Instead he gave them the time and the affection of a father. With stubborn hope the Community went ahead with what seemed like an impossible task, for "the people here are mostly merchants who care much for money and little for education. We are very poor and cannot draw pupils." The New Year saw fifteen cents in the Treasury. "Calumnies have been spread against the Nuns; the school is practically ruined," and a little later: "the last boarder has left." In May a visit from Mother Hardey brought them new courage. She did what she could to relieve the situation, even begging her own sister, Mother Matilda Hardey, from the southern Vicariate to help in the emergency. The Bishop moved them to a house more centrally located, but Mother Brangier fell ill, and Mother Cruice came to take her place. Their poverty approached destitution and there was constant sickness, but as the weeks passed the pupils, never more than a handful, caught the spirit of the Sacred Heart; "our children begin to understand us." Then in August, 1852, a visit from Reverend Mother du

Rousier brightened the skies. She took a special interest in the struggling house, and returned to it frequently during her stay in the United States. At her first visit there was hopeful talk of a new house in the country, at Ellysville, but on the day before her departure the shadow of the cross fell blackly. Cholera reached the Convent and with terrible swiftness three Nuns died.

September was a nightmare month. The epidemic in the city was such that no priest could come for Mass. There was no opening of school, and the house became a hospital. The confessor went from room to room, where, in profound silence, death and prayer stood hand in hand. The Bishop determined to move the whole Community to the outskirts of the town, into a house of his own. He brought four carriages, into which he helped the sick. The procession then slowly moved, "like a funeral without a hearse," through the streets of Buffalo. On the way one of the Nuns became violently ill, and nearly died. On reaching the house the Bishop went about the neighbourhood, begging broth from door to door. He heated, seasoned and blessed it, then carried the hot cups from bed to bed. The touch of his blessing brought peace and sometimes healing to the sufferers.

Spiders had long been the sole occupants of the tiny house in which they found themselves, but the Bishop would not let them be without a chapel. He had a wooden altar built and hung it cheerfully with yellow calico. He sent to the cathedral for a choir of seminarians to come and sing, and the walls shook to the sound of the strong young voices. A few pupils who were too far away to go home devoted themselves to housekeeping, and soon the stricken Community began to recover. When the worst seemed over they returned to their house in town.

Then a greater sacrifice than any they had yet faced was

asked of them. Reverend Mother Cruice fell ill of typhoid fever. Mother Hardey came at once from New York, bringing brief joy in the midst of heartbreak, but she was called away by unavoidable business, and it was Mother du Rousier who came in time to be present at Mother Cruice's death on October 22, 1852. She told the Community that their Superior had offered her life for the cessation of the scourge, and assured them that God had accepted the offering. No more deaths occurred, but a dismally cold winter settled down over Buffalo, in the midst of which the kitchen pump broke, the heating system failed and blizzards sent snow and ice drifting through every crack. Mother Gray, the new Superior, brought them artificial roses from Louisiana which glowed with warm colour on the altar on Christmas Eve, but by New Year's Day the owner of the house had turned them out, and they moved glacially into another.

A third visit from Reverend Mother du Rousier in the spring revived hopes of prosperity. Grapevines were planted on the property at Ellysville, and the new house was consecrated, before its building, to Our Lady of Victories. Funds arrived from Mother Hardey, the cornerstone was laid with pomp, and the work began. The walls had risen to a height of eight feet before it was discovered that the foundations were too badly laid to bear the weight of the superstructure. Outwardly it seemed symbolic of the Buffalo Convent, but an unerring Architect had blessed and strengthened those hard beginnings and the walls at last rose, permanent and foursquare, not in Buffalo but in Rochester, whither Bishop Timon reluctantly allowed them to move in June, 1855. Mother Barat, who had been watching anxiously from a distance, blessed the change and wrote of it to Mother Hardey:

> Our help is in the Divine Heart; He will never fail us when we place our confidence in Him and try to serve Him with fidelity

and love. Be assured that His mercy will follow us all the days of our life. "He has carried me in His arms; I shall want for nothing."

No sooner was the Convent established on North Saint Paul Street than prosperity began:

It would be difficult to tell of all the evidences of joy and expressions of kindness which have welcomed us to Rochester. . . . Soon Mother Hardey arrived to share foundation joys with us for a few days, sleeping on the floor like the rest of us that first week. . . . Thirty-five pupils quickly enrolled and there are prospects of steady increase. Bishop Timon is, as formerly, prodigal of kindness and constant in solicitude for us. He often comes from Buffalo or from an outlying mission, arriving early in the morning with his episcopal regalia in an old carpet bag to offer the Holy Sacrifice in the Convent chapel. "Make your Community holy," he says, "and you will be assured of success."

In a few years the Convent was transferred to Prince Street, where the "flower blooming on Calvary" struck root and grew fragrantly strong. Surely neither Bishop Timon nor Mother Hardey would have been surprised to know that in future a remarkable number of religious vocations would come from the School at Rochester, which settled happily down in its city surroundings, a home in which still "our children understand us."

Mother Hardey's next move carried her far inland. The foundation of Detroit was linked by direct causality with Mother Duchesne, who had written in the Florissant Journal in 1821: "Father Aquaroni came to visit us today with a Father Richard who has been for many years a missionary in Detroit. He has begun to build a fine church and urges us to make a foundation there. This is impossible." To say that anything was impossible was not characteristic of Mother Duchesne; her missionary spirit soon got the better of her, and she wrote a little later to Mother Barat: "In my last letter I spoke to you of the proposal of an establishment in Detroit, Michigan, about two months' journey from here. Monseigneur Dubourg was not pleased that I gave Father Richard even so vaguely hopeful an answer." Father Richard had as sanguine a soul as Mother Duchesne. He continued to cling to the "vague hopefulness" of her answer, and when it became apparent that the time was not yet come, he wisely planted his hope deep in the heart of someone who would outlive him.

Father Gabriel Richard [7] was one of the busiest and most influential men in Detroit, perhaps the most picturesque, and certainly the best loved. He had come in 1798 from France to the little town on the frontier of nowhere shortly after its surrender by the English to the United States, when its French atmosphere, its beaver trade, the memory of Pontiac's rebellion and of its own heroic days still clung to it.[8] A few years after his coming the whole of Detroit, with its whitewashed, green-doored houses, its proudly crooked streets and its venerated Church of Sainte Anne, was swept away by fire raging in a high wind. Father Richard went up and down the river banks that night begging food for his children from scattered settlers, and as the new town rose from its ashes he became the soul of its progress, though his clothing never caught up with the fashion. His lank form was everywhere at once; his face was scarred with traces of the French Revolution; his lively, sympathetic eyes peered into the future, while his soul lived aloof in a place of intense prayer. He set up the first printing press in the Northwest Territory that turned out spellers, primers, and French Fables. Six Professorships in the "Catholepistemiad—or University of Michigania" were handed to him simultaneously, together with the Vice-Presidency of the new Institution at its founding in 1817. He was the first Catholic priest to appear in Congress, having been elected as territorial representative in 1823 after a disgracefully exciting campaign in which he was imprisoned by his opponents for having done his priestly duty in a marriage case. He still wore his French Revolution clothes and manner when he appeared in the House, but he secured for Michigan an appropriation for its first Government road.

However, he could not stay away for long from Detroit, where lay the work closest to his heart: education. This born educator not only had a personal library of forty-two volumes in almost as many fields of learning, but he had established, for the purpose of "procuring the greater glory of God, the advancement of religion, and the instruction of the young," an Association with the ambitious title of "Society of Catholic Schools in the Territory of Michigan." He opened schools in which the curriculum, even for girls, included Latin and geometry. Unique among them was the Spring Hill Academy, probably the first industrial school in the country, where the time of the little Indian and white children was divided between intellectual and manual work, and where this energetic and inquisitive priest set up, besides many fine looms and spinning wheels, a "static electrical machine."

For this work Father Richard had called upon the aid of the lay apostolate and four young women gave their lives to this cause, Angélique Campeau, Elizabeth Williams, Elizabeth Lyons and Monique Labadie.[9] They took the greater share of teaching and organizing in his scattered schools, but this was not enough. The four had caught sight of Father Gabriel's own spiritual vision, and an attempt was made to form a religious Community. At first the venture was known as the Monastery of Saint Mary, but in 1826 the Founder reported to the Propagation of the Faith: "I have established a girl's school kept by a Sister of the Sacred Heart; she has twenty pupils; she comes from a nascent Convent near Detroit." Can it be that Father Richard's visit to Florissant in the interval had anything to do with this change of name?

Certain it is that although his attempt at establishing a religious Community dedicated to the Sacred Heart was not to succeed, the devotion to the Sacred Heart which he spread so earnestly among his disciples never died out. Through Monique Labadie the essential part of his dream eventually came true.

Monique was the only one of the four who married. In 1829 she became Madame Antoine Beaubien, and her new name linked her with Angélique Cuillerier de Beaubien who had heroically saved Detroit from destruction in 1763 by revealing the strategy of Pontiac to the colonists. Monique was now wealthy, and she continued to help Father Richard in his school-work until he died in 1832, a victim of his own charity during a cholera epidemic. As Monique advanced through life into the state of eccentric, lavish-handed old age, she grieved that devotion to the Sacred Heart no longer flourished in the City of Detroit, then in its gawky stage of rapid growth. When her only son died she determined to devote part of her fortune to the care of orphans, and looked about for a Religious Order to help her. She had never forgotten Father Richard's talk of Mother Duchesne, and now she somehow got in touch with Mother Hardey and gave her no rest until, in the spring of 1851, a little colony set out from Manhattanville on its journey up the Great Lakes to Michigan. Mother Hardey was unable to accompany them, but she gave the best that she had in Mother Trincano, "my second self," whom she named Superior. This young Italian Religious, exactly Mother Hardey's own age, had come to America in 1847 and had at once shown the rare gift of winning hearts which resulted in her being called upon wherever and whenever there was special need of a worker full of the spirit of God. She found plenty to test her spirit in Detroit.

On the lake boat they were accosted by a Canadian missionary:

"You are Papists, are you not," he asked abruptly. On our affirmative reply he left us brusquely but returned a few minutes later. "Yesterday," he told us, "I said to the Captain, who is a Protestant, 'I am a poor missionary who lives on alms; you can take me for half price. Your boat will not go any slower for that, and I shall pray for you.' He consented. Now, I have just said to him, 'Captain, there are some poor Religious on board who are going to make a foundation for orphans in Detroit. I have nothing to give them in charity, but you can give back to me what I gave you yesterday for my passage.' He did so, and here it is."

Thus assisted, they entered the city, and were driven to the home of Madame Beaubien in a flutter of triumph. An altar to Our Lady stood in the parlour where servants and neighbours crowded through the door to hear Mother Trincano sing the *Magnificat*. Before it was well over, their benefactress burst into joyful applause. "That's what I call Latin singing. I never understand what the singers here are saying, but you I understand! Mary has triumphed; the good French Sisters have come in her month." Then, to Monsieur, "I tell you, *mon vieux*, that if the devil has any horns left now, they are very short!"

But Madame's business capacity was not equal to her zeal, and by an "inexplicable error" it was found that the house secured for the Religious had been rented to someone else. So the work began in another and most unsuitable house, where the Feast of the Sacred Heart was celebrated with calico altar-drapes, borrowed candle-sticks, and a one-voice choir, while the congregation wept with devotion and muttered aloud, "On chante comme les anges; c'est terriblement beau." Madame Beaubien went to the core of the matter, exclaiming in her excitable *patois*: "Thanks to you, good Sisters, the fire is burning; it is you who have kindled it. Devotion to the Sacred Heart has been hidden under the ashes since the death of Father Richard. . . . I shall tell the priests and the Bishop that if these Sisters had not come the Devotion would not have spread."

But the devil still managed to use his shortened horns. A legion of Beaubien heirs arose to contest the donation of property, and this time Mother Hardey set out herself for Detroit, after appealing for help to one of the best of New York's lawyers, Mr. Charles O'Connor, who answered briefly: "I need a vacation; I shall take it in Detroit." He soon discovered legal flaws in the deed of donation, and the signing of a new document became imperative. Père Beaubien refused to do so, for no other reason than an illogical suspicion of pen and paper. Mère Beaubien took Mother Hardey in her carriage to have an interview with the obstinate Antoine. "On the way," related Mother Hardey later, "having no rosary with her she counted her *Aves* by striking her fingers against her breast, while her mind remained fixed rather upon the object of her prayers, which she kept interrupting in this fashion: '*Ave Maria, gratia plena,* O Reverend Mother, you forgot something, *Dominus tecum,* I must tell that to Monsieur Bieubien, *benedicta tu,* we must not lose such a chance for giving glory to God!' " Once in the presence of her husband she went straight to the point. "How stupid you are, *mon vieux*. Don't you see that we are giving our money to the Heart of Jesus, and we could not put it in better hands? Stupid! As for me, I shall challenge the Divine Heart to keep the conditions. If He doesn't, that's His business. . . . See, my Antoine, it's for the Heart of Jesus that we are doing this, all for Him, all for Him." The deed was signed, and when the couple were asked separately by the Court whether any pressure had been brought to bear Madame Beaubien retorted: "I should like to see anyone influence me! I have done my own will since I came into this world, and it is with my whole heart that I make over this property to the Society of the Sacred Heart of Jesus."

Things were going happily and on Mother Trincano's Feast the new children of the Sacred Heart expressed their feelings in a vivid little charade on the word "Felicité." The foundation was dedicated to Saint Philomena, the forgotten little martyr of long ago whom the Curé d'Ars had just made into the friend of all the world, and who showed special favour to the new house entrusted to her. Then the clouds gathered again. Madame Beaubien died suddenly, "a simple and prayerful soul," as Mother Trincano said of her, and the whole City grieved over her loss. Antoine promptly remarried and left the Convent to the mercy of the Beaubien heirs, who at once renewed their suit. The consequences were avoided for the time being by a hasty and clandestine transfer to another house over which there was no dispute, a move in which their devoted chaplain, Father Hennaert, and Bishop Lefèvre himself connived by sending carts and helpers in the early light of dawn.

Troubles multiplied, and in June, 1853, Mother Hardey came in person to the relief of the Community, staying six weeks this time. She moved the orphans, in compliance with the last expressed wish of Madame Beaubien, to a house in Sandwich, Ontario, and bought for the Academy a new house in the suburbs known as Elmwood. When she went away she took with her Mother Trincano for whom other work was waiting, and left Mother Regis Hamilton as Superior. The latter had to face the worst crisis of all. In accordance with certain advisory remarks made by the General Council of the Society in 1851, and with more explicit arrangements made by Reverend Mother du Rousier, none of which could be lightly set aside by Mother Hardey, no day scholars were to be accepted at Elmwood, and certain disciplinary measures were to be enforced which were not to the liking of Bishop Lefèvre. Like a thunderbolt fell his verdict: the Convent was placed under interdict, and the Nuns left to pray in sorrow before an empty Tabernacle, without Mass or Sacraments. Mother Hardey came back at once to face one of the most difficult and delicate situations of her life. She alone understood all sides of the question. She knew, as the Bishop could not, what were the Society's motives and what wisdom lay behind its stand in the matter. She also knew, as those in Paris could not, the special needs of the Detroit house and the Bishop's reasons for his stand. Her loyalties were stretched in every direction, but with strong patience she held true to them all. While the weeks of negotiation were dragging on she lifted the spirit of the tried Community to her own serene level of thought:

> She told us that we did not apply ourselves strongly enough to a practical study of Our Lord, and that any want of progress in the spiritual life came from that cause. What makes our work of little avail for the glory of God is that we are not in contact with the hand which must hold us as an instrument. Thus the means of doing our work well is to draw close to the Sacred Heart; for even as a workman cannot handle his tool with ease if it is remote from his hand and thus leaves the work incomplete, so if we withdraw from the hand of Our Lord the Divine work cannot be done.

In the meantime Mother Barat had written to the Bishop in that fearless, humble way of hers which Prelates were accustomed to find completely disarming:

> Our Constitutions, which have been approved by the Holy See, do not permit us to leave our enclosure either for Church services or for works of zeal. Have our Mothers failed in their duty to your Lordship by any want of that respect and submission which our holy Rules prescribe towards ecclesiastical authority, and have they thus merited to be the first examples of their present painful position which the Society has yet witnessed? I ask myself with anxiety all these questions, and I know not what to conjecture. If your

Lordship will deign to inform me of the cause of your displeasure, I shall earnestly seek to remedy it. In the meantime I venture to appeal to your charity in behalf of my daughters. If they have failed in their duty to your Lordship, I unite with them in imploring pardon. . . . I beg you to consider that it is not in my power to permit them to infringe their rules of enclosure, so that if you will not restore to them the spiritual help which is ordinarily granted, they will be placed under the necessity of giving up their mission in your Diocese. . . . Your Lordship knows well that these Rules have been wisely ordained, and that they are the safeguard of religious spirit. I am convinced that you would not wish to see them set aside, and thereby open the door to abuses which would be doubly deplorable in a Protestant country. . . . Deign to be favourable to my prayer, and restore to my family your fatherly protection.

Another letter to Mother Hardey gave leave for the admission of day-students and so a reconciliation was gradually brought about. The Bishop expressed his pleasure upon hearing that the Convent would be moved back into the City once more, and the pleasure soon turned into active friendship. In the meantime Mother Hardey was having other troubles with the Beaubien heirs, and in the course of endless litigation she revealed a brilliant talent for the law profession. The legal adviser of the Beaubiens declared that he "would rather contend with ten lawyers than with Mother Hardey," and he confided to a mutual friend "Mother Hardey has missed her vocation. If she were a partner in my firm I should be a rich man, for she is the cleverest woman I have ever met." This same mutual friend was asked by Mother Hardey to take some deeds to Mr. O'Connor in New York for examination. He merely asked: "Has Mother Hardey seen these?" "Yes." "Then you may roll them up and take them back to her, for if she has examined them it is needless for me to do so."

Thus by prayer and skill, by suffering and energy, Mother Hardey smoothed the way for the flourishing and peaceful life of the Detroit Convent on its Jefferson Avenue site. The walls of the new building rose in 1861, and at her visit the following year she found a large Academy and a larger free-school basking in the light of episcopal patronage, while through sodalities the dearly bought influence of the Convent reached out in all directions. So tranquil was the atmosphere that Mother Hardey chose to make her retreat at Jefferson Avenue, while the Journal remarked: "So peaceful and uniform has our life become that there is little of interest to record." In this peace work was to go vigorously on in many forms for half a century, until the apostolic spirit of Jefferson Avenue was transferred with the corner stone of the old building to its present site on Lawrence and Wilson Avenues, where from the walls the portraits of Monique and Antoine Beaubien still look down in old-world approval upon the fruits of their generosity. "You will see," Madame had said, "devotion to the Sacred Heart will flourish here."

For five years after coming to Manhattanville Mother Hardey had watched the river-boats grow small as they moved against the flow of the Hudson, up into the hill-crests to the north. At last, in 1852, she followed them to where the newly erected See of Albany was calling for a Convent School. Its Bishop, the future Cardinal McCloskey, was an old friend of Astoria days. As usual, the first foothold was found in the heart of town, on South Pearl Street, and here the new Community under Mother Ellen Jennings took possession in July. They found themselves in a stronghold of politely astonished Protestantism, facing a Young Ladies' Seminary of rigorous notions, and surrounded by neighbors more curious than bigoted. Invitations of a social nature arrived, one addressed to "Mr. and Mrs. Sacred Heart." "Our house was open to every wind, and to all the curious strangers who had a mind to come in silently, watch the Nuns at work, look at whatever was new to them, and withdraw without a word," while the Foundresses were cheered by a visit from Reverend Mother du Rousier, who shared their gaiety and poverty, "with bread and milk on the table, and no knives."

The work grew so fast that it soon had to be moved to the edge of town, on Troy Road. Mother Hardey had no doubts about the Albany foundation, especially when she saw the very marked way in which devotion to the Sacred Heart took possession of the first pupils, and she showed her prophetic spirit by purchasing, in 1859, a house on a hill, a place where rivers rise "to make glad the City of God," Kenwood, beautiful and beloved among houses. It was called the Rathbone estate when Mother Hardey first saw it, lying among the hills south of Albany and looking out upon horizons wide enough for even her generous soul to find rest and assurance there. Against the blue sky the crests of the Heidelbergs stood out more deeply blue, while the fields and foothills lay mistily green below, cut by the sharp sinuous silver of the river as it looped from sight to the south. Here, where forest silences clung to the fringes of work by day and possessed the air by night, it was easier than it had been in the city to remember what footsteps had passed before her over this ground, under the leaf-mould of two centuries.

Where Albany now stood a Dutch stockade had been built around Fort Orange in the same year in which a wall changed the tip of Manhattan Island into New Amsterdam. Furs were traded and gardens bloomed in the town of Beverswyck under the guns of the Fort when, in 1634, a Saint could be seen limping along the river bank, guarded by hatcheted Mohawks. Isaac Jogue let the air of Fort Orange drink deep of his tormented, peace-anchored prayers for the conversion of this land, until the uncomprehending but kindly Dutchmen helped him to slip from his captors.[10] They smuggled him in a boat down the Hudson to New Amsterdam and then out to the wide seas and to safety beyond. But Jogue came back again to the headwaters of the Hudson, and this time it was the soil that drank deep of his outpouring, not of prayers only but of his blood. He was tommyhawked one moonless night in a village some miles to the northeast of Fort Orange. Twelve years went by, and almost on the very spot where he died Kateri Tekakwitha was born.[11] Her uncle, Chief of the Turtle Clan, was among the important braves who stalked silently in and out of the Fort at the time when it changed its Dutch flag for the English; her tribe hunted and fished in the neighbouring Vale of Tawasentha, or the Valley of Many Dead. Kateri, shy but brave, hidden but shining like a pine-torch in the Indian lodges, was baptized by a Blackrobe, and having once tasted of prayer lived for nothing else. She was persecuted by her people not for being a Christian but for being a holy one, and at last she fled north up the Mohawk Valley through the crimson autumn of her twenty-first year. In a Christian village of Canada her life quickly burned itself out in a holocaust fit to bring graces showering upon the land of the Mohawks and upon the people who should live after them in their silent places.

Mother Hardey, standing on the south edge of Kenwood's terraces, could look down upon the Vale of Tawasentha. Longfellow would soon tell the nation how:

> In the Vale of Tawasentha,
> In the green and silent valley,
> By the pleasant water-courses
> Dwelt the singer Nawadaha.
> There he sang of Hiawatha,
> Sang the song of Hiawatha.

Mother Hardey made swift, complete plans. As soon as an ample house had replaced the residence now standing, she would bring the Novices from Manhattanville to Kenwood.

In keeping with its spirit, prayer and sacrifice would be offered in this lofty place.

The Civil War brought a lull in the founding of houses, on United States' soil at least, but not long after the close of hostilities Mother Hardey was in Philadelphia to arrange for the opening of a City House. It was very much desired by the Children of Mary of Eden Hall who were happy to see their venture placed under the patronage of Mater Admirabilis on October 20, 1865, when the first Mass was said in a rented house. The following year the school, already numerous, moved into the Edwards House on Walnut Street. At each of her visits Mother Hardey saw the new Convent's multiple works of charity reaching out more broadly even into such fields as that of the City Almshouse where the Children of Mary did heroic service for many years. Twenty years later, in the very month of Mother Hardey's death, it was to move again into a specially built Academy on Arch Street, where for thirty more years a rich inheritance was prepared for the Overbrook Country Day School which was to succeed it. In 1920 a beautiful Tudor Gothic house lifted its high façade over the rolling outdoors, while still carrying on the busy work of a city house.

In the meantime Cincinnati had not given up its tenacious claims on Mother Hardey. Ever since 1836 Bishop Purcell had been trying to bring her to his episcopal city, and at one time he had nearly succeeded. But Mother Barat, then in great difficulties, had been forced to disappoint him, and for the next thirty years he continued to plead. Finally in 1869 his hopes grew strong, for he found a powerful ally in Mrs. Sarah Peter.[12]

This remarkable woman was a warm admirer of Mother Hardey, who in return considered her "a truly apostolic soul, on fire to fill up those things that are wanting to the Passion of Christ by devoting herself to the neglected and the suffering." She liked to stop in New York on her many journeys to Europe where she went to collect art treasures, and to interest every royal and ecclesiastical personage of note that she could manage to meet in her good works. With an irresistible combination of shrewdness and charm she collected art treasures from them for purposes of civic uplift, and large sums of money for the convents and hospitals that she had founded. Her handsome and imposing figure leaned heavily upon a cane at her last visits to Manhattanville, but nothing could quench the electric sparkle of the broad blue eyes under white curls. The family of Sarah Ann Worthington represented that aristocracy of mind that had kept culture and dignity abreast of the American frontier. She had first married Edward King, and from their Cincinnati home the young couple kept in touch with the intellectual life of the east and middle-west. After her husband's death she married an Englishman, William Peter, and lived for many years in Philadelphia, active in fostering art and social betterment. She usually managed to combine the two, as in the Philadelphia School of Design which she founded, a pioneer school for teaching industrial art to young women. Wealthy, attractive and of forceful personality, Mrs. Peter drew the best of life into her hands only to give it out again to others. Her soul was as keen as her mind, and on one of her journeys to Rome she met a number of distinguished converts to the faith, both English and American, and followed them into the Catholic Church in 1855. She then spent a spiritual honeymoon at the Sacred Heart Convent of the Trinita from where she wrote: "My life here at the Convent is as delightful as heart can desire, and you may imagine the self-denial it costs me to leave it. I come in and out and receive visits at pleasure, and all sorts of kindness from the dear, good sensible and most lady-like *religieuses*."

As a Catholic she added supernatural zeal to her already

boundless philanthropy. After establishing the Good Shepherd Nuns, the Sisters of Mercy and the Sisters of Saint Francis in Cincinnati she set her heart on having the Sacred Heart there as well, and so it happened that Mother Hardey received a letter from Mrs. Peter which renewed Bishop Purcell's old appeal:

> It is so long since I have seen you that I fear that I have become almost a stranger; still I am sure you have not forgotten one who has so long loved you and so well. You would perhaps laugh if you were to know how many efforts I continue to make to bring your dear congregation and yourself also to our neighborhood. I have only desisted when my attempts seemed almost hopeless. Yet now, just now, for it is not half an hour since I left the Archbishop, all my hopes are renewed. Without any hint from me or any thought of it, his Grace mentioned that a magnificent property, beautifully situated, two or three miles out of the city had been offered to him, and he thought it would be altogether suitable for a Convent of the Sacred Heart.

The Archbishop's brother, Father Purcell, undertook the arrangements, and by November Mother Hardey had taken possession not of a magnificent property but of a temporary house on West Sixth Street, where a Community recruited from Kenwood and Manhattanville soon joined her. She stayed with the foundresses for three weeks, and "all the days during which our dear Mother remained in our midst were as bright as June days within, though all without was gloomy and dismal." These weeks gave Mother Hardey a chance to indulge in the hard manual work which she loved, and to plan all manner of conventual festivities for the young Community. The Bishop and his brother came in season and out with ornamental and useful objects, and the Blessed Sacrament had made its home with them before Mother Hardey went away, leaving Mother Hogan as Superior. It was January before any pupils arrived, but the Sodality of the Children of Mary was formed with Mrs. Peter as the first President. Mother Hardey managed to visit Cincinnati from time to time by making long detours on her journeys to other houses, "and of course, everything was invested with a new brightness as soon as she made her appearance." She formed far-sighted plans for the removal of the Convent to a better site, though only later, as Assistant General, would she climb Clifton's beautiful hill and taste the warm, affectionate joy of its special spirit. It was at her second visit to Cincinnati that she gave a conference to the Community which sums up as no other words could do all that she herself had put into her thirty years of founding houses:

"Be ye perfect as your heavenly Father is perfect." The soul that lives in the presence of God is interior, however distracting her occupations; the soul that lives in the presence of God is peaceful, however troublesome and annoying her labours. The soul that lives in the presence of God is humble, however exalted her position. When we live in that divine presence we are always humble, and what virtue is more essential than humility to the members of a foundation? What does it mean? The very word is its own meaning. It is to establish a dwelling where souls may come to learn of the love of the Sacred Heart, the foundations of which are formed of the solid virtues of humility, charity, fervour and zeal. . . . A deep responsibility rests upon those who are chosen to be foundation stones in the house of God. How then shall this responsibility be discharged? By living in the presence of God, and becoming perfect even as our heavenly Father is perfect.

XIV

TO THE NORTH

IT IS SOMETIMES in a round-about way that dreams sent by God come true. There had been a day when the Society of the Sacred Heart had numbered three members, the youngest of whom was its unsuspecting Foundress, Sister Sophie. Canada was their first dream, in the Convent of Amiens where

in the evening, after the fatigues and exhaustion of work, when the children were in bed, the three of us found ourselves free. Then our souls swam in the waters of refreshment. . . . It was our consolation, in a great purity of union in God alone. We talked together over the fire in the kitchen. There, our three heads close together, we exchanged our happy confidences. Sister Sophie, full of zeal, spoke her longing for the missions of Canada; Sister Grosier was drawn in the same way, while I listened.[1]

This Canadian dream was exciting, a trifle over-coloured perhaps by stories of the Jesuit missionaries of the seventeenth century and ending in longed-for but improbable martyrdom under the knives of Indians. Forty years later, under far different circumstances, the Sister Sophie of old arranged for the realization of her dream when she could no longer take part in it herself, and when the utilitarian architecture of the nineteenth century had replaced Indian lodges in the wilds of Canada. The foundation in Montreal was made by way of New York, and Mother Hardey faced not martyrdom but twenty years of incessant self-donation and long traveling when she assumed responsibility for this "mission" in 1842.

Bishop Bourget had come to Houston Street the year before to beg for a Convent of the Sacred Heart in his Diocese, and it was Mother Galitzin who had first visited the proferred site. Upon arriving, she took possession of Canada in the manner of William the Conqueror by tumbling out of the carriage into the mud in such wise that Canadian soil clung to her willy-nilly and she accepted the foundation, leaving its accomplishment in Mother Hardey's hands. The latter could not go with the foundresses, but she speeded them onto a Hudson River boat in the dead of December. There were four of them, led by Mother Sallion, and they sailed straight into northern snows. That night the passengers were advised to go to bed early to avoid freezing, and before many hours the boat was helpless in the clutches of an ice drift. The Captain announced his return to New York. Anyone who cared to go on, he said, would be put ashore. "We were told to go, not to go back," said Mother de Kersaint quietly. "Let us be like the Holy Family and go on. Perhaps we shall find a shelter." So the four Nuns were left standing in a snow-drift in the windy dark. They walked blindly towards a light in the distance which proved to be a postoffice where they spent the night sitting on benches by a roaring fire. With the morning mail-coach they were off again until they reached the Saint Lawrence. Montreal lay beyond, and they astonished the Parish priest of La Prairie who had offered them shelter by demanding sleds immediately for the dangerous crossing. The sleds came after an hour's wait on the ice in a bitter wind, and the drivers declared that never had they seen women cross the river in such weather. It is no wonder that Bishop Bourget greeted them with some amazement. "I had not expected you till spring," he said, "but now that I have you here I shall never let you return to New York," and he took them skimming over the ice to their new house at Saint Jacques l'Achigan.

Mother Hardey followed them later to Montreal. She had brought the Society of the Sacred Heart to this queenly place exactly two hundred years after Paul de Chomédy, Sieur de Maisonneuve, had taken possession of the river-island and built his Ville Marie.[2] In her quiet, business-like way she was not only fulfilling the youngest missionary dream of her Mother Foundress, but acting in response to a far older one that had first summoned this city to rise out of the wilderness on the slopes of its Royal Mount. There are not many great cities of the world of which a tourist's Guide Book could say:

> The main point to be remembered in connection with the early settlement of Montreal is that it was the result of religious enthusiasm. It was an attempt to found in America a veritable "Kingdom of God" as understood by devout Roman Catholics. The expedition was fitted out in France solely for that purpose, and the inception of the enterprise has many romantic particulars of "voices and revelations" and "providential occurrences" by which the zeal of its founders was supported and stimulated.

The first Jesuit *Relations* sent home from the new world, in the early seventeenth century, had set hundreds of persons "en route vers le Christ." More than priests were needed, and Père Le Jeune called out for stout peasants to come and build homes, land-tilling homes, cells of the Body of Christ in His New World; he called for Hospitalers to reach the souls of the Indians through healing and well-being; he called for "a brave school-mistress, whom zeal for God and affection for the salvation of the people will bring to Canada, with courageous companions." His call was heard. Young artisans, defying Jansenism, cried out: "Follow Jesus Christ! The faith is leaving France, let us go to Canada!" Fine ladies at court sent over-seas for little Redskins to be brought to Paris, there to be clothed in silk, baptized and sent home to do likewise to their people. Within the Carmelite cloister, a special oratory was built where prayers might be said for the salvation of New France. Thirteen Ursulines signed a vow to go there in person, when permitted. "Nature has no power to light such a glow," commented Le Jeune. "These flames come from a fire that is all divine." It kindled Mère Marie de l'Incarnation through mystic visions till she came to Quebec in 1639 and opened the first Convent on North American soil, where she planted her own devotion to the Sacred Heart deep. "May our drawing-near to It," she wrote, "cause true sanctity to flow into our hearts, for it is from this Sacred Heart that come all the treasures of grace and of love." [3] With her came the Hospital Nuns of Dieppe to open the Hôtel-Dieu, and Quebec had become an intense center of spiritual life among unchristened solitudes when the ships of Maisonneuve appeared on the Saint Lawrence. He resisted the temptation to anchor in the shadow of the rock, and pressed on to his island of vision.

This consecrated soldier was sailing in conscious obedience to the Liturgy of Candlemas Day, as a "light to the Revelation of the Gentiles." Some years before, on that very Feast, Monsieur de Dauversière, collector of revenues at La Flêche, had been inspired to establish a Religious Order which would open a hospital on the then unpeopled Island of Montreal. Six years later, on the same Feast Monsieur Olier, future founder of the Sulpicians, received a divine intimation, less precise but no less strong, that he also was to be a bearer of light to Canada, while at the same time two women were moved, through mystic intervention, to cooperate. By strange yet simple ways the plans of the four visionaries worked together towards fulfillment, and by 1641 the association of "Les Messieurs de Montreal" had been formed "pour servir Dieu et les sauvages," and Maisonneuve was chosen the civil and military leader of the enterprise.

Dawn on May 18, 1642, brought Maisonneuve and his colony to their island. There were Jesuit missioners in the party, and an adventurous young woman. It was she, Jeanne Mance, who prepared an altar under the shadow of Mount Royal, where Father Vimont founded the city of Ville Marie by saying Mass. The Blessed Sacrament was left till nightfall on the log altar, to be adored in the hush of the unconquered forest by these builders of a new City of God, for not till the next day would Maisonneuve consent to break the stillness by felling the first tree for a house. There was no oil for a sanctuary lamp, but those who had come "lumen ad revelationem Gentium" caught a bottle full of fireflies and let it shine before God in its wavering woodland way.

Mother Hardey put foot in Montreal not far from the spot where Maisonneuve had landed, but her destination lay miles to the north of the City; to reach it she must pass over the now-paved trail of the "Croisés de Montréal." She passed Fortification Street, and its name said enough of wars with the Iroquois whose Providential mission, according to the Jesuits, had been to people the Church Triumphant by cutting down the Church Militant. To her left rose the mountain to the top of which the settlers had toiled with a great cross to be placed in the crown of New France. Somewhere on the slope below was the site of the stone stable in which Marguerite Bourgeoys had taught the children, Red and White, until her work grew into the Congregation of Notre Dame which has been teaching Canada ever since.[4] Somewhere too in these streets, at a time when they were paths, Tekakwitha had peeped from behind her blanket at Marguerite's Nuns, and followed them to their convent, where her soul's eye had opened to the beauty of consecration which she made a reality in the brief remnant of her life. There too was the Hôtel Dieu where Jeanne Mance, after years of single-handed toil, established the Hospital Sisters of Saint Joseph, in realization of the vision of Monsieur de Dauversière. The Mystic City might look drab and worldly-wise enough as time went by, clad in utilitarian masonry and in commercial prosperity, and Mother Hardey herself, so deft and so alert, managing her time as carefully as a financier, might seem to be thoroughly of the same age, but as she approached the palace of Bishop Bourget in that spring of 1844 there was no other force controlling her than that which had sent Marguerite Bourgeoys over the sea to an intangible continent where "Christ prowled after the souls of His lost children." She, like Marguerite, believed that the Divine Explorer could be best served by winning and keeping the children for His Heart, and here was the Bishop to tell her the ways and means of her own day.

He was a white-haired man whose gentle, sensitive features softened the effect of his tremendous administrative energy and whose sanctity worked miracles during his own life-time.[5] Bishop Bourget was riding on the crest of the wave. Canada's "Heroic Age" had come to an end in 1659 with the appointment of its first Bishop, Monseigneur Montigny-Laval, who from Quebec had organized his incalculable diocese as "a holy man, father of the poor and of the public" and a few years later Ville-Marie had been given in fief to the Sulpician Order. Since then, through the turmoil of uneasy union with its English conquerors, through the Penal restrictions brought to bear upon French Catholics, and through the attempt to Protestantize all forms of education, the church in Montreal had grown steadily until its erection into a separate See in 1836. When religious independence had been assured by the Act of Union soon after, an immense impetus for the development of all forms of Catholic activity had set in, due largely to the zeal of Bishop Bourget. In a short span of years five Religious Communities of men and sixteen of women had either been founded on Canadian soil or introduced from elsewhere. He was eager to have the Society of the Sacred Heart among them, and assured Mother Hardey that, with its bilingual customs, it was well adapted to draw both French and English-speaking children. Then he guided her through flowering apple-orchards to Saint Jacques de l'Achigan.

It was a village on the banks of the Assumption River. Though snow-buried much of the year it bore a strange resemblance, in tongue and in customs, to the sun-drenched Opelousas of Mother Hardey's childhood, for it too had been founded by refugee Acadians. Four *arpents* of land had been promised the Religious when they came, but the surreptitious generosity of the Pastor had so increased the gift that Mother Hardey found the little Convent set in a wooded, watered stretch of three hundred and sixty *arpents*. Here the first-comers had been received by an outburst of civil and ecclesiastical pomp on the Feast of Saint John, when the house was blessed as for Easter Saturday while roaring stoves kept the cold at bay. Since then it had been enlarged by a chapel designed by Mother Sallion. Mother Hardey saw that ignorance was rolling away like a cloud from the scattered homes nearby, thanks to the Free School; she rejoiced in the simplicity of life among the *habitants;* she saw that an Apostolate was being carried on by a circulating library, by a long-distance Sodality for Children of Mary in Montreal; above all she saw the nucleus of a Noviceship. All this was good, but Mother Hardey was not easily blinded where there was question of a greater good. She knew that during the winter months most of the work came to a stand-still and so before she left she had started plans for buying property nearer the city. This resolve was made easier by the fact that the villagers rose in open protest when they saw most of the places in the School being given to children from Montreal, and they had started a semi-rebellion which must have reminded Mother Hardey of the Acadian Trustees of old in Saint Michael's.

Two years later the change was made. The Community of Saint Jacques was divided, leaving Mother de Kersaint, or "de Coeur Saint" as the people called her, to carry on the work there for five more years. They were difficult years with the Nuns doing all their own hard work and with fish from the river as their only unfailing sourcc of supplies, until the house was turned over to a new Order, the Sisters of Saint Anne, which Bishop Bourget had founded and which was specially equipped for the work in rural Parishes. The Religious then joined the Community of the new Convent at Saint Vincent's on the Ile Jésus. There it carried on its work successfully for ten years, but in Mother Hardey's mind it was only meant to be one more stepping-stone nearer to Montreal, and when she next came North she determined upon a further move.

When the news transpired a veritable tumult broke out in the Village of Saint Vincent. Father Lavallée was inconsolable at the thought of losing his Convent, and a town-meeting was called. The result was a document sent to the Administrator of the Diocese in which the Village, in an extremity of self-righteous pride, dared to pit itself against the mighty Montreal. The petition pleaded in behalf of this

> refuge prepared by generous piety for young girls, where they may adorn their minds by study of letters and science and form their hearts to the love and practice of virtue. . . . This establishment is destined to plant all virtues and spread consolation in the cottages of the poor and happiness in Christian families.

Enclosed in the petition was a Memoir drawn up in the form of a balance between:

Montreal where there are: taxes of all kinds, insalubrity of the climate, terrible ravages of pestilence—situation peculiar to the city of Montreal—probability of the seeing the number of Know-Nothings increase, enormous expense for the construction of a building, of fuel, etc. . . . Numerous visits to the great detriment of the rules of the Convent, proximity to places of scandal, forced withdrawal of pupils, etc., etc.

At Saint Vincent de Paul: enchanting site, picturesque outlook, delightful woodlands, agreeable and healthy grounds for recreation. Seclusion from the noise and tumult of the world, exemption from taxes. Practically no danger of fire. Construction and enlargement of building at low cost. Moderate expenditure for fuel. Less frequent visits from parents. . . . Position of the town of Saint Vincent de Paul incomparably superior to that of Montreal as far as sanitary conditions are concerned—and this on the word of doctors.

These overwhelming arguments were crowned by the promise that a stage-coach line—fare $1—would soon do away with Montreal's argument of distance, while gifts of property and money were added to the verbal appeal. It was hard to resist but Mother Hardey's decisions were notoriously firm, and another equally determined Pastor, Father Vinet, had offered lands in the Parish of the Sault-au-Recollect, easy of access from the City and far enough from it to be free of the fearful menaces enumerated in the Memoir.[6]

On August 7, 1856, Mother Hardey was present at the blessing of the corner-stone of a completely new building, and watched with pleased amazement an outburst of popular feeling which more than justified her choice. The local newspaper gave a vivid account of the scene the next day:

The citizens have shown remarkable zeal in making the ceremony imposing. Carriages lined the road from the Church to the edifice a mile away. Garlands and green festoons made the Church a charming sight. From early morning skilled musicians filled the air with the sounds of joy. . . . Towards noon the bells rang out, the canon spoke with majestic voice, the musicians poured forth their sweetest harmonies, while his Lordship, the Bishop of Montreal, appeared and blessed the respectful crowd. . . . After solemn singing by the pupils of the Sacred Heart themselves, the crowd set out for the Church, following the banners that were carried high. The Cavalry was proud and happy to render military homage to our Venerated Pontiff, and to mingle their warlike uniforms with the white surplices of the priests and levites.

The house was two years in building, but at last the goods from Saint Vincent's was sledded over the ice-bridge in the dead of winter, and life at the Sault began. When Mother Hardey arrived again on the scene she found the Gothic greystone Convent standing with austere yet gracious dignity, lifting its tower in a tract of semi-wild woodland. From the homes of farmers scattered about the tiny Parish Church, a little gem of Roman architecture in a setting of God's handiwork, the children came in crowds to the School of Sainte Sophie into which the original Meilleur house had been transformed. In the boarding-school a dual system of classes in French and English met the needs of the children, who came in great numbers from Montreal and from far beyond. Bilingualism would not die out here, as it would inevitably do in the United States. Mother Hardey came in all seasons to the Sault, loving its strict simplicity, its gay warmth in a cold setting. On a January night she saw:

a sky scintillating with a thousand fires, and the moon shining in full brilliance over a sparkling white country-side which reflects all the beauties of heaven in its crystal ice. Then, at seven in the evening, when the cold is thirty or forty degrees below zero, we can walk outdoors and play in the snow without the slightest discomfort, so calm and pure is the air. These are among the joys of our beautiful Canada!

She saw the children watching the shrouded sugar-maples impatiently for the first stirring of sap that would bring out the sugar buckets and set the fires burning rosy-red in the snow. As warmth crept into the air, she heard the grinding, roaring sound of the ice breaking under the windows as the uneasy river stirred. Even in summer the Rivière des Prairies shot in wild self-will through its rapids, making a perpetual voice in the silence to which Mother Hardey listened, unaccustomed, as she led the Community to a leaf-screened place on the shore of a cove for a brief, soul-precious gathering. Here, said the talkative waters, a brave soul sped to God. In 1625, Father Nicholas Viel, the Recollect, "le bon Père Nicolas" as all the *Relations* called him, was voyaging in his canoe with Ahautsic, a newly-baptized Indian lad, when his treacherous Huron guides threw them both into the swiftly devouring rapids.[7] Eighty years after his martyrdom a Jesuit Mission was established on the site for a brief time, and the murmur of the Mass was heard under the overtones of the stream. It was still heard now, indoors, in a Gothic chapel, a sound more unchanging than the river's flow, while later missioners taught their pale-faces. Unaltered by years both sounds went on together, and not even the fire which later destroyed the greater part of the building that Mother Hardey loved could check the continuance of the work that she had begun.

Reverend Mother Trincano, in whose hands the care of the Sault was left, was resolved at all costs to keep its character of high simplicity, and to make its influence felt in the City, where there was hope for still another foundation. The carrying out of her first resolve achieved her second.

The Bishop was at the Sault for an ordination ceremony on the last Sunday of 1860, and was served at breakfast by some of the older pupils of the Academy. The courtesy of their manner and the simplicity of their dress seemed to impress him as never before. "I see that crinolines are banned here," he said to Reverend Mother Trincano. "Yes," she answered, wondering what would come next. "Well, I wish you would come to preach in Montreal; I give you full permission." . . . Three weeks later the Bishop came for Confirmation. "Monseigneur," ventured Mother Trincano, "you invited us to preach in Montreal. I am quite ready to do so, but I have to have a little ground on which to stand. I could then have the meetings of the Children of Mary there, and by this means perhaps accomplish much good. And there could be retreats for them."

So a day-school was opened in 1862 on Saint Hubert Street. The foundresses came in from the Sault with a vast amount of luggage but no bread, so the neighbors provided them with cake. In pomp and poverty the house was blessed, and "everyone was intoxicated with joy," remarked the usually sober Journal. The house was to be, in the words of Bishop Bourget, "a temple of peace in the midst of a bustling world," and it bustled a bit itself in carrying on the multiple works which soon developed, including an unofficial but powerfully effective "Apostolate of Modesty." Within a year it became necessary to move to larger quarters, the first of five changes of locality which eventually brought the house to Atwater Avenue on the side of Mount Royal itself. There it stands on the ground once covered by Marguerite Bourgeoys' Indian Mission, whose old wall still fringes it. It looks out over Ville Marie, still thinking the thoughts of de Maisonneuve for his City of God.

In the meantime, Mother Hardey was as busy on the Atlantic as on the Saint Lawrence, for in the May of 1849 she had herself led a new colony from Manhattanville to Halifax. It was the Eve of Ascension Day when they set out and the cannon on the Jersey shore saluted their boat as it moved away in a burst of wind-stirred sunshine. They landed in Halifax in the dark of the wee hours three days later, and saw the dawn pour up from the sea and set the harbour and the sharp military outlines of the City on fire. They went at once to the Bishop's palace. As Mother Hardey wrote:

> Bishop Walsh has shown us unequaled kindness and generosity, and likes to say that the day of our entry into his city is one of the happiest of his life. He was shaving when informed of our arrival, but threw aside his razor and came running to meet us, one side of his face shaved and one not. He kept us at his house all day while the ladies of Halifax were making ready for us at Brookside.

Two carriages called to take them to the Convent in the late afternoon, and although their new home was practically next door to the Cathedral the Bishop saw to it that they passed all the spots of interest in the city on their way. They were now in the land of Acadia itself, but Mother Hardey had seen and heard more that was Acadian in southern Opelousas than here in this very English northern city with Redcoats and Blue-jackets everywhere in evidence. Yet just across the semi-island lay Annapolis, the one-time Port Royal, oldest of French settlements in the western world, where the first Indians had been baptized with their chief, the redoubtable Membertou who, at the age of one hundred, became Henry and a faithful Christian. An attack by the English in 1613 had scattered what colonists it did not kill, and so the Acadians wandered the woods, peopling them and planting their faith there as deeply as the rooted trees. Only in 1749 was the strong English garrison of Halifax founded by Cornwallis, where the forthright life of England throve under its Citadel and flowered into homes, orchards and commerce. There were Scotch and Irish Catholics among the settlers who came flocking in; and they had in common with the Acadians and the converted Indians interests deeper than racial differences. To address such a congregation a priest had need of the gift of at least four tongues, French, English, Gaelic and Micmac. As Mother Hardey's carriage drove along the water-front on the present Barrington Street, it rolled past the spot where the greatest of the missioners of Halifax had all but achieved the miracle.[8] The Abbé Pierre Maillard had said Mass there in a barn. He was brave, wise, gentle, a book-lover and a leader of men, who had come to Halifax in 1760 as Vicar-General of the Bishop of Quebec. Even politically he was influential, and maintained a precarious peace between the disputers of the land, while his leisure time was given to composing books in the Micmac tongue. All the Catholics of Halifax came, half surreptitiously, to his barn where the Blessed Sacrament was housed with a lamp, kept alive out of their poverty, for its guardian.

A little beyond this site the Bishop asked the party to alight and walk through a pine wood near the water. Here Mother Hardey was invited into an Indian tent, lit by a fire in the middle and furnished with an old trunk, some cooking pots and a gun. Sitting about in friendly silence were the descendants of Abbé Maillard's Micmac children, Catholics still and proud of it. Their Pastors could no longer speak their tongue, so they entrusted the tale of their misdoings to an old woman who alone could serve as their interpreter in confession, and thus they remained true to the Sacraments. Perhaps Mother Hardey's alms, always generous, had never been received with more proudly contented indifference.

They reached Brookside at the end of the circling drive. It was a pleasant frame house, screened by fruit-trees and furnished throughout by thoughtfulness, while a picture of Saint Margaret Mary in the chapel told them that they were at home. Not far away the grim crest of the Citadel rose protectingly over them, and their steps could not help falling into time with its martial music. The ocean stretched magnificently into the distances, with its come and go of boats. Near at hand was the Cathedral where they heard Mass the next day, enthroned against their will by the Bishop on carpeted prie-dieux near the altar, that the Congregation might be impressed, and might be prepared to read shortly an advertisement in the local paper announcing that:

> An Academy for Young Ladies has been opened at Brookside, where a solid and refined education will be given. . . . Music, the Modern Languages, and every branch of a polite education will be taught. The formation of the hearts of the Young Ladies to virtue, and the culture of their minds by the study of those subjects which are intended to constitute a superior education being the great object which the Ladies of the *Sacré Coeur* have in view, no pains will be spared to attain the desired end. The system pursued is strictly parental, and the mild influence of virtue is the guiding principle which enforces their regulation.[9]

The opening of Brookside coincided with the coming of age of Catholic Halifax.[10] It had been erected into a Diocese in 1842, and formally consecrated to the Sacred Heart, while Saint Mary's College had been opened a few years earlier. The last traces of the Penal Laws, once very heavy here, were vanishing. Great gallantry of spirit had been shown by the Catholics in resisting these Laws, and legend had somewhat magnified the matter, as in the case of the "One-Day Church" standing in Holy Cross cemetery. It seems that the Bishop, fearing that the erection of the Church would be prevented, had marched some two thousand men out to the site after Mass on July 26, 1843, and the enthusiastic army had managed to clear the ground in one day. The Church rose very rapidly, in the space of a few weeks, so much so that "in the memory of the people the event of July 26th assumed very large proportions, and soon it was thought that the Church had been built in one day."[11] The story reached Mother

Hardey in its legendary form, and she was much impressed, but not even exaggeration could alter the fact that the time was ready for rapid and fruitful work among the children of this enterprising Halifax. She returned very pleased to New York after a two-weeks stay.

Two years later she was back again, to find the Community in a new house not far from Brookside, high and overlooking the sea, and referred to by its friends as "the Crystal Convent." An epidemic of scarlet fever had brought trial and grief, carrying away two children and forcing the day-school to move to a temporary house elsewhere, but by now all was prosperous. She noticed an unusual number of vocations in the Academy, of whom she was to welcome twenty to the Manhattanville Noviceship in the next few years. Before the end of her second visit she had arranged for the opening of a Free School of which even her future-reading eyes could hardly have guessed the outcome. It became the famous College Street School for girls and boys, under Government control after 1864 when Halifax's Public School system came into effect.* It would send out its steady and continuous influence through the City, while the Convent property grew larger and the spirit of the Academy, largely a day-school, grew stronger through the years to come.

Halifax, lying so far from Mother Hardey's beaten track, received fewer of her visits, perhaps, than any other house, but the days that she spent there were marked down as "époques de grâce." She busied herself continually about her distant foundation, to such an extent that she had to defend herself against a charge of undue preference for it. She said,

* According to this system, Public Schools are provided for Catholics and non-Catholics alike. These schools are supported and the salaries of the teachers paid by the Government out of the public taxes. Catholic teachers, who may be Religious, are in charge of the Catholic Public Schools. Religious art may be displayed in the class-rooms, but Christian Doctrine as such must be taught after school hours.

writing to Reverend Mother Peacock: "You shall have everything that has been destined for your pet foundation, though I should say my pet, for it is generally so called by the Buffalo Nuns. Deeply interested as I am in your establishment, I must confess that I am equally so in all the others. I do not, nor did I ever, understand the spirit of partiality."

This Mother Frances Peacock, former Novice of McSherrystown, was a sister of the Cornelia Connelly of Grand Coteau, now the Foundress of the Society of the Holy Child Jesus. Mother Hardey must have learned to know the latter well at their short meetings, for during the trying months of 1846, while Cornelia was feeling for her vocation in the dark while living as a Postulant at the Trinita dei Monti, she had written to Mother Barat: "Mrs. Connelly is better fitted to found a new Order than to enter an existing one." Mother Peacock, to whom both Mr. and Mrs. Connelly indirectly owed their conversion, suffered much at Halifax during the storms that tried her sister's new Order. Incidentally, we may be thankful to her for having been, apparently, the only Superior to disregard Mother Hardey's injunction that all letters written by herself should be destroyed. "I hear that you are keeping my letters," she wrote to one Superior; "this is the last that you get from me till I hear that you have burned them." Letters to Halifax are among the few that escaped this ultimatum, and their rapid sentences, marked by dry humour and unaffected love, show how much we have lost of the pepper and salt that should season a life of Mother Hardey:

You will be obliged to wait for your goods, as I do not wish to send them except in the care of some trustworthy person. Madame Thompson has purchased the articles you desire, and as she does not seem inclined to charge for them I shall not insist. All here are greatly interested in Halifax. The altar linen was given by ladies and children expressly for your chapel. The candelabra are a present from Saint Aloysius, and you may thank me for them. . . .

I feel at times very uneasy, knowing how much you have to do. I hope the Heart of Jesus will watch over you and give you strength and courage. We can expect consolation from Jesus alone. Let us apply to Him in our difficulties. It is useless to seek assistance elsewhere. I beseech you, dear Mother, write often. You need not take such pains, nor write so large a hand, but let me hear everything concerning yourself and your little family. I hope you pray for me. . . . The cocks are crowing! Instead of wishing you good night I should say good morning. I hope you will be able to read my letter.

Again she wrote, after the scarlet fever trial:

I feel deeply the cross that it has pleased Our Lord to send you, though it may be a blessing for the house, as it was for the dear innocent child called to her eternal home before sin sullied her soul. She will no doubt pray for those who taught her to love the Sacred Heart of Jesus. . . . Trials of this kind may cause the parents to withdraw their children for a while, but believe me, they will never cause the ruin of a house in which God is faithfully served. I regret sincerely having disappointed you and His Lordship in regard to the pecuniary aid you asked. I really did not mean that you should not have the few hundred dollars needed at the present moment, but that for the next two years I could give you nothing more. How could it be possible for me to lend you money when we have to raise $6000 at 7 percent? As I mentioned in my last letter, if we succeed in finding a good purchaser for our twelve acres we shall be able to assist you at once, but not otherwise. . . .

I am delighted to hear that you have received a letter from our saintly Mother General. What will you give me if I send you her portrait, or rather for having sent it? As for the altar linen, I have none for you nor for anyone else. I fear your box has been lost. Pray to Saint Anthony. Before I can authorize the use of the History of England please send me a copy, that we may judge of the merits of it, for, as you are aware, no book can be introduced into the school unless approved. I shall have the arithmetic book examined and give you the answer. . . .

I have a favour to ask, dear Mother. It is this: please spare my eyes and not your paper. Do not cross your writing any more. I will send you a quire of paper if needed. Pray for me.

Another letter contained one of Mother Hardey's rare confessions of weariness: "You see, dear Mother, I have much to contend against. Poor nature often murmurs, but it has to submit and to try to bear the cross graciously if not lovingly."

In the meantime the Vicar-General of Halifax, Monsignor Connolly, who had been, as he himself boasted to Mother Barat, "chaplain, confessor, architect and business agent" of the house there, had been named Bishop of New Brunswick. No sooner had he taken charge of his new See than a frightful epidemic of cholera swept into Saint John on a wave of immigration. The new Bishop inaugurated a public novena to the Sacred Heart and the scourge ceased, leaving him with a crowd of homeless orphans on his hands. If the Sacred Heart, he thought, had stopped the epidemic, why should he not appeal in the same Divine Name for his orphans? He set out accordingly for New York and for Mother Hardey. She made no delay, but at once sent the sixth band of foundresses to leave in as many years from Manhattanville. Again it was the tireless Mother Trincano who made herself Mother Hardey's second self. In 1854 she led her colony up the Bay of Fundy when the woods were burnished by September. There they found themselves welcomed as the first Religious ever to set foot in New Brunswick. They mothered the orphans until some Sisters of Charity were able to do so, then turned their efforts to the building up of an Academy where the children were "distinguished by that lively and practical faith which marks in a special way the people of this City," and which prospered until an unfortunate move in 1890 to an inaccessible crest of hill outside the city led to its eventual closing.

Mother Hardey visited Saint John on each of her zig-zags back and forth through Canada. The route was a complicated one, for after 1857 it included London, Ontario, where the little house at Sandwich had settled. This house prospered on the slopes of its beautiful Mount Hope, but its removal into the city brought it into still closer contact with souls until its closing in 1913. In that year its altar was sent to the western limits of Canada, carrying the sanctuary-fire of Mother Hardey's foundations as far as Vancouver. Thus there were five Canadian houses in 1864, but by that time Havana had been put on Mother Hardey's regular itinerarium, and the web of her activities had been stretched to the breaking point.

When she went to the General Council in Paris that year she took Mother Trincano with her. Upon their return the two went together to the Sault and there Mother Hardey herself told her Canadian daughters that they were no longer under her direct care, but in a separate Vicariate entrusted to its co-founder, Mother Trincano. Although something very like a wail of grief rose from the five houses, each knew that it would keep forever the mark that Mother Hardey had impressed upon its beginning. For twenty years she had kept every detail of their welfare in her busy mind and her thoughtful heart, and she had seen to it that their life had been woven through with traditions radiating not only from France from which so many of the members of their communities had been sent, but from the home of Mother Duchesne as well; for she had appointed Superiors who came from the first home of the Society in America: Mother Gray from Florissant, Mother Landry from Saint Michael's, Mother Peacock from Grand Coteau. The spirit that resulted was multiple yet simple, the spirit of a Society primitive still yet maturing.

Mother Hardey's own government of Canada had been carried on at long-distance range, and her visits had always been too short for anyone's liking, "constantly interrupted," as her daughters complained, "by visits from outside." Yet the Annals of those years, kept by different scribes in separated localities, are amazingly similar in their tribute. Each visit brings a deepening of some fundamental thing, charity, faith, zeal, regularity. Courage is strong, resolve is high, after she has gone. The Rule will be more fervently kept because of her brief presence. "She forgot nothing," says one record, "which could encourage us to work with ardour for the glory of God; the example which she herself had given us of continual devotedness spurs us on." Another account, written later when she returned as Visitatrix, gives us in one sentence a pen-picture of Mother Hardey, coming, then going, but doing an abiding work: "While waiting for the carriage we all gathered around her once more, and again she spoke to us in those burning and persuasive words that make us realize so well our duty as Religious."

XV

TO THE SOUTH

MOTHER DUCHESNE had never been able to pass a place by without an apostolic tug at her heart-strings, without a leap of desire into the future. Only a few of her divinely extravagant dreams were realized during her life, but "you will see," she had said undauntedly at its end, "after my death all will prosper." The lacey coasts of Cuba had been the first sight of the Americas to meet her eyes, and the island called to her unmistakably. On May 16, 1818, her Journal recorded that the *Rebecca* had "anchored before the capital, Havana. A vessel coming out from port brought a passenger named Martinez, a Catholic gentleman. Learning that five Religious were on their way to make an establishment in America with the hope of serving religion, he gave them forty dollars and urged them to return to Havana if they did not succeed elsewhere." The invitation was not heeded for some forty years, but Mother Duchesne had no sooner reached heaven than it was urgently renewed and accepted at a time when it was perhaps more needed then it had been in her own day.

When Columbus, borne by the west-blowing wind, had first caught sight of Cuba fringing the blue sea with foamy white and green he had described it in one simple superlative. "The Isle," he said, "is the most beautiful that eye has ever seen." [1] Through the disasters of his attempted colonization which dimmed for a time the glory of his discovery, Christopher Columbus never forgot that his name meant Christ-bearer, and later, when his work was more successfully taken over by Velasquez, the cross rose above the flag of Spain at every step.[2] Fray Bartolomé de las Casas, "Friend of the Indians," measured his steps with those of the conquerors, and the foundations of the future cities of Cuba had no sooner been laid than Bishoprics too were founded, first at Baracoa then at Santiago de Cuba, whose growth kept pace with the growth of the Island.[3] It was in 1604, as the legend claims, that the gracious image of Our Lady of Charity floated to Cuba over the waves, and took the place of Queen and Patroness in the hearts of the people. When Bishop Morel came to the See of Santiago in the mid-eighteenth century the Church in Cuba was at the glittering height of its prosperity, perhaps the richest in the world and not the least fervent. In 1787 Havana was erected into a separate See, and for a few brief years it reigned proudly over Florida and Louisiana. But the great Sugar-Kings were beginning their reign as well, and with over-gorged material prosperity the robustness of the Faith declined. Secular control in ecclesiastical affairs grew stronger as religious practice grew weaker.

But don Francisco Fleix y Solano became Bishop of Havana in 1846. He was a luminous-minded, far-planning Bishop, who spoke with the quiet courtliness of his own Spain and acted with vigour in the land of his adoption. Under his touch the Church awoke to a spiritual and intellectual revival. He introduced many Religious Orders, and looked to education to form tools for his work. There was already a University in Havana, in the hands of the Dominicans; there were Jesuits with several Colleges for his young men. What was to be done for his young women? About this time Archbishop Hughes of New York came to Cuba in search of health, and the problem was laid before him. "An appeal to Mother Hardey," was his solution, and he was forthwith appointed its spokesman.

The appeal was made at a rather bad moment for Mother Hardey, just when her own Vicariate was being spread thin from one new house to another, and she received it dubiously. The Cuban plan seemed one too many, but suddenly God played into the hands of don Francisco. The head-mistress of a fashionable boarding-school in Havana, Señorita Purroy, declared that she wished to be a Religious of the Sacred Heart, and that she would give over her pupils into the care of the Society if the Cuban foundation were made. At the same time Señora Espino, a wealthy lady who was anxious to make some generous act of charity to obtain the grace of her husband's return to the Sacraments, offered to provide a house. "All I ask," wrote Mother Hardey to the Superior General, "is permission to undertake the foundation and the help of your prayers,"[4] while in Paris Mother Barat said one day to her Community at recreation: "You know that for a long time they have been asking us to come to Cuba. The Captain General of the Island has offered me $10,000 to make a foundation there. I answered that it was not so much a matter of money as of finding enough people for all these American houses. And now, my Daughters, see how wonderful God's ways are! They tell me from Manhattanville that nineteen Postulants have entered the Noviceship since June, among them several Cubans. It is more than evident that Our Lord wants to be glorified by us in that Island. And just now Father

Munar, Rector of the Jesuit College of Havana, came to see me and declared that he would not go away without my formal consent."

The consent was hesitatingly given in a letter to Mother Hardey:

> I am told that foreigners are especially liable to take yellow fever which annually visits the island, and that consequently we must be prepared to lose many of our subjects. What a prospect! I do not shrink from it, for God is all-powerful, and though I dread the consequences, I cannot refuse the opportunity of procuring His glory. The fact that He has sent you those twenty subjects should excite our confidence and our abandonment to His Divine Heart. . . . It is with a trembling heart that I say to you, "Go, my dearest Aloysia."

In reply Mother Hardey sent her eager acceptance and her plans across the sea, and Mother Barat's comment was: "What a treasure the Lord has given us in the person of Mother Hardey! She is able to triumph over all obstacles when there is question of the glory of God."

Manhattanville had often turned its thoughts in a roundabout way to the Antilles, for Spanish-speaking children constantly enlivened the ranks of its pupils, and there were many Cuban families on the ever-lengthening list of Mother Hardey's friends. Years ago she had required Mother Tommasini to learn Spanish. For her, the special sign that God's hour had come was the presence in the Noviceship of several providentially gifted persons. There was Justina Casanova Lay, a young widow whom Mother Hardey mentally designated as the first Superior of Havana, and Rosa de Abreu who, after having managed her millionaire estate and its hundreds of slaves with the charm of a Christian chateleine of old and the canniness of a modern banker, had reached Manhattanville dressed like a servant and riding in the public omnibus in her new-found love of poverty. Two such as these could, with a contingent of Americans, lay the foundation of the Society's work in the South.

Mother Hardey liked to put an international stamp on her beginnings, so she chose for her companions Mother Tommasini, the Italian, Mother Fowler, an American Novice, and Sister Mercure, a Canadian. On the morning of the departure, December 28, 1857, Father Gresselin preached an unexpected sermon after Mass on the ill-boding text, "They fell upon Paul's neck, weeping for the word which he had said to them that they should see his face no more." Perhaps he did not realize that the hearts of his listeners were already heavy with fear at sending Mother Hardey into the land of yellow fever, and he was somewhat startled when the chapel broke into audible weeping. Mother Hardey alone remained calm, and leading her fellow-travelers to the altar-rail she made an act of complete abandonment to the Sacred Heart, then left with her characteristic farewell: "I count on you all."

The party picked its way through a blinding snow-storm to a pier at the traffic-muddied foot of Robinson Street where they boarded the *Caoba* [5] without the help of the usual crowd of friendly seculars. This clandestine departure was deliberate, for among Mother Hardey's friends was a certain old maid who, with embarrassing devotion and complete lack of tact, dogged her steps whenever she went abroad. But the party was no sooner on the snow-muffled boat than a loud and happy voice called across the deck: "Surprise! I am going with you to Cuba!" And she went.

Snow and gray waters yielded to sun-filled blue, while the fragrance of the south crept into the air. No one on board knew that they were Nuns, yet as the days passed Mother Hardey became the center of attraction, and by the end of the voyage found that she had made lasting friends. An extreme correctness of manner, a dignity most frequently described as queenly, might veil but could not hide her spontaneous, friendly interest in people, no matter who, and while a few were awed, most were drawn to her at first meeting. Among the passengers were some families prominent in the Southern States, and later on she unabashedly made use of the influence that she had gained over them to secure assistance for the Sacred Heart Convents in the South during the Civil War. Her power of winning admiration was one which she had the knack of turning consciously to good after having unconsciously exerted it. A shock of astonishment went through the boat when on the last day of the journey she appeared on deck in her religious habit. The new friends then came forward with offers of assistance which she a little mischievously accepted.

Mother Hardey first saw the straight-lined harbour of Havana open before her under the level sunset light of the First Saturday of January. The Morro Castle stood steeply to the left; its sixteenth century foundations, half-cut from living rock, tapered sharply to a more modern lighthouse. Those lower walls had sheltered one of the most heroic bands of men in all history when in June, 1762, Velasco and his tiny garrison had withstood heat, starvation, guns and the undermining of the briefly victorious English. The red and gold of Spain flew over it now. Blue, white and yellow, the houses crept down to the esplanade that curved along the jeweled water, and their red-tiled roofs seemed to meet across the streets. All Havana was still old Havana then.

Through the swarming craft, fish-piled, fruit-piled, importunate, they saw a single lordly launch making its way driven by fourteen oarsmen, and soon men in glittering government uniform boarded the *Caoba*. The passengers stepped back as the Officers came forward, straight to the Religious. The warmth of their Spanish salutation left no doubt that a literally royal welcome was being given to the new foundation.

Behind Señor Espino came his black-clad wife, leading little Maria, an angelically beautiful child dressed all in white. "Take her," said the Señora to Mother Hardey, "I give her to you. Bring her up for God and for the Church." Mother Hardey took her, and with her multitudes more of Cuban Señoritas, future home-makers devoted to God and to the Church.

The party broke through all red tape, and once on shore were bundled into *volantas,* microscopic carriages which looked, declared Mother Tommasini, like high-shouldered birds buzzing through the narrow streets. Hay-piled donkeys made way before them, shrill, lilting street-cries followed them. Tawney walls faded in the purpling air, and lights appeared behind the gratings of windows that reached down like doors to show a gleam of marble floors within. Evening quivered under a bell-stroke, and there were the Cathedral towers, lucently massive, standing over the body of the Christ-bearing Columbus. They stopped on the Calle del Prado before the house that Señora Espino had furnished for them with every luxury, including instruments of penance in each cell. As they passed from the patio into the parlour they saw a large painting of Our Lady under title of the Immaculate Heart, and recognized in it the features of its model, little Maria Espino.

The next morning they saw a strange procession drawn up at the door, waiting. It consisted of five *volantas,* each drawn by a horse with a fantastically dressed postillion on its back. What followed was enormously enjoyed by Mother Tommasini at least:

The three front carriages were filled with chairs, carpets, coverings, books *in quarto* dating from the discovery of the Island. We filled the fourth carriage, the servants the fifth. I could not smother my laughter, and Reverend Mother, in spite of her dignity, was in the same state. This is how we went into Church. A little page carrying the carpet and the chair of his mistress opened the march; then the Señora Espino, then Mother Hardey and her daughters in their rank places, then Miss McB. . . . . [the old maid] whom everyone took for the house-keeper. Lastly there followed chairs, shawls and books, almost hiding their bearers.

Once installed, they could appreciate the full splendour of the scene. They were in the great Jesuit Church of *Belen*, and it was still Christmas time. The entire sanctuary was a Bethlehem, where shepherds and their sheep, full sized, were descending a mountain to a grotto where the Holy Family, clad in brilliant brocades and jewels beyond imagination, awaited their homage; and all the time castanettes, triangles and tambourines played dartingly over the surface of a rolling tide of organ music.

Home-life in the Calle del Prado began when their own chapel was installed, and troubles arising from very excess of good will began also. The house could hold three Religious and accommodate a handful of day-scholars, and this, it appeared, was what the Señora had intended, a very exclusive school—for Maria. Her husband understood better Mother Hardey's determination to plan for a full-sized boarding-school, and he offered her a grandiose but impractible property outside the city to which he would in time, he said, append a railroad. It took greater tact to refuse such generosity than to make demands upon the unwilling. Moreover, there was no sign of the $10,000 promised by the Captain-General. Discreet questioning discovered that Mother Hardey's nationality was the reason for this. Cuba was tense at the moment, torn between the Spanish Loyalists and those who favoured annexation to the United States. It did not matter that the United States was afraid of annexation on account of the slavery question; those in power were afraid of Mother Hardey, and no one dared to take the initiative in raising the promised subscription. She may well have felt uneasy, seeing that Mother Barat had written warningly: "It seems to me that you are going rather fast, my Daughter, with your Havana foundation," and had insisted that Mother Hardey make sure beforehand of the Governor's support, and of the acceptability of the Society's Constitutions. "I don't know what to do," she confided to Mother Tommasini, from whom she never hid her moments of weakness. "I feel that the whole foundation depends upon the decision that I make now." She prayed, and her decision was to return to New York after visiting the Captain-General and frankly laying her reasons before him.

As it turned out, her very frankness won the day by winning the Captain-General. The two Religious were led by Señor Espino across the Plaza de Armas, through the fairy-like courts of the Vice-Regal Palace, into the presence of don José Concha. Mother Hardey did not trust herself to speak in Spanish, but she could follow what Mother Tommasini was saying and guided her spokesman with the flicker of her eyes. They told the simple truth, that the City did not seem ready to receive them and that they would come back at another time. "But I shall forbid any boat to carry you," cried his Excellency. "You shall not leave until the foundation has been made." Then, turning to his Officers, "Why has the subscription not been taken up?" With a speed that left all good Cubans stunned, he summoned the leading citizens to a meeting next day and organized a systematic drive throughout the city, while his secretary was sent house-hunting. Señor Espino gasped. "Mother Hardey is the only person who has ever given wings to our Captain-General," he said.

A house was at last found in the peaceful suburb of the Cerro, with a distant view of the sea from its roof. Mother Tommasini was put in charge of the arrangements. She was a good person to have on hand in upsetting circumstances for she had a way of bursting into song at any time and in any place, "pour égayer ma Mère," as she put it, and Mother Hardey gave her full rein. Now, however, she was at her wits' end how to cope with the leisurely ways of local tradesmen and negro workers, and even suggested sending to New York for needed things. Mother Hardey only smiled and said, "Patience; the graces of a foundation are obtained by suffering." Then she added a bit of worldly wisdom which betrayed the secret of her own power of getting what she wanted: "It is better, even at your own expense, to buy from local dealers. Win their good will, and let them understand that you have come to render service in a city, not to get money elsewhere. That's justice, and at the same time it is to the interest of your own school, for you will be looked upon as belonging to the city where you are."

One morning in February Mother Hardey received a letter from Father Gresselin in which he persevered in the thought of his late sermon. "No good is done without the cross; if that divine seal is not placed upon your foundation, do not look for any success." That afternoon she was walking quietly in her room, reciting her Spanish lesson to Mother Tommasini, when she was suddenly prostrated by an illness which proved to be a bad case of yellow fever. The news spread over the city, where prayers were offered in all the Churches and Convents. Friends arose on every hand, generously helpful. The Captain-General called every day and waited patiently in the parlour till news of the invalid could be brought to him. Señorita Purroy hastened to take charge of the house, and invited various ladies of Havana to come and play portress. It was her experience that suggested the remedy that was finally effective. For five days the issue was doubtful, while in the chapel the great candle given to Mother Hardey on the Feast of the Purification, burned itself out before the altar.

On the morning of the crisis, Father Luck, the Jesuit Rector, spoke to Mother Tommasini gravely. Was she resigned, accepting the divine will in advance? She shook her head violently. "Then how do you dare to ask this cure of God, without accepting His will?" The words forced submission upon her; she made her sacrifice, and in the peace of heart that then came flooding upon her grief, hope arose and seemed like certainty. Just then she was told that some one wished to speak to her in the parlour. There, framed by the sunny flowers in the patio beyond, stood a young girl with simple, serious eyes, holding her fortune tied up in a handkerchief. She was Rafaela Donosa, she said, and the very name of Sacred Heart had drawn her to the Society. Might she be admitted at once as a Coadjustrix Sister? "I cannot settle that question," said Mother Tommasini. "But if you will obtain by your prayers the cure of our Superior, I shall try to arrange for your admission." Determination came into Rafaela's face, strengthened by her great longing. She went off to the Jesuit Church, where she knelt the length of the day. What could she give to God for this cure when she possessed only her desire to belong to the Sacred Heart? There was nothing left in this world that she could sacrifice, but what of the next world? She offered to remain for three extra days in Purgatory when her time should come, that Mother Hardey might now recover. Her confessor sanctioned the offering, and before night she learned that the crisis had passed. Mother Hardey's first act when life came back to her was to admit Sister Donosa into the Society.

In the meantime nothing was known of all this at Manhattanville. Mother Tommasini's letter had been entrusted to the pocket of a forgetful messenger, whence it found its way back to her eleven years later. Accordingly the second band of Foundresses arrived from New York, to find Mother Hardey still too weak to see them. But her strength was soon restored, and on March 19th military bands bespeaking the presence of the Captain-General played around the Cerro, and although the pupils of Señorita Purroy were more than enough to fill the house by themselves, two hundred delighted guests poured in and out all day. School had begun.

Mother Justina Lay was made Superior of the new house, where the children became Children of the Sacred Heart with satisfying rapidity. Although she had only made her First Vows the year before, she wore a cross and ring for appearances' sake, and governed the house with gentle energy through its makeshift days of squeezing, doubling up, and doing without. Mother Hardey sailed for home in May, and not long after learned that the intention for which Señora Espino had assisted them so generously had been granted, for on the Feast of the Holy Heart, to which the house had been dedicated, Señor Espino received Holy Communion in the Convent chapel.

The Community had its own reasons for gratitude, and sang the Magnificat every Saturday in thankfulness for Mother Hardey's cure, while back at Manhattanville one of the promises that Mother Tommasini had made in the dark hour of the illness was carried out. A votive chapel was dedicated to Mater Admirabilis, where Our Lady with lily, distaff and open book silently educated the children who came, in silence too or with singing, into her small Temple. Very special graces, including some cures that bordered on the miraculous, were granted there in the first years. Like Mother Hardey, this chapel was spared for a double span of life, for the picture of the *Madonina* was saved when the house about it burned down, and in a new chapel, given by the Alumnae at the time of Manhattanville's Golden Jubilee, went on with its noiseless work. Mother Hardey herself had not been indifferent to her own cure; her promise had been characteristically fundamental and practical: to undertake some special work to spread Devotion to the Sacred Heart. The result was the translation and publication of Gautrelet's *Month of the Sacred Heart.*

Sister Donosa had not long to wait before her offering too was completed. After a brief stay at Manhattanville she was sent back to Cuba, where it became evident that her real life was being lived not in herself but in the Tabernacle. She declared one day in recreation, laughing but with complete seriousness, that she would die on Assumption Day, and no one was surprised when she fell ill at the approach of the Feast. For three days she lay silent, luminous with suffering and with love, while those who watched could only wonder if these were the three promised days. She died just as the priest was exposing the Blessed Sacrament for joy of an Assumption.

The Cerro prospered so effectively that within four years Mother Hardey was back in Cuba to plan for a second foundation. On the other side of the Island, not many miles from Havana as the plane flies now but separated from it by the still unsubdued jungle and by the Island's mountainous backbone, lay Sancti Spiritus. The Society of Saint Vincent de Paul of that town had asked the Religious of the Sacred Heart to take charge of thirty orphans, assuring their maintenance and leaving liberty for the opening of an Academy. Mother Hardey set out at once, though to reach the place meant more than a pleasant journey on a steamer. From Havana she sailed around the western tip of Cuba in a small boat open to sun and wind, then veered uneasily along the southern coast. One night was spent in the home of an old pupil of Havana, another in a forest hut. Finally she and Mother Lay took to a springless cart conducted by negroes who led the oxen on through the blinding curtains of the jungle. The trees were tall and kingly, mahogany, cocoa trees, and the royal palm, but rank undergrowth crawled up from the ground between them, swinging its treacherous arms from trunk to trunk.

Clearings here and there showed where monster sugar plantations were busy building up the economic life of the country in the heart of its wilderness. Here fires glowed hotly day and night under the great vats of crude sugar, tended by their armies of slaves, now silent, now singing at their unresting work.

Then, in a valley by the sea, Sancti Spiritus opened out. It was an old and sleepy town with three cobbled streets, but it boasted a sixteenth century church with steeples crowned by mosque-like balls, and a low stone bridge, quite as old, which sternly held up a road over the fickle Yayzabo River. Here the hills took on the colour and the illusion of Killarney, and by way of lakes shining tide-pools crept in and out through the cane-fields. Some of the oldest and finest of Cuban families lived here, holding to their colonial traditions with tenacious grace.

Señora Natividad del Valle, the wife of General Acosta hastened to welcome them and to give them her own house. It was peeling and venerable like all the other houses, but it had a fine location, fronting on one of the three streets and backing on another in such wise that its verandahs and the sidewalks were indistinguishable. It was soon furnished by kindly friends, and during Mother Hardey's brief stay the orphans were housed and the Academy opened for the children of planters who rumbled in from Trinidad and Cienfuegos in ox-carts, while bare-footed children of every shade of black, brown and white trudged in from hill and forest to the free-school.

The people of Sancti Spiritus took strongly to Mother Hardey. One negro workman became so devoted to her that he made himself a nuisance, in the opinion of other people, by stealing in to stand behind her chair, in season and out, but Mother Hardey would not let him be molested. "If it gives him pleasure to follow me around," she said, "why not let him?" Other admirers peeped through the grated windows to watch her as, broom in hand, she gave an astonishing example of manual labour. Thus in a glow of affection she left Sancti Spiritus to pursue its briefly tranquil life. Only after she had gone did she tell the Religious of the personal sorrow that had come to her there in the news of the death of her father, in Louisiana just beyond the blue Gulf.

Five years passed before things went any other way but well with the Cuban houses, but then Mother Hardey heard news that made her catch the next boat. Bishop Fleix y Solano had died, and his successor, a Spanish Capuchin devoted to the old régime and suspicious of all things American, soon discovered that the privileges accorded to the Sacred Heart Convents in his Diocese had not been registered at the Chancery Office. Bishop Martinez disapproved of many points of a Rule that was unfamiliar to him, and especially disapproved of authority exercised at a distance by an American Superior Vicar. He had withdrawn the English-speaking confessor from the Cerro, leaving several nuns without the possibility of confession. Among them was Sister Anne Leveau, who was at the point of death. Mother Hardey arrived so promptly on the scene that she appeared at the front door unannounced. There she learned that Sister Anne had died that morning without the Last Sacraments but comforted by the visit of an English speaking Jesuit who, though without faculties to minister to her, had left her completely happy. "She is an angel ready for heaven," he told Mother de Abreu.

Mother Hardey prayed by Sister Anne's body, then, with a trepidation that she could not conceal, asked for an interview at the Episcopal Palace. She entered it by one door as the Bishop went out by another, leaving word that he would not see her. That night she told the Community that their prayers had won for her a great grace, adding only "a humiliation is a great grace." "We have not gained the ends for which we came," she told Mother Tommasini, "but we have done all that God wanted us to do, and that is enough," and she went back to New York. There seemed nothing to do but suppress the Cuban houses, but when the matter was referred to Cardinal Bofondi, Protector of the Society, his answer brought her the strength of the Holy Father's own decision:

> The Holy Father, having been solicited to authorize the suppression of the two houses which your Society has in Cuba, does not favour this measure, as it would deprive that country of the great spiritual good which is being accomplished there, as elsewhere, by the Religious of your Institute. An academy, which according to the Bishop's own letter contains more than one hundred and fifty pupils, must enjoy the esteem and confidence of the public, and thereby refutes most triumphantly certain assertions made by Monseigneur in his famous letter. His Holiness has expressed himself in the most benevolent manner with regard to the Institute of the Sacred Heart. He sympathizes with the Religious who must remain in Havana, but he reminds them that in order to acquire any merit we must be disposed to suffer something for it. In the meantime the Sacred Congregation of Bishops and Regulars will write again to His Lordship requesting him, in the name of the Holy Father, to have all possible regard for the welfare of the Religious, and to procure for them the means of accomplishing what is prescribed in the Constitutions which have been approved by the Holy See, and also of conforming to the particular usages established. The Holy Father trusts that the Religious on their side will strive to correspond to the wishes of the Bishop in such matters as do not affect the fundamental points proper to the whole Institute.

Reverend Mother Goetz, who communicated this letter to Mother Hardey, added some advice of her own as to a procedure usually found irresistible. "Humble yourself," she wrote, "throw yourself at the feet of his Lordship, and beg pardon for the pain we have caused him, assuring him that we have no other desire than to be his most humble and obedient daughters."

So once more Mother Hardey and her faithful interpreter found themselves in Havana, where she carried out Mother Goetz' directions to the letter. Monsigneur Martinez began to relent. He was about to set off on an episcopal visitation, and Mother Hardey determined to press her advantage by getting to Sancti Spiritus ahead of him. The ensuing journey turned out to be one of the most remarkable that she had ever undertaken. She tried to go *incognito,* as one of the grievances against her was her habit of "trotting about the world." Moreover the countryside was in a turmoil. The Bishop was making his visitation *in pompis,* and the Captain-General elected to make a tour of his own at the same time, *magna cum laude.* He ordered the bells to be rung in all the churches at his approach. The Bishop forbade them to be rung for a civil authority. The pastors in every town had to choose between excommunication and prison. By some unforeseen combination the two dignitaries found themselves travelling on the same boat which, to Mother Hardey's horror, turned out to be her boat. The Nuns lowered their veils over their secular bonnets, but in the mêlée of passengers Mother Tommasini, the irrepressible, peeped around the corner of hers and found herself looking straight into the eyes of the Bishop who recognized her, while at the same moment she was approached with a great show of honour by an officer of the Captain-General. A strained journey followed, but at every sign of excitement from her companion Mother Hardey only said: "Tommasini, say your prayers and let me say mine." Finally she decided to brave an interview, and the Bishop capitulated before the unswerving graciousness of her humility. All passed off well a few days later at Sancti Spiritus, where he and the Captain General were received at separate *fiestas.* Gradually all the privileges of the Cuban houses were restored. Not long after this Monsigneur Martinez was recalled to Spain, and stopped for a visit at Manhattanville in the course of which all misunderstanding blew away like smoke. The Bishop reversed the rôles; he poured out the story of his own long difficulties, and ended by saying: "O my friends, we are reconciled now. Never again will I make such mistakes."

It was hard to end by suppressing Sancti Spiritus after all, but the measure was at last forced upon Mother Hardey by political events, for by the end of 1869 the Island was in the throes of a considerable uprising of the Independentists. On Christmas Eve the military were the only people abroad in the streets of Havana, while behind locked doors the Religious of the Cerro were praying at Midnight Mass for their Sisters in the other house, which was caught between two opposing garrisons. The Community got away in safety, but the situation in that part of the Island was so altered by events that they never went back, and the work at Sancti Spiritus came to an end. Before another house could replace it Mother Hardey had ceased to be Vicar in Cuba. The houses there would multiply, would stretch to Puerto Rico, combine for a time with those in Louisiana and then with those in Mexico, and finally become a Vicariate of their own with branches reaching into Colombia. The forty dollars given in alms to Mother Duchesne had borne interest many hundredfold. Mother Hardey had been the agent, investing it generously and leaving the fructifying to others. After dreams comes doing, after the path-finders come the house-builders. The houses that they build are of many styles, strong-set for northern snows or wide-arched for the warm beauty of the south.

XVI

THE HOUSE ON THE ROCK

MANHATTANVILLE ALL THIS TIME very virtuously felt that it was doing its share of the work of expansion. "Can we complain," it wrote, "of the privation which Mother Hardey's absences impose on us when we see her giving us such constant examples of zeal for the glory of God and for the interests of our dear Society?" "Our hill," as Manhattanville was familiarly called, was her home, and when Mother Hardey was at home she was there completely, "working like our first Mothers" said those who watched her. The continuity of her presence was never really broken, for during absences life was lived as though she were still there. "Everything goes on peacefully and quietly at Manhattanville," she herself wrote, "and it would be difficult to find a more united and devoted family. Pray that this blessing may always continue." "I know of no place," said Father Gresselin, "where a soul can enjoy greater peace or serve God more abundantly."

There were, however, outward difficulties and alarms, especially in 1860 when Mother Hardey was seriously ill. During her convalescence several fatal accidents to men working on the grounds gave her shocks from which she did not easily recover. Then one night there was an alarm of fire, and as a result her illness returned. Her moral vigour assured recovery, but it soon afterwards became evident that she had lost the use of her right hand. A few lines to Mother Barat, traced with difficulty, were the last that she ever wrote. From then on those who came into her room had not to apologize for stopping the swift movement of her pen, for her right arm lay lightly along the edge of her desk. No one ever heard from her a reference to what it cost her, during twenty-five more years of life, to rely on others for every written word.

There was a policeman who assured the outer tranquillity of Manhattanville. At one time his name was Adam Myers. He lived in a lodge near the grand entrance to the grounds on 127th Street, through which a driveway passed to sweep up to the front door. Policeman Myers patrolled the property from "Hell," a rural gorge along the future Convent Avenue, through "Purgatory" on the brow of the hill, to "Heaven" on the rocky points behind the house. A fountain splashed in the back gardens which stretched off into orchards where Policeman Myers met his worst enemies. Beyond the orchard lay the cemetery, as remote and tree-embowered as though no city existed. The solid S-shaped block of buildings traced dignity against the sky. All the rooms beneath spelled dignity, from the library where plush coverings hid the legs of every table and where the ornamental book-cases stood at respectful distances from one another, to the dormitory where beams crossed in severe arches over the alcoves. So pure was the air over Manhattanville that doctors recommended the school to the parents of ailing children, and so bracing was the moral and intellectual atmosphere that the number of students crept higher and higher. They came from everywhere, even from

California where the frontier was making its last stand, enticed by a Prospectus which read:

Academy
Under the direction of the Ladies of the Sacred Heart
New York

The Sacred Heart Academy is about eight miles from the city of New York in the vicinities of Harlem and Manhattanville. The site is elevated, healthy and beautiful. The grounds for recreation and promenade are neat and spacious, surrounded by shrubbery and pleasantly shaded by forest and grove trees.

This Institution, in its plan of education, unites every advantage that can be derived from a punctual and conscientious care bestowed on the pupils in every branch of science becoming their sex. Propriety of deportment, politeness, personal neatness, and the principles of morality are objects of unceasing assiduity. The health of the pupils is the object of constant solicitude, and in sickness they are attended with maternal tenderness.

Difference of religion is no obstacle to the admission of young girls, provided they be willing to conform to the general regulations of the school. The knowledge of religion and its duties being of primary importance in a good education, it is treated with the attention due to so important a matter, and enters as the basis into the plan of studies followed in every class and department of the school.

Terms

Board and tuition, per annum, payable half-yearly in advance $200
Postage, books, stationery, washing, are charged to the parents
Use of library, per year $2
Physician's fees $3
Medicines charged at apothecary's rates
Each pupil will pay on entrance for use of bed, etc. $5

The usual extra charges are made for instruction in the Spanish, Italian, German languages; for music, use of the Piano, Harp, Guitar, and Organ, for Drawing, Painting, Oil Painting, etc. The

French language being universally spoken in the Institution, forms no extra charge.

The annual vacation commences the last week of July, and scholastic duties are resumed the first Monday of September.

There will be an extra charge of fifteen dollars for pupils remaining during vacation.

Besides the uniform dresses, which differ according to the season, each pupil will be provided with six regular changes of linen, two bathing gowns and sheets, six table napkins, two silver spoons and goblet, knife and fork, two pairs of blankets, three pairs of shoes, one counterpane, one white and one black plain bobbinet veil, work-box, dressing-box, combs, brushes.

At first the children wore uniforms only on Sundays, then Mother Hardey decided for week-days as well. Foreseeing resistance, she cannily closed her announcement of the change with the statement: "Of course, those whose parents have suffered loss in the late financial crisis will not be asked to comply at present." Needless to say, all promptly appeared in rosy pink uniforms.

The study-hall was a large room at the junction of several stately corridors. Each of its unornamental desks held two students, and those full pink skirts fell, severely deflated with no crinolines under them, to the shining floor. During the writing lesson there was no sound but the scratching of some hundred stiff pens. Then the door opened quietly and one of those currents of communication so powerfully felt in a schoolroom told each writer that Mother Hardey was present. The pens scratched with self-conscious industry. Untidy strands of hair were patted into place, for nothing would escape Mother Hardey. The children were not supposed to rise when she came *incognito* like this to their writing-lesson, but one child after another became aware of an interested presence by her side. Here drooping shoulders were drawn into line; here a word, here a smiling question established understanding. As

Mother Hardey went up and down, heads turned ever so slightly to hold her look as long as possible. With one writer there was an earnest moment of conversation. This child was a day-student and that night her parents said to each other knowingly, "Margaret must have seen Mother Hardey today; she is so happy and peaceful." On the way out of the study-hall she met another child coming late, one whose scowling look showed that she was more or less deeply in trouble. Mother Hardey gave her first a searching look then a smile, and the child had to smile back. "What has happened to change you so?" whispered her desk-mate a moment later. "I met Mother Hardey." "And what did she say to you?" "Nothing."

Perhaps Mother Hardey knew—perhaps not—that at least one desk in the great study-hall contained an autograph-album in which the very best of the penmanship laboriously acquired during the writing-lesson was squandered at other times. One of these, known as "The Forget-Me-Not Album," of heavy gold-tooled leather, was illustrated with ultra-romantic scenes of fair girls, bereaved wives, and towers with ivy growing out of their tops like hair. It had been given to a certain Mary Abraham by her brother, who had inscribed its fly-leaf in agonizingly correct script as follows:[1]

To Mary. In presenting you this album, my dear Sister, I do so with the proud conviction that it will be filled with the real feelings of the companions whom your kind and amiable manners, your mild demeanour and sensible qualities have drawn towards you; that it will be a depository wherein will be contained, in various styles, the esteem in which you are held by your school-mates, the friendship of those who subscribe their names to the choice pieces, or Floral Productions culled from their own imaginations, in which the Young Ladies of the Convent *de Sacré Coeur* are adepts; and that it will be a fond object in after years to look upon and see its pages filled:

"With fond device and loving lore,"

recalling to memory:

"The happy hills, the pleasing shades"

of the Convent and the dear companions of your youth.

Though I know, Mary, that you are adverse to flattery, yet without some such praise to act as an incentive to something great and good, my dr Sister, our existance [sic] here below would be cold and dull.

Your affectionate brother
Joseph

Mott Haven, May 26, 1861

The pages within the album, faintly blue and pink and yellow, called for poetry of a heart-moving timbre, and were duly filled with it. The first entry records that:

When the harp's sole touching chord
Is roughly frayed and torn,
When of all tunes the string that poured
The fullest is outworn;
When it is heard to breathe and break,
Its saddest music shed,
Then, then will thy warm heart bleed and break
And cherish the absent friend.

Written with sincere wishes for your welfare,
Ada,
Enfant de Marie

Our Convent Home
June 7, 1861

Another, of brighter outlook, wrote:

When far away my friend you go
Will you on me your thoughts bestow,
And in your memory keep apart
The hours we spent at the Sacred Heart?

With the best wishes of your school friend,
M. Ritchie

There were elaborate signatures of whole classes grouped dizzily on a page; there were acrostics, verses written upside down, verses in French, and occasional lapses into prose. The prose, however, lost little in the way of poetic feeling:

> May thy pathway here be ever bright as the star which is thy guide to heaven. The "Distant Hills" seem far away, and a misty viel [sic] of blue sometimes hide their beauty; but, each day and hour brings us nearer, until our journey ended, we meet at last above.
>
> Your friend,
> Hattie

If Lydia Languish herself had penned these verses they would belong to the tenderly satirical field of literature. Such melting sentiment, it would seem, needs the pen of a Sheridan or of a Jane Austen to sketch in its background of ringleted girlhood, fragile and tight-laced, living in a world of dainty unreality which a hearty laugh might shatter into disillusion. Actually the poems were written by living children two generations after Miss Austen, children made serious by the outbreak of a Civil War. The Victorian Age is at the far swing of the pendulum from us, more remote than many an age farther away in time; its pastels play over a silken surface to our eyes. To Mother Tommasini these little Lydias were of flesh and blood, and she wrote of them: "The children of those days were of a strong and energetic type; several were as difficult as possible, but it was rare to find one in whom some chord could not be made to vibrate. There was at that time a strength of character which is scarcely to be found in more peaceful days."

So the same child who could sit at her desk with the autograph album open under her geography writing such lines as "When I forget thee think of me as dead" and meaning it, would at the next moment be shouldering her blue ribbon and exercising really womanly judgment in her rôle of school-leader. It took an unchildish courage and common sense raised by its motive to something approaching vision, to be a real child of the Sacred Heart in that epoch which Mother Tommasini called the Golden Age of the boarding-school. These were the children whom she had to watch with care lest they injure themselves by their self-imposed penances during Lent, whom she prepared by virile handling to brave human respect at New York balls when they left school. Some of them refused to go home when the pupils were dispersed during times of epidemic, preferring to stay and help with the extra work of nursing. So practical was their understanding of their devotion to the Sacred Heart that during the years following their departure stories came back to Mother Hardey of conversions effected, missions and churches supported, and spiritual wonders wrought by the vibrant contact of holy lives upon a restless or too complacent world. When Pius IX was asked to bless one of them he was heard to say: "Oh, the children and grand-children of the Sacred Heart are true children of the Church." Mother Hardey was not surprised; for many years she had been saying to those who bore the burden of teaching: "Make valiant women of your pupils by training them to the heroism of self-denial so necessary for the fulfillment of their noble mission in the world."

The eighteen sixties believed in polish, not a glitter applied with a brush but the kind of polish achieved by rubbing a strong substance till the grain shows. Mother Tommasini wrote in reminiscence:

> We took every care to perfect our children in correctness of language and distinction of manner. . . . Not quite so much Latin and algebra was asked of young girls then, but a perfect manner was insisted upon, and they were expected to be able to carry on a sensible conversation or to write a letter worth reading. One of the means employed for forming our children to cultivated

speech and to that complete self-possession which is the jewel-box of virtue was the teaching of plays or of pieces to recite. . . . The children sang in five different languages, English, German, French, Spanish and Italian, and these songs were intermingled with recitations and addresses in English and in French. Mother Jones composed and taught them so well. Once an *entrée* was played on ten pianos by thirty little girls. Our celebrations were distinguished but gay; we would not have thought it respectful to have Church music at them. The French dialogues were always sparkling with wit.

If this element of the old world and of the foreign attracted pupils to the school it certainly was not because New York liked what was too conservative. Mother Hardey could only have kept up with New York by keeping up with the times. As it happened, a good deal of what was most significant in Catholic intellectual life was taking place in New York itself just then. Saint John's College, later to be incorporated as Fordham University, was supplying leaders and scholars through whom the Church might make her impress upon secular culture: [2] John Hassard, the journalist, who wrote for Horace Greeley on the New York *Tribune;* Martin MacMahon, who distinguished himself as a Union General in the Civil War; John Gilmary Shea, first winner of the Laetare medal and also the first—let us hope not the last—to see the interest and the magnificence of the history of Catholicism in the United States. Although before 1870 only ten or twelve men graduated annually from Saint John's, great Professors and Presidents of the College were developing the University to come, and it was on the stage of Fordham's auditorium that, accidentally, a dramatic scene took place which brought into relief the fact that Catholic thought was striding into the future.

Orestes A. Brownson, who by 1861 was already known as "the old lion," had opened his *Review* as a battle-ground for all the conflicts that must be fought out when the dogmatic teaching of the Church is brought to bear upon political and social questions which, though largely ephemeral, touch upon eternal issues. In that year he spoke at the Commencement Exercises of Saint John's; he spoke vehemently, seeing before him young men whom he hoped to sway into what would now be called Catholic Action, or the Lay Apostolate. Sitting upon the same stage, listening, was Archbishop Hughes, then an old man whose simpler lines of thought could not curve into the complexities of a new age. He rose at the end of Brownson's speech and silenced the applause with more than a gesture. The episode was indicative of the misunderstanding that must arise at cross-roads.[3]

Brownson, always submissive to authority, continued to suffer, and to think and write his way ahead. The Archbishop had written in the *Metropolitan Record* for December, 1856:

> Young men born in this country imagine themselves an auxiliary corps to aid the Bishops. . . . Their general idea for the accomplishment of this was a combination of lay elements to aid indirectly in the work of the ministry. Their reliance was principally on the press, but in connection with it on associations which they have tried and which have all failed, viz. Catholic Library Associations, Catholic Lecture Associations and last of all and least profitable, Catholic Clubs.

This was intended as a condemnation of Brownson, but through it shone, unknown to its author, the outlines of strong American Catholicity of a later day. The things condemned would in time achieve the very ends for which the Archbishop had fought so valiantly during a long life, and with different weapons.

Mother Hardey subscribed to Brownson's *Review*, and at one time was quite naturally afraid, in view of all the controversy, that it was leading its readers astray, but Father Gresselin wrote to her from Fordham: "Do not give up your subscription to the *Review*. . . . Let us not forget the eminent services that Brownson has rendered to religion, and which he is yet to render. If he is wrong on many points, those who pursue and abandon him are still more guilty." So Mother Hardey continued to subscribe to forward-looking movements.

Brownson had once written: "There is a respectable Catholic-American literature springing up among us, and Catholics have their representatives among the first scholars and scientific men of the land. In metaphysics, in moral and intellectual philosophy, they take already the lead." Mother Hardey's interest in such literature was strong, and she showed it practically by helping struggling Catholic authors. She even contributed to it indirectly, and in the slight measure open to her, by having some of her Community translate French biographies of the saints, and some narratives of America's heroic age such as *The Missions of Oregon*. She likewise encouraged the writing of textbooks, like those of Mother Kate White whose *Mythology* and *History of the Church* took their place among the standard works in use in secular as well as Catholic schools. This Apostolate of the Press received a powerful impetus during the years of Brownson's activity from the work of the Missionary Priests of Saint Paul the Apostle, founded in 1858 by Father Isaac Hecker, the one-time baker-boy of Brook Farm. As the Paulist Fathers made their influence felt, Father Hecker wrote: "The special battle-field of attack and defence of truth for half a century to come is the printing-press," and his own contributions to the cause included *The Catholic World*, *The Young Catholic*, and the Catholic Publication Society. In the spiritual life of his sons, as in their work of preaching and writing, he advocated a thoroughly orthodox form of modernism:

So far as it is compatible with faith and piety, I am for accepting the American civilization with its usages and customs; leaving aside other reasons, it is the only way by which Catholicity can become the religion of our people; and their institutions must find themselves at home in our church in the way those of other nations have done; and it is on this basis alone that the Catholic religion can make progress in our country.[4]

He underlined one word in preaching on the text, "the wise house-holder brings out of his treasury *new* things and old."

The educational world is peculiarly sensitive to such currents of thought, and Mother Hardey was an educator. The broad lines that she followed had already been laid down. The Plan of Studies in her schools came to her from the Mother House; for the teaching methods of the Society, like its spiritual life, reach from the Center outward. Yet the Plan of Studies was dynamic from the beginning; the further it must reach, the more life it would put forth. The version of 1852 was the last upon which the Foundress put the seal of her personal approval, and its opening paragraph must have seemed to Mother Hardey like a modest statement of the all-American principles of Father Hecker: "In the revision of this Plan experience has been consulted, and without scorning old methods or rejecting new ones, there has been drawn from both the one and the other whatever seemed to favour true intellectual development." In her last Circular Letter Mother Barat had written:

Education is not as it was in former days. Many institutions have yielded to the tendencies of the times. God forbid that we should ever wish to make any compromise in regard to those duties and sacrifices which are our chief aim, but it is necessary to examine again the points that can be conceded, to review the Plan of Studies, that we may modify it and bring it nearer to completion.

In accordance with this, a further revision was made in 1869, offering a liberal and thorough plan for each class up to the Superior, the syllabus for which stated that "it may be modified to suit pupils and circumstances." It was Mother Hardey's responsibility to see that this Plan was exactly carried out, yet so effectively had she met modern requirements in so doing that she received recognition from an unexpected source. She was offered a place on the Board of Regents of the State of New York when no other woman had as yet been accorded that honour, while a New York newspaper stated that "few persons have been more instrumental, under the blessing of God, than Madame Hardey, in propagating conventual life and conventual education in America."

With regard to the formation of young teachers, it was not so much a question of curriculum to which Mother Hardey looked as of the moral qualities required by the good teacher. She said to the Aspirants:

> The secret of bringing up children well lies in the knowledge of the human heart, in patience, in influence, in example. An education which does not give self-possession, personal discipline, is an *éducation manquée*. Remember that the children often become like the mistress whom they most love. . . . Some of you are too agitated, always running about. That's time lost. Hold your children through the heart, through their sense of honour, reward them generously, but three or four times a year it is well to come down upon them with the majesty and thunder of the Last Judgment.

The young mistresses waited in wholesome awe for the weekly meetings at which Mother Hardey enumerated the faults of the children by attributing each to some corresponding lack in the teachers, but a still more efficacious form of correction was her quiet: "You have disappointed us." Self-education, she insisted, would increase their influence:

Remember that you are consecrated to the education of youth. Your profession is not one that you are at liberty to take up or abandon at pleasure. . . . You must yourself love to study if you wish to give your children a love of it. We cannot impart what we do not possess. Understand well that your own education is never finished, therefore continue daily to cultivate your minds that you may be better fitted to cultivate the minds of your pupils. They will be just what you make them, and you will make them just what you are.

Best of all was the constant, even, moulding influence of her own manner. When speaking to her one was drawn to rise to the level of her "intelligent and serious conversation," free from all unreality. If anyone asked her a flighty question she would only say, "I did not ask about that . . ." and to the remark, "they say that . . ." she would reply, "Who are *they*?" She was her own best lesson in the womanly qualities which she formed in those around her, an unfailing courtesy of speech, neatness and decorum of person. Education ranges beyond books; sewing contests and constant object lessons in house-keeping and husbandry were placed first in her modest scale of extra-curricular activities.

Mother Hardey's personal influence on the children themselves was perhaps most directly felt in the remarkable number of conversions, sometimes ten or twelve a year, which took place in the school. Often the turning point was a well-timed word from her. She would, for instance, content herself with patient listening during months or even years of a soul's struggle to find the light, then suddenly bring matters to a close with a firm remark: "Confession is your stumbling block. Prepare yourself at once, for I will not let you leave here till you have made your peace with God." There were strong souls among these little converts, many of whom worked upon their friends and then brought them triumphantly to Mother Hardey for the final conquest. There was a child of seven who had teased her way to baptism through the opposition of her parents. Her mother then fell ill, and Leila poured out by her bedside all her own happy thoughts of God until the mother wrote to Mother Hardey, begging to come into the Church. A priest was sent to her and the whole family was baptized. These conversions were like ripples spreading out through time, so that many are living now who owe their faith to Mother Hardey.

Sometimes one interview with a child was enough to give a life's anchorage. One whom she met in a Canadian School wrote later:

> I had remained at school only to keep my promise to my Catholic mother that I would not ask my father, who was a Protestant, to take me home. Mother Hardey's sympathetic heart divined the cause of my sadness. That same evening she sent for me, and began to speak to me gently, but with such earnestness that I can never forget her words. . . . After some months, however, my longing for home returned and I left the convent. When the Academy was opened in London Mother Hardey's words came back to me so forcibly that her appeal to my sense of duty left me no peace and I asked and obtained permission to enter the school. When next I saw the dear Mother I had felt the call to a higher life, and she strengthened and encouraged me to be faithful to grace. Her every word was full of light and consolation.

Although vacations were short and the children's *sorties* into the city rare, the city made up for it by thronging the Convent parlour on visiting days. With a swish and whisper of striped taffeta and the thump of a heavy walking stick, Mother and Father appear at the door, she jaunty with bows and feathers over the sober amplitude of her gown, he stiff with black broadcloth and a bow cravat. They settle down in the uncompromising parlour chairs while their daughter,—who has more than likely watched through the back of her head as the calèche drove up,—is being requested from one intermediate authority to another. They are very determined, for they have come to ask a special favour for their one and only. But a dignified figure is moving across the room. Mother Hardey, with her graciousness and her shrewdness, is before them. She opens the conversation with the regretful information that their daughter has lost her notes for good conduct that week. They would not, of course, think of showing her any special favour just now. They nod their heads in entire agreement; for Mother Hardey has flattered their judgment by assuming from the beginning that they would support the cause of justice. In fact, she has turned them around her little finger.

On another occasion it was the father who requested to see Mother Hardey alone; he knew that she wished to ask him to make a concession. "I shall not do it," he had told his daughter briefly. "Wait till you see her," was the answer. After the interview Father had the grace to submit to his daughter's "I told you so." "What a woman!" was his only defence. "I wonder whether there's a man in the world who could say *No* to her when she wants a *Yes*." "The fact is," another fond papa told his wife, "the devil himself couldn't resist her. She actually made me believe that I did not want to take my daughter out." It seems usually to have been the fathers rather than the mothers who matched their wits with hers and were enlightened. One came ready to do battle because a class-mistress had lowered his child's mark by one point for a fault which the child herself had pointed out. The quiet question: "Would you want her to have a point which she did not deserve?" touched his sense of honour and he surrendered. But another time it was the child whom Mother Hardey defended. The class-mistress, a foreigner, had written at the end of a faulty exercise "What a spelling!" "What a grammar!" retorted the culprit. "What penance should I give

caller was not only bigoted, angry and unbalanced, but hungry as well. She listened to the story and read the article without paying the slightest attention to their implications, then gently questioned the furious woman about her family and her work. The air began to clear, and at an opportune moment a tray appeared loaded with substantial refreshments, while an alms quite as substantial was slipped into an empty pocket. Tears of gratitude came; another friend had been won and another soul lifted above itself. "What has happened to me?" asked the repentant visitor in wonder. "When I came into the house I hated that Nun, and now I would give my life for her."

In one case Mother Hardey had to admit defeat. "Mother Barat's Julia" would be controlled by no one but Mother Barat. This strange black-haired girl was only Julia; no one knew whether she had a last name or not. She may have been a gypsy but she was certainly a waif and a stray speaking an unintelligible tongue, distrusting the world and giving it more than enough reason to distrust her, when Mother Barat had taken her in, given her the anchorage of religion and cultivated her talent for painting, finally sending her to America in the hope that Mother Hardey might find purchasers for her pictures. Julia crossed the sea in the company of Mother du Rousier, and Manhattanville did its best to welcome her. But the shifty black eyes would rest on nothing long enough to read its true value, and the girl slipped about the big house like a restless shadow. Patrons were found for her, but Julia refused to paint, and wasted materials so that debts for her unfinished work were laid to the Convent account. Every move that Mother Hardey made was met with insolence and duplicity, while calumnious letters did mischief abroad. Mother Barat appealed to the heart which she knew was hers at bottom; "How often you are in my thoughts, dear Julia. I think of you when I go into the garden where you used to like to come to me and tell me your faults and your troubles." Mother Hardey was at last obliged to send her back to France where Mother Barat forgave and forgave through many more wayward years. Julia finally died repentant, saved by the love of a Saint and by the heroism of the man who married her for her soul's sake.

One day another strange character called upon Mother Hardey, a fascinating little person about seventeen years old, who has told of the visit herself: [5]

I asked for Madam Hardey who in a few minutes made her appearance. She invited me to be seated beside her and questioned me about myself. I merely told her that I was a Miss St. John; that I was poor and an orphan; that I wished to educate myself; and, that if she would take me, I would be forever grateful. While I was speaking Madam Hardey looked me full in the face. . . . Her attention was drawn from me, for a moment by a religious coming in and asking "if the dog should come with them too." "Certainly," replied Madam Hardey; "they expect to see the dog as much as they do you." As she spoke these words she smiled so sweetly and her face lighted up so beautifully that I felt I could be happy near her; and I waited with breathless impatience for her reply. She paused as though waiting to hear if I had anything more to say; and as I looked up into her eyes to catch her words, she spoke, and her words thrilled my very soul. She said, in a kind, decided tone: "I will take you; you may come as soon as you choose."

The child went away stunned with happiness; but she did not come back. For all her intuition Mother Hardey could hardly have guessed that Miss St. John was a daughter of Maria Monk, an abused, eccentric, brilliant, soul-hungry child of misfortune known as "Tick" who had escaped from slum life and tested by bitter experience every form of misunderstanding in her brief career. She was so eager to be beautiful that she had strapped her pug nose with elastic bands till it became classic in contour, and so determined to have a good education that she had braved going to a Convent in spite of her mother's *Awful Disclosures*, as she had been told that Catholics were the only people in the world who would educate her gratis. Mother Hardey had proved the truth of the promise, but all was spoiled by Tick's jealous half-sister who threatened to reveal her identity, adding "Then that *good* Superior will tear you limb from limb." So Tick did not go back, but became instead Mrs. Eckle, dazzling, wealthy and ever more eccentric until, in the midst of fantastic adventures in Paris, she found her way along a strange path of her own into the Catholic Church. She finally reappeared at Manhattanville, this time to place her own little girl at school. Mother Hardey instantly remembered having seen her before. Then:

> I told her that I was that poor girl, and I related to her what prevented me coming: how a lady had threatened to go and tell her that Maria Monk was my mother, and said she would tear me limb from limb if she knew who I was. "O," exclaimed Mother Hardey with indignation. "How foolish." . . . At parting she embraced me, and I left her that afternoon with the same sentiment of admiration and gratitude that I had experienced the first time I had seen her seventeen years before. The only change that I could see in her was that her cheeks had grown pale. The first time I saw her they were tinged with a deep roseate hue; yet the same sweet expression, and the same compassionate look and smile which animated them seventeen years ago still remained and seemed to defy the ravages of time.

So the grand-daughter of Maria Monk became a docile pupil of Manhattanville, and Mother Hardey undertook the direction of Mrs. Eckle. She made her a Child of Mary, checked her extravagances, righted her only too obvious want of balance, and turned to the best account the fugitive but strong gleams of spirituality in her strange, appealing nature as only a person gifted with the discernment of spirits could have done. One day she advised her protégée to say the Thirty Days Prayer for a certain intention, which was granted.

> Then Madam Hardey said to me: "Why are you so surprised that God should have answered your prayer? He always answers our prayers when we pray for that which will add to His Glory. You should not make such a wonder of it." . . . Her words impressed me so much that I kept thinking of them all the way home. I felt that Madam Hardey ought to know. That I loved her no one can doubt, and I was determined to pray more earnestly than ever.

Such intuitive interest in other people brought it about that Mother Hardey was loved in every circle. There were, of course, the old pupils who named their children after her, and brought them back to see her through succeeding generations. On one occasion she held one such spiritual grandchild in her arms while it was baptized. "What is the name?" said the priest. "Pauline." "No," said Mother Hardey firmly, "Mary Pauline," and so it was. Then there were those whose intercourse with her was more hidden. There was the poor woman whose husband she rescued from a worse than vagabond life by giving him self-respect and a farm to cultivate near the Convent grounds where she could watch him at work. There were the labourers, always present on account of her ceaseless building activity, whose cans of cold coffee were carried off by Mother Hardey to be heated, and the organ-grinders to whom she opened the gates wide in the spring. There was the Negro woman whom she met on the grounds one day and ended by bringing into the Church, so that Father, Mother, and a procession of pickaninnies were all baptized in the Convent chapel. There was the boy unable to get an education for the priesthood who found himself in a Jesuit College because his story reached her ears. When the Convent engineer was killed in a boiler explosion Mother Hardey cared for his family. When the little Princess Clotilde of Savoy, exiled in a New York hotel, found loneliness or officious attention too much for her, she would escape to Manhattanville and hide among the pupils, and in gratitude for Mother Hardey's understanding she dropped at her feet one day, kissing them with swift Italian impulsiveness.

It was the Village of Manhattanville that felt proudest of its associations with Mother Hardey; or rather it was the Annunciation Parish, for the Village had by now nearly lost its identity. A railroad passed through it, and a new ferry over the Hudson had been opened, "to import cattle from the west." Manhattan College had long been sheltering the religious activities of the neighbourhood when, in 1853 a Parish Church was erected close to the academic buildings in a hollow blasted out of the rocks on Bloomingdale Road, now Old Broadway. It was "truly an Angelus in brick and mortar," handsome without and prayerfully beautiful within. Then the overflowing school, which had been in session since 1847 in the renovated Lorillard barn, became a Parish School indeed, and Mother Hardey made plans for the larger building which was finally erected in 1872. The Brothers at Manhattan College had a similar school for boys, and parochial fervour mounted high. It has never ebbed.

One day in 1856 Mayor Woods addressed the Common Council of New York in congratulatory mood. He had his reasons for complacency. There were horse-cars on Broadway, a Crystal Palace stood at one end of the new Park fit to house a World's Fair and to entertain the Prince of Wales at a gala ball. A plan had been submitted for an elevated railroad, to reach which, said the sanguine inventor, "the passengers will not need to walk up the stairs, but ascend by a screw-shaft containing a sofa." If the first "model tenement" to be built gave sorry promise of what its successors were to be, the brownstone houses that pushed their way in the wake of Fifth Avenue were, noted a visitor, "of a richly decorated style of street architecture; all the windows are of plate glass and the door-handles, plates, and bells are silvered so as to impart a chaste and light effect." From a higher point of view also the Mayor was glad to note development. Columbia University was so crowded that it had to move uptown to 50th Street, the Astor Library and the Hudson River School of American Landscape Painting had lately been opened. Jenny Lind had sung in Castle Garden and Thackeray had lectured to good audiences. "So," said Mayor Woods, "with the laying out of the Central Park, the almost entire union of Harlem and Manhattanville, the connection made by the actual settling of the City proper and what was once the village of Bloomingdale, have left indeed but a few rural spots untouched by city life." This will result "in the complete and entire consolidation of the people of New York into one compact Community." The Convent, which stood aloofly on its hill, which had just concentrated its inner strength by establishing perpetual adoration of the Blessed Sacrament, was ready to be a part of city and national life.

"Religious life is not always as monotonous as is generally believed" was Mother Tommasini's comment on one national event in which Mother Hardey became involved. The fanatical outbreaks of the Native-American Party in 1844 had died down, but ten years later the same spirit of blind hatred boiled up again, made more formidable by thorough organization. The rise of the Know-Nothings not only threw the country into a ferment but entangled it in international difficulties till the United States Government itself was compromised. Orestes Brownson, who treated the question with tremendous vigour in his Journal, penetrated its depths and found justification for the existence of the party.[6] But he showed at the same time that even at best "its platform is too weak and too narrow for a full-grown man to stand on," and "its condemnation is that it is not truly American, and proposes a remedy for an evil which every American deplores that would prove far worse than the disease." But while Brownson was making a rational if passionate analysis of the Party, its members rushed irrationally into pure passion. The storm-center was New York where Bishop Hughes was at the height of his power, swaying opinion and leading action in Catholic and non-Catholic circles alike.

Sheer bigotry might not have stirred up such trouble had it not been coupled with the question of liberty, always capable of arousing response in a self-conscious democracy. The relation of liberty to the Church had become intensified with the accession of Pope Pius IX in 1846, and the political liberalism of the new Pope during the first years of his reign met with feverish acclaim in the United States. At a mass meeting held in the Broadway Tabernacle in New York the most influential non-Catholics of the day made a gesture to join hands with the Pope. Horace Greeley (whose daughter was later a pupil at Manhattanville) proclaimed him "the heaven-appointed instrument" of the resurrection of Italy, and James Buchanan, then Secretary of State, closed his message to the meeting with the words "that he may prove successful must be the wish of every lover of liberty throughout the world!" Bishop Hughes, seeing more deeply into the complications of the matter, showed great reserve; and his attitude was justified soon afterward when Mazzini and the Young Italy League swept the movement from liberality into revolution, and the Pope, thwarted in his plans for an enlightened liberalism, became the Exile of Gaeta. The Bishop in the meantime was engaged in various other battles on his own account, all concerned with some species of liberty—Irish, abolitionist, or anti-clerical, but when the news of the events in Italy reached him he threw all his energies into defence of the Pope. New weight was given to his words in this same year when the See of New York was raised to the dignity of an archbishopric, and the Archbishop elect went to Rome to receive the pallium on April 3, 1851.

Grave business was awaiting him in his Diocese upon his return in June, but on the morning of the twenty-second the new Archbishop suddenly decided that he would give himself a pleasant interlude, an hour of relaxation at Manhattanville. It was the day after the Feast of Mother Hardey, which had been celebrated on a large scale with an elaborate French dialogue, and:

> At nine o'clock word was brought to us that the Archbishop, who had just returned from Rome, would be here in an hour, that he was already on his way. Great confusion, while the children were sent hastily to the dormitories to put on their white uniforms and the Nuns and servants arranged the room. A large inscription which had been made for Reverend Mother's Feast was altered so that it read "A notre Digne Père" instead of "A notre Digne Mère." We were about half way through when the bells announced that Monseigneur was in the house. The children came down four by four, and the dialogue which had been prepared for Reverend Mother was repeated. The children showed a really admirable presence of mind, and changed all the feminine pronouns into masculine without once making a mistake. Never had Monseigneur seemed more pleased.

If the Archbishop suspected anything clandestine about his reception he gave no sign of it, and in expressing his thanks to the children compared them, in the most popular metaphor of the day, to a garden of ever-blooming flowers. Regretfully he tore himself away and plunged into a vortex of trouble, for the Know-Nothing movement was absorbing all smaller Nativistic parties into itself. The pseudo-patriot Kossuth arrived from Europe before the end of the year, and stirred up the city. The new Archbishop issued a warning to Catholics not to greet him, for he said, "I regard him as an arch-enemy of the Catholic Church and of the peace of mankind."

Kossuth was bad but Alessandro Gavazzi, an ex-priest who arrived in New York two years later, was worse. Dressed in a monk's robe with a blazing cross woven into it, he drove his audiences to the maddest excesses against Popery and the Papacy as "the fiercest tyranny the earth knows." Just at this moment the Papacy itself, with little advertence to Gavazzi and his like, was quietly arranging a demonstration of its true ends and means. On June 30, 1853, Archbishop Gaetano Bedini, Nuncio to Brazil and personal ambassador of good-will from the Pope to the President of the United States, landed in New York and was met by Archbishop Hughes.[7]

Monseigneur Bedini was a quiet, gracious Prelate, bearer of semi-official messages from one Ruler to another, and charged with investigating such questions as new Sees in the United States, the Catholic school-system, and the protection of Church property against the aggressions of Trusteeism, still rampant in the middle west. His attitude was full of friendliness and hope, and the hearts of all open-minded Americans turned to him in the same spirit. But the unenlightened trouble-makers had already fastened upon an episode of his past life for his present undoing. While he had been governor of Bologna, which lay in the Papal States, some murderous agitators had been put to death by the civil authorities. Bedini himself had had nothing directly to do with the execution, but now an ugly undertone was heard through the cheers that greeted him as he drove to the Archbishop's house: "Butcher of Bologna."

Just across the woody ravine to the west of Manhattanville lay the Donnelly estate, and here the representative of the Holy See was a guest during his stay in New York. While there, he dedicated the new church of the Annunciation. Mother Hardey's invitation to visit the Convent reached him speedily, and one fine Saturday morning a chorus of fifty children's voices raised the triumphal song *Pio Nono*. After that the Prelate said Mass in the Convent chapel every morning during his stay at the Donnelly estate. The children's enthusiasm for the Holy See refreshed him, and he told Mother Hardey that he loved America because it was "a land restless with the fire of youth.'"

Bedini then swung wide into a tour of the country, bringing wise answers to old problems, noting with pleasure the vigorous life of the Church as she made her way into public consciousness. But Gavazzi was also going from city to city, one step ahead of him. His attempts to poison the minds of the people failed in some places, but met with ominous success in most. Placards appeared announcing:

> Bedini the Tiger, who is Guilty of the Murder of Hundreds of Patriots, their Wives and Children in Italia, who Ordered that Ugo Bassi, the Patriotic Catholic Priest, be Scalped before he was Executed; Will this Abominable Servant of Despotism Receive the same Honors as the Heroes of Freedom? [8]

The glitter of receptions, the enthusiasm aroused by his graciousness, the respect felt by the right-minded for the cause he represented, all this was like a triumphal march. But in the streets, in the lecture-halls, in the railroad stations, roaring, swaying mobs, made up of anything but Native-born sons of the Republic, made Bedini's nights and days hideous. With minds bloated by libelous newspapers they tumbled his effigy, together with that of Pius IX, into bonfires along his route. "I am frightened more than I will to be," he wrote to Archbishop Hughes, "but I am determined to satisfy even the slightest desires of the good Catholics and of the Bishops of the United States, cost what it may. God who has so evidently protected me till now, will continue the work of His mercy."

The climax was reached in Cincinnati at the end of December. In the official newspaper of the Radicals the hope was voiced that at least one man would be found brave enough to assassinate Bedini. Then, as the *Catholic Telegraph* reported next day:

> A mob was organized at Freeman Hall, and armed to the teeth, started, bearing transparencies with every manner of insulting devices and mottoes, towards the Cathedral. They were met by the police, upon whom they fired. The police then fell upon them, arrested about sixty and put the rest to flight. . . . God forbid that a band of aliens to our institutions, who scorn allegiance to our laws, should succeed in jeopardizing the lives of our citizens.

But as Archbishop Purcell wrote:

> The hand of God was in all that occurred. The wicked have been confounded. They were arrested at the dead hour of the night within a square from the Cathedral—not by the Catholics, but by the police. . . . We have kept all our appointments as if nothing had happened, and visited churches, institutions even miles from town, to a late hour of the night. The heart of the Nuncio abounds with consolation in the midst of tribulations which of course he feels.[7]

Mother Hardey was on her way to the chapel one evening when she was stopped by Mother Tommasini in an even greater state of excitement than usual. "You must come to the parlour at once," she was told, and rather unwillingly she went. There, waiting on her knees before a picture of Our Lady, was a young girl sobbing with fright. She was a member of a Club for Italian working-girls under the guidance of Mother Tommasini, and gradually her story came out. Her fiancé was a member of one of the most virulent groups of the Know-Nothings, and had revealed to her a well-formed plot to assassinate the Papal Nuncio upon his return from Cincinnati to New York, which would take place in a few days. The girl had come to Mother Tommasini, as to the one friend whom she could trust, only in the hope of finding some way of turning the young man from his share in the crime. It would be folly, she assured Mother Hardey, to go further and try to prevent the assassination, for if the intervention were discovered Manhattanville would be burned to the ground. She knew her fiancé and his friends well enough for that.

Mother Hardey spent the rest of the night in the chapel. What if the tale were due to excitable exaggeration? She could hardly take the responsibility of assuming as much, after what had happened in another city. And if it proved to be true, and she acted upon it, would her chapel be added to the half-dozen churches that had already been burned down? By morning she had made her decision. She told Mother Tommasini to write out the whole story for what it was worth, and she sent it by hand to the Italian Ambassador in Washington. "It is now my responsibility," she said to Mother Tommasini. "You must pray and know nothing about it." A close student of this sad piece of history says: "We have no accurate knowledge of Bedini's journey back to New York, or of the events which occurred between his return and his journey to Washington on January 10th." It looks as though his moves had been deliberately veiled, but it is too late now to be sure whether Mother Hardey actually saved the life of a Papal Nuncio.

Archbishop Hughes in the meantime had been forced by his health to spend the winter in Cuba, so Monseigneur Bedini went quietly about New York saying goodbye to his friends, while spies watched all the outgoing boats and the newspapers shouted "Freemen—Arouse—Bedini the Butcher of Italian Patriots, the Tyrant of Italy, is in our city." He did not go to Manhattanville, as though he had some special reason for not wanting to attract attention to the place, but he sent word to Mother Hardey to meet him at the Seventeenth Street Convent. There she found a pale but undaunted Nuncio in secular dress, who thanked her warmly for her services, great and small. His parting words had a significant ring: "Unworthy and miserable as I am, I can assure you that in my heart you occupy, after God, the first place." Then, after a silence, he added: "It is as it should be. The world begins with Hosannas, it ends with the *Crucifige*. I am happy to have some resemblance with our Lord and with His Vicar on earth." On February 3rd he slipped silently onto a steamer at Staten Island, and sailed for Rome, where he loyally reported to the Holy Father all that he had seen worthy of admiration. As for the rest, as he wrote to Archbishop Hughes: "I am leaving under painful impressions, but in spite of these unmerited and unexpected reverses, the memory of America will be a source of consolation to me all my life. . . . Let us live in God and love one another in God with our whole hearts." While the Senate was making public reparation for the conduct of a part of the country, Archbishop Hughes was grieving over the manner of the departure: "The part that afflicted me most was the mode of your leaving New York. . . . If I had been at home we should have taken a carriage at my door, even an open one, if the day had been fine enough, and gone by the ordinary streets to the steamboat on which you were to embark." For her part, Mother Hardey received a letter from Monseigneur Bedini saying that the album containing the verses of welcome so loyally spoken by her children, lay on the center table of his Roman salon.

In her desire to help everyone Mother Hardey sometimes created delicate situations for herself which she carried through with *sang-froid*. There were many Mexican children in the school, among them the three daughters of Señor Comonfort, ex-president of Mexico, whose persecuting habits at home were balanced by his devotion to Convents abroad, and especially to Manhattanville where he was a frequent caller upon Mother Hardey. It happened that at this time Monseigneur Labastida, Bishop of Pueblo, who had been ungently dismissed from his diocese by Señor Comonfort, was living in poverty and neglect in New York. Mother Hardey invited the Confessor of the Faith to live in an attractive little stone house on the grounds which had once served as the Noviceship. The Bishop accepted with gratitude. One day he spoke to the children so beautifully of the honour of suffering for the Church that at the next class one of them demanded "who is the monster who persecuted such a Saint?" "Mi Padre," said a small voice. Electrified, the children realized that this was a matter for discreet silence, while the portresses grew skillful in showing the Bishop out the back door whenever Señor Comonfort was seen approaching the front door. One day a new and very elaborate ciborium appeared at Mass, and a new embroidered veil at Benediction. They were gifts from "mi Padre" which Bishop Labastida recognized as having been stolen on a time from the Cathedral of Pueblo. Mother Hardey continued none the less to follow her policy of universal hospitality, and the Bishop wrote some verses in her honour on her Feast-day, and dubbing her "the Saint Teresa of our century." Each month he tried to pay for his lodging. Mother Hardey accepted his offerings, but when he left he found in his suitcase the equivalent of their sum total in gold coins with which to begin rebuilding his broken work in Mexico.

From then on Bishop Labastida's great determination was to bring the Society of the Sacred Heart to Mexico. To Mother Tommasini, who had been his interpreter during his stay at Manhattanville, he had often said: "You will be one of the Foundresses." Twenty-four years of slow, Providence-marked preparation passed before his prophecy came true, but by that time Mother Hardey was living in Paris, guiding from afar. She was known to many influential Mexicans, one of whom once said: "If Mother Hardey were only the Minister of our poor distracted country, how soon she would restore order there!" The way was opened for a foundation by devoted old pupils of Manhattanville, who kindled faith and courage among their tried countrymen by spreading devotion to the Sacred Heart. Rafaela and Adela Muñoz and Concha Lascurain were devoted to her, and never let her forget their hopes for a Mexican foundation. At school Concha had been an unbearable child whom only Mother Hardey seemed to understand and once, when a particularly distressing report had to be sent to Concha's mother, the Superior had written across the back of it: "Do not be discouraged, dear Madame; I am sure that your child will turn out admirably, and be an honour to us all." Later on Concha found this note among her mother's papers, and made it her life's work to live up to it. She had a Mass said every month for Mother Hardey and worked tirelessly in the interest of the Society. She was the first to welcome Mother Tommasini and Mother Moran when they came at last to Mexico in 1883, in disguise and moving among great dangers. Then it was that Bishop Labastida, white-haired but alive with zeal, repaid Mother Hardey's hospitality of old by helping, at deadly risk to himself, to found the first Sacred Heart Convent in Mexico, which, multiplied by many, has carried on its work ever since in trial and in triumph.

And so, whether we look from within at the life of the House on the Rock, or follow the influences that moved out from it, we find that Mother Hardey's work as Superior was characterized by the joining of many forces, by the give and take that make for solidarity. She had merged her personality into the life of her Society, and had thus freed it from all that was merely personal. So liberated, her remarkable gifts made of her person a link through which the lives and works of many crossed each other in constructive harmony. She, not in the least self-conscious, looked objectively over the play of events in which she was interested, of people whom she loved, while her conscious powers were lifted and turned to God.

As she moved about the corridors of Manhattanville she gave an impression of peaceful power. Hers was a generously built figure, not too tall or large; her movements were calm but decided, the hands invariably joined, the straight, blue-gray eyes alive with interest, an amused smile at the corners of the lips. In her youth she had been rebuked for too dignified a bearing, and until late in life her directors told her that her manner was apt to be cold, and might compromise the good that she could otherwise do. This pomp of bearing had its usefulness. One day she was followed in the street by a crowd of ill-mannered urchins who pursued her with songs and hoots. Mother Hardey turned and said simply, "that's enough, children, go away," and they went. "C'était son port de reine" commented her companion. It was useful in cowing lawyers and keeping familiarity at bay, but a child once found it chilling when she was introduced to Mother Hardey—in a crowd of other children, to be sure. She said afterwards: "I neither felt important, nor were my feelings hurt." But for one such child there were dozens of others who ran to her on the slightest provocation, and the littlest hid in her skirts from the whole of a less loving world. Aloofness was undoubtedly evident at times, and must be drawn like a cool shadow into any true picture of Mother Hardey, but for those who knew her it did no more than give an astringent quality to her devoted heart, freeing her love from the slightest touch of sentimentalism or unreality. Who knows but what it may have come from fear of those very qualities, or have been raised as a defence against the deep self-diffidence that is often present in persons of commanding temperament? One who lived closest to her has left a portrait in which magnanimity and affection are blended in this powerful Superior:

She prayed and weighed all before the Lord, then was slow to act, but when light was given to her she hesitated not one instant but went ahead with the virile energy of her beautiful character and with an admirable *savoir-faire.* God was with her. I hardly know how to picture the greatness of her soul. She was great, magnanimous in all her actions. Her words, full of vigour and of life, went straight to the mark; she lived the truth. This nobility of soul made her meet the most exalted with royal dignity, and it made her kneel humbly before the least of her daughters when she had committed a fault. . . . Always convinced of her own lowliness, she showed by her own example the beauty of holiness. Of broad mind and measured judgment, she knew nothing of prejudice; the clarity of her views gave perfect security when one consulted her. In thinking of her now I feel the tears rising, and I seem to hear her say in her inimitable tone, half-serious and half-teasing: "Tommasini, stop crying, I don't want to get my feet wet."

The devoted friend who wrote these lines could not stay with Mother Hardey forever. Mother Tommasini was named Superior of Havana, and had to leave Manhattanville. When the moment of departure came Mother Hardey wept, but she spoke through her tears and by her words unknowingly left to us her own portrait of the Superior that she herself was:

Let us be faithful, wherever God sends us, moving towards Him step by step, hoping, believing, that what happens is His will; so living as to draw souls to good through love of the Sacred Heart. Let us do our duty simply, gently. Let us strengthen the weak, be sympathetic, helpful, patient, smoothing the rough ways. The life of a Superior is a life of constant effort, of persevering abnegation; a word here, a look there, an intelligent and efficacious interest in the affairs of everyone. The life of a Superior must be made of kindness and affection, and that joyfully.

XVII

WAR AND PEACE

When, after years of tension, the country finally split apart along a jagged, bleeding line between north and south at the shock of a gun fired at dawn on April 12, 1861, Manhattanville found itself a small register of the whole United States. A great many of its pupils were daughters of southern planters, and though rumours of war had long troubled the air they had not been withdrawn from school. Mother Hardey, born and bred in the South, living and working in the North that she had made her own, was walking outdoors one day in the sun-peace of that dire April. It was recreation time and she noticed the school drawn up into two agitated camps, miniature forerunners of the pending conflict. When the children saw her, the nearest contingent, the Northern, ran up and closed about her. As usual, her presence had a quieting effect and the shrill voices subsided. "You are for the North, aren't you, Reverend Mother?" pleaded the little Patriots. "I am your mother," came the answer, "of course I am with you." But the Southerners were running up frantically. "But

Reverend Mother, you're from the South. You're for us." "Am I not your mother?" was the same unanswerable answer. To keep two such factions living together through the dragging months and years of war was a task that Mother Hardey accomplished by determination and by a boundless sympathy. While many of the large boarding-schools of the North were depleted to the point of ruin by the withdrawal of southern children, Manhattanville suffered little diminution from any quarter, though Mother Hardey's charity and tact were stretched to the utmost as southern fortunes vanished like smoke in the wind of devastation. One child of those days said: "Received during the war as a gratis pupil, a little Rebel refugee, I shall never forget her delicate generosity. . . . I was made to feel my position only by marks of particular kindness, a deeper interest, and maternal dealings towards me." So wide-reaching was this generosity that when Washington was threatened with invasion Mother Hardey invited the whole Visitation Community of Georgetown to come to Manhattanville in case of danger.

Within the Community it was not a question of calming factions but of supporting moral strength. "I well remember," wrote one of the Nuns, "the gloom that filled our hearts when the news reached us of the Battle of Bull Run. . . . Instinctively I left my place and seated myself on a low stool near Reverend Mother. I felt that by her side I should grow calm, nor was I mistaken. She read my thoughts, and quickly turning the conversation lifted up our hearts from the sad forebodings that oppressed them to a childlike confidence in God." Then, with her all-accomplishing energy, she set the Nuns to work packing boxes for the soldiers and collecting supplies for the army chaplains, one of them wrote afterwards:

In the name and by the request of the soldiers, who appreciated the thoughtful remembrance of their spiritual wants, I wrote to

Reverend Mother some letters from the seat of war. She took special interest in our little drummer boys, to whom she sent special marks of favour. The little fellows, with noble pride, exhibited through the camp these presents which they received, as they informed us, from the "Mother of all Nuns." One of her little protégés died, while regretting that he was not spared to go home and give the Mother of all Nuns the pleasure of hearing how many beats he could play on his drum.

Soon the blockade of the Mississippi valley cut off all communication with the three Convents in Louisiana. Sixteen months passed in which no word from them reached the Mother House, and there was reason for fearing the worst. Mother Barat knew to whom she could appeal, and in August, 1862, she wrote to Mother Hardey asking her to visit the Missouri houses which were unable to communicate with their Superior Vicar, Reverend Mother Jouve, who lived at Grand Coteau. Mother Hardey's Councillors took alarm. The Superior General, they said, would never have asked her to go had she realized the dangers of the journey. Such an argument was not likely to appeal to Mother Hardey who set off at once in spite of disrupted railroads and recent illness. She took a north-looping route which brought her to Chicago, then a raw young city rising on its shaking wooden sidewalks above primeval mud, but flourishing its head in the air and growing by the thousands every year. Here was the latest Sacred Heart Convent, founded only three years before from the Southern Vicariate; and here was Mother Hardey's old novice of Saint Michael's, Mother Galwey, busily building up an academy and flourishing works of all kinds. Behind a new house just built that year on freshly acquired property stood a large frame building. This was a Parish School which Mother Galwey had erected on the first site of the Chicago Convent. Not wishing to leave so serviceable an object behind her upon moving from Rush to Taylor Street, the energetic Superior had ordered the house to be rolled bodily upon a flatboat and paddled up the river to the new property, where it promptly welcomed three hundred children into its generous walls.

Mother Hardey did her best to take the place of Reverend Mother Jouve in encouraging the young foundation, which was growing into maturity as rapidly as Chicago itself, and when she left she carried off Mother Galwey to be her companion on the journey into Missouri. She reached Saint Louis in October. The year before a crisis had threatened the very existence of the Convent there, for that border city had undergone a small Civil War of its own, and the Republicans had expressed a noisy desire to have the house and grounds for their barracks. The price of vehicles had soared beyond reach as thousands of people fled the town, but the Religious could not flee, being responsible for too many children. So the windows were barricaded with mattresses, but in spite of threats and a temporary removal to a country house the school went on, and Mother Hardey found that all was tranquil in spite of straitening circumstances. This was the first time that she had ever visited the scenes of the life of Mother Duchesne. In the words of a later visitor, this house of hard beginnings was:

> . . . a low rambling brick building, dull grey, facing west. On this side it was bordered by a brick wall, at the edge of which are tall lilac bushes. Now and then, after late spring rains, their perfume scented the air. Inside the house there was always a fragrance which reminded one of Paris—a faint mixture of spiced foods and incense.

For Mother Hardey there was another and more austere fragrance in the air, the unpassing presence of a life too strong to be submerged by years of trifling change. More redolent still of heroism was Saint Charles. The house was poor still, as when she who was so rich in her poverty had lived there.

New wings had been added, but no walls that were relics had been demolished. There was a hump still in the attic floor, the mark of pioneer builders; there was a sense of energetic peace in the air, like the breathing of an athlete at rest. Only great detachment and great love together could have made such a spot on earth as Saint Charles was and is. Already, Mother Hardey found that the small room under the stairs where Mother Duchesne had died was becoming a sanctuary.

The house had nearly been closed a few years before, that its resources might serve the Chicago foundation; but once more Mother Duchesne, pleading this time through the lips of Mother Jouve, her own niece, had begged that its consecrated life be spared. Then the rumblings of war had rolled close but done no harm, and Mother Hardey walked through the stillness, over the grass that sloped from the house down towards the river, to the shrine in the garden where Mother Duchesne now lay. All the houses in America had contributed to its erecting, as well they might, and its foundation stone had been laid by Father de Smet, missionary of those Rocky Mountains to which Mother Duchesne's last impossible hopes had turned. She had crossed the ocean once, wind-blown and slowly, drawing behind her the first thread for the weaving of the pattern of the Society in America. Mother Hardey, before her work was done, was to carry the shuttle nineteen times back and forth over the same ocean more swiftly and easily while the pattern broadened. Now, in this deep moment between her ceaseless moves, she read the tombstone before her that spoke of great labour and of a crown of glory.

There was no possibility of penetrating to the South, but there was one more house in Missouri to be visited. Saint Joseph's had been founded in 1853 by Reverend Mother Shannon. The school there had leaped to the hundred mark in the first year of its existence, but Mother Hardey found it sadly shaken by fringes of the war that kept brushing over it, and by the threats of "Jay-hawkers." Here as everywhere she was looked upon as the direct envoy of the Mother House, and "may her visit" prayed the Annals of the house, "bring about those fruits that our Mother General desires of us." A letter from Mother Barat's secretary reached Mother Hardey soon after her return to New York:

Our Mother was happy to know that you were able to make the journey to Saint Louis. She thinks it advisable that the Western houses should correspond with you while they are unable to communicate with Mother Jouve. You must, therefore, direct the changes that may become necessary or useful. Your recent letter has relieved our Mother of a great anxiety, since it assures her that the business difficulties of the Convent of Saint Joseph have been satisfactorily settled. She begs me to tell you of her heart-felt gratitude for your goodness to her Western families.

By the following year the blockade was broken, and news from Louisiana began to reach the outer world. Mother Hardey then had the satisfaction of learning that one of her attempts to bring aid to the houses under fire had succeeded most opportunely. The story made thrilling reading after the pain of it had passed. High courage had carried the Communities of the South through days of adventure and of desolation, a courage personified in the slight, laughing, intrepid figure of Reverend Mother Shannon, whose buoyant nature had been tempered into flexible but unbreaking strength by Mother Duchesne herself in Florissant's Heroic Age. Now, when Federal gunboats were crawling with surly determination up the river and Blue-coats swarmed over the levees, when terror filled the plantations with restless refugees, and hunger stalked the cotton fields, Mother Shannon stood on the gallery of Saint Michael's and the Union Officers could not pass indoors on their self-invited visits without removing their hats, so courteous was her greeting.[1] "We can scarcely hope to be very welcome here," they mumbled. "I admit," said Mother Shannon, "that if God had heard our prayers you would not be here," and she spread refreshments before them. "It's your fault that I have not better to offer you, but your blockade is very effective." They immediately promised to send special supplies to the Convent. Later, when she had occasion to meet General Butler himself, he abruptly asked her if she had taken the Oath. "I have done better," she retorted, "I have taken three vows," and the General was too mystified to inquire further. Mother Shannon was mistress of the situation, and used her influence for the good of the countryside. She stung the Federal soldiers into realizing that she expected honourable behaviour, and she won it, while at the Convent the negroes remained loyal, food was somehow found for the many homeless ones who crowded into the charitably large house, and Mother Shannon's sympathy brought healing to many woes.

Grand Coteau had expected to be left in quiet in the heart of its land of plenty, and at first the school enrollment had increased enormously. Then troops came pouring into the Têche Country from two directions and settled down for a long siege. The fighting came so close that hand-to-hand combats could be watched along the Convent hedges. Caught between two fires, the children pluckily gave their time to preparing for a life different from any that they had known before. "Divided into bands, they were taught by their Mistresses to do all kinds of household work, caring for the dormitories, refectories and kitchen, washing dishes and ironing clothes. They even wanted to learn how to milk cows. The time for all this was taken from that formerly devoted to music lessons."

Then, just when the danger was greatest and the food shortage beginning to be serious, the hand of Mother Hardey was felt. The new Federal Commander of the Department of the Gulf, General Banks, made his headquarters at Opelousas, and on the very morning of his arrival an unexpected letter brought hope and protection to the Convent: [2]

Headquarters, Army of the Gulf
Grand Coteau, Apr. 20, 1863, 8 A.M.

To the Superior of the Convent of the Sacred Heart;

If you desire to send letters to New York you will please forward them to me by the bearer who is instructed to wait for them. I send a safeguard that will protect your school from the struggles in the rear of my column, and if you desire it will leave a guard. I regret that I cannot call to see you. My daughter is with Madame Hardey at New York. Mrs. Banks, who visited the school but a short time since, writes that all are well there.

I am respectfully
Yr Obt Servant
N. P. Banks
M.G.C.

The next day a second letter arrived bringing assurance of the same kind interest in the Convent at Natchitoches, and a few days later came an even warmer message:

Dear Madame,

Accept my thanks for your note. The favor to which it refers is too slight for reference. I have ordered the Commissary-in-Chief to forward to your Order at the Convent small quantities of flour, coffee, tea, fine salt, and other articles which may be useful—which I beg you to accept—if you get them—with my regards.

Army movements are uncertain. If you have any requests to make, desire to go or send to New Orleans, inform me soon.

It grieves me that I cannot see you and your Sisters. I think we should be friends, as with your leave I subscribe myself,

Yours truly,
N. P. Banks

The promised "small quantities" of food arrived by the barrel and the hundred pound weight, and were followed by the unusually perspicacious gift of a bolt of black merino. As the fighting grew closer a sharply reassuring note arrived:

> Officers and soldiers will protect the property and persons of the Convent and College at Grand Coteau. The violation of this safeguard will be punished by death.

Accompanying this official message was a more leisurely one:

> Accept my thanks for your courtesy in informing me how I could serve you. It gives me great pleasure to comply with your requests. I have sent to New Orleans for some of the articles you desired, and have directed the Commissary, Captain Woodruff, who is much delighted that he has the opportunity to oblige you—to obtain others. For such as I can send there will be no charge. . . . My small service to you is the only real pleasure I have had in Opelousas.

When the campaign was over and General Banks had withdrawn from the Têche Country, he continued to be the obliging go-between, writing through his secretary in August:

> I have the honour to forward you a package addressed to yourself from Madame Hardey, whom I saw in New York in June last, and I promised that this should be delivered. As I understood from her that there would be some papers in return, if you will please in some way forward them, or anything else that you may wish to send, I will see that they reach her in safety.

Later in the year Mother Shannon succeeded in making the perilous journey to Grand Coteau, and brought Mother Jouve a letter which, like the blowing of the Spirit of God, swept her once more into the full current of the Society. Mother Barat wrote of the sorrow that it cost her to put off the Eighth General Council on account of war, and continued:

They say that the coming months will see the end of it. If that is so, you will be called as quickly as word can reach you. Otherwise we shall have to find some other means, but I dread half-measures, especially at my age. If I may express one desire, it is to gather together my old Mothers and Daughters one last time in this land of exile, those who have helped me and who have shared with their First Mother the constant work of our difficult mission, who have so often sweetened and lightened it by taking upon themselves the most wearisome and thorny share of the labour. Oh, how I want to see them, to tell them my thoughts, my gratitude, to urge more intimately those who will survive me to double their devotedness, if possible, to establish our Society upon the firm basis of religious virtue, especially those which stop before no obstacle when there is question of the glory of Jesus, and as these virtues must be practiced until our last breath, who will have such courage and such perseverance unless she is guided by the habitual action of the Holy Spirit? So it must be interior spirit, union, and at least a tending towards the Heart of Jesus that will continue, strengthen and sustain this life of sacrifice and renouncement, which will assure the existence of our Congregation for the future which Jesus has prepared for it.

Although the war was still dragging on the call to Paris reached Mother Jouve the following spring, and she managed to sail from New Orleans to New York where Mother Hardey was waiting for her. This was not the first time that the two had travelled together. They had slipped overseas in 1860 for a month or so of Mother House air. A slight shock had met Mother Hardey to find on arriving that she was not expected, for the letter telling her not to come for business reasons had, as she openly rejoiced to find, been sent just too late. Now, in 1864, there was no mistake. There was instead an urgency in the words of invitation that left no doubt of the importance of the coming Council in the eyes of their Mother Foundress:

Ah, dear Aloysia, how many frightful things I have witnessed since my young days, and of how many of them I have been the victim. How much these remembrances help me to become detached from the things of this world. One hope alone enables me to keep up; it is the joy of being permitted to labour for the salvation of even one soul, and there are so many on the verge of destruction! Let us then steer our little bark courageously to the end. The Heart of Jesus is guiding us because we desire to save souls. The more useless and unworthy we are, the more we should rely upon Divine assistance. The great Saint Paul said, "When I am weak, then I am strong!" After this blessed Convocation your Mother will be ready to say her "Nunc Dimittis." Yet she must always add, "Fiat voluntas tua!"

It was mid-June when the Superiors Vicar finally met at the Mother House. It had been recently moved to a new building at one end of the sweeping gardens surrounding the Hôtel Biron, from which it was separated by a wall with a little green door. The children in the Junior School kept an anxious eye on that door, always hoping that Mother Barat would come from "The Castle of the Sleeping Beauty" as they called the Mother House, to pay a visit to her favourites. Before the Council opened there was a preparatory retreat on the text "Seek first the Kingdom of God," and a whole month of sessions followed, over each of which Mother Barat herself managed to preside. Her eyes were somewhat dimmed to the things around her by the nearness of eternal light and her voice was very small in the large-roomed house. One of her most observant daughters, the Mother Perdrau who in her youth had painted the picture of Mater Admirabilis, has left us a word-sketch of her: [3]

When I look at her she is profoundly recollected in thought; there is a deep serenity resting upon her face. She has grown old in the joy of the Lord, in spite of her hard trials. If a duty calls her, she literally runs to it, . . . but if she meets you she poises delightfully, ready to listen to you with a loving wish to be entirely yours—just as God is, we said to ourselves. . . . She seemed to have an intuition of the effect which the very sight of her produced, for with one swift word she would answer a thought which had not been spoken, which had been hidden perhaps through self-love. Then one would feel captivated, drawn, not towards our Mother who had the art of vanishing most charmingly and of leaving Jesus Christ in the place of her frail little person, as she would say. And if she saw that we still felt anxious over something she would whisper in our ear on meeting us: "Run to the tabernacle, and get along without the rest!"

Mother Hardey found herself one among fifteen Vicars. One hundred and eleven houses had been founded since the beginning of the Society, but of these twenty-five had been closed. Of the remaining eighty-six, forty-four were in France and twenty-two in North America, of which fourteen were under Mother Hardey's care. The readjustment which formed the Canadian Convents into a new Vicariate under Mother Trincano also divided the other American houses into two Vicariates, that of Louisiana under Mother Shannon, and that of Missouri, including Chicago and Saint Mary's, Kansas, under Mother Galwey. Mother Jouve was to remain in France. When these organizations had been made the Council proceeded to arrange for the future, for Mother Barat was looking beyond her own life. The Plan of Studies was made more flexible and a *Juvenat* established to provide for the studies of the young Religious. Between the meetings the Foundress gave away all that was left of herself in long talks with each of the Vicars, and at the close of the last session all heard her faint voice grow strong, though they could scarcely see her for tears:

Now each one feels the need of putting her hand to the work, of going with a truly apostolic heart to pour out upon others the graces that she has received. If we are full of these thoughts, it will be said of us what Scripture said of old of Israel about to meet its foes: "They rose as one man." Yes, Mothers and Daughters, you will all rise, one in mind and in heart; you will be strong as an army in battle array, and your acts will be blessed by God.

Before the opening of the Council Mother Barat had said to Mother Prévost, Superior of the House on the Rue de Varennes: "I want you to prepare for the Feast of Saint Madeleine in my old and dear Hôtel Biron. The Mother House is going to be a Cenacle during the Council; the Religious feast will be celebrated there *in pompis;* but the solemn feast of the Society, with all the Vicars present, cannot have the grace that is proper to it, intrinsic to it, without the presence of a school. What are we without children? I have lived for them, I shall die for them; you will make them understand that!"

So on the morning of July 22nd Mother Hardey, lost in a crowd of Reverend Mothers, followed the Superior General into the great study-hall of the Hôtel Biron. It was no longer a study-hall. A double row of orange-trees, more natural than life and dating, said Mother Perdrau *sub rosa*, from the days of Louis XIV, slanted back and up from the low ones in front to the tall ones enclosing the statue of the Sacred Heart at the end of the woodland lane reaching the length of the room. Light filtered in through garlands of greenery over the windows. In the spaces between the trees, arranged in illusive perspective, sat the children, demure in posture but with excited faces. To the strains of a symphony, Mother Hardey felt for her place in the formidable semi-circle of seats of honour. Mother Barat sat down in her arm-chair and closed her eyes, listening intently to the music, and then, through long habit, began to pray even more intently. The music ceased and her eyes remained closed. From behind the tree-trunks peeped out the faces of fifteen charming shepherdesses, waiting anxiously. Was Mother Barat not going to see their impressive, long-practiced entrance? But Mother Goetz, the Vicar-General, touched her on the arm and she came to herself. "Where am I?" said the voice they all loved, in mischievous surprise. "Is this a garden?" Then her laugh rang out. "It has been like this through my long life," she said. "I am always taken in by these illusory creations of your childlike love for me, and as your mother I shall enjoy, to the very end, entering into these beautiful perspectives that you make for me, opening upon the Heart of Jesus."

With measured grace the fifteen shepherdesses approached, carrying great silver crooks bearing the name of one of the Vicariates of the Society, all linked silkenly to the central one. The crooks were presented to the Vicars with a dignity reminiscent of the innocent pastorals of the Petit Trianon, to a flow of unimpeachable French verse of classic turn. Music wove the poetry together, but while the double harmony filled the room Mother Barat beckoned to Mother Perdrau, who was responsible for the performance, and whispered in half-mock anxiety: "Tell me exactly how much money you spent for those rainbow-silk dresses, those hats of fine Italian straw?" "The dresses are of satinette," Mother Perdrau whispered back, "and the hats are of straw-colored cardboard." "I am always taken in at plays," laughed Mother Barat low to her neighbors, and she gave herself up to the joy of the hour as her little shepherdesses, with their verse, their songs, and their flower-twined staves, drew the Society closely about her with delicate, unbreakable cords.

When Mother Hardey reached home on September 8th she felt that she was bringing a legacy to the Community. "I do not think," she said, "that we shall have our Treasure with us much longer, and I want you to know that the last impression carried away from our Mother was that of her humility. When we were going away, and were all gathered about her for a last painful farewell, she gave us this message for our

Vicariates: 'With humility one can do everything for the glory of God; without humility one is good for nothing.'" She then worked out her Conference on the theme of the Mother House retreat: "Seek first the Kingdom of God."

The following April the guns of the Civil War stopped rumbling, but in the relieved silence a single shot rang out that robbed the land of its leader. It was a lonely month for Mother Hardey. She had not yet grown used to the loss of Archbishop Hughes, whose strenuous career had ended on January 4, 1864, and of Father Gresselin, her director for many years, who had died while she was in France. Then as spring warmed into summer came word of another loss, foreseen but none the less overwhelming. The first warning was a Circular Letter from the Mother House saying that Mother Barat had been stricken beyond human hope of recovery on May 22nd. Mother Hardey read the letter to the Community and added, "although our fears are not yet confirmed I feel that on Ascension Day our Mother ended her pilgrimage here below."

She was right. All year since the Council Mother Barat had been walking up the side of Mount Olivet, her face catching the light at its top. During the summer she had often come in a rolling chair drawn by a dozen or two young Religious, to a terrace at the Rue de Varennes. There she sat for the evening recreation till it grew too dark for her to see the crowd of faces turned up to hers from the grass at her feet. She sometimes forgot everything but her thoughts and her love. "Let us begin on earth," she cried, "right now, at this moment, while we are gathered together here, the divine work of love that will be ours for all eternity—eternity! Then we shall love, and that will be joy." "After such flaming words," says Mother Perdrau, "she would make little pauses, and smilingly come down to some practical everyday matter. One could see that our Mother did not trust mere empty enthusiasms. And so her abandonment, the flights of thought which carried us on high, were suddenly controlled by her wisdom." During the winter she was scarcely seen by anyone, but strength returned in the spring and she asked hungrily to have the children sent to her in little groups, under a cedar tree planted by herself long ago in the garden and now in its prime. Then on the Sunday before Ascension Day she entered the Community Room saying, "I was eager to come to you today, for on Thursday we are going to heaven." On Monday she was prostrated, and God held her in a close silence from then till the day of His and her Ascension.

So Mother Hardey found herself back in Paris less than a year after she had left it, for the Ninth General Council which must fill the empty stall of the Foundress. Young Mother Josephine Goetz, the Vicar General, awaited the decision of the Council in positive terror.[4] "She will suffer as in the Garden of Olives," said Father Fessard, "until the Feast of the Nativity of our Lady when the grace of the Generalate will flood in upon her. It is a marked sign of the care of the Heart of Jesus for your Society that He has formed such a soul to govern it. She is completely above all merely human considerations. It is rare to find such a capacity for the supernatural." The Assistants General and the fifteen Vicars were of the same mind, and the voting was unanimous. Mother Goetz became the second Superior General of the Society, and in spite of the overwhelming business of the moment grew to know Mother Hardey well and to ratify with her a serious decision which was kept secret till the return to America. In the meantime Mother Hardey made the most of her opportunities. A young Religious who had come with her wrote back to Manhattanville:

If in America I always thought her a saint, I am sure of it now. Her humility and self-forgetfulness lead her to seek always the last place and to act as if she were the least of all. She misses our

Mother Foundress very much. I think she feels her loss all day long. Every morning she goes to her little room to pray, and I love to kneel just behind her, for I think our Venerated Mother cannot fail to listen to me when I am near one of her dearest and holiest daughters. Reverend Mother prays for everyone while there, and with the greatest fervour, so rapt, so intense, that it seems as if she was in sensible communication with our departed Mother. She says that she tells her all her troubles, all her difficulties and her projects, and then she is satisfied. And truly, when she leaves the room, the peace on her countenance is heavenly.

Back in America Mother Hardey went quietly about her business for a year, and then the decision made in Paris was carried out. She was to leave Manhattanville and take up her residence at Kenwood. In vain Archbishop McCloskey, who had taken the place of Archbishop Hughes, produced from the Cathedral Archives a letter from Mother Barat promising his predecessor that Mother Hardey should not be moved from New York. "Both parties to that agreement are dead," said Mother Hardey. "In a conference full of feeling," recorded Manhattanville, "Reverend Mother did her best to soften the pain of such a separation, then, speaking out from her heart, she let us see something of the strength, the joy even, with which she set herself to the fulfilment of such an important point of our Rule." Mother Hardey herself wrote to the Superior General: "How grateful I am to you for having given me the opportunity to obey," while on September 16th Kenwood recorded its own feelings: "Jour de grand bonheur."

XVIII

WHERE RIVERS RISE

THE DRIVEWAY into Kenwood, curving from the foot of the hill to the house near its top, seems to say to those whom it lifts upward, "I am doing a great work and I cannot come down." It sweeps with the grace of a single swift-drawn line out of one world and into another. It comes to rest on a terrace below which the old world falls away and stretches into unguessed perspectives, while above it fringing pines lead the way up one brief height the more, to where the sky waits. That sweep up the drive, momentously final for so many, is swiftly made today, but it must have been even more impressive in 1866, when even the friskiest horses were surely sobered by it to a slow walk. Mother Hardey could see the Novices waiting for her at the top as she looked up through the carriage window. They had left Manhattanville only a short time before her own departure, to refound the Noviceship in Kenwood's silences. Fifty had entered in the past three years from the Eastern Vicariate alone, and the city could no longer hold them. She dismounted among them, and found herself at home on her hill.

Hills are the place where rivers rise; headwaters are lofty and hard to trace. It is hard to follow a stream back beyond the breadths that carry boats of commerce and of pleasure, back from the obvious gleam of its surface to its overshadowed springs. Mother Hardey had found a place high among hills where the headwaters of the Society in America could rise, where the first sacrifice that makes a religious life could break from the ground into a small clear spring of living water, then move outward to find its momentum. The secrecy of springs is proverbial. Mother Hardey knew where to find them, how to channel their course in other people, but she kept her own secret jealously. Those who knew her often wondered about the springs of spiritual life that fed her own overflowing action, guessing much and sure of little. Latecomers can hardly hope to do more, but that little can best be done, perhaps, while she is at Kenwood where rivers rise.

Spiritual writings since the days of the Desert Fathers have told stories to prove a truth that would be self-evident were it not for the "bewitching of vanities" to obscure it, the truth that outward works without inward grace are as nothing in God's eyes. There are many variants of the tale of the preacher, golden-mouthed, who swayed a congregation to fervour only to have it revealed to him that his triumph was due to the sacristan who sat on the pulpit steps and prayed. Bishops and Builders enlist the prayers of holy sufferers; Missioners write to their cloistered Sisters to turn the current of prayer in their direction; and Founders of Religious Orders declare that houses and numbers do not matter in comparison with holy lives which alone can make the work of the Order efficacious. Those who pray help those who work but things are perhaps at their best when there is no division of labour, in other words when saints do the work. So Mother Barat wrote to Mother Hardey, her hard-working daughter, and said: "You have no idea how often I am occupied with you and your household before Our Lord; and it is you who are first in my thoughts. I desire perfection for you; more than that, I desire your high perfection."

When a person is known for striking executive gifts and is singularly unrevealing of herself, when her development has been marked by uniformity and unusual exterior perfection, it is hard to know much of that inner life which is closer to self than personality, since it comes from grace possessing personality. In a life like Mother Hardey's no spiritual crises stand out as in the lives of converts, of penitents, of persons of uneven temperament or unusual qualities who bring catastrophic changes upon themselves. She began to serve God too young for there to be much to undo, and her path was determined for her. Obedience carried her along simply. The world could see little of inward drama, with its climaxes and anticlimaxes. So busy and so successful a life as hers might easily have been self-guided and ended in self-possession, yet, when activities came to rest and habits were indistinguishable from nature, it was seen that God possessed her.

The story of how it came about is faintly traceable in fragments of conferences—quoted from notes or hazardous memories, in a little book of Maxims, in passages taken from undatable letters from her directors, in some scraps from her own pen, and in the *vox populi* of her day. This is all that is left of written evidence, but still stronger is the evidence of those who came into contact with that indefinable quality visible in one who prays and lives her prayer.

It happened that one of her Nuns, more admiring than discreet, determined to outpray Mother Hardey, just for once. They all knew that she took for prayer much more than the length of time required by Rule, for Mother Barat had written to her: "Try to manage some half-hours during the day to gather strength near the Source of life." So one Feast day, when the rigidity of time was somewhat relaxed, the admiring Nun watched her chance, slipped into the chapel behind her Superior, where she carefully copied the erect, mortified attitude, and set to work to pray, feeling that she could do so indefinitely with such an inspiration before her. But two hours went by and Mother Hardey gave no sign of knowing that there was anything in the world but the tabernacle, while her would-be rival left the chapel, vanquished. When Mother Hardey finally left, she carried the atmosphere of the sanctuary with her. Her daughters grew to know when she had just come from the chapel; the evidences were more tangible as her years became more serene. Something luminous rested upon her; it was a radiance that could only be called heavenly, a light upon her face. A proverb says: "He who looks on the sunset shall have his face golden." Those who saw it spoke of it to each other, guardedly, but Mother Hardey kept her secret. A young Religious came into her room one day on some business or other, and was so overwhelmed by the supernatural beauty still resting on her face that she could say nothing. There was a long silence before Mother Hardcy spoke, not with annoyance but with finality: "Sister, if you have come only to look at me, you may go."

It was, apparently, at the famous retreat made at Lyons in 1842 that her spiritual life came of age. Father Barrelle must have recognized great aptitudes for things of the soul in the young American Superior, for he continued to direct her for many years by letters that aimed at keeping alive the realizations gained at Les Anglais. He wrote in the first months after the retreat:

I thank God for the betterment found in your life, and I pray that He will make you understand more fully every day, touch with your finger, the necessity of being all His; yes, all, with no reserve. For, Reverend Mother, when we have well understood this necessity, not only is there kindled in our hearts a strong desire of knowing what our good Master wants of us, whether within ourselves or without, to prove to Him how real is our desire of being all His. . . . I have read over your plans, and they seem to me good. Go to your prayers as epicures go to their finest dishes, as starving men go to food. What they do through fleshly craving, let us do through desire for our sanctification.

As time passed and difficulties arose, he wrote again:

I see that spiritual help is lacking to you, but you will find everything in the Holy Eucharist, in the wounds of the Crucified. Look there, turn your desires there, your prayer, your gaze, your whole hope.

Some years later she had consoling reports to give, to which he answered:

Blessed be God, my daughter. I am delighted with Him and with you! With Him because He now gives you sensible proofs of His merciful love, yes, more than in the past when He hid His tenderness from your soul. Today He reveals it to you, and makes you feel it more clearly. I thank Him with all my heart, as though it were for myself. And I am also pleased with you, because of the victories which you have begun to win over yourself, with the help of the great graces which your loving Spouse has given you. You have only one thing now to do: let yourself be led interiorly by the spirit of Our Lord, in conformity with the spirit of your Institute and the virtues which it requires, for that is a circumference beyond which you must never go, no matter what motives may urge you to overstep it by ever so little; and obey always in conformity with that same Institute. I like your state of indifference, with the abandonment which it implies to the least wish of Our Lord. Trust yourself blindly to His wisdom and to His power. I was very happy over your letter, for it reveals you completely. Your contempt of yourself will make you more meek and gentle with others, and more devoted in your service of souls.

The guidance that she received from Mother Barat was asked for in the spirit of a Novice and acted upon with child-like exactness, while the Foundress for her part openly exulted in dealing with a soul of such earnest docility. Only one letter in Mother Hardey's own hand is extant, written from Astoria, when she was still very young yet burdened with authority. She has just made her retreat, and:

> If Our Lord is satisfied with my efforts, I must be satisfied also with all that He plans for me. He has reproached me with many an infidelity and negligence, with luke-warmness and indifference in His service, with a great want of generosity and of zeal. Yet the sight of these miseries has not discouraged me. The words of Father Suddé have helped me: "Let him who fears that he is wanting in prudence in fulfilling his charge consult his Rule, and he will know as much as the most able. Inferiors, superiors, all, fail only when they abandon the way of their Rule." These words have encouraged me and made me take the resolution to become an able Superior, since I know the means, and they are within my reach.

She then goes on to enumerate minutely all the little clouds that have come between her soul and the God for whom she hungers, the difficulties that arise from her own temperament and the temperaments of others. She describes, rather diffidently, the means that she has taken to strengthen her prayer, adding wistfully: "I want so much to become an interior soul! Give me a practice for that, Very Reverend Mother." If only, the letter seems to cry between the lines, her Mother were not on the other side of the sea! Among the Religious in America, she says, there are two whom she would most gladly consult, for she trusts to the spirit of God in them; they are Mother Boilvin and Mother de Kersaint, but they live far from New York. This clear-sighted leader of others had her moments of helplessness, even of fear, and a strongly felt need for dependence underlay the decisiveness of her character. To give herself anchorage she asked permission to make two private vows: "Never to put off what I think God or my duty asks of me, and to make all my spiritual exercises, especially meditation, with most careful attention, seeking my happiness in it." Another time she asked to bind herself by vow never to commit the least deliberate fault. The permission was granted.

The matter of these vows was far from extraordinary; she was simply using them as an extraordinary means to insure the doing of ordinary things. No shadow of illusion is visible in Mother Hardey. She did not bind herself by promise to reach unusual heights, but, wide-openly aware of her own weakness, bound herself to what God expected her to do anyway, trusting in Him to lead her where He would. Imagination, whether in its desirable or undesirable rôle, seems to have played little part in her spiritual life. Reason counted for much and desire for still more, so, lest desire should fail of effectiveness, she vowed to do what was reasonable. This attitude appealed to Mother Barat, who prized reality above all, and Mother Hardey maintained it as youth passed into a maturity that never became self-reliant. As late as 1860, when she was at the Mother House, she asked leave to make out in writing a detailed account of her own character and of her spiritual life. "Yes," said Mother Barat, "I want to know you through and through, so write out your *compte-rendu* and give it to me; then we shall talk it over together." Distance made no difference, and Mother Hardey wrote faithfully at each step of her way:

I have just made my retreat, a really good one, though I had not the slightest human help. What Our Lord is asking of me above all is that I should enter generously into the practice of the third degree of humility, to be thought ill of—which has already happened—to be accused of a want of straightness, to have my mistakes spoken of to those who need not know them, to have my actions blamed; that is how the Lord wishes to detach me from creatures, and I see the will of God in it so clearly that it does not pain me. The fruit of my retreat will be a general perfecting, both for myself and for others. Please, Venerated Mother, bless these resolutions and add to them whatever you think best. Bless also your poor child, who is at this moment at your knees, asking pardon for the trouble that I have caused you.

The trouble referred to seems usually to have come from precipitous action on Mother Hardey's part; she would now and then move too rapidly in the matter of foundations, or trust people too easily. When blamed she wrote:

I thank you most sincerely, very Venerated Mother, for telling me the things that you have heard about me. I promise to look into them, to correct what is true, to avoid what is not. Please lay the blame upon me, but spare X; her head could not stand it. I have just received your letter of April 18th, and I thank you a thousand times. Your reproaches have gone through my heart, but I think I can say that I have accepted them in the same spirit in which they were made. I would not for the world be spared hearing them. I know how far I am from having what I need for responsibilities such as mine; necessity alone has placed me in my position, and it is only by knowing my mistakes that I can correct them. How could I not be willing to hear them from you, my Mother, to whom I have belonged for twenty years, and who knows all that is wrong with me?

On one occasion when difficult circumstances had arisen she was found sitting silently before her crucifix, and when asked why she looked so sad answered, "I have just been asking Our Lord to take me out of the way if it is I who am the obstacle to good." And when the troubles penetrated still deeper, and interior anguish was added to the outer burden, she wrote again to Mother Barat:

It is a sweet consolation to me to be your daughter, although so unworthy, but your charity reassures me in the midst of my interior dryness and torpor of soul. O, my Venerated Mother, how you would pity me if you knew how much I suffer, and how hard it is for me to bear with myself and my miseries. If I could only love Our Lord with tenderness! But all I can do is to throw myself upon His mercy and try to resign myself to my sad condition, trusting that with His grace I will overcome the obstacles to my union with Him.

She was happy to find a successor to Father Barrelle in a director who resembled him. Father Gresselin was also French, and was stationed at Fordham in 1858 when he became acquainted with Mother Hardey. He understood the spirit of her Rule, and its obligations upon a Superior Vicar; he said: "Meditate for some time every day upon the destinies of your Society in this New World, and when you have understood the immense good it should accomplish you will see that such gain cannot be too dearly purchased." He guided her for six years, at the time of her greatest striving, on to the moment when it would seem that God Himself stilled the striving and granted moments of the union for which she thirsted. He allowed her much in the way of penance and mortification, and wrote in a strong strain:

The time has come for you to enter into the third and last period of your life, the period not so much of progress as of perfection. You must die to all, that you may live to Jesus Christ alone. Take to heart the words of the Apostle "I die daily." Try to understand them in their fullest extent, for they imply death to all desire, to all fear, to all affection. You must take up the cross and say with Saint Paul: "With Christ I am nailed to the cross." You have no time to lose. . . . Do not hesitate then to sacrifice to Him all that His love asks, and in return He will give you all that is most precious, His cross and His divine Mother. The cross of Jesus Christ pours itself out in charity for others. He bore it for our salvation, that was the purpose of His passion; such must be the purpose of your own life. You have a great mission to fulfill, and you must become the living image of the gentleness and sweetness of the Heart of Jesus.

He did not spare her sense of responsibility:

You are a Mother in your Community; you must then have the care and love of a mother who guesses when there is illness or suffering in the hearts of her children. You have a remarkable penetration on that score. . . . If there has been negligence in the past, God gives you powerful means for reaching your end. He has given you extraordinary influence over the Religious of whom you are the Superior and the Mother. They all respect and love you as much as it is possible for them to love and reverence a human being. He confides to you thousands of children to fashion for Him according to the designs that He has for them. Any negligence or indifference that might be noticeable in you would produce great voids in their lives. . . . But do not attribute to yourself the imperfections of your Community; at least do not do so too much, for it is true that if your charity had been more effusive certain faults might have been prevented.

His requirements for prayer were uncompromising:

There is one point which I have not sufficiently stressed: the direct communication with God which must be the soul of your life. We cannot always be occupied with our neighbor, but it is different with God. Instead of thinking about ourselves, which is time lost, we should be exclusively absorbed in God, so that nothing can turn us away. . . . I know that you are aiming at that perfect liberty, that death to nature, in order to live in God. You have made some progress, but you are only touching upon that state, and Jesus Christ loves you too much to be satisfied with half measures, with weak efforts and mediocre success. I would not be surprised if the time of great trials is approaching, when thick clouds will envelop your soul and God will withdraw His sensible presence, so that the enemy can raise up storms about you. Your virtue has need of that, to be strengthened. . . . This is the third period of which I spoke, the period of perfection into which you must enter with all the ardour of which you are capable, with the help of divine grace.

When it came time for her retreat he showed what he thought of her ability to launch out into the deep in prayer:

> The retreat is a time of sweetness and peace, not of agitation and sadness, as too many of your past retreats have been. This one must be a continual act of love, in which you will taste the sweetness of the Hearts of Jesus and Mary. Take no particular resolution. In passing eight days in the hearts of Jesus and Mary, your soul will receive an increase of light and strength sufficient for all future needs. If God should will you to give Him something special He will speak to your heart with clearness. Whatever is doubtful or cloudy comes not from Him. Do not be surprised that I hold very little to your having fixed hours for everything. I prefer that you should not. I ask of you something far better, eight whole days in the Hearts of Jesus and Mary.

It is the lost half of this correspondence that would tell most. There is silence along Mother Hardey's way of prayer, and it is best only to wonder about what lay behind the hints found in the last letters from Father Gresselin. Speaking of self-immolation he said: "That is what must result from your interview with Our Lord in Cuba." And he added:

> There was later another interview in the same place. The Heart of Mary also showed itself to you, and made you understand that God has poured into her heart all the treasures of charity, and He wishes you to see and love only her, and what is offered through her. Never forget that you then understood and were convinced that you must go to the Heart of Jesus through the Heart of Mary. This was a choice grace, and you must never let the memory of it fade from your mind. . . . The grace of December Eighth is also a grace of the first order. It is not extraordinary, in that God wills to give it to many souls. It is not extraordinary as are visions and ecstasies which are outside the way of Providence. It is extraordinary only because few persons

find the way that leads to it. With you it was a reward for your ardent desires to give glory to Our Lady.

If these were great graces they were not given to Mother Hardey for herself alone. Letters might be lost or destroyed by her own orders, but the impression that she made could not be effaced. She was called to give to others all that was hers to give. In guiding souls she could not help but reveal herself, and they have given testimony to the virtue that went out from her. The coolness that sometimes checked sympathy seems not to have been noticed once a soul had come definitely under her guidance, for then the action of the Holy Spirit was felt to take control. Mother Tommasini, when very young and new to the country, at first found in Mother Hardey's imposing air another reason for homesickness, which, added to the complications of spiritual adolescence, made her half-ill.

But one day Mother Hardey called me and questioned me gently. . . . Then for the first time I opened my heart fully to her, and what good it did me! My kind Mother read me through and through. She saw my fear of being unfaithful to grace, my ardent desire to become a perfect Religious, and she told me not to be anxious, that Our Lord was not offended by the liveliness of my character; that I must not try to quench my nature but to sanctify it, and for that to be obedient.

Then came Probation, and the Long Retreat:

As there was much of the merely human in me, the fear of losing God took possession of my soul. Mother Hardey saw how pale I was, called me and questioned me. I do not know why she quoted to me the Psalm *Nisi Dominus aedificaverit domum*, but suddenly a great light came. I heard no more of what she was saying. I think she saw this, for she sent me away, saying while giving me her blessing: "Conformity with the will of God is your star." I had not heard more because I had seen where my place was to be.

Light comes from one who is in the presence of God not so much through as above the spoken words. It was the effect of a single sentence which, years later, saved a vocation:

I was a Novice, and it seemed to me that she read my most secret thoughts. When I had received her blessing after my first visit with her, and she had assured me that she would pray for me, I was about to go when she called me back and said in a penetrating tone, "Sister, always be faithful to God." The words went to my heart. Soon after, Mother Hardey left for France. I had terrible trials to undergo; my soul was sorrowful unto death. Faith, hope and charity seemed to have fled and my life appeared a failure. My vocation was shaken to its depth, but in the midst of the shadows the solemn words "always be faithful to God" rang in my soul, and the memory of Mother Hardey's loving kindness helped me to persevere in spite of all obstacles. So it is to her that I owe the joy of being today a Professed.

One who had been her Novice found herself followed for many years by letter:

I cannot let this opportunity go without a line to my oldest and I wish I could say my best daughter. But you will promise to become so, will you not, during my absence, that God may bless me and my mission? The first thing I ask of you is great fidelity to your spiritual exercises. Our Rule says that we must love prayer; then the indifference that you complain of will disappear, and your fidelity will make up for the want of sensible fervour. Try to become an interior soul; you have fit dispositions for that, and believe me that the difficulties which you feel come from failing to develop them. Promise me that you will go directly to Jesus when you want to speak to me; I have given Him all my messages for you. If you turn to His Sacred Heart you will overcome your sadness; it comes from the strong desire you have to be united to Him. No need to ask me to pray for you;

I never fail to do so. Your happiness is as dear to me as my own.

And again to the same:

"Blessed are the clean of heart for they shall see God." Yes, even in this world, for Our Lord dwells in hearts that are watching and praying. Our difficulties come from our too great eagerness for the things of this world and our desire to see and hear all that is going on. Our Divine Spouse is jealous of our affections and He cannot tolerate in our hearts anything that does not belong to Him.

To another she wrote:

Let the thought of our Master be continually before your mind, so that you will always consider how He would act in like circumstances. For example, when you are teaching, represent Him to yourself as a Teacher. What patience, what sweetness in His voice and manner! No harsh words pass His divine lips, no cross looks, no deep-drawn sighs! How does He teach? What effect do His explanations produce? Now compare His class with yours. . . . Our study of Him must be made practical, and then by persevering we shall become familiar with His every word and work. . . . You are right in thinking that distance will never change my feelings towards you; it only makes me a little fearful that my child might forget what God asks of her fidelity.

It has been said of Samuel Johnson that he was one of the few men for whom there are no platitudes. For him they were simply the plainest and therefore the best statements of something true, and he could utter them with as much surprised conviction as if he had discovered them by himself. Without resorting to a Chestertonian paradox he could startle other men into believing them. Mother Hardey's literal, straight, take-it-for-granted way of stating spiritual truths had the same effect; it carried conviction. In Johnson's case the roar, the "Sir," the thump of the big fist, added a dramatic appeal to his truisms which, thanks to Boswell, clings to them even in cold print. With Mother Hardey there was no mannerism, rather a manner as simple and as momentous as her words. This would escape from print even had some religious Boswell taken it down. Yet where we find her conferences clear, practical, fundamental, her contemporaries described them by such words as burning, persuasive, inspired and profound. They even called them eloquent and *pleines d' onction*, so completely did her own conviction of their truthfulness supply for brilliance of expression.

As I listened to that never-to-be-forgotten conference on earnestness in the service of God, the truths, the entreaties, the hope that she expressed fell like words of fire upon my soul, and since then have ruled and shaped whatever there has been of effort or of worth in my religious life.

The sentences in these conferences move with the marshalled power of those in *Rasselas*. They are brief, and there are no figures of speech to grace their geometric lines. They did their work starkly.

When we wish to retain a thought a very good thing is to divide it into parts, and, as I wish you not only to retain but to practice, I thought during my meditation this morning that I would say only three words to you, and with these we will be able to go very far in the way of perfection. The first is the love of the Sacred Heart, that Heart that has done so much for us, that has loved us and suffered for us, a love which will make us have constant recourse to that Heart, for we naturally apply to a person whom we love and who is able and willing to assist us. The love of the Sacred Heart of Jesus is our vocation; there is no vocation to the Society without it. It is not sufficient, however, to say "O Divine Heart, I love Thee." No, we should have a practical love that will enable us to make any sacrifices to please that Heart. Nor is there any love where there is not union; our aim therefore should be to live in close union with that Heart, and this I love to repeat.

The second word is love again: love of the Rule. Let nothing prevent our observing our Rule; no, nothing should come between us and the observance of our Rule; that Rule which has been so praised by spiritual authors, that Rule by which we shall be judged. But of course we cannot practice it unless we love it. In doubt we should apply to the Rule and say "Does the Rule ask this or forbid it?" Then act.

The third word is love, yes, love again, love of one another. The Rule says that charity is the bond which serves to unite one with another and the Head. This love is a necessary consequence of the love of the Sacred Heart and of the Rule.

During a Retreat of Renovation of vows she said:

Everything in the world has need of renewal, because everything has within itself the germ of decay; hence the necessity of a religious renovation, which means a renewal of fervour, of fidelity, in pursuing the end of our vocation. The law of sterility, of advancing age, is attached to persons and things, and leaves its impress all too soon. So it is in the moral order. There is a decline which fastens itself upon our thoughts, our desires, our sentiments, even our holiest resolutions. Hence the necessity of having spiritual things presented to us in a novel manner.

To a group of Probanists, she said:

A Religious of the Sacred Heart must be another Christ. She must possess His spirit and be directed always and everywhere by it. Jesus was meek and gentle, He was modest and simple and humble. We must never speak in a manner that is too arrogant or proud. There must be no levity, no affectation, no self-seeking in our manner. Why do we win so few souls? It is because we have not the spirit of Jesus, poor, humiliated, crucified, nor have we the form of His virtues, which is to be studied in prayer and exercised in practice, for then only shall we win hearts to His love.

Once, at the beginning of Advent, she said:

> Let your fast consist before all in denying your passions. Let the excitable control their impulses, the tepid become more fervent, the self-seeking more devoted, the procastinating more prompt to obey the voice of duty. . . . Fervour, like sanctity, is not measured by time. Though you must give to prayer the time prescribed by Rule, it is not the minutes that God counts but the amount of love that you put into your prayers.

A typical opening to her conferences was "Let us examine the meaning of this," or "It is well to have clear ideas," and a typical close is found in one given to the Novices: "Give all to God and He will give all to you. Let these few reflections penetrate deeply into your hearts; it is not I who speak but Jesus who speaks in me. Listen to His voice then and profit."

Even more stark of ornament are the brief sayings for which she was known; they were axiomatic. All were, in some form or other, re-expressions of the Rule. Since she lived by the Rule she spoke in terms of it; and because the living came first, words which might be called trite had the force of life. "She inspired us to fidelity to Rule" is the comment repeated over and over again upon the fruits of her visits to Communities. Her sayings were so easy to remember that they passed into Maxims:

> Of ourselves we are worth little. It is the Society that gives us influence and reputation.
>
> Whenever you look at a crucifix, pray that union and charity may reign in the Society.
>
> Study to keep your thoughts under control if you wish to become a soul of prayer.
>
> Try to see only what you are obliged to see, that the eyes of your soul may remain fixed upon God.
>
> An immortified soul will never be a soul of prayer.
>
> True charity is ever ready to prove itself by suffering.
>
> To do good to souls is the craving of a heart that loves God.

We should know how to speak *to* God before we attempt to speak *of* God.

Love should be the motive of your actions, for the spirit of the Society is essentially a spirit of love.

As an apple seeks the ground, one who so penetrated the Rule went to its heart. As the years passed it was noticed that more and more her words, her conferences and what could be known of her prayer, concentrated upon Devotion to the Sacred Heart. There was her warmth, the fire of her life. "Devotion to the Sacred Heart is our element," she said, "those who dwell in it are free from illusion." And again: "We need have but one fear, that of not corresponding with the love of the Sacred Heart." She once took up a book to prepare her morning's meditation, read one sentence and closed it again. "I find all in that one sentence," she said. It was "Heart of Jesus, ocean of goodness, have mercy on us." And towards the end of a life eaten up by zeal she revealed how quietly her soul had rested in the flame's core; she admitted that for the past sixteen years the sole subject of her meditations had been: "Behold this Heart."

She herself, if asked, could have stated the meaning of her life in a single phrase, a phrase repeated again and again in the chapel on the hill where rivers rise: "In the name of the Father and of the Son and of the Holy Ghost, and for the greater glory of the Sacred Hearts of Jesus and Mary." These are the opening words of the vows that make a life in the Society of the Sacred Heart what it is. She had said them, irrevocably, and by them a life bounded at both ends by the nineteenth century had become an expression of the age-varying but age-abiding life of the Devotion to which those words give tongue, that "Devotion the keenest-edged, which glorifies the Sacred Fire of Love which the Son of God came to cast upon the earth that it might be enkindled." [1]

Saint Madeleine Sophie, towards the end of her long life,

was talking once with revealing abandonment to a group of her young Nuns, and her words showed the double form which Devotion to the Sacred Heart needs must take in religious life. A heart means love, and love is the source of inward living and of outward giving. And this, she said:

> was my primordial idea of our little Society of the Sacred Heart, to gather about me young girls to establish a little Community which, day and night, would adore the Heart of Jesus outraged in Its Eucharistic love. But, I said to myself, when we shall be twenty-four Religious able to replace each other upon a prie-dieu in perpetual adoration, that will be much, but little enough for such a noble end. If we had young pupils whom we could form to the spirit of adoration and of reparation, that would be different. And I saw these hundreds, these thousands of adorers become an ostensorium, universal, lifted high over the Church. That is it, I said as I knelt before a lonely tabernacle; we must combat the traces of Jansenism which have caused a falling away; and upon the revelations of Jesus Christ to the Blessed Margaret Mary, upon that Devotion to the Sacred Heart which repairs and expiates, we will raise up numberless adorers from all nations, even to the farthest limits of the earth.[2]

From the hill at Kenwood one seems to look to those farthest limits of the earth. Mother Hardey was playing an active part in the realization of the amazing vision of Saint Madeleine Sophie, that verified vision of what Devotion to the Sacred Heart can do. She was rooted in the first traditions of a Society consecrated to It, whose spirit is "essentially based upon prayer and the interior life," and she was called to labour mightily in spreading that Society in America. The ground-breaking and planting had been done by the time responsibility was laid upon her; she reaped from that grain as it ripened and made her second sowing.

XIX

THE FULL CIRCLE

When Mother Hardy first reached Kenwood she found the Novices and children packed cheerfully into the Rathbone House, which was monastic enough in appearance with its carvings and its stained glass, but quite incapable of corresponding with Mother Hardey's hospitable plans for her House on the Hill. Behind it, and preparing to swallow it up, the excavations of a new house yawned in the ground, straight-lined and broad-laid like her own ideas.

Those plans rapidly took on reality in the presence of the planner. Winter could stop neither the work nor Mother Hardey's supervision of it. Foundations have to be laid deep in hilly ground under-eaten by springs, and one day the foreman remarked with a shade of satisfaction as he peered into the damply dangerous caverns prepared for pipes, "that's one place at least that Mother Hardey won't see with her own eyes." But just then she appeared on the scene. To his horror the foreman saw her pin up her skirts and ask a nearby workman for the loan of his oil-skins. She was accustomed to going to the bottom of things, and she did so now. The main section of the house, skirting the brow of the hill, was ready for use while the snow still lay thick, and by the time spring stepped lightly over the hill the cornerstone of the chapel in the central wing was ready to be blessed. Then with the unfolding of summer the old Rathbone Mansion vanished noisily to make room for the east wing. Thus Mother Hardey lived at Kenwood literally while it was rising, though she left before the east and west wings had reached completion. Her stay was brief, only four often interrupted years, but the house that was coming into being took the stamp of her presence. It became the center from which she moved outward in an ever-widening ring of final journeys through America which at last brought her to rest in the Mother House when the work of foundations had come full circle.

"Reverend Mother seems to think only of our happiness," was the verdict of the Kenwood Community upon Mother Hardey's stay among them. This could be true only if she had the gift of thinking of many things at the same time. Long before the house was finished one hundred and sixty children were disputing every foot of it. As in the first days at Astoria Mother Hardey lived in a handbag, which took up less space than a room, and did housework when she was not supervising the farm and the orchard. One new building was not enough for her, and soon a second was under construction on a level stretch below the brow of the hill. This became Saint Anne's Parish School, where the First Friday of each month was made such a day of joy that its glow spread, drawing new children and new sodalists. In the meantime a separate Academy for day-students, which only existed for a few years, was thriving on Beaver Street in Albany, and its Community, locally known as the Beavers, spent their holidays at Kenwood.

These holidays had only one shadow, that "Reverend

Mother is carried captive to the parlour," where she remained an unconscionably long time, but when she returned "the evening passed in song and music till the night-prayer bell warned us that our day of pleasure had come to an end, like everything earthly." One of the most popular of these songs, of home-composition was known as "The Yankee Postulant," and there was a special edition of a religious newspaper with "the sad tale of Cock Robin, which we will never hear without reverting to the happy group that gathered around our Reverend Mother at Kenwood." One of the most appreciated gifts offered on her Feast-day was a pin-cushion filled with pins that the Parish School children had gathered, for these were days of hard-working poverty as well as of gaiety. One day, for instance, was recorded as "memorable for the renovation of all the old stockings and clothing that could be picked up." Kenwood's center of gravity was found when the new chapel lit its sanctuary lamp on October 20, 1869, the feast of Mater Admirabilis, and two years later the temporary altar was replaced by the marble one which has since become the altar of consecration for the whole of the Society in North America.

One familiar but sadly changed figure could be seen moving about on the terrace in the sunlight, "taking walks in the garden of abandonment to God's will and weaving together the threads of my wasted years," as she put it. Mother Hardey on a visit to the Sault had found Mother Trincano so ill that she had brought her to Kenwood, to have the joy of making a return to her for all her giving. The two had worked together in companionship or separation for twenty years. Mother Hardey had sent her from one new house to another, that her holiness might be stamped like a seal upon its beginnings. Her virile intelligence was able to cope with difficulties that needed quick solution, but her special gift was an eloquence in speaking of the things of God that made all else seem of passing consequence. She brought a touch of Italian colour to many an American scene. She spent the winter at Kenwood under Mother Hardey's grateful care, but died soon after her return to the Sault, going to heaven in a flame of joy. Her last words to her community were strong: "rigorous silence, fraternal charity, perfect union of minds and hearts." Years earlier Mother Barat had written to her: "Let us refuse nothing to the divine Spirit of Jesus, who wills that all our actions should become supernatural through their union with his Sacred Heart." Mother Trincano's death was like a transparency of a soul which had lived these words to the full.

While thus helping Canada by caring for its Vicar, Mother Hardey also showed her unfailing interest in the Southern Vicariate. Reverend Mother Shannon had appealed to her generosity on behalf of Saint Michael's where the Community was sadly overworked in the bitter days of the so-called Reconstruction. She was always more than ready to help where she could, and here she had an opportunity to repay a debt of gratitude, for Saint Michael's had been extremely generous to Manhattanville in the days of its beginnings. She promptly sent six Coadjutrix Sisters south, entrusting them to a coasting steamer, with a special prayer to Mary Star of the Sea. The day after their sailing the headlines of the paper screamed at her that the ship had been caught in a violent storm off the shores of North Carolina, and had sunk in the dark. It was days before her anxiety could be relieved by a letter from an old pupil of Manhattanville living in Virginia which brought reason for pride as well as gratitude. It gave an account of the storm, and then went on to say:

About one in the morning there was a terrible crash which caused indescribable terror and confusion among the passengers. In a few moments the steamer lurched to one side, and the water rushed through the open holes, for the ship had struck a rock. . . . The danger was imminent, and the only alternative was to climb up on the side of the vessel which was out of the water and wait there until daybreak would enable them to get into the life-boats.

This was no easy task, as the side of the vessel was very high, and in order to reach the boats each passenger had to be tied around the waist and let down the length of the vessel to the frail bark below. The sea was so rough that none of the passengers was willing to take the risk. It was then that the Captain, who had noticed the self-composure of the Sisters, appealed to them to set the example of courage. The youngest Sister asked to be let down first, then the others followed, while tears and cries of terror resounded all around them. Others soon followed their example, but the greater number fell into the raging waters and were drowned. In fact, out of three hundred on board only twenty-eight were saved. From the life-boat the Sisters were transferred to a fishing smack where they remained all day and the following night exposed to winds and waves but still calm and courageous, full of trust in God's fatherly care, and by their heroic example inspiring their own spirit of peaceful resignation into the hearts of those around them. Many of the rescued passengers declared that they owed their lives to the example of the good Sisters.

In the May of 1869,—one of her most travelled years during which Kenwood scarcely laid eyes on its Superior—Mother Hardey set off on a less perilous journey of her own to the Missouri Vicariate. She went first to Saint Louis where there was question of a new Academy just outside the city. All property matters involved great financial difficulties in the depression that covered the area of the Civil War, and Reverend Mother Goetz had entrusted the negotiations to Mother Hardey whose business acumen was known to real estate men all over the country. She took Maryville to heart; nothing, she felt, should stop the building of a new Convent here in the city of Mother Duchesne. The site chosen for it was magnificent, overlooking the Mississippi, and Mother Hardey could see a future in keeping with the view. She decided that the plan must be carried out, and for the next few years watched over its realization. When more money was needed she suspended work on a still unfinished wing of Kenwood, and sent the funds to Maryville.

At Saint Charles she found Mother Lucille Mathevon,[1] old now and living like a second Mother Duchesne a life vibrant with prayer and penance, she whose youth had been spent with Mother Aloysia Jouve on the zeal-swept heights of Sainte Marie d'en Haut, and who had lived for twenty years after her departure for Sugar Creek in cabins which she cheerfully shared with cold winds, rattlesnakes, and ragged, silent, loving, importunate Indians. She had led the way, literally, by cutting down the tall grass ahead and shaming the braves into following her when the Potawatomis had been driven from their reservation at Sugar Creek to another farther west on Saint Mary's River, Kansas. There, as Superior, she served her Indians as the least of them; and they, it was said, "used her as one uses water, without thinking, because one is sure of finding it always fresh and always new." Her laughter rang out at hardships beyond imagination, she sang aloud when suffering gripped her, while prayer clothed her impulsive little person with steady sanctity. She had been recalled in old age to Saint Charles, but her eyes were full of longing as she saw Mother Hardey and her secretary Mother Hoey take the boat for Saint Mary's.

There they saw one worn face that shone with excited joy at their arrival. Sister Mary Layton rushed forward to greet Mother Hardey, her Mary Ann of the first days of Grand Coteau, whom she had cooked for and mothered in the days when there were two instead of twenty-two Convents of the Sacred Heart on the American continent. The place of their meeting seemed like a return to those early days. The small

Community was living in a house with plank floors and walls covered with white-washed muslin, and Mother Hoey wrote back to Kenwood:

We visited the class-rooms, where we found about sixty girls of every hue and grade, from full-blooded Indians to whites. Near the Convent are two little huts; I cannot give them any other name. In one we found the kitchen and the pupils' refectory. Of course I did not expect to find white table-cloths and napkins, but the tin plate and cup, iron fork and spoon, surprised me not a little. In the second hut was the refectory of the Community. The room was rather miserable looking; we had white stone-ware instead of tin, and everything looked neat and clean. The next apartment was the Community dormitory. In the middle of the room is a little altar, on which is a statue of the Blessed Virgin resembling a squaw, and pasted on the wall are four angels in gilt paper cut in the most fantastic shapes. We named it the "Chapel of the Angels." . . . After supper we took a walk to the wash-house, about half a mile distant near the river, and on returning we had a view of the tents in which the Indians were encamped on the brow of the hill, having come many miles to assist at Mass on Sunday.

As Mother Hardey watched the Indian children running about barefooted in pink and red calico dresses, she realized the sorrow of the purpose that had brought her to Kansas. Lovingly and persistently the Society had tried to carry on the work which had brought Mother Duchesne to America. It had sought out the Indians and followed them west, giving all that it could to them while realizing that this was not the chief work that it was called to do. The Mission had undoubtedly prospered. One of its Jesuit patrons, Father Gailland, had written in 1853:

Whatever is noble and generous in their [the Indians'] young souls can, by the powerful motives of religion aided by the grace of God, be trained to every Christian virtue. This is the fruit which is being produced in our schools. . . . Now we have reason to believe that this fruit is solid and lasting. And further, when we see how the Sacred Heart pupils have already renewed whole families, by their good example and by making themselves useful in household work, sewing, knitting, and every womanly art, we have hopes that the good fruit will go on increasing.

But white men less zealous than the missionaries were also following the Indians, and white civilization was crowding them out of their homes. In 1861 the Potawatomis had signed a fatal treaty with the Government which left them no choice but gradually to abandon their reservation and slink away to poorer lands in the west. The effects of the Treaty were not immediately noticeable, and when a Government agent visited the tribe he reported that the school was doing admirable work, and that priests and nuns: "devoted their entire time to its interests without pay, and with that self-sacrificing spirit which the love of God and the labour of elevating the human race should inspire in every breast." But in a few years white children had begun asking admission, and the Nuns wrote: "Since we have opened our school to these children, our Indian girls have become very difficult to manage," and again a year later:

The Indians are few and scattered now. We have had to follow the course of this progress, and our Superiors have judged it best, for the glory of God, to abandon the type of education we gave the Indian girls who are now received only as day pupils in the Free school. Since September 1869, our dear Nazareth of Saint Mary's has become like the other Academies of the Society. . . . The needs of this country are great; may we be docile instruments in the Master's hand.

It was to regulate this difficult situation that Mother Hardey had come. As usual, it was her rôle to represent the advance of the time, and to call in new means of spreading

God's kingdom. Her first act was to arrange for a division of the property between the Jesuits and the Religious of the Sacred Heart who till then had owned all things together in a sort of apostolic Communism, even down to the cows. This required a visit to Leavenworth, where the deeds had to be signed in the presence of Bishop Jean Baptiste Miège, Vicar-Apostolic of the Indian Territory.[2] They found the Bishop in his severe little wooden house under the shadow of the first permanent Cathedral to be built on the great plains. It was romanesque and massive, ruggedly simple yet rich with frescoes, bearing the name of the Immaculate Conception. The Bishop resembled it as he towered over Mother Hardey in warm greeting. There was an abiding smile on the great, square face, chiselled by wind and sun and long, hard, prayer. A Savoyard by birth, he had seen the tumult of Europe in Revolution move like a storm across the background of his sunny youth. He had left home on hearing an Indian-call in his soul, and had straightway been made a Bishop and presented with four hundred thousand square miles of prairie land for a Diocese, lands scattered with rough, wild, wandering souls to be pursued for Christ. For four years he had lived at Saint Mary's Mission where he had played big brother to the Indian girls and father to the Nuns, of whom he wrote to Mother Galwey:

> They have eighty boarders; they work far more than they should, which is your fault, dear Mother, more than mine. . . . They are loved, respected and admired by all who know them, above all by their Bishop who does not know how to show it, nor how to contribute to their happiness which he desires as much as he does to save his own soul.

He had chosen Leavenworth as his See, and tried in vain to draw the Religious of the Sacred Heart after him. He travelled in what he called his "mule-steamer" in circles that touched the Rocky Mountains and Canada, while all around him the Free-Soilers and the Slavery-Men brawled and seethed and farmed until the States of Kansas and Nebraska emerged from the turmoil. Then the Missions began to vanish like a mirage as the Union Pacific Railroad drew its thin line of wealth and adventure across his Diocese, and the United States came rolling after it. Now his health was breaking and his soul was sick to return to its true home as a Jesuit among Jesuits. He watched Mother Hardey shrewdly as she signed the papers that regulated the affairs of his beloved Potawatomis, the children who called him "Chief of the Blackrobes." She was a remarkable business woman, he told his friends later, but still more she had "a singularly just appreciation of things temporal and eternal." "To my mind," he added, "she is the finished type of a true Religious of the Sacred Heart."

Mother Hardey returned home, while as a result of her visit a four-story brick building known as "the sky-scraper of the prairies" rose at Saint Mary's. Kenwood scarcely had time to welcome her when she was off again, this time to Paris where a retreat was to be held for Superiors from many lands. In establishing the custom of such retreats Mother Goetz was carrying out one of the last wishes of the Foundress. It was given by Father Olivaint, so soon to fall a martyr to the Commune. The retreatants marvelled at the assurance and penetration with which he spoke of the inner spirit of the Society; he might well do so, for he had before him on his table copious notes written by the Superior General herself which he had borrowed from her without telling her to what use he intended to put them. While she listened with dismay to her own wisdom, the Superiors profited. The retreat tended, said one who was present, to eliminate all purely personal action by establishing more deeply than ever the uniformity of spirit and of Rule which alone could set free the full life of the

Society. A council of Studies followed the retreat, but Mother Hardey had to hurry home. No one could have guessed that she was carrying a heavy secret in her heart.

Manhattanville claimed her again as Superior for a short time, and she returned to New York in the fall of 1870 to face a thorny practical problem. The Village of Manhattanville was vanishing in the city proper. Street car lines ran through it, though muddy strips here and there still did duty for streets. A few big estates stood firmly and lifted their feathery green in the midst of a new commercial bustle; Manhattan College, humming with boys, with baseball and with books, held a large space free from intrusion. But the Board of Public Works had made some unswervingly geometric maps in which new streets were made to cut straight across the grounds of the Convent and obliterate the historic contours of Lot 15. The Board selected a Committee of its most bewhiskered members, dressed them up as for a funeral in black coats and creamy waist-coats, and sent them with the maps to brave Mother Hardey.

She let them wait in the parlour, knowing already what was on their maps and in their minds. The delegation grew uneasy. "Gentlemen," said the spokesman, "do not permit yourselves to be magnetized by Madame Hardey. Be determined not to yield an inch of the ground mapped out. She has a wonderful power of bringing everyone into line with her views." The gentlemen renewed their oath of fidelity to the Board of Public Works. Then Mother Hardey entered, greeted her visitors as though they had come to tea, and waited. They served their ultimatum while she listened with alert interest and said not a word. When they had talked till they had nothing left to say, a silence fell; they were obliged to beg for her opinion. It came in a tone of reproachful surprise. "Surely, Gentlemen, you cannot intend to carry out the extreme and ill-advised measures which you have proposed?"

There was a gasp. Mother Hardey ran her pencil over the maps, pointing out obstacles which they had overlooked and proposing other plans, all to the greater good of the Board of Public Works. Then she produced a pen with which each member of the Committee signed a formal statement that the Convent property would not be touched. Before anyone of them had recovered from his astonishment the tea for which they had not been invited appeared. Mother Hardey served them, and soon a roar of laughter sealed the compact of good will. As they went away the spokesman could be overheard saying, "Did I not warn you, Gentlemen?" [3]

About this time Mother Hardey came into direct contact once more with her family traditions by events which led to an interesting but ephemeral foundation. Her father, not long after the death of Sarah Hardey in 1846, had married Miss Elizabeth Millard of Baltimore and had taken her home with him to the Opelousas plantation. Soon after Mr. Hardey's death in 1864 she decided to return to Maryland and came east with her little daughter Pauline, or Lena as she was always called. It was no easy matter to get from Grand Coteau to the Mississippi just then, and the two joined Reverend Mother Shannon, who was returning to Saint Michael's on the last stage of her perilous journey in and out among fighting armies on behalf of her convents. The party of ten had an exciting time which Lena, aged thirteen, enjoyed to the full. They spent long days sitting on a raft which was poled cautiously over the waters of one black bayou to another, and at night slept on beds of moss by a campfire which sent its light-shafts quivering up into the secret hearts of the cypresses.

From Saint Michael's travel was tamely civilized and soon Mother Hardey was welcoming them to Manhattanville. The second Mrs. Hardey was young enough to be her sister, an attractive, gentle-mannered woman, still somewhat of a

Belle, who was fond of displaying the endless pretty things that her husband had lavished upon her. She was on her way to the magnificent three hundred acre estate which the Millard family had acquired on the shores of the Saint Mary's River, known as Rosecroft, which she wished to make into a home once more. Two devoted former slaves, Ole' Washington and his wife Caroline, had come with them from Opelousas. Mother Hardey noticed that the aged Mammy was shivering in the northern air; she left the room and returned with a shawl which she put over the bent shoulders. "O, Miss Mary," burst out Ole' Washington, "de Lord bless you! You just like ole Massah. Yo' his true chile sure!"

Lena remained at Manhattanville. Mother Hardey felt a very special affection for this half-sister some forty years her junior. She was a tall, lively child whom one of her friends called "a great big sunbeam." She sometimes went with Mother Hardey on her travels, especially to Cincinnati in its first years, where she moved the children to tears by singing "Robert of Sicily" most effectingly in her beautiful contralto at a holiday concert. When she finished school she joined her mother at Rosecroft. It was an exquisite place, but life was lonely there and Mrs. Hardey's thoughts were turning to her old home in Baltimore. She gave Rosecroft to Lena, but Lena had already made up her mind to enter the Noviceship, and so it came about that one of the loveliest and most historic of Maryland's colonial homes, standing near the place where the Calvert pilgrims had landed, was offered to Mother Hardey for a Convent.[4]

Early one morning in April, 1869, Lena looked out of the window at Rosecroft and was startled to see Mother Hardey walking towards the house across the lawns that stretched so high and green against the blue water behind her. She had arrived on the weekly boat from Baltimore which had dropped her at four A.M. on a neighboring point, leaving her to find a rowboat for the rest of the journey. Lena rushed downstairs. The house into which she welcomed her sister stood on a bluff on the junction of Saint Inigoe's Creek and Saint Mary's River where it broadens to meet the Chesapeake. It was shut in by woodlands behind which the first Catholic settlers moved in memory in and out of Saint Mary's City. The land had been laid out in 1641 "to be used" said the old record "by Cuthbert Fenwick as a dwelling place." The house itself, built in 1650, was long and narrow, of white clapboard save for the brick ends where the giant chimneys rose. Flagged porches ran the length of it front and back, and dormer windows looked out inquisitively from the steep roof. As Lena drew her into the "great room" Mother Hardey's eyes ran over the soft gray-blue walls, and over the fine carving in the hood-shaped alcoves of shell design near the fireplaces, but they lingered longest at the windows which framed one of the most beautiful dreams of Tidewater Maryland. An endless stretch of water sparkled in the sunshine, with the Virginia shore mistly in the distance.

The ground on this April morning was shimmering with thousands of flowers, for Cuthbert Fenwick, besides being a great Catholic legislator and colonizer, had been fond of beauty, and had once filled the arms of all his little slave-children with bulbs, jonquils, narcissi and tulips, and told them to run and plant them where they liked in the deep grass. Before the house were gigantic masses of boxwood grown from slips brought over in the *Ark* and the *Dove* from a still older home, while everywhere climbed and bloomed the roses that gave the place its name. Daniel Wohlstenholm, first Royal Collector of Customs for Saint Mary's port, had next owned the property, and in those early days it had seen exciting deeds stirred up by the smugglers who hid their ships in the near-by wooded coves, such deeds as those that form the plot of John P. Kennedy's novel, *Rob of the Bowl.* Rob, the legless buccaneer, had rocked in his bowl under the windows of Rosecroft, through which, says the legend, the lovely Blanche Warden had been kidnapped; but she had found her way back to live happily ever after among the roses with Rob's handsome son. The Neales and the Coads had owned the place; then the Millards. Then Lena Hardey planted a white rose-vine which still twines today around a mulberry tree that casts a great pool of shade in the warm sunshine.

Lena and Susie showed Mother Hardey round the property. Susie MacLean was one of her dearest protégés; she was half-Chinese, and a Princess at that, who had been brought to Manhattanville at the age of four, where she was for many years the favorite play-mate and travelling companion of the Mother Vicar. Now she, like Lena, was waiting for the Noviceship door to open to her. They took Mother Hardey to "de quarter's shade", the one-time slave-huts where Ole' Washington and Caroline were sitting on the porch, against the white-washed log walls. The batten doors on their huge hand-wrought iron hinges were open, and spinning wheels purred a song of the past within. They took her to the little round chapel behind the house, and Mother Hardey wondered doubtfully how often a priest would be able to row across the Creek from Saint Inigoe's Jesuit house, near which Father Andrew White had once lived, to say Mass.

On her way back to New York she stopped in Baltimore to see Archbishop Martin J. Spalding, who was anxious to see Catholic life restored to vigour in the place where it had first found a home in the United States. He remarked of Mother Hardey after she had gone: "She is a woman created by God for the accomplishment of a great work." By September Reverend Mother Grasser with a community of four and a school not much bigger took possession of Rosecroft. The healthy air and beauty of the place made its charm, but, wrote one of the foundresses later: "The post-office and general supply store were six miles away, and all our needs had to come from there, but we had no money to buy and there was not a foot of ground under cultivation. Large fields were left in furrows as before the Civil War. It was a place of desolation except for the oysters which abounded on all sides." One day the Jesuits across the stream received an unexpected visit from the Archbishop and appealed to the Nuns for help. A complete hot dinner on the Convent's only china dishes was ferried over to them. The next day the boat brought back thanks but no dishes, and when the Archbishop arrived at Rosecroft he was served on the cracked ones used by the Community. Such difficulties could have been overcome in time, but not those of isolation and of lack of spiritual help. The too-few Jesuits found that they could not serve the Convent, and no other chaplains were at hand, so in 1873 Mother Hardey, who was then in France, was obliged in spite of the pleas of Archbishop Bayley to close the foundation. The school was transferred to Elmhurst, a newly-opened Convent in Providence, Rhode Island, where one of her nieces, Cora, was among the first pupils. Rosecroft passed into other hands, the old house burned down in 1906, and Catholicity still awaits its full flourishing in the home of the Calverts. Lena, who had brought Rosecroft into touch with the Society, died while a Novice. Mother Hardey, who had reason to fear that her health would not allow her to make her vows, only said: "Lena's death is a matter of joy and not of sorrow; she belongs to the Society in heaven."

In the meantime grave danger had been threatening the Mother House and the Convents of France. In July, 1870, the Prussian army rumbled over the frontier. House after house was either evacuated or converted into an ambulance, while cannon balls fell into the gardens of the Mother House.

Hunger walked the streets, and so many horses were killed and eaten that, as one of the Sisters remarked, "dead people had to go on foot to their own funeral." Mother Goetz had been persuaded for the sake of the Society at large to take refuge at Laval. She left Paris with the words: "Let us make gain out of everything, even the most painful events, to grow in the love and service of God, for it is for this end that He sends them." She had scarcely settled down in her retreat when a letter from Mother Hardey brought a fresh suggestion: "Will you allow me, Very Reverend Mother, to come to France to get you and bring you to our American shores?" When this plan was found to be quixotic Mother Hardey devoted all the money that she could or could not spare to the relief of the houses in the war zone. Soon the Commune enclosed the Mother House behind seven lines of barricades, but the Stars and Stripes flew over it, in honour of a spirited American, Mrs. Blunt (daughter of Francis Scott Key) who took up her residence there to protect it. In May the hostages of the Commune were shot, among them Father Olivaint. The peace of exhaustion settled down over France, but new sorrow came with the expulsion of the Religious from all the Convents in the grip of the Kulturkampf.

With astonishing calm Mother Goetz lost sight of no part of the Society in caring for those most afflicted, and in December, 1871, Mother Hardey received the word for which she had been prepared during the Superiors' Retreat. There was a vacancy in the General Council and Mother Barat had advised that as far as possible the Assistants General should be chosen from the various countries in which the Society had houses. Who could better represent those of North America than Mother Hardey? So she was called to leave them all, and to bring to the Center with full hands the work with which she had been busy for thirty-five years. The new Assistant General wrote:

Your letter of December 12th has overwhelmed me. My first exclamation upon reading it was "My poor Mother General! She is increasing her burden by choosing an aid who is incapable of giving her assistance." Yet obedience is everything to me, my Venerated Mother. I am ready to go. As for the sacrifice of my native land, I can say in truth that I have always considered the Society as my country and my home. With regard to my works, I know full well that God has need of no one. . . . To be stationed near you, and to learn at last how to obey after having been so long obliged to command, will be a real happiness to me.

Mother Goetz had asked her to make a tour of the twenty-five American houses before coming to Paris, and Mother Hardey made only one request, that the news of her nomination should be kept secret till after the journey. To travel with the simple title of Visitatrix would save a heavy pull upon many heart-strings. Mother Goetz willingly agreed; she knew what a thunderbolt would fall at the departure of Mother Hardey. She confided to Mother Perdrau that she had had a strong light on the subject while in exile at Laval. It had come to her, with the force of a divine inspiration, that she should:

Unite the houses of America by a living link with those of our old Europe, overthrown and torn with different nationalities, while heresy and schism are taking from the Church the nations that have been lead into error. It seems to me, as I go about Europe, that the New World offers more hope to the Church for the future. The Sacred Heart has had its apostolic outposts there. That alone should influence our zeal in Christ Jesus. I will name an American Assistant General in the place of Mother Prévost. For such a coup d'état I shall consult the Sovereign Pontiff, my Council, the clergy, the Jesuit Missionaries, even the Father General, so devoted to our Society. The affair is grave. . . . It is God who had moved me to this; He has spoken through me.

It was now January, 1872, and Mother Hardey was urged to lose no time; she was needed at the Mother House. A tremendous distance of over five thousand miles had first to be covered before the wheel could come full circle. For the next six months she was hardly to have time to feel solid ground under foot, while house after house passed before her vision with the speed of the still uninvented moving-picture. She knew the past of each of them, from Saint Charles the oldest to Rosecroft the youngest; she must now do her best to read the future of each, and to give to each in the present all that her long experience had stored up. In her pocket or more often in her hand was an ingeniously subdivided note-book in which to make entries for the Superior General whom she now directly represented.

So literally did she take the injunction to make haste that she and Mother Hoey caught the boat for Cuba on one day's notice. Circumstances facilitated matters. She could by now carry the cloister, so to speak, on her person, for at the last Council Mother Shannon had secured permission for travelling in the religious habit. This was well, for the full skirts of other days were beginning to congeal into bustles, and the bonnets to shrink into pancakes on tops of chignons. Trains were on their way to being stream-lined; the bell-shaped smoke-stacks had vanished. George Pullman had made night-travelling less of a night-mare, even though his first sleeping car was lit by candles. But although the Central Pacific and the Union Pacific had been riveted together with a golden spike, the line of railroad spanning the continent was as thin as a spider web. Even where the spider had spun most thickly there were gaps, and Mother Hardey's journey was an odd combination of rapid transit and primitive inconvenience.

Cuba was in the bloom of its February summer. Mother Tommasini, now Superior of the Havana Convent, was sitting at recreation one evening with her head bent over some photographs when a gentle touch drew her eyes up. There had been no time for letters to announce Mother Hardey, who stood smiling till she was overwhelmed in a flood of Spanish joy. Two sunny weeks were hardly long enough to bless the plans of the new house in the Cerro which was to replace the old one, to see the flourishing zeal of the good works established by Mother Tommasini, and to receive presents of rich altar lace from the devoted Cuban families who considered Mother Hardey as their own possession. On the way back to the boat she passed unknowingly the site of the future City House of Havana, the Tejadillo. As she sailed away, the beauty of the island flashed brightly back at her; virile devotion to the Sacred Heart was set in its dreaming loveliness like a ruddy jewel.

She paused at Manhattanville where the oral examinations were in progress. As though she had no houses to examine, she asked to see all the children's exercise books, models of high-wrought hand-writing and full of compositions on such edifying subjects as "What constitutes Real Happiness," "A True Woman," and "A Dialogue about Pearls," interspersed with mingled history and geography in letter form. Easter Monday saw her off to Chicago. Here she found the house in mourning for the death of Reverend Mother Gauthreaux, one of her old novices of Saint Michael's. The city itself was still a vast wreck after the fire of the preceding October which, driven by an eccentrically twisting wind, had demolished the greater part of the business and residential districts, but had paused as though before a curtain of prayer at the Holy Family Parish. The Sacred Heart Convent had thus been one of the few to escape the flames, and for weeks afterwards it had sheltered homeless Benedictines and Good Shepherd Nuns with their charges. Mother Hardey saw a new Chicago standing up and shaking off the ashes of the old.[5] It was ready to give new work to the Religious of the Sacred Heart when, in the future, the Convent on West Taylor Street had taken fresh root in the country soil of Lake Forest and grown into a College, and when a City House opened in 1876, had come to rest on Sheridan Road. There an unusual and most successful venture would proudly bear the name of "Hardey Preparatory School for Boys." Unsuspecting of this honour, Mother Hardey left Chicago after a visit of five days, during which she arranged for the transfer of the Noviceship to Maryville, where it was to remain until merged with that of Kenwood in 1899.

Saint Joseph's was the next halt, and here she helped to place the school on so sure a financial basis that a time of lasting prosperity followed her passage. Each visit was planned with as much economy of time as lavishness of interest, and she set out for Saint Mary's by pullman. But the new system was so defective that she and her secretary and her trunk were dropped at a desolate junction at 3 A.M. As the telegraph also failed to function there was no one to meet them. "We have only to sit on the trunk," said Mother Hardey. "In the meantime let us ask Saint Joseph to come to our aid." They sat till the cold compelled them to walk, and then saw a light in the distance. It proved to be a lonely store, whose proprietor was with some difficulty aroused.

He invited us into his best room, and made a fire in the big stove which seemed to be the chief article of furniture. Learning that we were from New York, he plied Reverend Mother with questions about trade, stocks, politics and every imaginable subject, and in spite of her fatigue she entertained him while I dozed in a chair. A messenger was dispatched to the Convent and at about five o'clock the farm wagon and team took us to our journey's end.

Life in the "sky-scraper of the prairies" was not what it had been in the log cabins of old. Mother Lucille Mathevon had come back from Saint Charles the year before, recalled by the love of the people of Saint Mary's who had clamoured to the Superior General for her return. Her old mission was new to her eyes, but there was now a chapel under the same roof with the Nuns, and in the peace of that Presence Mother Mathevon was praying out her life. Mother Hardey could see what was coming to Saint Mary's. She negotiated a loan which saved the convent for some years and installed steam heat for its immediate warming, but the school was dwindling to nothing. It would be closed in 1879 and from Paris Mother Hardey was to see what becomes of a seed instinct with the immortality of zeal. In a missionary leap as wide as Mother Duchesne's own dreams, the life of Saint Mary's sprang to far places after its apparent death. The closing of the house was to make a new apostolic venture possible, when in 1880 the Vicariate of Saint Louis sent a band of missionaries to New Zealand. Mother Boudreau, child of La Fourche, novice of Saint Michael's, and Mother Hardey's fellow worker at Manhattanville, passed the Rocky Mountains, out through the Golden Gate to a land poised on the limits of the West where it merges again into the East. She reached Timaru, only to die twelve days after landing. "If Our Lord," she said, "sees that my death can avail for the good of this foundation, I willingly, gladly, offer my life for its success."

Mother Hardey went from Saint Mary's to Saint Charles, where there was little time to do more than entrust her imminent sacrifice to Mother Duchesne, the fruit of whose earlier sacrifices she was so soon to carry back to their common center. Her conference here, as in many of the houses along her route, was on interior life, as though the sheer pressure of her travels kept throwing her back upon her true center of gravity. At the Saint Louis City House the children had composed their own dialogue of welcome. It was the era of flower-imagery, and Mother Hardey saw seven pupils advancing towards her with the rigorous grace of movement which comes of hard training in *maintien*. Each gloved hand held a flower, whose mystery was revealed in verse. The initials of these flowers spelled "Aloysia", and Mother Aloysia was bidden carry the sentiments of the bouquet to the Mother House in the name of Mother Duchesne's inheritors. In Saint Louis the Nuns were kept even busier than elsewhere supplying relics of Mother Barat to devoted clients, for a child in the school, Nancy Bakewell, was a walking witness to her holiness. In 1867 Nancy, then eleven years old, had risen from bed one morning instantaneously cured of coxalgia during a novena to the Mother Foundress, for whose Beatification the miracle was later accepted.

The Community of Maryville had not yet settled in its new home, but Mother Hardey walked through the stately building that she had helped to erect, delighting in its broad corridors and high ceilinged rooms, empty as yet but ready to hold a College one day, and to be a center of that active life of mind and soul that it was Mother Hardey's aim to cultivate. When she had boarded the Louisiana train on April 30th, Mother Tucker wrote to the Superior General: "I might almost say that Mother Hardey has been the salvation of this Vicariate. She has effected great things everywhere . . . and has gained the confidence of all by her goodness, her devotedness, and her love for the Society."

Delays on the south-crawling train were constant, but at each Mother Hardey quieted her secretary with a determined: "Let us thank God for this." In New Orleans they drove straight into the heart of the *Vieux Carré*, little changed from the time when it had first welcomed Mary Hardey, aged seven, to the South. Here, nestling tightly among the mellow old houses on Dumaine Street not far from the Cathedral was "Mater's" the Sacred Heart Convent opened five years before and already overflowing. Some day, as The Rosary, it would expand in the freedom of flower-filled courtyards and generous galleries in a more spacious quarter of the city, but it would always keep the charm of New Orleans, old or young. Mother Hardey could stop only for a few hours among its eager little Creoles this time, for a swift boat was leaving for Saint Michael's at once. It brought her to the landing late at night. All was hushed in darkness except for one pair of keen old eyes that had refused to sleep for three nights in the fear of not being the first to see Mother Hardey come home again. It was "Old Black John" who claimed to have known her since he was born. When he heard the sputter of the boat he waited only long enough to identify her figure on the lamp-lit deck, then rushed off to rouse Saint Michael's from end to end with loud cheers. It was May time and Mother Hardey was back among her own after thirty years, but she refused to be enchanted by the beauty of the new day as it dawned, for she at once caught another boat, this time for Natchitoches. She had been told that the Red River would soon be unnavigable, so Saint Michael's must wait.

As the boat meandered through the enchantment of Louisiana, through the green things that grew from water and dipped their arms back into it, then parted to show the mystery of flat lands that somehow rise and fall, she kept her secretary busy. "Is yo' daughter writin' a newspaper?" asked one of the curiously friendly negro women on board. "No, only a letter," was the answer. At the word "letter" a gleam of longing came into many pairs of rolling eyes, so for the rest of the day Mother Hoey wrote at dictation all manner of letters to Sams and Jims and Sallies. Mother Hardey, unable to write herself, sealed and stamped each letter after reading it aloud more then once to its enchanted sender.

Natchitoches, the oldest town in the state, allowed its streets to curve along the windings of the river and lived in peace behind its leafy verandahs. But yellow fever, flood, drought and famine had tried the mettle of the little Convent there ever since its foundation in 1847. Its history had been worked in the lights and darks of sacrifice, and she pondered it beside the grave of Mother Catherine Thieffry, a co-founder of Houston Street who had spent her last twenty years here in such holiness that she had been called the "lightning-rod of Natchitoches." Mother Hardey foresaw the near closing of the house, but entered fully into the joy caused by her visit before going back to Saint Michael's.

The house whose foundations she had laid stood queenly still through the sorrows that had passed over its head. Flowers burned tropically under the cool-branched trees that held their moss so high; cactus plants stood with stiff, elaborate gestures against the creamy walls. It was Mother Hardey's first house-dream come true. Double-galleried, with crenellated roof and massive doors and windows, it stood for generous dignity. Its soul was expressed in the amplitude of the great rooms within, in the aristocratic curve of stair rail, in the hungry fire-places, in the touch of simple carving along the corridors that brought grace to its austerity. The outhouses reached from the brick courtyard in the rear, and a fruit-lined road led past the graveyard to labyrinths of woods and tilled fields. Three hundred children at a time had made the school a great and gracious place before the War, and even now Mother Shannon's cheery energy would not let go of that greatness.

And here was an old friend, moving with determined dignity to greet Mother Hardey, strong-featured under her turban, wearing black mitts, ear-rings, silk shawl, and a large crucifix. It was Liza, who wept with joy to see her. Liza was happy, for after her marital experiences Mother Shannon had allowed her to make a vow, a very beautiful vow of charity to the Nuns of the Sacred Heart. She renewed it every year on the Feast of Pentecost, when, holding a lighted candle and dressed in a new white dress and bandana which Mother Hardey never failed to send to her each time, she would kneel beside the Superior who read aloud the Act of Consecration. Then Liza would go solemnly down the ranks of the Community, shaking hands. Now she exclaimed: "Mother Hardey will not go away till Ah open mah soul to her." After the visit she declared: "Ah'd like to go away with you, but I'se goin' to stay here and take care of yo' chillun." Each of the nuns was "chile" to Liza, so she stayed loyally at her post, and kept her vow through the years. As each loved Superior left Saint Michael's Liza's prayers and her dictated letters followed her. When Reverend Mother Moran went to Mexico to make a foundation there, she was warned by Liza in this fashion:

> You's a long time in dat Spanish town, and its time now to come home. You're needed here, for what's a home without a mother? You don't know dem people over dere, and you'll get yourself into trouble with 'em. Instead of comin' home you're goin' backer and backer. You're sendin' for dem chillun here to go dere and soon you'll empty de house here. I'se begged the Sacred Heart and Saint Joseph to hold dere arms over you, but deyse tired now, and can't do it no more, so take my 'vice and come home; you'se been away long enough.

"That chile has a mighty 'tractive face," added Liza to her scribe, "and she'll draw all dem people to her, and dey'll make her b'live dey're goin' to do much and dey don't do nothin'."

None of Liza's letters to Mother Hardey can be found, but one written to Mother Randall in 1880, a letter that reads like a poem in its pathos, its truth and its tears, expresses her gratitude to her old "chile" and a grievance that she had against her as Assistant General:

It seems as what it is an age since I received de letter what you sent me fur to have a Mass said fur your 'tentions, and fur to have all de darkies in dese parts to exist at de Holy Sacrifice. But I has been so upside downwards fur dese last six weeks dat I ain't had no time to think ob nothin' but my pore ole soul what has had a heap o' sorrow and tribulations. But I wants you to have a good understandin' of what fur I had not sent you a letter long afore dis present time. First and foremost I was awaitin' fur dis here Lady what is sittin' in my cabin now, writin' down all that I tells her to say; cause she knows you and all dem Yankees up in your part ob de world. An' I knowed she was comin' up here wid my chile, Madame Mary Moran, fur to see our ole Archbishop, [Archbishop Perche of New Orleans] what is stayin' on dis here convent plantation fur to be took good care ob till he gets over his spell of sickness. Dat is de why and de wherefore dat you ain't done got a letter from Liza long afore now. I hopes dat you has a good understandin' ob my 'pology, 'cause I was riz by de Ladies ob de Sacred Heart an' I don't want to bring no disgrace on dem by bad manners. Fur Madame Duchesne an' Madame Aloysia Hardey was mighty partiklar when dey was raisin' me to show Liza what was right and what was left. So I knowed politeness most as well as de white folks and fifty times better den any ob my kin' or color.

All de members ob dis here colored congregation sends dere bes' love an' compliments to all you Ladies. Dey will join in de Mass when our Director says it next week. Dey has all been invited to exist at de Mass an' communicate. Maybe I'll go and maybe I'll not, 'cause you see I's in great 'fliction at dis present time. My legs is swelled up like two drums, an' my feet is so sore I can't put on my shoes. De Father says: "Liza, put on a long gown an' go to de Holy Table in yer bare feet." But I says: "No, I ain't goin' to make any show like I was so virtuous when all de folks knows dat Liza ain't no saint." I ain't goin' to do no such thing. De Lord 'flicts me, an' when He thinks I done suffered enough, den He'll make de way smooth. But now its all hills and hollows, an' de pebbles an' de sharp bits ob rock sticks in mighty smart. But, den, de Lord knows how many thorns He put on de briar-bush an' it seems like He'll soon tell it to quit, dat He's tired 'flictin' pore ole Liza an' wants to give her a rest. I don' say dis to grumble 'bout His hand what is laid so heavy on me, but to 'splain de reason dey may prevent me to exist at your Mass. But de Lord is in my ole cabin, 'an I can pray dere fur all you Ladies ob de Sacred Heart.

My chile looks mighty smart; but I done cried a hogshead ob tears, 'cause she can't be 'suaded to come an' live here quiet at St. Michael's. Since she's been Superior she's like a spirit goin' everywhere. I blames Madame Aloysia Hardey—I do—fur givin' dese superiors here in Louisiana dose idees 'bout flittin' from house to house. Afore she was come down here, dey was always quiet an' contented to stay in de same convent from de beginnin' to de end ob der days. But she comes an' gives 'em a taste for cars an' boats an' since den dey is every one like de moon, what's always a changin' an' a changin'. But I ax de Lord to leave my chile here to me, so I can keep an eye after her health. She's so valuable to dis here Society dat she ought to be took double care ob. Ef I see her cheeks a-sinkin' in an' her complexion gittin' white, like whitewash, I'll keep a-jawin' an' a-grumblin' till dey send her back to dat dere Halifax; fur I don't ever want again to see her look like chalk, like she used to.

I's taxed wid de rheumatiz an' a heap of other misfortunes, an' it 'peers to me like ole Liza won't do much more in dis worl'; it seems like her web is most spun,—dat dere ain't much yarn left on de spool, an' de Lord's pretty nigh to settin' His foot again de wheel fur to stop it from whirlin' round any more. So if you don' hear any more from Liza, you needn't be 'sprized. Please present my compliments to all you Ladies ob de Sacred Heart an' tell "how-do" to every one ob dem. I love dem all; dey is all locked up in my heart, 'cause dey was 'fectionate and 'tentive to my pore sick chile, Mother Moran. I draw my letter to a close wid love.

LIZA NEBBIT

Colored chile ob de Sacred Heart,
first slave what was brought in dis
convent by Mother Duchesne.[6]

Liza may have taken special pride in signing herself "coloured child of the Sacred Heart," but she was not to be the only one with a right to do so, for Mother Hardey found a large coloured school at Saint Michael's. One of the most important questions considered by the Bishops at the Second Plenary Council of Baltimore of 1866 had been the evangelization of the Catholic negroes of the South, who were in a pitiable state during the painful years of the Reconstruction and the reign of the Ku Klux Klan. Archbishop Odin of New Orleans come straight to Mother Shannon after the Council and asked her to undertake a work which no one else seemed willing to face at the moment. She accepted at once, even though it meant refusing a prospective foundation. She opened a Free School for negro children at Saint Michael's, and carried it on in spite of opposition and misunderstanding. Grand Coteau followed with a similar school in 1875, and soon Sodalities for adults were carrying the work far afield. At Grand Coteau it was to go on through the years, until "coloured children of the Sacred Heart" could be counted by the hundreds. Mother Hardey might have been happy to know that in the distant future the house most associated with her name would take part in a further development of this apostolate. The time would come for the coloured members of Christ's Mystical Body to receive their rightful share in the cultural gifts of the Church, and then it would be a College that would welcome not "chilluns" but coloured students of the Sacred Heart.

But time pressed, even at timeless Saint Michael's. Mother Hardey found that she could reach Grand Coteau more speedily by taking a train on the other side of the Mississippi, so she put her trust in a small, uncertain rowboat. The goodbyes were said under a lowering sky, and a wind-squall struck the river just as the boat reached mid-stream. For a time it looked as though it would never reach the bank again. Mother

Hardey sat praying as quietly as though no eddies were turning her round and round, while the black oarsman muttered prophecies of immediate death. At last the farther shore was gained, and Mother Hardey, looking back, saw a last gleam from the sky fall upon Saint Michael's before it grew dim behind a curtain of driving rain. The conditions of the countryside had been so wrenched awry by the Civil War that never again would the stately place hold court as in days of old. Even the river would turn against it and eat away the royal sweeps of lawn till only defiant levees, two stories high, could keep it from the house itself. Five times cyclones would pass over the old mansion, until the terrible one that shook the life out of it and leveled the oaks and pecan and camphor trees in the year following the centenary of its foundation. For a few years more the house would do its appointed work, welcoming bands of Religious and pupils exiled from Mexico to soil friendlier to religion, but when these returned to their own land a final silence would close over it. Completely empty, swept by winds from lonesome fields that rock the old slave-bell in its tower, Saint Michael's stands today white and stately still, gallantly dying on its feet. Clover fragrantly smothers the graves in the orchard where Mother Galitzin lies among her Louisiana daughters. The clean vast rooms and stairways within are vibrant of past greatness, while in the chapel, stripped as bare as renunciation itself, a word of eternity can still be read in high letters over where the altar stood: *Cor Jesu, Salus in Te Sperantium.*

The train that Mother Hardey caught at such risk failed to persevere as far as Grand Coteau, so she approached her old home in the good old way, riding in a mail-coach. All was strange at first. The house that she had known was hidden modestly behind its successor which stood among the roses, creamy gold and triple-galleried. There were gala receptions in her honour, while from the neighboring plantations came relatives, family friends, one-time slaves bearing the name Hardey after their former master, to see "Miss Mary." Then one evening Mother Martinez asked her to come on a pilgrimage. No sooner had they entered the old Convent than its short corridors were filled with the sound of the Magnificat. The Community had gathered in the one-time chapel where a prie-dieu stood on the spot where Sister Aloysia had taken the veil. Mother Hardey knelt down on it, and for once failed to check her tears, for it seemed as though Mother Duchesne and Mother Audé were there in the room with her.

This was not the only shrine in Grand Coteau. In 1866 a Canadian postulant, a recent convert named Mary Wilson, lay dying in terrible suffering. Holy Viaticum was given to her on December 14th, the last day of a Novena made for her cure through the intercession of Blessed John Berchmans. She was then left alone for an hour, but when the Superior returned to the room she found Mary aglow with health and with a joy more than earthly. Blessed Berchmans had stood by her bed, and after placing something cool and healing on her tongue had said, "You will get the holy habit you desire. Be faithful, have confidence and do not fear." She did receive the habit soon after, and went about as actively and as happily as any other novice, but her heart had gone to heaven beyond recall. In a second apparition on the same spot Blessed Berchmans assured her that she would soon be there. She died the following August, and Mother Hardey found her grave, among many others bearing names well known to her, in Coteau's rose-grown cemetery which lies in the sun and silence like a bit of heaven to which she had escaped so young. The infirmary where the apparitions took place had already been changed into an oratory from which graces continued to go out, and the miraculous cure was eventually accepted as one of those that led to the canonization of Saint John Berchmans.

Mother Hardey left Grand Coteau after only one week, and as she looked back she saw it through a long avenue of pines and another of oaks which had been planted by Mother Murphy in the beginning. They stood very high now, gigantic in marshalled magnificence, their trailing robes of moss creating a strange moonlight under them while their tops stood steady in the sun. The disasters of the War would ebb away in time from this land of loveliness and simple peace; the turn of the century was to bring a new prosperity. Wings added to the already generous house would one day shelter a College as well as an Academy, while two Parish Schools across the fields would brim over with children, white and black. Reality lies in simplicity, and "God is very present at Grand Coteau," said one who knows.

Mother Hardey returned to New Orleans to finish her visit, then journeyed north on a long diagonal. She reached Cincinnati early in June, where her Conference was on the words "Behold this Heart", a theme that now recurred so frequently as to become almost continuous. She then set on foot a search for a new house which would eventually bring the Community to Clifton high on its hill among hills, with valleys winding about its feet. She then travelled east, pausing at Rochester and Detroit and cutting north into Canada to include London, Ontario. Manhattanville, which had a new Parish School under construction to entice her home, caught her and held on for a few weeks in June, weeks which she shared with Eden Hall and Philadelphia. Then she went north on a wide sweep through the Sault, Montreal, Saint John, and Halifax, and came back to pause at Kenwood for a brief space, where she said: "Do well what you do; be sincere before God, doing from your heart what He asks of you." Not one of the houses through which she passed realized that her parting blessing to each was a goodbye.

She returned to Manhattanville just as the Community

went into retreat late in August. She told them the night before they went into solitude that she must set off for France to give an account of her journey, but neglected to mention when she would return. The Father who gave the retreat seemed to leave nothing unsaid on the subject of sacrifice; it was the Holy Ghost that so inspired him, insisted the Community later. On the morning of September 11th when the first autumnal austerity tinged the trees, they all pressed around Mother Hardey's carriage. There was the usual delay in getting off, during which the postman passed with the mail. Mother Hardey asked for it and began to open letters with provoking calm, deliberately deaf to the sorrowful clamour around her. Then, she gave them a swift look, and with the suddenness with which the inevitable always happens at last, the horses were off down the drive. Mother Hardey gave Manhattanville into God's hands as something done for Him and not to be taken back.

XX

IN THE CENTER

THE BOULEVARD DES INVALIDES was a cobbled street in 1872; *carosses* rattled over it lightly but noisily. The sound blended with the indeterminate hum of a capital city, of Paris. Royal coaches had once passed this way, then tumbrils for a brief and terrible time, now briskly trotting traffic. The huge shadow of the tomb of Napoleon fell over the Boulevard when the sun was in the west. A little distance away curved the Seine, whispering history to each bridge that it passed under. All these sounds, the heard and the unheard, drifted up to the shuttered windows of Number 33. Feathery trees, still young and spindling, blurred those windows to the humming distractions of the world. It was very quiet behind them, especially in the room at the north-west corner of the steep-pitched, gray building that had been the Mother House of the Society of the Sacred Heart since 1857. The room was as bare as it was quiet; shaded light fell on a prie-dieu under a crucifix, on a walnut desk piled high with letters. Mother Hardey sat at the desk saying her beads, her impotent right hand held still.

For the first time in her life she was experiencing that unbroken tranquility that can be monotonous or thrilling according as the soul makes it so. Each day was very much like the one before and the one after it. She had time now to say her beads when she wished to, or to slip across the corridor to the room opposite and stay there with no sense of pressure. It was the room in which Mother Barat had died, now an oratory where the business of the Society was worked out before God, in silence. After forty years of more or less turbulent works of zeal and of unresting action, she was learning how to serve by waiting. This was an interspace; she could, for a while, rest in it. She could let her past life sink back into the streams of tradition so strongly felt here in the Center where they converged to flow out into the future. Paris had shaped the beginnings of the Society of the Sacred Heart. It had now made Devotion to the Sacred Heart its own, for the Basilica of Montmartre was rising slowly on its hill, pressed like an aura of peace from the anguish of the Commune, where *Gallia devota et repenta* might crowd up the broad steps and pray its life clean and strong again in the votive shrine of the Heart of Christ, and where a lamp burned for the intentions of the Society.

Reverend Mother Goetz went by the door of her new Assistant General and heard no sound. "Go and visit Mother Hardey," she said to Mother Perdrau whom she happened to meet. "I feel sorry for her. Take her with you on a walk through the gardens of the Rue de Varennes, but be sure to suggest some charitable motive for the walk or she will not change the plan of this new life of hers, which is to remain hidden unless some duty makes her appear." Mother Perdrau, talkative and affectionate by nature, was only too glad to entertain Mother Hardey, and as the late light measured the shadows of the linden alleys the two passed across the quadrangle of the Mother House, fringed with lilacs that were bare now but heavy with the promise of a fragrant spring. They opened the green door in the wall that separated it from the more spacious ground of the Hôtel Biron. They passed the statue of Our Lady of Victories standing dizzily high on its pedestal in the center of the richly formal gardens crossed by paths where Mother Barat had walked. They passed the famous cedar tree, her *rendez-vous* with the children. It bore an inscription which read: "This cedar was planted in 1820 by our venerated Mother General. Under its shadow she often rested. 'She did not labour for herself alone but for all that seek out truth. The root of wisdom never faileth' ". The Hôtel Biron faced in upon the green peace of the garden, with its back to the street, one of the most exquisite houses in Paris, built in 1729. It was flanked by the high Roman chapel that Mother Barat had erected. Mother Perdrau watched Mother Hardey as they walked back to the plainer, newer Mother House whose quiet dynamism was controlling some ninety houses in other parts of the world, and her admiration deepened. As she wrote later:

> How heroic we thought this Reverend Mother who in America controlled at a sign Religious, houses and works, who even influenced Protestant civil authority! She had not sought her own glory in America; she did not seek it in France. She now made it her business to be totally and completely dependent, to reflect only the authority of the Superior General. So thought all at the Mother House.

Sometimes it was Reverend Mother Borget, the Treasurer-General, who took Mother Hardey walking among the unfinished walls of the Maison des Anges being built adjacent to the Mother House to shelter the many good works which were growing up. She said with energetic humility: "I am going to learn how to facilitate our works and our employments by leaving to holy poverty all that simplicity which is at variance with worldly comfort. In the past I have erred somewhat on this point. Here at the Center I shall learn to do better". It was in this way that Mother Hardey interpreted her greater authority as Assistant General. She would make herself a helpful disciple, then transmit what she learned to the houses in America for which she was now more than ever accountable. One who had known her in her own land said of her: "I found her manner different in Paris from what it had been in America; at home it was watchful responsibility, in France it was a daughter's trustful love of her Mother General. I was greatly struck by her attitude in the presence of her Superior General; she looked radiantly happy."

Reverend Mother Goetz,[1] whose favorite reading was the *Summa Theologica*, whose favorite Choir of Angels was that of the Thrones because they represented the stability of wisdom, whose moral strength overcame her shyness and physical frailty, and whose humility lifted her high above self, owed what she was to her childhood grasp of devotion to the Sacred Heart. An appeal made in Its name had turned her rebellious will-power into a steady act of love. A clear, almost masculine intelligence measured her actions. She looked to the future, and found long hours for study and for reflection on the religious and civil trends of her day, learning how to put first things first. When Mother Hardey came to know her in 1872 she had just made a fourfold plan for the rest of her generalate, which she knew would be short: to classify and edit the Decrees of the General Congregations; to settle the Society unshakably on the bases laid down from its beginning; to have the life of its Foundress written by a priestly theologian; and to ground the studies pursued by the Society on the Scholastic Philosophy of Saint Thomas. Mother Hardey could watch the gradual completion of the first two points, and she had reached the Mother House just in time to hear the Life of Mother Barat as it came chapter by chapter from the pen of the Abbé Baunard and was read aloud before those who had seen a Saint in the making. On the final point concerning studies, her own experience was called upon.

As a young Mistress in the school Mother Goetz had taught logic in such a way that her pupils found it "delicious", then while Mistress of Novices she had followed the Debates in the Senate on liberty of education in order to learn how to test the principles involved in passing mental fads. She had called her little room at Conflans with its high grated window her "laboratory", because in it she made practical experiments in the scientific psychology that she acquired from Jesuit guides like Father de Ravignan. She fed her spiritual as well as her intellectual life on the *Celestial Hierarchy* of Denis the Areopagite, and as for Saint Thomas, she declared that when she read him she "swam in the truth", adding that he had given her a philosophical touchstone with which to try the minds of others. She refrained from any public mention of the word "philosophy", which savoured of Voltaire just then, but she declared to the Mistresses of Studies that a knowledge of it, even for young girls, would assure "a real triumph of the spiritual nature over the sensitive, for want of which women often allow the noblest faculties that God has given them to fall into decay. . . . We must strengthen our studies by scholastic philosophy, even in our lower classes, in an elementary form, in order to accustom our children to using their judgments rather than their memories." As Superior she saw to it that books on natural science were added to the classical library at the service of the young nuns, and now as Superior General she conferred with Mother Hardey upon the plans for the formation of an advanced *Juvenat* that she had been maturing for twenty years. She asked for her views with regard to higher studies, which she knew were favoured for women by the majority of American Bishops. Mother Hardey had consistently aimed at strong studies by unfolding the

Society's Plan. Together they drew up tentative schemes which were submitted to Monseigneur Pie, who said later: "Mother Goetz, with her humble and powerful intelligence and virile firmness, will lead her Society into the new paths of those masculine branches of learning of which women who rule our Christian homes must no longer remain ignorant." Mother Hardey did not forget all this on her subsequent visits to America, where she set certain Religious to studying Latin, "that our girls may know as much of it as their brothers," and when it was suggested to her that Manhattanville might one day be a Women's College, she answered, "It may come."

In the winter of 1873 the health of Mother Goetz was failing, but it gave her new life to see a stream of all sorts and conditions of people, the beggar woman on the Rue de Varennes, Matthieu, the Convent man-of-all-trades in his Sunday best, and silk-fluted ladies of rank, coming to the Mother House to give their testimony before the Tribunal of investigation of the Cause of Beatification of Mother Barat. In the spring she went outdoors to see the children of the Free-School as they played in the garden, "in order to keep my fourth vow," as she said, or to meet the little group of *Affiliées*, the first of its kind, that she had formed from among the Children of Mary. Then in May she said to Mother Hardey: "Come; we are going to open the packing boxes of the new house at Pau," and the two set off for the south. After a year's peace Mother Hardey entered upon another ten years of travelling.

The purpose of the visit to Pau was to restore the Mother General to health, if possible, and Mother Hardey reasserted her magisterial manner of old; she decreed a régime of knitting in the sunshine for the invalid while she herself gladly plunged into the well-known work of bringing order out of chaos of foundation days. She conducted the recreations in French so recklessly that she brought tears of laughter to Mother Goetz. She even persuaded the latter to be daringly modern and face a camera, which Mother Barat had never been brought to do. Mother Goetz yielded on condition that Mother Hardey stand behind her chair and be photographed with her.* But the crowning joy of Pau was the pilgrimage to Lourdes, undertaken at the wish of the Bishop. There was no cure—the invalid had not asked for one—but a river of grace was flowing by the river of waters, and Mother Hardey felt close to its springs in Our Lady.

Before leaving Pau she listened to one of Mother Goetz' last conferences, which closed her message to the Society with a final expression of thought that had made her what she was:

> It is for you to kindle here the fire of Devotion to the Sacred Heart. I am always afraid that this devotion is not all that it should be among us. Persons of the world sometimes understand it in too exterior a manner, one that appeals to the senses, but for us, Religious of the Sacred Heart, it must have a much deeper and more intimate note. Union with Our Lord is its basis; without that union there is no true Devotion to the Sacred Heart, and no true Religious. There is nothing solid to be hoped for without it; all is futile, light, superficial. I am always struck by the sterility of souls in whom there is no union with Our Lord. Those who are united to Him are, on the contrary, capable of anything; they can be counted on; their works are blessed by God. Union with Him is the surest way of reaching the perfection asked of us by our vocation.

Mother Goetz died almost suddenly on the fourth of the following January. "I loved her too much," said Mother Hardey; then she set herself to the task of cheering the Mother House until the elections of May had placed Mother Adéle Lehon at its head.[2]

* It is from this photograph that the frontispiece of the present book was drawn.

The new Superior General had already spent a long life in the service of the Society, mostly in Italy. Tall and so thin that she seemed almost incorporeal, she had a soul of fire that shone through the actions of a strong, vivacious, practical and affectionate nature. Hers was the vision, intuitive yet concrete, fitted to guide the Society through twenty years, peaceful for most part, of expansion and consolidation. At her election she made a compact with herself: "You are now sacrificed," she said, "sold to others; you are at the service of all." Reciprocally she drew out the best services of others. Knowing well what capabilities Mother Hardey was holding so exquisitely in balance, Mother Lehon gave her a triple task for the ten years during which the two worked together: to knit the Society in France and in America as closely as possible; to visit the European houses on special missions, and to exercise authority at home, first with the Probanists, then as the Superior of the Maison des Anges, and finally as local Superior of the Mother House itself.

America came first, and July, 1874, saw her back at Manhattanville. Reverend Mother Jones was now Superior Vicar of the Eastern houses. The keen legal mind inherited from her father, the experience gained from long association with Mother Hardey, found full swing in the government which she carried on with the courtly manner of the old school and the energy of great zeal. Mother Hardey, never self-sparing, set off at once on the rounds of her former houses. Elmhurst had by now been added to the list, and was flourishing to such an extent that she authorized the opening of a City House in Providence. This foundation was not to be lasting, but the work for which it was intended went on when the Parish School, numbering seven hundred children, was entrusted to the Ursulines a few years later. Elmhurst itself was a homelike, charmingly inconsistent house hidden among great trees. Here Bishop Hendrick delighted Mother Hardey with an account of his recent visit to Leo XIII, saying, "I told the Holy Father that a Convent of the Sacred Heart had just been established in my Diocese. With that he stood up suddenly and put his arms around me, saying, 'My Son, devotion to the Sacred Heart will save the world'." The autumn passed thus in visits, into each of which she wove some precious thing gained from abroad. At Seventeenth Street, for instance, she established a new work which she had admired in the French Convents. When leaving the Mother House she had packed some special trunks with materials for making vestments, and these she spread enticingly before the Children of Mary. She came to each of their weekly meetings as long as she was in New York, and before the end of the year the Tabernacle Society had begun the great work which still offers a port of hope for poor priests and missionaries.

The winter was spent quietly at Manhattanville, where her stay was prolonged by an accident. During an epidemic among the children she went every day to see those in the infirmary, and on one of her visits overturned a lamp full of boiling oil on her foot. She returned to Paris in April, but her intercourse with America was renewed soon after. In 1877 a retreat called many Superiors to Paris. She followed the Exercises with them, but it was all too clear that fatigue had at last overtaken her, and a sea-trip was prescribed. The trip as such failed of its object, for it turned out to be the most unrelentingly stormy passage recorded for many years. An eight-day hurricane made sport of the *Russia*, and even the crew had need of being heartened by the sight of Mother Hardey's calm. Her name became a by-word in the vessel, for her answer to every despairing remark concerning the weather was "God rules the sea as well as the land."

This second visit lasted from October, 1877, till the following July. Although she travelled and settled property matters here and there and authorized the building of a brick addition to the chapel-wing of Manhattanville, these months were, on the whole, unusually quiet, and later they became known in all the houses that she visited as "the passage of the Lord" in which He was "to prepare for Himself a perfect people." Mother Hardey seemed remarkably expansive; she was moved by a spiritual force which could now show itself without let or hindrance. It possessed her, and she must needs share it. One hour of each day she devoted to the young Religious of the Community, letting her own vision of the Society shine before their eyes. The lucky ones faithfully took notes which resulted later in the publication of a little Book of maxims, which, in their very brevity and plainness reveal the quintessence of her wisdom: "Seek God sincerely and you will find Him. . . . It is better to do than to teach. . . . The grace of God does not accompany an infidelity. . . . When the will disapproves difficulties begin. . . . Provided Jesus loves us and trusts us, what matters all else?" She multiplied her formal conferences; and the same spirit was manifest in them: an intense desire to see the hundreds of daughters for whose formation she was directly or indirectly responsible rise to their full stature. She drew up a detailed form of examination of conscience in which points of the Rule were unfolded relentlessly, inspiringly. There were two keynotes to her words: Love of the Heart of Jesus, and Fidelity to Rule. "You have in these," she added, "a pledge of happiness in this life and in that better one where partings are unknown." In the last conference given at Manhattanville on the eve of her departure she said:

We must love one another as Our Lord loves us. If He loved only the perfect He would love very few. Therefore let charity unite us all as one in the Heart of Jesus. To assist us in attaining this blessing Our Lord has sent us today a precious book, the Life of Mother Duchesne. You will find here the spirit that she brought to this country. You will see what her sufferings and her love of the Cross have purchased for us. It is my desire and my earnest prayer that you may learn from her heroic example to labour generously for the love and the glory of the Sacred Heart of Jesus, by your love for the Rule and your love for one another.

There was one more visit after this to her own country, in 1882. Once again the Board of Public Works was threatening the very existence of Manhattanville by cutting streets through the heart of the property, and many friends counselled moving the school elsewhere. But Mother Hardey could not believe that Manhattanville should be abandoned; its life was still ahead of it. Before leaving France she spent a day in prayer at Conflans at the tomb of Mother Barat, then sailed to face the business men. The negotiations took her a year and a half. When Mother Lehon wrote anxiously to know when her Assistant could come back, Mother Hardey answered drily that she would come at once unless the loss of a half a million dollars counted for something. She was busy selling lots, and succeeded in diverting the proposed streets from the center to the edge of the property, thus reducing the grounds to approximately their present size, and she then built a row of so-called cottages along 130th Street to keep the City at bay. Ownership of lots beyond the new streets was retained for some years more, after which they were sold to assist the foundation of Puerto Rico.

In the intervals of all this business she took time to explain the School Rule to the children at their *rentrée* in September, and made her usual round of visits to other houses. There were three more now on her route. In 1880 a Convent had been opened in the historic center of American culture, Boston, where, according to the Foundresses, "the work of the Religious is facilitated by the Bostonians' innate love of study and ambition to excel in things intellectual. . . . Devotion to the Sacred Heart is striking deep root and working transformation in these young people. . . . But there is little opportunity to inaugurate external works of zeal because of public sentiment which is still hostile to Catholicism." This last difficulty disappeared by the time the Boston Convent found its way many years later to a permanent home in the Country Day School known as Newton, Gothic and spacious in free outdoors. In 1887 a second City House had been opened in New York on Madison Avenue, a house which gradually absorbed its two neighbors and for more than fifty years carried on a vigorous apostolate, with loyal and tightly-packed children in its zigzag rooms. Skyscrapers finally squeezed it from its place and it moved to Ninety-first Street where it could stand up with grace and look out over Central Park, still bent on the sanctification of a city. In Detroit also there was new activity. The Society had long owned property on Lake Saint Clair, where the sun rises across bands of purple and green water; and now, at Mother Hardey's visit, the foundations of the Grosse Pointe house were laid, a house which would one day add a handsome wing to itself larger than the original building.

After so much business Mother Hardey fell ill, and was among those first to profit by the advantages of still one more foundation, that of Atlantic City. This little house, with its breezy verandahs and its sharp cross-tipped cupola, looked to the limitless sea across the board-walk of fashion. During its short life it would do well its work of caring for the instruction of hundreds of religiously neglected children. It was closed in 1900, but as one of the Community wrote: "Seeds of virtue and of Christian life have been sown; if the Sacred Heart reaps a harvest of souls, that will be worth all the labour." It justified its health-giving mission the very first year of its existence by giving Mother Hardey strength to face her last sea-voyage in the stormy February of 1884. With her sailed her new secretary, Mother Grasser, and Sister

Gartland whose devoted care as nurse was to accompany her everywhere as her health failed. As she left Manhattanville she was scarcely able to walk, but her voice had lost none of its energy as she left them her last Testament: "Goodbyes are always hard, but obedience is sweet, and now we are all going to begin to become saints."

The boat moved away from the shore. Forty-five years ago brick houses among tree branches had welcomed Mother Hardey to New York; now the sky-line was writing its own version of "America" in grey hieroglyphics against the clouds. Brooklyn Bridge clasped its steel hands over the East River, steel strong-holds of Big Business towered up around it, not yet into skyscrapers whose height could give grace to their gauntness but into raw blocks where money made itself from money. The corrupt "rings" of "Boss" Tweed were circling invisibly among them, just as the wider rings of great Trusts and Corporations circled out to bind the whole land. Half in protest, half in league with them, Labour was uniting, forming itself into the social problems of the future. 1884 was midway in the years that have been called the most lawless age of American life, lawless in politics and finance, but there were strange, tense, sensational attempts to balance all this by pseudo-religion; Christian Science and Spiritism were the thrills of the hour. Yet through those loose energies a constructive force was gaining strength day by day. There to the South, in the Primatial See, was Archbishop Gibbons, "an American among and of the people", whose favorite study was American History and Civics, who wanted all his priests to be in touch with their country and their times. He was busy preparing the Third Plenary Council of Baltimore, to be held in June. He was to make of it "a strong fabric for the American Church." In the next few years he himself would be made a Cardinal, would win the sanction of Rome for organized Labour, link the Far West with the older East in a common harmony of spiritual progress, and lay the corner-stone of the Catholic University. More than ever would his action, that "religion of action" for which he stood, prove true to his own words: "A Catholic finds himself at home in the United States," and again: "A wonderful future is before the Church in this country if we are only true to her and to ourselves. . . . Let us be cordially American in our feelings and sentiments, and above all let each individual act in his personal life and character the spirit of his Catholic faith." [3]

As the ship gained speed the horizon widened. In the broad land behind it education was stirring busily where Colleges for Women were being founded and where Universities were adding Graduate courses to their studies. Whistler, Lafarge, French and St. Gaudens were justifying the new passion for opening museums for native talent. Great writers were few at the moment, but Emily Dickinson, had been beating her wings against bars for many years, and there, in the blur of vanishing buildings, the forerunner of a new age of poetry was raising his lusty voice. Walt Whitman sang:

> Come Muse, migrate from Greece and Lonia. . . .
> For know a better, fresher, busier sphere, a wide, un-
> tried domain awaits, demands you.

Catholic writers and artists had yet to find their pens, their brushes. Father Tabb had dared to begin:

> O little bird, I'd be
> A poet like thee,
> Singing my native song.

And at the Sacred Heart Convent of Elmhurst Louise Imogene Guiney had been preparing to lift the Catholic strain in her own fine woman's fashion, invoking:

Spirits of old that bore me
And set me, meek of mind,
Between great dreams before me
And deeds as great behind.

Catholic culture in the new world would grow slowly from branch to flower to fruit, but behind the flat blue line of Mother Hardey's horizon, growing too thin to see, were the schools that she had helped to shape, and the children in them who would be the mothers of children, womanly thinkers and doers of the Church to come in America. Suddenly there was only ocean before her eyes, and she turned to the other horizon.

The sense of empty distance between the Center and the circumference of the Society that had been Mother Duchesne's greatest cross, had now all but disappeared. There seemed to be as much of America in France as there had been of France in America in the beginning. Mother Hardey brought many Novices overseas to Conflans, besides the Probanists who now came regularly every six months to the Mother House. At no time had the two countries seemed more closely interlinked than at Mother Hardey's Golden Jubilee. This event, which is usually celebrated only after fifty years of Profession, was for some reason kept on that of her First Vows, March 15th, 1877.

Mother Lehon gave notice of the event to Manhattanville, with the result that no fewer than seventeen extra trunks full of presents crossed the Atlantic under the nervous supervision of a group of Probanists. Their nervousness increased at the Customs-House, and still more at the Mother House, for Mother Hardey was known to have a habit of assisting in person at the opening of every trunk that came from America. When she saw the seventeen uncalled-for pieces of luggage her lips closed in a non-committal line. She had the cover of each lifted, examined the innocent top layer of clothing just enough to tease the pale Probanists, and walked away.

On the Eve of the Feast Reverend Mother Jouve, then Superior at Orleans, arrived at the Mother House, and at Mass the next morning American Novices from Conflans and children from the Rue de Varennes filled the chapel. Among the Probanists that year was Anna Radley, the child of prophecy whose mother had been invited to the first Prizes given at Manhattanville. It was she who read in English the address from overseas. The last of many tender verses ran:

Unseen, we all are kneeling by your side,
O Mother whom our love forever calls your own,
The best and truest Mother we have ever known.
Each heart among your children in your native land,
Bows, joyful, tearful, down in spirit here,
To ask the tender blessing of your voice and hand.
The seas divide us not, O Mother, on this day;
Our hearts and yours are one, as we together say,
Praise and glory be to God for fifty sacred years.

Sister Radley then presented Mother Hardey with the most golden of the gifts that had come in the seventeen trunks, a rosary each bead of which was a gold coin to aid her in her apostolic work. All day happy celebrations went on with every manner of conventual joy, even to a dance performed by some of the negro dolls from Louisiana. At night Mother Hardey turned to her Superior General saying: "I have been so touched today that I would have wept had you given me time." It was just as well that she did not know what was going on at Manhattanville. The Reverend John L. Spalding, future Bishop of Peoria, was asked to preach at the Mass of Thanksgiving. He chose to make his sermon into a panegyric as though the ceremony were a canonization instead of a

Jubilee, claiming that "absence gives in a measure the privilege of death."

Mother Hardey's zeal was by now active in Europe. She devoted her Jubilee rosary to a work which she had built up and which was unique in the history of the Society. She founded an "Apostolic School", to provide an education for young girls who had a religious vocation and no means of fitting themselves to follow it. She hoped to train candidates not only for the Society but for other Religious Orders as well. She chose the Convent at Beauvais for her school and set to work energetically, begging and buying if not stealing for her protégées. The work was difficult by its very nature, and it met with criticism. School-girl vocations are apt to be ephemeral, and Mother Hardey's efforts ended in frequent failure. One young Canadian girl, beautiful and brilliant, consoled her for several disaffections by becoming a fervent novice at Conflans, but her health broke down and she returned home to die. "God punished me," said Mother Hardey, "I was too proud of my little Canadian." Another promising subject was sent to the Noviceship at Kenwood, but when the time came for taking the habit she showed the unreality of her vocation, declaring that if she had been left alone she would probably have been happily settled in life by then. "That child is right," said Mother Hardey when she heard of it. She sent her back to her own home and continued for years to supply her with pretty clothes. The Apostolic School was not marked by the success which is almost legendary where Mother Hardey is concerned, but when it closed it had already sent some twenty young girls on the road to happy religious life. Mother Hardey would have done as much for one.

Once she had started travelling in Europe she hardly stopped. Her journeys were on the old grand scale, through the distances were negligible to her. On account of her knowledge of Spanish she was sent in February, 1876, to visit the Convents in Spain. She and Mother Seymour went over the Pyrenees in a *diligence*. They left from Perpignan and passed through the spurs of hill not far from where they rise from the Mediterranean blue. On the way Mother Hardey made an unusually literal impression of queenliness:

Reverend Mother was so enchanted with the grand spectacle of the mountains that she forgot the fatigue of the journey; I think her heart was all the time lifted up in prayer, and even on the heights of the Pyrenees the sad story of a lost cause enlisted her deepest sympathy. The army of Don Carlos had just surrendered and detachments of the conquered troops passed us on the way, fleeing across the frontier to seek refuge in France or some other foreign country. Spain was in a state of political agitation and a rigid inspection of luggage was therefore enforced on the frontier village of Jungera, but our trunks were not opened, owing to the kind intervention of our travelling companions, chief among whom was an officer in the army of King Alphonso. Whenever a halt occurred in the journey he was at her side to offer assistance, and seeing this other officials pressed forward with added courtesies. On arriving at the hotel in Figueras we were conducted to the handsomest apartment, and served as travellers of the highest distinction. The next day we heard that Reverend Mother was believed to be Queen Christina travelling in disguise, and so the honours she received were marks of respect intended for the grandmother of the Spanish King.

They then moved away from the rocky backdrop of the mountains across on undulating plain to where it dipped to the sea at Barcelona, the old capitol of Catalonia. Here the warmth, vivacity and faith of Spain closed round them. Barcelona, Don Quixote had claimed, was the "seat of courtesy, haven of strangers, mother of the valiant, champion of the wronged." Mother Hardey drove beyond the milling cosmopolitanism of its streets to the village of Sarria, where she found the oldest Sacred Heart Convent in Spain, founded in 1845. It owed its existence to the ingenious loyalty of the Spanish children at school at Pergignan who had dared, on their own initiative, to address a *Supplique* to Mother Barat asking her to found a convent in their native land. She had sent her letter of consent directly to them, and now their successors gave Mother Hardey a laurel crown with leaves of silver and gold to be laid on the tomb of Mother Barat.

The travellers then went straight west into Aragon, across a desert-like plain to where rivers and canals were laced together into the great garden that held Saragossa. Here each home in the old town was built to be a fortress, but among the newer houses was a Convent opened but a few days before. It was in the state of upheaval with which she was so familiar from long experience with foundations, and she was there in time to welcome the first children who arrived. They were children of Our Lady of the Pillar for, said the legend:

> Saint James the Great was in Saragossa in the year forty of Our Lord Jesus Christ. He went out to pray with his disciples on the evening of the second of January, and turned to the shores of the River Ebre. While they were praying, the Blessed Virgin, who was still alive, appeared to the Holy Apostle upon a column of jasper, carried by angels and encircled by countless heavenly spirits singing sweetly in praise of their heavenly Queen whose image they gave to the Saint, and which is still venerated in Saragossa.

Then came Madrid in the heart of Spain, standing in the royal accoutrements of Philip II upon a high and leafless barren. The travellers passed the palaces and homes of art to find Chamartin de la Rosa. This beautiful estate had been presented to the Society in 1859 by the Duke of Pastrana, upon the mere expression of a wish to buy it. The Duchess straightway became a fast friend of Mother Hardey.[4] Doña Dionisia de Pastrana's rôle in the world was that of God's Lady Bountiful, and her husband more than seconded her lavish generosity. She was not only a benefactress of many Convents, but a fervent Child of Mary and a sharer in the spiritual privileges of the Society. Mother Hardey had ample opportunity to see the wonders of Madrid, for the foundation of a City House was in project and she visited one stately home after another in the search for the right one. The Duchess was anxious to present the Society with her own city residence on the street called Isabel la Catolica, but the moment had not yet come. A year after Mother Hardey's visit the Madrid Convent opened on the Cabellero de Gracias, and only eight years later did the Duchess' exquisite home become a second City House, named Saint Denis in her honour.

Mother Hardey could hardly have guessed, in spite of the political agitation on all sides, how soon the flames of anti-religious hatred would devour the walls of Chamartin, and what answering fire of heroism would be struck from the souls of all Spanish Religious in the great persecutions to come. She left Spain in mid-March, leaving a glow of appreciation behind her. "I shall never forget," wrote one of the Religious, "the great simplicity and strong religious spirit which Mother Hardey united in so high a degree. There appeared in her two qualities which at first seem contradictory, a childlike candour with the intelligence and experience of age, and the ripest virtue."

A few years later Mother Hardey visited England and Ireland as the interpreter of Mother Lehon. As early as 1802, when the Society had scarcely begun to exist, Mother Barat had been tenaciously drawn towards the British Isles, hoping to kindle Devotion to the Sacred Heart to new ardour from the faith of the Irish, and to use it as a means to draw back to the faith those who in England had lost their heritage. "We must go there," she had declared "at the price of any sacrifice." In 1842 foundations had been made simultaneously at Roscrea in Ireland and at Berrymead in England. Mother Barat herself visited the latter house before it was transferred in 1850 to Roehampton. It was here that Mother Hardey arrived in March, 1880, driving up an avenue of great elms and acacias, past the lake that mirrored the pillars of the semicircular porch that gave such dignity to the white house beyond the lawn, a house that was to be dear to the Society not only in England but over the whole world through its associations with Mother Mabel Digby and Mother Janet Erskine Stuart, until it became a whole-burnt offering at the unleashing of total war. Mother Hardey did not meet Janet Stuart,[5] who was still following the hounds over hedge and hazard, a recent convert who had not yet made up her mind what Convent to enter, but Mother Digby, then Superior Vicar, welcomed her to Roehampton.[6] The commanding personality, the deep blue eyes that searched the eyes of others with such fearless and affectionate insight, were already familiar to Mother Hardey, who knew the fact but not the inner secret of the miraculous moment of grace that had changed Mabel Digby from a defiant Protestant into a great-souled Catholic. It had occurred at Benediction as the Sacred Host was lifted, and throughout her life it was noticed that Mother Digby seemed irresistibly drawn towards the chapel at the same hour of every afternoon. Later on, Mother Digby often repeated to others a remark made by Mother Hardey at this visit which had impressed her: "Whenever your propose a difficulty to a Superior, have a solution for it prepared to offer her, in order to spare her unnecessary trouble."

The English houses passed by in quick succession. At Roehampton the children had been in a fever of expectancy and presented the Mother General with fifteen hundred garments for the poor made by themselves. Wandsworth, a Normal College, was next visited. The staff had been specially prepared by Mother Digby who had faced and met all government requirements for training and equipment. The first troubles were over by now, and Mother Hardey could admire the maps and other educational projects made by the students. As the travellers left for Brighton, they heard a farewell salute—novel to Mother Lehon at least—of "hip-hip-hurray!" The Convent of Brighton, overlooking the sea from its smooth steep hill, was a recent foundation, and Mother Hardey assisted at the consecration of the altar in the new chapel.

There were four Convents in Ireland. Roscrea was a white house looking down over the green of Tipperary. As the carriage drove up the hill three hundred children from the National School with shining cheeks and eyes cheered and held up their bunches of shamrock, quite unmindful of the pouring rain. Here, as in each house, Mother Hardey entertained the school with stories of Mother Duchesne while Mother Lehon was giving her conference to the Community. Armagh, the next house, stood in the heart of the Orange Land and taught not only the children in its schools but large groups of mill-girls who came for religion lessons at night. It had fought stout battles for the Church, and the Convent dog who wagged his tail at Mother Hardey was a confessor of the faith, for his ear had been torn by a stone hurled at him in malice during an uprising of prejudice against the Popish school. That spirit was dying out, as the charity that goes with zeal was felt throughout the countryside. Lastly, Mount Anville near Dublin, and a City-House in the capital itself, had thriving works to show the Mother General before the return to Paris in May.

It would be too difficult to follow the net-work of visits that

Mother Hardey paid to the many Convents of France and Belgium. Each of these houses was a chapter in itself of the earlier history of the Society, which she helped to perpetuate by her decisions regarding rebuilding or expansion. Here and there she took part in a new foundation, and everywhere made the history of the New World as vivid to the various Communities as that of the Old World was to her. "In listening to her," and said, "we were reminded of the *Book of Foundations* of Saint Teresa, and each of us felt stronger, readier to love and make loved the Divine Heart, that Heart which we all realized was the center of the life of Reverend Mother Hardey." These visits were all very short, for year by year her duties in Paris were increasing.

During one winter, in the absence of Reverend Mother Desoudin, she was placed in charge of the Probation. This responsibility seemed to alarm her as few others had done. One of her Probanists wrote:

> She seemed very diffident, and based her explanations of the Rule upon the words of those who had preceded her. Love for the Society seemed to overflow from her, but above all when she spoke of the incomparable Devotion to the Sacred Heart, which she seemed to have a special gift of communicating to others. Although her usual way of speaking was very measured in expression, on this subject her voice took on a special ring of fervour which made her speech almost precipitous.

Before relinquishing this charge she placed a picture of the Sacred Heart in the Probation Room where it remained after her in life-giving memory. Her usual connection with the Probation consisted in keeping a motherly eye on the American Probanists, and if she met one of them shivering in the unaccustomed climate she would smuggle her some extra-warm clothing. Mother Lehon used to send the Americans to her in groups, to give them the pleasure of speaking English, but Mother Hardey, while complying, said: "You are here to learn the language of the Mother House; the language of our Mothers General is the only true one for us, and for that you have come across the Atlantic and the Pacific."

While she was in charge of the Maison des Anges, which had been opened in September 1875, she organized a new work, a school for Parlour Boarders. The young girls who came were foreigners for the most part, and Mother Hardey's rare understanding of their troubles and their desires helped them to take full advantage of their stay in Paris. One day a little group of Irish girls got into trouble by acquiring some tea, off bounds, in the hope of having a real tea-party in spite of their French surroundings. The plot was discovered and the tea confiscated. Mother Hardey heard that they were in disgrace. It was not her way to reverse the decisions of those in immediate authority, but after a few days the Irish girls were specially invited to a tea-party, where Mother Hardey served them tea prepared with almost Irish skill. There was no reference to the escapade, only a healing of hurt feelings. As Superior of this house, with its many good works she once more had the opportunity of making others happy by discreet giving, till priests, foreigners, beggars, and friends old and new found their way to the *Trente et Un*. Within the small community she lifted up hearts as ever, by her deeds and by her words, saying:

The Rule tells us that the Spirit of the Society is based upon prayer and the interior life. Keep them united to the Sacred Heart by recollection. Never allow the multitude of thoughts which constantly pass through your minds, or the occupations of daily life, to so absorb you that you forget to look upon your Divine model. Think how philosophers study for years and years to discover some secret of science, and when they find it how happy they are. Study the Sacred Heart. You will discover Divine secrets in that book, and your happiness will increase in proportion to the earnestness with which you practice its lessons of wisdom.

In January, 1884, Mother Lehon wrote to the whole Society: "Let this year be a year of love from its first moment to its last." Mother Hardey made the words her own, for soon love alone was to be her work. She took part in the General Council in February with keen interest in the main question under discussion: how to meet the movement towards University education for women. She was unchangeably cheerful, but Mother Jones felt that there was something almost too heavenly in her bearing, and left for home full of foreboding.

Mother Hardey was now local superior of the Mother House. A last busy winter passed quietly over her head, but in the spring she received a shock in the death of Reverend Mother Cahier who had been Secretary General for over twenty years. The past seemed suddenly to be cut away, and she found that she had no strength to face the future. Only God counted, God and the "everlasting Now". She grew so weak that in July Mother Lehon sent her to Calais for a breath of salt air, but before she reached there an abrupt movement of the train caused a heart attack. She rallied, but a second attack a few days later brought her swiftly within the reach of death. Within a few hours Mother Lehon was by her side, and in the silence of early morning the Last Sacraments were given. At their strength-giving touch Mother Hardey's power of speech came back, clear and forceful, and she spoke out the only thought of herself that was left in her mind; she tried in words of humblest contrition to fill up the voids that she saw in her full life. Mother Lehon gently silenced her; and then there was no thought left but for her End who was also her Beginning.

"I can do little," said the doctor. "Her organs are simply

worn out." "Yes, they are worn out," interpreted Mother Lehon, "solely for the good of souls, and in the interest of the Divine Master." She recovered slightly as the days went by, and in September it was found possible to take her back to the Mother House. Soon her wheel chair began to appear in the Community Room and in the chapel. She dictated cheerful letters to America, sent for the Probanists to come and see her, and let Sister Gartland lavish care on her. Healing spring sunshine came, but by that time suffering had made Mother Hardey its own. "For the last ten months," wrote Mother Lehon, "we have seen her always self-controlled, abandoned to God and to authority like a child, sometimes accepting the hope of working again then giving it up with the same tranquility of soul, and going through these painful alternatives without ever losing her peace in God."

During a brief period of betterment Mother Lehon thought it safe to make a short journey into Belgium, but she was recalled at once by cable. A stroke had left no hope. Mother Hardey counted the hours until her Superior General's return, and then "we spoke of God, and for the rest not a single disquiet came to trouble her soul until the end. After a government of more than fifty years, such calmness and gentle serenity showed with what admirable straight-forwardness she had always acted." She wondered how far across the Atlantic was the boat that was bringing Mother Jones to France, but let the hope of that last joy go. From the tenth to the seventeenth of June the poised soul waited. The air in the Mother House tingled as night does when dawn strikes upon it, when star-blinding morning has touched the dark, unheard and still unseen. The bitter-sweet breath of a death that is more joy than pain came and went through those days like a wind blown from pungent pines or from a far salt sea. She received Holy Communion almost daily, and the Last Sacraments brought strength again, not now of body but of soul. Beyond a murmured "yes" she did not speak, except once when her voice rang out unexpectedly after Communion: "I ask pardon of everyone, yes, of everyone."

Mother Lehon stayed on one hand, Sister Gartland on the other, while lonesome American Probanists peeped in the door. Mother Hardey was conscious to the end, and as though listening for a last obedience waited for the words, "Go forth, Christian soul," before she slipped without sign or motion into God's presence. It was eight o'clock on the morning of Thursday, June 17, 1886. "Can this be death, so peaceful, so calm?" a wondering Probanist asked herself. "Where is the horror of death? Then the thought came to me, that to die such a death one must live a holy life, as had our Mother."

XXI

LIFE AFTER LIFE

Mother Lehon came early the next morning with an armful of white roses to where Mother Hardey lay in the serenity of candlelight. "How beautiful she looks!" she exlaimed. almost startled. The many visitors who came that day received the same impression. There was colour in the strong face, and "she had the same sweet smile that she wore when pleased or amused." The piles of flowers by her side grew higher, and a magnificent wreath was laid at her feet by the heart-broken Duchess of Pastrana. The next day the funeral procession moved west, across the Seine and out to the suburbs. For two hours it went slowly on while a fine drizzle of rain began to fall, tinging the grey houses and streets with silver and whispering on the carriage tops. The windows of the Convent of Conflans, standing in a long gabled row on a hill along the river's edge, welcomed them through an increasing downpour. The horses turned into the gardens near the Pavillion. The Community and Novices stood with shining candles along the corridor that led to the chapel. Here a Requiem

The drawing for this chapter was made by Carol Putnam.

was sung, and the coffin was carried down into the shadows of the vast crypt beneath. Mother Hardey was laid to rest in a cell not far from that of Mother Goetz, among many other builders of the Society. A tree-lined alley stretched from the end of the chapel to the shrine of Our Lady of Sorrows where Mother Barat herself lay buried, she who through God had brought the Society into being and who was now calling her first daughters one by one to her side.

That afternoon Mother Lehon wrote a Circular Letter to all the houses, placing Mary Aloysia Hardey among those whose memory is to be held in veneration:

> You all share, as your letters prove, the deep grief which her death has caused, for she was one of the strong pillars of the Society. In America especially she cultivated and spread abroad the seed sown by the Holy Mother Duchesne, reliving the solid virtues of the first foundresses. Her works, which will be recounted in detail later on, prove this sufficiently. I only wish to recall here how noble, generous and straight was her character, how kind, compassionate, strong and invincible in trial was her heart, how devoted she was to the interests and to the glory of the Heart of Jesus, active in procuring them and at the same time filially submissive to the voice of obedience. . . . Let us profit, Reverend Mothers and Sisters, from such precious lessons, and thus, ever faithful to our holy vocation, we shall all meet in that Divine Heart.

Mother Jones reached Paris two days after the funeral and was met by the Superior General with the words: "Now I am doubly your Mother." When she learned that Mother Hardey had expressed a wish that her body might remain in France she gave up her desire of taking it back to America, although it had been sealed into a leaden coffin ready for transportation. So for twenty years more Mother Hardey lay at rest at Conflans while the life of the Society went on above and about her, inwardly at peace—that strenuous peace that wars unrestingly for perfection—but outwardly under a darkening cloud of persecution.

A radically Masonic government had gained control of the French Parliament, which began its attempts to strangle the Religious Orders by secularizing education. On this point the Orders met their foe more than half way and fought them with their own weapons by developing the curricula, but the Brisson Law attacked on the financial side. Other laws continued to add odious and flagrantly unjust taxation. Reverend Mother Lehon, then eighty-four years old, summoned the Twelfth General Council of the Society in 1890, and an energetic plan of resistance was mapped out. The valiant Superior General died four years later, after celebrating her diamond jubilee of Profession. The next Generalate lasted scarcely a year, for Reverend Mother de Sartorius died under the heavy burden, leaving a radiant memory of holiness to light the coming storm, and the joy of daily Exposition of the Blessed Sacrament at the Mother House. Prayer deepened at every step.

Reverend Mother Digby succeeded her, to face great joys and a heavy sorrow. She brought about a stimulating advance in the matter of studies, and made a long journey through America; then came the Centenary of the Society. Three years of preparation were not too long for that November 21, 1900 "on which," wrote Mother Digby, "let us look to the past and the future; to the past to thank God for numberless and inestimable graces; the future to promise that, come what may, we will not come down from the high thoughts that have inspired our Society, and in which its foundations have been laid." The splendours of the day passed, but not the renewal of the primitive spirit which it had brought about, and which was strengthened incomparably eight years later by the Beatification of Madeleine Sophie Barat. On that day the Society seemed to hear again the words with which its Foundress had closed her last Testament to it: "I beg our good Master to bless you all and to engrave deeply in your souls the will, the incessant need of spending yourselves until your last breath for the love of the Divine Heart of Jesus; and, for His sake, for the salvation of souls, according to the end of your vocation."

Between these two joys came the bitter task which Mother Digby was so well fitted by the clarity of her judgment and the firmness of her will to face and overcome. In 1901, under Minister Coombes, the right to teach was withdrawn from fourteen of the French Convents of the Sacred Heart. The movement spread until one by one within the next eight years forty-five houses were closed and three thousand Religious dispersed. As each house was lost a new one was opened somewhere else in the world, and each Religious found a new home like to the old. On August 10, 1907, Mass was said for the last time in the Mother House, and Mother Digby's carriage, the last to leave, drove her late that afternoon to Conflans. The fate of this house too was foreseen; the body of the Mother Foundress was sent to Jette Saint Pierre in Belgium, while rows of empty niches in the crypt showed that the first makers of the Society were resting elsewhere. Thus it came about that in the summer of 1905 the body of Mother Hardey crossed the ocean to a home not new but old. It was her twentieth transatlantic crossing.

In America her memory was still potent, beyond the Convent as well as in it. At the time of her death the *Catholic World*[1] had published an obituary notice in which it spoke for the public:

> Madame Hardey had the gift of mingling in the world and of being an excellent administratrix without losing anything of the exalted asceticism of the religious life. Although obliged from her care of the temporalities of the institutions over which she presided to come into relation with things and persons naturally

calculated to wear off the sheen of high spirituality, she preserved among seculars the fervour of the novice. This rare excellence of leading a contemplative in the midst of an active life arose from her punctilious fidelity to the rules of her Order, from the observance of which she never allowed anything to make her swerve. Thus, faithful to every point of her Rule, she edified the religious community in which she lived, while her sweet yet firm character, her cultivated manners and magnetic virtues, won the respect and the love of seculars.

Some years later Bishop John Lancaster Spalding spoke in his turn for the Clergy and the educational circles when he closed his book, *Religion, Education and Agnosticism,*[2] with a tribute to Mother Hardey:

What a fund of good sense, what balance of judgment, what a sentiment of justice, what endurance of labour and trial, what power of love and helpfulness, what a strong and serene spirit there were in her! She had the gift to make authority lovable; and where she ruled the wise and virtuous wished that she might never cease to rule. She was born to govern, and in obeying her all felt that they were hearkening to the voice of reason and doing the will of God. How wholly unselfish, how free from vanity, how incapable of deceit she was! How tolerant, how large of mind and heart, how able and ready to sympathize with all who have good will!

Though loved with a tender devotion that few have known, and followed with a confidence that never questions aught, though honoured and consulted by the rich and fashionable, not less than by priests and Bishops, she retained always the perfect simplicity of speech and action which belongs only to the most innocent or to the greatest souls. No one ever left her presence without having been made braver and better. To know her was to understand the supreme worth of a soul that is moulded by religious faith and love. . . . One felt that her wisdom and strength came from within—from a soul that dwelled in habitual loving communication with God. Apart from Him she understood that no good could possibly come to her, and that as He was the end so was He the principle of her being.

When Mother Hardey's body reached Manhattanville it was placed in the chapel. This was the chapel that she had built, yet it was new. The stones that she had seen placed in its walls reached only half way up in the taller, younger, more simply beautiful house of God. The outer surface of the older stones was blackened by the fire which had swept away her Manhattanville, all but the foundations. On the evening of August 13, 1888, a small stove had been left burning by some workmen in the attic. By eight o'clock flames had under-eaten the tower, and it fell in a pillar of fire. A high wind carried the destruction throughout the building while the heroism of the firemen and of friends from the neighbourhood was powerless to save it. A Nun, standing in the chapel of Saint Joseph, looked into the blazing courtyard through the laced branches of the oak tree that was too strong and green to die. She was heard to cry: "O Mother Hardey, why will you let Manhattanville burn?" Mother Hardey, from heaven, saw to it that the foundations stayed. They were enough, and before a year had passed a new Manhattanville had arisen upon them. "So as by fire" its life went on, and was again humming about her when her body came to receive grateful honour in the new chapel. Then for six months longer she rested in the burial vault in the hill behind Saint Joseph's chapel, where her stepmother and Lena were buried among the many Religious whose bodies had been placed in the vault when the city had taken the site of the former cemetery.

The children of 1905, with their skirts no longer hooped or bustled but trailing flatly, with their leg-o'-mutton sleeves and the high pompadours that made them look unaccountably old for their years, might still have looked familiar to Mother Hardey. But she might have some difficulty, at first sight, in recognizing their short-skirted, short-haired successors of today. She who represented so well that blend of the progressive and the traditional that makes for the permanent, may well be called the remote founder of the Liberal Arts College that has inherited the place of the Academy. *In Exultatione Metens* is the motto of the College; it reaps where such as she has sown, and exults in the reaping. Nearly four hundred students fill the house built on the foundations that she laid for a future that she could not guess. They lead the life that she began for them; they have a receptiveness, an energy and a joy that must make glad her now unhampered vision. Modern buildings extend the work of the College over the whole campus, and a larger Parish School spreads its influence even farther than of old. All activities are bound together by song, joy perfected and lifted to the plane of worship by the Pius X School of Liturgical Music.

Thus the cross-bearing Tower is the center of a life ever more multiple,

> On the heights so proudly standing,
> Strong against the blue.

The Catholic Action foreseen by Orestes Brownson is in full swing; though perhaps even he did not see that young women as well as young men would conduct the meetings of Associations devoted to the Lay Apostolate. Students go each week to the site of Mother Hardey's old home on Houston Street, to do work that would please her in the Barat Settlement. Giving and taking goes on, the work of the heart; the pursuit of higher study goes on as strongly and as deeply as possible, the work of the mind. Together, they are "doing the truth in charity." Mother Hardey had said to the children of Manhattanville: "Let your religion be practical; your faith must find expression in works." To the students of the College their President has spoken words which show time's development of that earlier ideal;

> The very life of a movement is its soul; its soul must be spiritual, and a soul raised by God's mercy to a supernatural end and committed by that fact to supernatural means. The soul of Catholic Action comes from its union with Christ's Mystical Body. The human means which it uses are divinized by the grace of God which vivifies them, and by prayer which multiplies indefinitely their power. The end is that which from your earliest childhood has been placed before you as the one reason for your existence—the glory of God. So let us throw ourselves with ardour into the work of bringing about the reign of Christ in His world and particularly in our beloved country.[3]

On December 12, 1905, the casket containing Mother Hardey's body was laid before the altar for a last Mass at Manhattanville, and then taken to Kenwood where the Absolution was pronounced in the chapel by Bishop Burke. Reverend Mother Mahoney, then Vicar, was present, and so too were Mother Hardey's old and faithful fellow-workers, Mother Jones and Mother Tommasini. From the chapel a candle-bearing procession wound up the hill; and in grey December peace, without snow, without sun, the coffin was lowered into a central grave. The candles were blown out, and Mother Hardey was left alone on her hill.

She was back in the place where rivers rise, at the summit of that uplifting hill. The lower levels had not held her; she had passed them by. If a bird sings while one is alone in God's Acre at Kenwood, one fears—or hopes—to become like the monk of the legend who, listening for a moment to bird-song, found on its ceasing that a hundred years had passed. Perhaps, in the same way, time may cease in such a place at a snatch of the music of the mind. Perhaps Mother Hardey's life may best be seen—now that the story has been told—by looking forward and backward in time, seen not in itself only but as part of a great unfinished history from which it was drawn and into which it has returned to live its life after life.

That history is the history of the Devotion of the Sacred Heart.[4] Time has a way of disappearing in matters which have an element of the divine. The Church, which is both divine and human, eternal and yet progressing, draws individual lives into its vaster self, giving to each a wider meaning than its own, even as at Mass one insignificant worshipper may offer the whole of worship. At Mass the words are so quietly spoken as scarcely to brush the air; they move rapidly, but their meaning towers, motionless. Their giant power walks out and takes possession of the unmoving heart of time. The reality is that of a fact, of a thing done, of a thing that is. Christ on the Cross abides, transfixed, while the centuries revolve about Him; and even so a life devoted to the Sacred Heart shares in the whole range of the Devotion's work in the world.

On the Cross, said Saint John, "one of the soldiers opened His side with a spear, and immediately there came out blood and water." The spear had gone to the Heart. He who saw it was the Disciple whom Jesus loved, "and we know that his testimony is true." Longest-lived of the Apostles, he stretched the apostolic age to its limit. The Church by then was rooted in Rome, deep-rooted in the catacombs, watered in its own blood. Then came peace and release; it marched into the open, holding its processional crosses high in the sunshine. After the days of martyrdom came the Golden Age of the Liturgy, then the spread of monasticism and the conversion of the nations. Church history unfolded, year after heroic year of it, active and life-giving. But the life of the Church is the life of Christ led within His Mystical Body, the social body that He took, the body that is made up of mankind.

That life is led within as well as without. It is an unfolding of prayer, the mystic Christ loving His Father under the wings of the Spirit. As time went on and the Church worked mightily in the world, men holy of heart penetrated that inner life. Three memories came back to them; the soul prefigured in Solomon's Song, whose heart watched, who hid in the caverns of rock; then the Beloved Disciple who leaned on His Master's Heart; then the opened side of the Master on Calvary. From meditation, preaching and writing on these three texts, Devotion to the Sacred Heart first stirred and took shape in the Church, in the days of the Fathers, the mighty years of the crumbling and the forming of civilization. "Saint John," says Saint Augustine, "drank deep secrets from the inner Heart of the Son of God." "The wound in His side truly is the cave in the rock," said Saint Gregory the Great; and the Venerable Bede went further: "in the wounded Heart is seen the greatness of the love which the Spouse has for His Church."

As the centuries went on and the Feudal Ages took shape, love became more strongly revealed: "The open side has revealed to us the charity of His Heart," said Saint Anselm. By the twelfth century, when the silence of the cloister was opening the way to the piercing mysticism of the Middle Ages, Saint Bernard found that "the secret of His Heart is discovered," and William of St. Thierry, later, desired "to enter wholly into the wound, even into the Heart of Christ." The Devotion found its synthesis in the anonymous *Vitis Mystica,* from which were later drawn some of the Lessons for Matins in the Office of the Sacred Heart: "Since we have reached the most sweet Heart of Jesus, and it is good for us to abide in it, let us not readily turn away from it. . . . Draw me, then, wholly into Thy Heart."

In the thirteenth century came the flowering of Mediaeval contemplative life; the shouting of the Crusades was dying away, but stone-hammering in the great Cathedrals was unceasing. Hidden in the Monastery of Helfta Saint Gertrude and the two Saint Mechtildes lived familiarly with their Beloved who said to them: "Behold, I deliver to you the richest consolation and the sweetest delight of my Divine Heart, that you may give of them generously to all, as much as you will." It was the theology of the Sacred Humanity that found its interpreter in Saint Gertrude, who clothed her expression of it in the language of the Liturgy. In using the symbolism of a human heart to express Divine Love she was using the speech of humanity in all ages, for whom the heart is the index of the inner, moral life of affection and volition.

Then the Cistercians, ascetics of a living penance, the Dominicans, guides in the wisdom of the interior life, the Franciscans, romantic realists of the Passion and of the gladness of the Son of Man, all these preached and practiced, wrote and sang Devotion to the Sacred Heart throughout the fourteenth and fifteenth centuries until it reached the rank and file of the faithful. They in turn shaped their prayers by it, and engraved its symbol in stone and wood. The Devotion which had expressed exuberance of love in the ages of faith, now served as an astringent against the evils of the days of decline; and when in the sixteenth century the Reformation rent Europe apart, it took organic shape as if to stand for unity. It passed from the domain of mysticism to that of asceticism, and its theological foundations began to be analyzed.

In the seventeenth century came the turning point. The social character of the Devotion began to be stressed; in Spain, the Low Countries, in France, it was found to be a potent way of linking man to man, group to group, in common action. Saint John Eudes based his new foundations, his new works, upon it, and the time was ready for the great revelation to Saint Margaret Mary. She was the means by which Devotion to the Sacred Heart became an integral part of the social and liturgical life of the Church. No longer was it to be a matter of sporadic, personal prayer; it became official and universal. "My Divine Heart," said the Master to her, "can no longer contain the flame of the fire of its love, but must spread this flame through you, and manifest itself to men, to enrich them with its precious treasures. These I show you; they contain the sanctifying and saving graces needed to draw men back from the pit of perdition." A Feast-day, public worship, group consecrations and outward symbols, reparation each for the other, all these Saint Margaret Mary asked of the Church and of the world, in the name of Him who used her to gain possession not only of the inner prayer of this soul or that, but of the entire prayer of men united in one Heart and one soul, working together, body and hand and mind.

Because it was now official the matter moved slowly. Saint Margaret Mary died, but before her death the Jesuits had placed their militant ranks at her service. Their theologians sounded its depth; their writers and preachers spread it indefatigably. Through the eighteenth century with its cold philosophism the Devotion of love made its way until, just one hundred years after the Great Vision in which Our Lord had asked for the establishment of the Feast, it was permitted by the Decree of Pope Clement XIII. It was inevitable that Religious Orders should arise in response. Father de Tournély, some twenty-five years after the Decree of Rome, conceived the Society of the Fathers of the Sacred Heart while meditating upon the pierced side of the Crucified. His was the first religious society in the Church to bear the name of Sacred Heart. When its members were drawn into the ranks of the Jesuits upon their reconstruction the name passed to the corresponding order of women. The Society of the Sacred Heart paid every price to keep that name that held the meaning of its existence.

As Saint Madeleine Sophie's work advanced, so did the nineteenth century, running on through its extremes of placid conservatism and of restless doubt, materialistic on the surface yet evolving in other ways than by its Evolution through the spiritual forces at work in it. Lourdes recalled the power of miracles to the minds of men; the Curé d'Ars the power of asceticism; mighty mission movements spread the power of zeal; and then Montmartre built into stone the uncapturable power of Devotion to the Sacred Heart.[5] As its fire had burned into the cold abstractions of the eighteenth century, so, as the pendulum swung the other way, its keen sacrificial spirit cut against the excesses of romanticism of the nineteenth.

Mother Hardey's life was lived to the swing of these great movements, but she died before they reached their full momentum. She laboured, prayed and lived greatly, then gave her life back into the Society where it lived on. It lived through the intensifying generalate of Mother Janet Stuart who, by her personal influence, by her wide travelling and her books, reached all hearts with a message of confidence in God Who is all; through the concentrating generalate of Mother Marie de Loe, in which the Mother House moved through pain and stress as though drawn by a magnet into its place in the shadow of Saint Peter's bark in Rome, and in which the final splendour of Canonization came to Saint Madeleine Sophie; then into the troubled days of Mother Manuela Vincente, who saw the beatification of Mother Duchesne shine on the edge of the storm.

Each step of these rapid and momentous years has seen a corresponding manifestation of Devotion to the Sacred Heart. Fifteen years after Mother Hardey's death Leo XIII, the Pope of the *Rerum Novarum*, consecrated the human race to It. As the Encyclical said: "since there is in the Sacred Heart a symbol and a sensible sign of the infinite love of Jesus

Christ which moves us to love one another, it is fit and proper that we should consecrate ourselves to His most Sacred Heart." Leo XIII knew that the world was on the verge of an upheaval and he wrote:

> When the Church, in the days immediately following her institution, was oppressed beneath the yoke of the Caesars, a young Emperor saw in the heavens a cross which became the happy omen and the cause of the glorious victory which followed. And now today there is another blessed and heavenly banner offered to our sight—the most Sacred Heart of Jesus, with a cross rising from it and shining forth with dazzling splendour amidst the flames of love. In that Sacred Heart all our hope should be placed, and from it the salvation of men is to be confidently sought.

As the twentieth century advanced the cataclysm foreseen by Leo XIII drew nearer. Pope Pius XI looked to the same banner to lead the way. He gave to the Feast of the Sacred Heart the utmost sanction and solemnity of the Liturgy, the Liturgy which Pius X had called "the primary and indispensable source of the true Christian spirit." And now in our day the storm has broken. The skies grow darker, the Banner more brilliant against them. As totalitarianism, potent only because it is a twisted truth, battles and bombs for the dominion of the world, the truth against which it fights stands out revealed. The human race is one body. Our century is conscious of this, more clearly perhaps than other ages have been. The human race is, actually or potentially, the Body of Christ, and in the Body is the Heart of the Body. One individual life that lived these truths, half lost in the mightiness of the whole yet integral to it, is the life of Mother Hardey, who said in her straight and quiet way: "Devotion to the Sacred Heart is essentially adapted to the wants of our age; it supplies every need and satisfies the highest aspirations of the soul." This is her life after life.

The Society which was everything to her is now caught in the wine-press, with the Church, with mankind. Sundered house from house but still "one heart and one soul," it shares in the redemptive sufferings of the Heart of Christ here and now, and it looks beyond. It is praying the prayer that Saint Madeleine Sophie once spoke aloud in a more tranquil hour: "Thy kingdom come, Thy will be done, in the Society of the Sacred Heart as it is in Heaven."

SOURCES

(1) This biography has been made as historically accurate as possible, and imagination has been used to fill in the background only where there is a strong probability in favour of the "might-have-been." There are no fictitious scenes, conversations or letters in the book. The aim has been to present a readable account of the life and times of Mother Hardey, made as attractive and as vivid as possible while resting on a sound factual basis.

For this reason it has been thought best not to employ the type of scholarly apparatus required in a thesis. All the bibliographical and source material has been placed together at the end of the book, to avoid overlapping and repetition. Numbers inserted in the text will refer to this informational section, whereas an asterisk in the text will refer to a footnote on the same page. Frequently used sources are given only the first time that they occur. Page references have not generally been given, as the bibliography is meant only as a guide to enable those interested to make further explorations into the field of American Church History.

The basic sources are:

A. For the personal events of Mother Hardey's life:

1. Garvey, M.; *Mary Aloysia Hardey*; Longmans Green; 1925.
2. *Vie de la Révérende Mère Hardey;* privately printed; Paris.

These two lives contain the greater part of the correspondence of Mother Hardey, most of whose letters have been lost.

3. Memories and anecdotes handed down by tradition; all authenticated as far as possible.

B. For the history of the Society of the Sacred Heart:

1. *Lettres Annuelles, 1838–1890.* Accounts of the events of each Convent and of the lives of individual Religious, written yearly and privately printed.
2. *House Journals* of the respective Convents, and other documents kept in the Archives.
3. Cahier, Adèle; *Vie de la Vénérable Mère Barat*; 2 vols.; Paris; 1884.
4. Duval, Marie-Thérèse; *Histoire Abrégée de la Société du Sacré Coeur*; Rome; 1926.
5. Letters from the Mother House Archives, or in privately printed collections.
6. Biographies of Religious, which will be referred to separately.

7. Callan, Louise; *The Society of the Sacred Heart in North America*; Longmans Green; 1937.

C. The History of the Catholic Church in the United States.

This has been taken largely from special studies made for Historical Societies, as well as from the few standard works on the subject. The references will be grouped according to topic as they occur in the text.

Chapter I

(2) Buchanan, Scott; *The New Program at Saint John's*; Supplement to the Bulletin, 1937–38.

Chapter II

(1) Richardson, H. D.; *Sidelights on Maryland History*; Williams and Wilkin; Baltimore; 1913.

Valuable information concerning the early members of the Hardey family and their property holdings has been furnished by Mr. J. H. Bell of Arlington, Virginia. He states in a letter: "An accurate list of those who came over with Governor Calvert seems not to have been preserved, but the following names have been recorded: . . . Nicholas Hardy. . . ." (Quoted from John Clagett Proctor in the *Washington Star*, Nov. 12, 1933.)

(2) *Relation of Maryland*; Maryland Historical Society; Fund Publication No. 35.

(3) *A Declaration of Lord Baltimore's Plantation*; Baltimore Press, 1929 (facsimile)

(4) Hall, C. C.; *Narratives of Early Maryland*; Scribners, 1810; Quotting: *Instructions to the Colonists by Lord Baltimore.*

(5) Ibid. *Briefe Relation of a Voyage into Maryland.*

(6) *Relatio Itineraris in Marilandiam;* Maryland Historical Society; Fund Publication No. 7.

(7) Davis, G. L.; *A Day-Star of American Freedom;* Scribner, 1855.

(8) O'Daniel, V. F.; "Cuthbert Fenwick—Pioneer Catholic." *Catholic Historical Review*, July–October, 1919.

(9) *Archives of Maryland*; Volumes 1–5, 7–8, 10.

(10) Ives, J. M.; *The Ark and the Dove*; Longmans, 1936, pp. 146 and 261.

(11) Shea, J. G.; *History of the Catholic Church in the United States*; 4 vols.; New York; 1890.

Maynard, Theodore; *The Story of American Catholicism*; Macmillan; 1941.

These two works are the basic sources for the broad outlines of historical periods and movements in the present work.

(12) Brumbaugh, G. M., and Hodges, M. R.; *Revolutionary Records of Maryland*; Darby, Washington, D. C.; 1924. See Vol. II, "Patriot's Oaths of Fidelity and Support."

Chapter III

(1) Spalding, C. W.; *The Spalding Memorial*; Chicago; 1897.

(2) Spalding, M. J.; *Sketches of the Early Catholic Missions of Kentucky*; Louisville; 1844.

(3) No record of the marriage can be found, but Prince George County Records show that the license was issued on October 25, 1806. Many Church records in Southern Maryland have been lost through fire.

(4) Frederick, Rev. J. A.; "Old Saint Peter's" (Baltimore); *Historical Records and Studies*, V, 354.

(5) For this and all further descriptions of costume see: McClellan, E.; *History of American Costume*; Tudor Publishing Company; 1937.

(6) Brumbaugh, G. M.; *Maryland Records, Colonial, Revolutionary, County and Church*; Darby, Washington, D. C.; 1915.

(7) Sargent, Daniel; *Our Land and Our Lady*; Longmans Green; 1939, p. 88.

(8) For this and further descriptions of travel see: Reck, F. M.; *The Romance of American Transportation;* Crowell Co.; 1938.

(9) Hart, A. B.; *American History Told by Contemporaries*; Macmillan; 1917; Vol. III, p. 462; "A Voyage down the Ohio," by Henry Brackenbridge.

(10) Dickens, Charles; *American Notes;* Pollard, 1888.

(11) Semple, H. C.; *The Ursulines of New Orleans, and Our Lady of Prompt Succour*; Kenedy; 1925.

(12) Ditchy, J. K.; *Les Acadiens Louisianais et leur Parler;* Johns Hopkins Press; 1932.

(13) Colliard, B.; "Historical Sketch of the Parish of Opelousas;" *Saint Louis Historical Review*; III, 14–18.

Chapter IV

(1) Cited from a lecture by Frank J. Sheed.

(2) *Abridged Plan of the Institute.* Privately printed.

(3) Beaulieu, Agnes de; *Léonor François de Tournély et son Oeuvre*; Vienna; 1886.

(4) Guidée, Achille, S. J.; *Vie du Révérend Père Joseph Varin*; Paris; 1854.

(5) Baunard, Mgr. (Louis); *Histoire de Madame Barat;* 2 vols.; Paris; 1876. See also the *Life* by Cahier, from which the greater number

of documentary quotations concerning Mother Barat and her foundations have been taken.

(6) Shea, J. C.; *Life and Times of Archbishop Carroll* (Volume II of *History*); p. 502.

(7) Baunard, Mgr. (Louis); *Histoire de Madame Duchesne;* Paris; 1878.

Erskine, M.; *Mother Philippine Duchesne*; Longmans Green; 1926.

CHAPTER V

(1) Amiens Archives, quoted in Callan, p. 43. Many documentary sources not available in the original have been quoted from this exhaustive work, where full bibliographical information concerning all the Sacred Heart Convents in North America may be obtained.

Many details and quotations in this chapter have been taken from the *Journal of Mother Duchesne*; copy in the Archives of Saint Charles.

(2) Garraghan, G.; *Saint Ferdinand of Florissant*; Loyola University Press; 1923, p. 251.

——; *The Jesuits of the Middle United States*; 3 vols.; America Press; 1938.

(3) Kenny, Rev. L.; "The Mullanphys of Saint Louis," *Historical Records and Studies*; XIV:70.

CHAPTER VI

(1) Callan, Ch. 21, "The Educational System."

(2) O'Leary, M.; *Education with a Tradition*; Longmans Green; 1936.

CHAPTER VII

(1) Manuscript *Life* of Mother Aloysia Jouve; Archives of Saint Charles.

Gigord, J. de; (editor); *Réligieuses du Sacré Coeur: Quelques Contemporaines de la Fondatrice*; 2 vols.; Paris; 1924.

(2) Archives of the Visitation Monastery, Riverdale-on-Hudson. These also give information concerning the Hardey and Smith families.

(3) Spalding, M. J.; *Sketches of the Life, Times and Character of the Right Reverend B. J. Flaget*; Louisville; 1852.

(4) Code, J. B.; *Great American Foundresses*; Macmillan; 1929.

(5) Colliard, *loc. cit.*

(6) Sennegy, René de; *Une Paroisse Louisianaise, Saint Michel*; New Orleans; 1877.

CHAPTER VIII

(1) Garraghan, G. J.; *The Catholic Church in Chicago*; Loyola University Press; 1921; p. 70.
Godecker, Sister M. Salesia; *Simon Bruté de Remur, First Bishop of Vincennes*; St. Meinrad's, Indiana; 1931.
(2) *Life of Cornelia Connelly*; Longmans Green; 1922.
(3) Galitzin, Prince Augustin; *Vie d'Une Réligieuse du Sacré Coeur*; Paris; 1869.
(4) Lempke, P. H.; *Life and Works of Prince Demetrius Augustine Gallitzin*; Longmans Green; 1940, p. 6.
Flick, L. F.; "Gallitzin;" *Catholic Historical Review*; XIII:394.

CHAPTER IX

(1) For details of the history of New York in this and succeeding chapters, see:
New York City Guide, Federal Writers' Project; Random House; 1939.
Valentine's Manual, volumes from 1840 to 1890, and contemporary Guidebooks.
Ulman, Albert; *A Landmark History of New York*; Appleton; 1901.
Oldboy, Felix; *A Tour Around New York*; Harpers; 1893.
(2) Hassard, J. R. G.; *Life of the Most Reverend John Hughes*; New York; 1866.
Brann, H. A.; *Most Reverend John Hughes, first Archbishop of New York*; Dodd, Mead; 1892.
O'Daniel, V. F.; "Documents—Archbishop John Hughes;" *Catholic Historical Review*; October, 1917.
(3) A large picture of Our Lady painted by Mother Galitzin was given to the Sisters of Charity in gratitude for their hospitality. The College of Mount Saint Vincent has generously given this picture to Manhattanville College.
(4) Talbot-Smith, J.; *History of the Catholic Church in New York*; 2 vols.; New York; 1890.
Bennett, W.; *Handbook to Catholic Historical New York City*; New York; 1927.
——; *Catholic Footsteps in Old New York*; New York; 1909.
(5) Ryan, L. P.; *Old Saint Peter's*; United States Catholic Historical Society; Monograph 15; 1935.
Walsh, Thomas; "Saint Peter's of Barclay Street;" *Commonweal*; May 6, 1925.
(6) Guerin, Mother Theodora; *Journals and Letters of Mother Theo-*

dora Guerin; Published by Sisters of Providence, St. Mary's of the Woods, Indiana; 1882.

(7) Guidée, Achille, S. J.; *Vie du Révérend Père Kohlman*; Paris, 1854; (under title of *Vie du R. P. Varin*).

Parsons, W. J.; "Father Anthony Kohlman;" *Catholic Historical Review*; IV: 38.

(8) Meehan, Thomas F.; "Catholic Literary New York"; *Catholic Historical Review*; IV: 399.

A special indebtedness is due to Mr. Meehan for many articles, documents and letters bearing upon the early Catholic history of New York. These have been constantly used, though it is not possible to refer to them each time.

Foik, P. J.; *Pioneer Catholic Journalism*; Catholic Historical Society Monograph, No. IX; 1930.

Baumgartner, A. W.; *Catholic Journalism; a Study of its Development in the United States*; New York; 1931.

(9) Binsse, H.; "Pierre Toussaint, a Catholic Uncle Tom;" *Historical Records and Studies*; XII: 90.

Ryan, L. R.; "Pierre Toussaint, 'God's Image Carved in Ivory';" *Historical Records and Studies*; XXV: 39.

(10) Meehan, T. F.; "Andrew Parmentier and His Daughter, Madame Bayer;" *Historical Records and Studies*; III: 440.

(11) *An Apostolic Woman; Life and Letters of Irma Fer de la Motte*; Catholic Publication Society; New York; 1882.

(12) Owen, D.; "Our Lady of the Woods;" *Catholic World*; CI: 303.

Chapter X

(1) Chazournes, Léon de; *Vie de Révérend Père Joseph Barrelle*; Paris; 1868.

Chapter XI

(1) Archives of the Sisters of the Good Shepherd, Louisville, Ky.

(2) Pasquier, H.; *Life of Mother Mary of St. Euphrasia Pelletier*; 2 vols.; Burns and Oates; 1893. Tr. from the French.

(3) *Memoirs of the Pittsburgh Sisters of Mercy*; New York; 1917.

(4) MS Life of Mother Jones, and Memoirs of Miss Cornelia Craigie.

(5) Stokes, I. N. Phelps; *Iconography of Manhattan Island*; Dodd; 1915–1928; 6 vols. This exhaustive work is the source of many quotations from contemporary documents and newspapers, taken from the *Chronology* in volumes IV and V.

(6) Emerson, R. W.; *Works*; Houghton Mifflin; 1876; II: 4.

(7) Burton, Katherine; *Paradise Planters*; Longmans Green; 1939.

(8) Whalen, Doran; *Granite for God's House;* Sheed and Ward; 1941, p. 126.
(9) *The Centurion*; Fordham Centenary Year Book; 1941.
(10) Sargent, *op. cit.*, p. 179–80.
(11) Riker, James; *History of Newton*; p. 259.
(12) Browne, Eliza; *A Girl's Life Eighty Years Ago*; Scribner; 1887, p. 167.

Chapter XII

(1) *New York City Guide*; Federal Writers' Project, p. 257.
(2) Riker, James; *Harlem; its Origin and Early Annals*; printed for author; New York; 1881.
(3) Collections of the New York Historical Society, 2nd series, Vol. I: 325, 300.
(4) Yates and Moulton; *History of New York*; New York; 1824, p. 238.
(5) Johnston, H. P.; *The Campaign of 1776*; Brooklyn, 1878; See map, p. 259.
(6) For information concerning the property of the Sacred Heart Convent at Manhattanville from 1712 to 1889, see: Deering, J. A.; *Abstract of the Title of the Female Academy of the Sacred Heart*; New York; 1889.
(7) For information concerning the district of Manhattanville, see: Brislin, Genevieve; *Manhattanville has an Historical Background*; unpublished B.A. thesis, 1930.
Woolston, H. B.; *A Study of the Population of Manhattanville*; Columbia University Studies in History, Economics and Public Law; Longmans; 1909.
Annunciation Church Jubilee Book, 1938.
(8) *Mémoirs de la Révérende Mère Maria Stanislaus Tommasini;* Roehampton; 1918.
(9) Ernemont, Madeleine de; *La Vie Voyageuse et Missionaire de la Révérende Mère Anna du Rousier*; Paris; 1932.

Chapter XIII

(1) *Essays in Catholic Education in the United States*; edited by Roy J. Deferrari; Catholic University Press; 1942.
(2) Watts, H. C.; "Conewago: Our First Shrine to the Sacred Heart;" *Historical Records and Studies*; XX: 28.
(3) Collection of Quigg letters, Archives of Sacred Heart Convent, Maplehurst.
(4) Gorman, R.; *Catholic Apologetical Literature in the United States*

(1784–1858); Studies in American Church History, No. XXVII; Catholic University Press; 1939.

(5) Berger, J.; *Life of Right Reverend John N. Newmann*; New York; 1884.

(6) Deuther, C. G.; *Life and Times of Right Reverend John Timon*; Buffalo; 1870.

McAndrews, A. J.; *Charitable Activities of the Right Reverend John Timon*; Buffalo; 1870.

(7) O'Brien, J. J.; "The Reverend Gabriel Richard, Educator, Statesman, and Priest;" *Historical Records and Studies*; V: 77.

(8) Catlin, G. B.; *The Story of Detroit*; printed by The Detroit *News*; 1923.

(9) Rosalita, Sister M.; "Four Women Lay Apostles of the Old Northwest;" *Historical Records and Studies*; XXXI: 119.

(10) Talbot, Francis; *Saint Among Savages*; New York; 1935.

(11) Walworth, E. H.; *Life and Times of Kateri Tekakwitha, the Lily of the Mohawks*; Albany; 1926.

(12) McAllister, A. S.; *In Winter we Flourish*; Longmans; 1939.

Chapter XIV

(1) Reminiscences of Mother Genevieve Deshayes; Cahier I, 42.

(2) Goyau, G.; *Les Origines Réligieuses de Canada;* Paris; 1924.

(3) Bainvel, J.; *Devotion to the Sacred Heart of Jesus*; London; 1924; tr. from the French, p. 218.

(4) Drummond, M. M.; *La Vénérable Mère Marguerite Bourgeoys, sa Vie et son Temps*; Paris.

(5) Langevin, F.; *Monseigneur Ignace Bourget*; Montreal; 1931.

(6) Beaubien, Charles P.; *Le Sault-au-Recollect*; Montreal, 1898.

(7) *Jesuit Relations and Allied Documents*; ed. Kenton, E.; New York; 1925.

(8) Burns, Rev. John E.; *The Abbé Maillard and Halifax*; Canadian Catholic Historical Association; Report, 1936–37.

(9) *The Cross*; March 9, 1850.

(10) Johnston, Rev. A. A.; *The Right Reverend William Fraser, First Bishop of Halifax and of Arichat*; Canadian Catholic Historical Association, Report, 1935–36.

Catholic Diocesan Directory of Nova Scotia; Halifax; 1936.

Burns, Rev. John E.; *The Development of Roman Catholic Church Government in Halifax from 1760 to 1853*; read before the Historical Society, 1933.

(11) Correspondence of Rev. John E. Burns.

Chapter XV

(1) Sargent, D.; *Christopher Columbus*; Bruce; 1941, p. 108.
(2) Currier, C. W.; "The Church of Cuba;" *Catholic Historical Review*, I: 128.
(3) Lancaster, C. M.; "First Fruits of Cuban Catholicism;" *Historical Records and Studies*; XXX: 54.
(4) *Tradiciones de Familia*; Cuba.
(5) Dana, R. H.; *To Cuba and Back*; Boston; 1869.
(6) Guerra y Sanchez, Ramiro; *Manual de Historia de Cuba*; Havana; 1938.

Chapter XVI

(1) Album presented to the College of Manhattanville by Mr. Joseph Carey, son of the owner.
(2) *The Centurion*; op. cit.
Campbell, Thomas; "St. John's College, Fordham, in 1859;" *Historical Records and Studies*; III: 88.
(3) Hurley, D.; *Granite for God's House.*
(4) Elliot, W.; *Life of Father Hecker*; Columbia Press; 1891.
(5) Eckel, L. St. John; *Maria Monk's Daughter*; New York; 1874.
Bonn, J. L.; *And Down the Days*; Macmillan; 1942.
(6) Frese, J. R.; "Brownson on Nothingism;" *Historical Records and Studies*; XXVII: 52.
(7) Guilday, P.; "Gaetano Bedini;" *Historical Records and Studies*, XXIII: 87.
(8) Billington, R. A.; *The Protestant Crusade*; Macmillan; 1938, p. 302.

Chapter XVII

(1) *Vie de la Mère Anna Josephine Shannon*; Roehampton; 1920.
(2) Collection of letters from General Banks; Archives of the Convent of the Sacred Heart, Grand Coteau.
(3) Perdrau, Pauline; *Les Loisirs de l'Abbaye*; Vol. I; Rome; 1934. Memoirs of Saint Madeleine Sophie.
(4) ——*ibid.* Vol. II. Memoirs of Mother Josephine Goetz.

Chapter XVIII

(1) Ghéon, Henri; *The Secret of Saint Margaret Mary*; Sheed and Ward; 1937.
(2) Perdrau, *op. cit.*, Vol. I, p. 423.

Chapter XIX

(1) Gigord, *op. cit.*, Sketch of Mother Lucille Mathevon.
(2) Mary Fitzgerald, Sister; "John Baptist Miège, S. J., A Study in Frontier History;" *Historical Records and Studies*; XXIV: 284.
(3) For the Manhattanville property, see *Bromley Atlas of the City of New York*; editions of 1879, 1893, 1911.
(4) Notes on Rosecroft, by Mrs. C. M. Robinson.
(5) Garraghan; *The Catholic Church in Chicago*.
(6) American Catholic Historical Society of Philadelphia.

Chapter XX

(1) *Vie de la Très Révérende Mère Marie Josephine Goetz*; Roehampton; 1895.
(2) *Vie de Très Révérende Mère Adèle Lehon*; Roehampton; 1895.
(3) Will, A. S.; *The Life of Cardinal Gibbons*; Dutton; 1922.
(4) Gigord, J. de (editor); *Enfants de Marie du Sacré Coeur*; Vol. I. section on the Duchess of Pastrana.
(5) Monahan, Maud; *Life and Letters of Janet Erskine Stuart*; Longmans Green; 1922.
(6) Pollen, Anne; *Mother Mabel Digby*; Longmans Green; 1914.

Chapter XXI

(1) "Mother Mary Aloysia Hardey;" *Catholic World*; XLIII, 1886.
(2) Spalding, J. L.; *Religion, Agnosticism and Education*; Chicago, 1902; p. 238.
(3) Dammann, Mother G. C.; *Address to the Alumnae*; 1933.
(4) Bainvel, J.; *Devotion to the Sacred Heart of Jesus*; London; 1924. Richstaetter, K.; *Mediaeval Devotions to the Sacred Heart*; London.
(5) Ward, Maisie; *Insurrection versus Resurrection*; Sheed and Ward; 1937. Ch. I.

Grateful acknowledgment is made to the publishers of all the above books from which direct quotations have been made for their kind permission to reprint the passages quoted.

INDEX

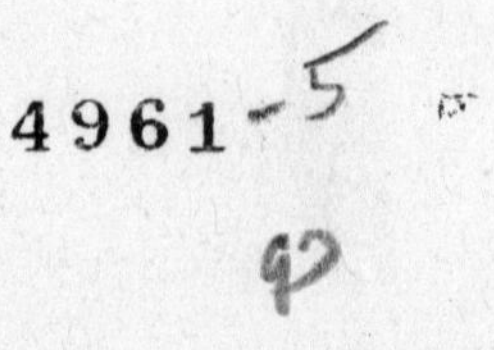